THE PUBLIC AND
ATLANTIC DEFENSE

THE PUBLIC AND ATLANTIC DEFENSE

Edited by
Gregory Flynn and
Hans Rattinger

ROWMAN & ALLANHELD
PUBLISHERS

CROOM HELM
LONDON & CANBERRA

ROWMAN & ALLANHELD

Published in the United States of America in 1985
by Rowman & Allanheld, Publishers
(a division of Littlefield, Adams & Company)
81 Adams Drive, Totowa, New Jersey 07512

and by
Croom Helm Limited,
St. John's Chambers, 2-10
St. John's Road,
London SW11 1PN England

Copyright © 1985 by The Atlantic Institute for International Affairs

Library of Congress Cataloging in Publication Data
Main entry under title:

The Public and Atlantic defense.

Includes bibliographical references and index.
1. North Atlantic Treaty Organization—Public opinion—
Addresses, essays, lectures. 2. North Atlantic Region—
Defenses—Public opinion—Addresses, essays, lectures.
3. Public opinion—North Atlantic Region—Addresses,
essays, lectures. I. Flynn, Gregory. II. Rattinger,
Hans.
UA646.3.P78   1984   355'.031'091821   84-15894
ISBN 0-8476-7365-0

British Library Cataloguing in Publication Data

The Public and Atlantic defense.
1. North Atlantic Treaty Organization
2. Military policy—Public opinion
I. Flynn, Gregory II. Rattinger, Hans
355' .0335'1821   UA646.3

ISBN 0-7099-1056-8

85 86 87 / 9 8 7 6 5 4 3 2 1
Printed in the United States of America

Contents

Tables and Figures

Preface

Few can deny that the subject of this book has been one of the most controversial confronting the Atlantic Allies during the past several years. Since "the public" in our countries has become a justification for policies on all sides of the same issue, we decided that an independent group of specialized scholars should take a closer look at what has really been happening to public attitudes toward defense and security questions.

This book stems from a major international research effort of the Atlantic Institute for International Affairs in collaboration with the Atlantic Treaty Association. The authors were brought together in Paris with a prominent group of international experts at the end of June 1983. This meeting was especially designed to confront the "macro" world of security policy analysis with the "micro" world of public opinion analysis in order to force each to come to grips better with the assumptions of the other. The work presented here has thus been tested not only against rigorous methodological standards but against all of the various predispositions existing about the role of the public in today's security policy debates. It stands up well against the former, however, as the editors argue in their introduction and conclusion, few people in the "macro" world find that the work of this project confirms very many of their assumptions.

This project would not have been possible without the efforts and support of a great number of people and institutions. Dr. Peter Corterier, a member of the Institute's Board of Governors and President of the ATA, was instrumental in bringing together this support. We would particularly like to acknowledge the aid of the German Marshall Fund of the United States, the Robert Bosch Stiftung, the Ford Foundation, the NATO Information Service, the Bundespresseamt of the Federal Republic of Germany, the United States Information Agency, the British Foreign and Commonwealth Office, the Planning Staff of the Norwegian Foreign Office and the French Secrétariat Général de la Défense Nationale, Ministère de la Défense and Ministère des Relations Extèrieures.

We must here give special acknowledgment to the late Gilbert Sauvage, Deputy Director of the NATO Information Service, who saw the importance of this project from the beginning and did everything he could to help in its realization. His passionate devotion to the ideals of truth and liberty in the Western system was a very particular factor in motivating us and our colleagues. This work is a tribute to his energies and dedication.

Richard D. Vine

Editor's Note

In order to facilitate the readability of the considerable volume of public opinion data used in this book, the presentation of sources has been simplified as follows:

1. In the text, the name of the polling agency and the date of the poll are to be found in parentheses at the end of the sentence in which the data is mentioned unless reference is specifically to a table.

2. The references in tables occur in three formats:

   a) If the data comes from a single polling agency and a single poll, the name of the agency and the date of the poll are listed in parentheses following the title of the table. The key for acronyms is given in the Appendix of each chapter.
   Example:

   Table 5.39: Attitudes toward INF deployment among educated Italians by age (DXUS 3/81)
   Polling done by the Doxa Institute for the United States Information Agency in March 1981.

   b) If the data comes from a single polling agency but from polls taken at different times, the name of the agency appears in parentheses after the title of the table and the dates of the polls appear at the head of each data column.
   Example:

   Table 3.3: Judgment of French policy toward the Soviet Union (SOFRES)

	3/80	5/80	10/80

   Polling done by SOFRES in March, May, and October 1980.

   c) If the data comes from different polling agencies at different moments in time, the name of each agency and the dates of the polls appear at the head of each data column.
   Example:

   Table 7.9: Attitudes toward the NATO double-track decision

NOI	NMD	NOI	NOI	NMD
11/82	12/82	1/83	2/83	4/83

   Polling done by NOI in November 1982 and in January and February 1983; polling done by NMD in December 1982 and April 1983.

In this way, it is hoped that the reader can easily identify the source of the data and the date of its collection. If more precise information is needed, this citation should be adequate for anyone to trace the specific question wording (if not given) or the specific dates of polling, and to acquire the breakdowns according to background variables if desired.

1 *Introduction*

GREGORY FLYNN and
HANS RATTINGER

The motivation to produce this volume is both political and intellectual. During the past several years, debate has raged over the wisdom of NATO's decision in December 1979 to modernize its nuclear forces and simultaneously to negotiate with the Soviet Union in an effort to limit nuclear arms in Europe reciprocally. This debate has focused on two interrelated issues: first, the requirements for deterring aggression in an age of nuclear parity and second, the requirement to reassure Western populations that Western strategy is a lesser threat than Eastern strategy (compare Howard 1983).

A viable security policy requires not only the capability to organize and to maintain the military prerequisites for deterrence and defense, but also a degree of societal acceptance of these measures. That current debates over security policy have assumed such proportions suggests how much the domestic context of security policy has changed in many Western countries. The current policy disputes in fact are about (1) exactly what has changed and (2) the dimensions of that change.

People focus on how best to reconcile the requirement to reassure with the requirement to deter without at all being sure what the requirement for the former is (or the latter, for that matter). In the process, the public becomes the reason or the excuse for almost everything. Mutually exclusive hypotheses about what has happened within Western publics over the past few years are easily developed, with selective use of overabundant data. Public opinion is being used to justify simultaneously demands for change and demands for continuity. The public is both a participant in and an object of current debates. Yet all affirmations about what "the public" believes contrast starkly with the lack of serious, systematic analysis of public opinion on national security issues.

The purpose of this book is to contribute responsibly to the current political debate by providing a more adequate profile of the patterns of popular support and of popular discontent that Western governments must confront in security policy. It seeks to do so first by sober assessment of popular attitudes in the security policy area from all available sources, not just selected sources. It will also seek to clarify the conceptual, theoretical, and methodological problems that are posed for attempts at more accurate description and explanation. The reader will thus, it is hoped, gain greater insight into what can, and perhaps more importantly, what *cannot* be said about public attitudes on defense and foreign policy and hence also into the political judgments that can (and cannot) be made about the public's role in current Western policy dilemmas.

Recent contradictory assessments about what has been happening in Western publics have each assumed significant changes in public attitudes. One disputed issue concerns the extent to which these putative changes are permanent or transitory. Some, for example, argue that we are witnessing a long overdue "democratization" of defense policy, that popular participation in determining defense priorities is natural and irreversible. The population at large is considered no longer willing to accept certain basic premises that have underlain Western defense efforts over the past thirty years. Accordingly, it is argued, governments must adjust both their policies and the way they make policy in order to take account of the new realities that are here to stay.

Others argue public involvement in national security affairs is not permanently entrenched and that we are witnessing a period of public anxiety about the future unprecedented since the early postwar period, stemming as much from economic as other factors. Feeding this is a profound lack of public confidence in the ability of governments to resolve difficult problems. In any case, security policy decisions are held to involve calculations that cannot always be adequately grasped by populations at large. The problem of recreating a viable consensus is, therefore, considered to be one of governments modifying their rhetoric to correspond more closely to the realities as perceived by populations in order to help reinstill confidence.

People differ just as widely over the second issue: whether this change should be regarded with sympathy or concern. Those who apocalyptically subscribe to the notion that societal acceptance of a viable Western deterrent is diminishing draw the conclusion that internal social evolutions in the Western democracies are eroding the capability of these nations to survive in freedom and security. On the other hand, others rejoice that now, finally, popular unrest and pressure could force governments to abandon their trodden paths of national security policy, to abandon the inhumane dependence on nuclear deterrence, to initiate unilateral arms reduction, or to search for entirely new security arrangements that would no longer rely on the threat or the application of military force.

The very nature of these arguments points to the urgent need for a careful analysis of the "new realities" surrounding national security policy in Western nations. It is in fact surprising that better, more responsible use has not been made of the wealth of public opinion data available. Analysis of the criteria and intensity with which publics evaluate the threats to Western security, on the one hand, and how governments provide for security, on the other, is simply inadequate. Yet this is a precondition for determining how deterrence and reassurance can best be reconciled with one another, and therefore how best to resolve the public policy problem currently the source of this tremendous political dispute.

This book obviously addresses a complex network of interrelated problems. At the same time its scope is inevitably limited at the operational level. We want to look here at what is going on in the publics of Western nations with respect to their perceptions and attitudes on national security. The only raw material we have is public opinion data. Moreover, these data are one of the vehicles of current political strife, if not products of it. This must be borne in mind throughout the remainder of this book. We can strive hard to deliver nothing but scholarly investigation and interpretation, but we have to be aware that our most important material is also used for quite different purposes, including manipulation and propaganda.

A simple example may serve to illustrate the need for a more serious and detached perspective toward these data. In the Federal Republic of Germany, the Forschungsgruppe Wahlen in Mannheim has in recent months regularly asked respondents in its monthly surveys how they felt about deploying new nuclear weapons in the Federal Republic vs. continuing negotiations in Geneva. In May and June of 1983, the percentages of respondents rejecting new nuclear missiles were almost identical; in July this figure was slightly higher, but within limits explicable by sampling fluctuations.

The May and June figures were reported by the second German television network (for whom these surveys were taken), but the slightly higher July figure was not reported on the premise that it was not really news. The July figure became known to the German peace movement, who then held a press conference, expounding on the rise of rejection of new nuclear weapons in the Federal Republic and denouncing the second TV network for "suppressing" this information. As a consequence, the July figure (which conveyed no other political message than published data from previous months) was assigned even greater importance by the peace movement. It was televised and broadcast widely both inside and outside Germany, and all those who thought they had anything to gain spread the news that something dramatic and quite unprecedented had happened within West German public opinion on the issue of missile deployment. This example clearly demonstrates that a considerable clarification of our knowledge and analytical tools is necessary.

Our ability to convey to decision makers a clearer notion of the context and constraints within which they have to operate is limited by two considerations. First, this volume almost exclusively deals with mass attitudes. The formation of opinion within groups of "opinion leaders"; their organization and activities, their interaction with political parties, social groups, the media, and with mass opinion will not be investigated systematically. For decision makers the knowledge that their policies are supported by a "silent majority" offers little consolation if resistance of minorities is based upon intensely held attitudes, well organized and publicized, and echoed by key social groups, political parties, and the media. Consensus on a particular national security policy has much to do with mass attitudes, but it is not an exclusively quantitative concept.

Second, the intellectual side of our problem prevents us from giving definitive answers to what mass attitudes on defense currently really look like, at least beyond a certain level of generality. We frequently encounter more problems than answers, and upon close scrutiny apparently certain and stable results of mass opinion on national security and defense can dissolve into speculation and guesswork. Mass opinions on national security and defense in many ways prove to be extremely diffuse and intangible.

The media today carry regularly the most recent survey data on nuclear weapons, arms control negotiations, and the Atlantic Alliance. However, this abundance of *current* data is an additional part of the problem we face, as it stands in stark contrast to the lack of earlier data. In the sixties and seventies national security was largely uncontroversial; there was little public interest and involvement. Therefore, there was little incentive to include appropriate questions in opinion surveys. In many cases we simply do not know whether the mass attitudes reported now are any different from those of earlier years. Some of the attitudes or contradictions in attitudes that we find and that worry or delight us today may actually not be new at all, but in earlier times we did not know about these attitudes, and we did not want to know about them for lack of political relevance.

For the same set of reasons there also has been little serious social-psychological and political science research on the origins, formation, structure, and dynamics of defense-related mass opinion. One could even go further and say that there is rather little research on foreign-policy-related mass attitudes in general, as the accepted notion has long been that foreign affairs and international relations are issue areas that are very remote for the average citizen (Rosenau 1961, 35; Hughes 1978, 23). For all practical purposes, the "public" attentive to and knowledgeable on foreign affairs for many years has been conceived of as a rather limited "elite public."

Many of those actively involved in the current political debates surrounding defense policy believe that this has changed dramatically. Yet it remains probable that sizeable segments of populations still have rather little interest in and information about this issue area and rate it rather low in personal importance. Under these conditions, reactive measurement as applied in public opinion polls can lead to very undesirable results. Current polls investigate surprisingly detailed aspects of national security attitudes. It is entirely conceivable that sizeable shares of samples are required to indicate perceptions or evaluations of matters on which they have almost no information at all, and about which they have never before been required to form an opinion or even think. Of course, they could refuse to reply or say that they "don't know." But perhaps they choose not to do this, in order, for example, not to appear ignorant or to please the interviewer.

Applying reactive measurement in such situations invariably provokes a certain number of "non-attitudes" (Converse 1970). Respondents may choose randomly from the alternatives they are being offered, they may reply on the basis of what they think is socially desirable or acceptable, responses may reflect attitude dimensions that are very different from the ones that are to be ascertained (and that are evoked by the particular question format used), and there can be sizeable effects of survey techniques. One could almost say that, with issue areas in which respondents know and care little, the person who designs the questions to a considerable extent determines the outcome of the poll. This is, of course, what makes this field so accessible to skillful manipulation.

It must be emphasized at this point that this embodies absolutely no value judgment about the public itself. The judgment being made concerns our methodological limitations in understanding public opinion on national security issues. In the chapters that follow there will be many instances in which the authors attempt to determine the extent to which the data they have gathered includes such nonattitudes. This is in no way meant to imply that "attitudes" should exist. Highly structured opinions, especially in response to detailed questions, will only exist on issues close enough to individual experience or interest, and national security policy falls into this category for only a limited number of people.

In order to get a complete and reliable grasp on the mainstream of public opinion on national security in various Western countries, we would really need to be able to draw on an established body of knowledge about how foreign policy attitudes in general and national security attitudes in particular are formed, how stable they are, to what influences they respond, what their basic dimensions are, and so on. This kind of research, at least any comprehensive work, is simply not available and it is certainly too much, in one volume, to develop and empirically test such a theory *and* to present an inventory of available findings, as is the purpose of this volume.

Such a theory probably would have to start from a classification of the substance that national security attitudes comprise, such as overall goals, derived instruments and strategies; facts (past, present, and future), and actors. Attitudes in these substantively delineated fields then would have to be differentiated further according to the familiar distinction of cognitive vs. affective vs. behavioral components (Rosenberg and Hovland 1960), and the relationship of the "salience" (Hartley and Hartley 1952) or "personal importance" dimension with these other three components would have to be clarified. Starting from this kind of conceptual inventory of the issue area to be investigated ultimately should lead to more precise notions than we have now of what aspects of national security mass opinions can be surveyed with what instruments with a reasonable degree of validity; what aspects are most susceptible to instrument effects; what components are most likely colored by what other attitude dimensions; and so forth. Such extensive theoretical and conceptual clarification of the mental structures we are dealing with here could ultimately lead to a series of empirically testable propositions which currently are not yet available.

Perhaps a small example would serve to clarify this. Imagine a survey question asking under what conditions different countries would be most likely to start a "nuclear" war (a question aiming at perceptions of hypothetical futures). It is entirely conceivable that this expectation of *circumstances* is almost completely determined by stereotypes and evaluations of foreign countries. What we would like to know is people's expectations about future possibilities for nuclear war, but what we actually may be measuring is what nations they like and dislike. Cognitions may be structured by affectively determined attitudes. In the field of mass foreign policy and national security attitudes, problems like this have almost never been seriously dealt with in the professional literature, all abundance of timely polling data notwithstanding.

The chapters on public opinion on national security that follow in this volume all attempt as seriously as possible to go beyond simple description of the available data to characterize important developments in the individual nations. We try hard to ascertain not only what the relevant data look like, but also what can and cannot be concluded from them. We try hard not to take the data at face value, but to produce some meaningful interpretations of the dimensions of attitudes that may be underneath the surface of the multitude of individual findings that are being presented. But, as should be obvious from the above, there are severe limits to the extent to which this book can perform a coherent and comparative critical evaluation of the available data base. Because the general theoretical and methodological inventory required to perform such a task in the field of mass attitudes related to national security is not yet available, the range of conclusions that can be drawn from the data presented in the subsequent chapters sometimes is very wide. Quite certainly, there are segments of public opinion on national security in which the interpretations of the authors represented in this volume differ widely, some deciding that their data measure what they are supposed to measure and that meaningful political conclusions can be drawn, although others would maintain that we cannot really be sure what the same set of data is measuring. This implies, of course, that there are aspects of the whole problem about which we and the authors on the individual countries would agree that prescriptions for policy should not be made at all, or only with the utmost care in view of the low confidence we can put in one particular interpretation of one particular set of data.

This volume comprises contributions from several different countries: first, the United States; second, Britain, Germany, Italy, and the Netherlands as Western European partners to the Atlantic Alliance that have been designated for the deployment of new American Intermediate Range

Nuclear Forces (INF); third, France as another major European member of NATO, but with a special position not only in terms of its membership in the Alliance but also in terms of its attitude toward INF deployment and of the absence of the antinuclear protest pervading all the other Western European countries that are treated in this volume; and finally, Norway as one of the smaller countries within the Alliance that borders on the Soviet Union but is not scheduled to receive INF. Even though this is probably a relevant sample of the member nations of NATO for the purpose of this book, its final composition, of course, also has something to do with the availability of authors who were capable and willing to prepare extensive and original contributions.

The differences among the seven nations investigated in the chapters that follow make the task of producing a truly comparative volume very difficult indeed. An attempt was made to assure a certain minimum of comparability by asking all authors to structure their contributions around four specific themes that clearly overlap, but with each representing one core element in public perceptions of Western security and security requirements. These four major analytical axes and the basic justification of each are as follows:

1. Images of the Soviet Union
   The Soviet Union is constantly referred to as a threat, but we have a limited understanding of the different concepts that exist of the Soviet Union in the populations of the nations of the Alliance. Such an understanding requires further exploration of the different bases for evaluating the Soviet adversary, especially the relationship of military, economic, and political factors. Do we continue to have two profoundly different views of the Soviet Union existing side by side in the West? To what extent are attitudes toward Western defense policies a function of specific perceptions of the Soviet Union?
2. Images of security
   The traditional boundaries between concepts of security, i.e. national, personal, economic, and so on, seem to have eroded. The problems of security as perceived by populations at large seem to be as much internal as external, as much economic as military. What in fact are populations most concerned about? Is military power, for instance, seen primarily to be a source of insecurity rather than security? To what extent, especially during prolonged periods of economic constraint, does defense policy risk becoming the prisoner of more immediate security concerns as perceived by populations?
3. Images of deterrence
   The growth of organized protest against nuclear weapons makes it imperative that popular perceptions of Western strategy be better analyzed. To what extent is the way the West provides itself with security truly considered more threatening than the Eastern bloc? What is the true extent of nuclear protest, and to what extent is it a

symbol or surrogate for other frustrations and fears? Is a shift toward greater reliance on conventional forces likely to diminish the strength of protest or simply to alter its focus?

4. Images of allies

   Currently, on both sides of the Atlantic, allies are frequently considered more a liability than an asset. There is a curious popular unwillingness to listen and to give credence to security problems as perceived by one's allies. The extent and the wellsprings of this mutual rejectionism need considerable exploration. Is it, for example, more the role of the United States than nuclear weapons as such that is at the roots of current European protest? Does popular opinion in the United States really reflect the often mentioned growing frustration with European positions on foreign policy issues? How much support do alternative arrangements to provide for security command?

By surrendering to these four general themes we have been able to concentrate each country "profile" on describing and analyzing related sets of attitudes, even though there are obvious constraints to the comparative approach. The problems of this present world affect our seven countries in quite different ways. Historically and culturally there is wide variance between them. Because of particular national contexts and experiences problems that are being surveyed in one country in a particular fashion are polled from a quite different angle in another nation. Therefore, even though a great deal of the substance that is being investigated in opinion polls in these seven countries is identical, question wording and the specific stimuli with which respondents are presented vary widely, so that the resulting data are not directly comparable in any strict sense. There also are big differences between the nations in the extent to which comparable data from earlier years or even complete time series ranging over ten, twenty, or thirty years could be found. Public opinion polls do not, of course, have the same traditions in all these nations. Finally, because of the prominent role of governments and official agencies in commissioning public opinion polls on measures of national security and defense, the accessibility of data is not the same in all countries. Some publish freely or at least supply almost all material to researchers upon request. Others pursue more restrictive policies. In spite of their common structure, the subsequent chapters thus exhibit considerable variance in terms of substance, and of style and extent of their treatment of particular aspects of our overall problem.

This introduction should have made the reader aware that the authors of this book have confronted a difficult task. In view of the complexity of the problems and of the scarcity of available theoretical or comparative empirical research the reader should be warned against expecting too much from this one volume. Its contributions set out to describe what mass public opinion on national security matters looks like in some important member nations of the Atlantic Alliance and how this has developed over the past several years. In that sense, the volume should also serve as an easily accessible cross-national data base, as a kind of "handbook" of defense-related public opinion in these seven countries. In addition, there will be some preliminary critical evaluation of what can and what cannot be concluded from these data.

Those seeking proof of dramatic shifts in popular attitudes on security policy, shifts that undermine the premises on which Western policies have been based, will not find it in the chapters that follow. Likewise, those who would believe that nothing of any significance has happened and that we can carry on "business as usual" will not find much comfort in this book. The reality, to the extent the research presented here has been able to bring it into sharper relief, lies somewhere in between.

This is not a study of elites, of opinion leaders, of peace movements. This is not a study of mass-elite, elitemedia, and other interactions that shape the process of political communication and the formation of political will. It is not a study of ongoing political battles in these countries, attempting to forecast possible outcomes or possible changes in policy. It is an inventory of mass opinions on national security in the nations of the Atlantic Alliance, something until now unavailable despite all of the regular assertions on what the public thinks. Under these circumstances, even a study with such limited aspirations should prove valuable in our current political debates over how best to provide for peace and security.

References

Converse, Philip E., "Attitudes and Non-Attitudes," in: E. R. Tufte, ed., *The Quantitative Analysis of Social Problems* (Reading, Mass.: Addison Wesley Publishing Company, 1970) Pp. 168–189.

Hartley, Eugene L. and Ruth E. Hartley, *Foundamentals of Social Psychology* (New York: Knopf, 1952).

Howard, Michael, "Deterrence, Consensus and Reassurance in the Defense of Europe," in *Defense and Consensus: The Domestic Aspects of Western Security* Adelphi Paper no. 184 (London: IISS, 1983): 17–27.

Hughes, Barry B., *The Domestic Context of American Foreign Policy* (San Francisco: W. H. Freeman, 1978).

Rosenau, James N., *Public Opinion and Foreign Policy* (New York: Random House, 1961).

Rosenberg, Milton J. and Carl I. Hovland, "Cognitive, Affective, and Behavioral Components of Attitudes," in M. J. Rosenberg et al., eds., *Attitude Organization and Change* (New Haven: Yale University Press, 1960) Pp. 1–14.

2 Britain: Two and a Half Cheers for the Atlantic Alliance

IVOR CREWE

Introduction

A report on the state of public opinion in Britain on defense, the Alliance, and East-West relations must begin with the disconcerting point that such opinion is faint and fragmentary and, until recently, has become increasingly so. One reason is Britain's decline as a world military and economic power since 1945. As economic problems have come to dominate the political agenda, as decolonization markedly reduced the direct involvement of British forces in armed conflict, so the attention of politicians and commentators has turned away from international affairs. Parliamentary debates on foreign policy have become few and far between. World affairs receive negligible coverage in the popular (as opposed to the "quality") press and bring up the tail end of news broadcasts on radio and television. The once preeminent status of the foreign office in the eyes of the Prime Minister and the media has slipped in favor of the main economic ministries. The second, and related, reason is that, with the occasional and spectacular exception, foreign and defense policies have not been the occasion of serious conflict between the two main parties. There have been differences of emphasis and rhetoric, of course, but these have been as marked within the Conservative and Labour parties as between them. Ever since 1945, for example, both parties have contained minorities hostile to the Atlantic Alliance (although for very different reasons) and in favor of an independently British or independently European defense and foreign policy. But, again until very recently, the Atlanticists have dominated the two governing parties, so that the question of Britain's international alliances, except for its membership of the European Economic Community (EEC), has not been a matter of partisan controversy.

As a result, interest in foreign and defense matters among the public at large has declined and indeed at times been almost entirely absent. According to the monthly Gallup polls, the last time that an aspect of defense or foreign affairs was considered "the most urgent problem facing the country at the present time" was in 1961 (see appendix A). In fact from 1964, when the deep-seated nature of Britain's economic problems first became generally apparent, defense and foreign affairs have barely loomed in the public consciousness at all. The Gallup polls reveal many years in which fewer than three percent mention any defense or international matter as the "most urgent problem" in any month. The impact of international crises, including those directly involving Britain, has been surprisingly small. For example, in 1966, at the height of negotiations with the illegal white-settler regime in Rhodesia, only 14 percent mentioned it as Britain's most urgent problem; when negotiations were resumed with the leaders of various black parties in 1979–1980, the proportion was smaller still. When Britain joined the EEC in 1971, a monthly average of 11 percent saw it as the main issue; in spring 1975, when the referendum on continued membership was imminent, the figure was about the same. During the Yom Kippur War, in October 1973, only six percent of the British public mentioned it as the most significant problem for Britain (although the subsequent energy crisis was more widely felt). Thus, for most of the past twenty years it is dubious to talk of public opinion about defense and foreign affairs in the sense of widespread and deeply held convictions based on knowledge, interest, and reflection.

An exception to this stark conclusion is provided by the last two years. A mass movement of protest against NATO's dual-track decision of December 1979 rapidly gathered support in 1980 and 1981 and attracted extensive publicity, notably by various forms of peaceful demonstration at the proposed bases for cruise missiles. The Labour party's adoption of unilateral nuclear disarmament as official policy (and its election in November 1980 of a veteran unilateralist as its leader), and the resulting strains within the party, ensured that the issue would enter party and electoral politics. By the time of the 1983 general election it was the second most important issue, surpassed only by unemployment.

The issue of nuclear defense and Britain's relations with the United States were fortuitously given extra point by the unexpected war with Argentina over the Falkland Islands in April-June 1982. Although a minor, short-lived, and anachronistic episode in the eyes of the rest of the world, the Falklands war had an enormous impact on the British public. Not since 1945 has any issue monopolized the headlines day after day for three months; never before has the public been able to follow the daily progress of British troops on their televisions. The Falklands war stimulated a general defense awareness in the public but also illuminated particular aspects of the defense debate. For instance, the Argentinian decision to invade was prevalently attributed to their belief, based on postulated cuts in Britain's naval capabilities, that Britain lacked both the will and capacity to deter an invasion; since then the Falklands war is often cited by advocates of deterrence theory. Another example is the ambivalent stance adopted by the United States to the episode, which is cited by pro- and anti-Atlanticists alike for their respective positions.

Despite the recent eruption of defense-related issues in British politics, the study of public opinion on such matters is made difficult by the wide gap between such issues and people's everyday concerns and experiences. This is particularly true when examining public attitudes to the *details* of defense policy. Attitude surveys assume that there is no subject under the sun on which the public does not have an opinion; that respondents are filing cabinets of opinion for which the key is the appropriate question. This assumption is fueled by the readiness of many respondents, out of vanity or politeness, to give a definite answer, rather than say "don't know," to questions on which in fact they have no real view.

Responses are not the same as genuine opinions, that is, stable convictions, based on knowledge or experience, that can be defended against contradictory opinions and counterevidence. Compared with opinions, responses are much more subject to nuances of question wording and format and to recent, and perhaps transient, events recorded by the media. Being so much more dependent on ephemeral factors they are more changeable over time and less consistent in relation to a series of logically linked questions. Thus it has to be recognized that many public attitudes to defense and foreign relations take the form of immediate and unreflecting response rather than deep-seated conviction. This does not prevent us from discerning the rough outline and broad structure of opinion and tracing trends over time, but it renders pointless the search for perfect consistency or the construction of elaborate explanations for inconsistency and change.

Some caveats also need to be made in the light of the public opinion data available. Numerous attitude surveys have followed in the wake of the emergence of the nuclear defense issue. These have not been sophisticated academic surveys but, typically, fairly brief surveys commissioned by the media or a defense-related pressure group and reported in the press, on television, or more fully in the regular publications of the major opinion poll companies. Where the client waives confidentiality, the survey report can be obtained; occasionally the printout of the standard cross-tabulations is available.

The opinion poll sources of this chapter are cited in the text and listed in appendix A. They are numerous, yet they provide a frustratingly incomplete picture, for three reasons. First, the phrasing of questions differs even for very similar topics, making precise comparisons over time impossible. The availability of trend data over a long period, based on identically worded questions, is scarce. Second, the questions are often *structured* differently. For example, most questions are closed-ended: the respondent is offered a fixed choice of answers. But sometimes the question is quasi open-ended: respondents are shown a list of statements or phrases and asked to say which, if any, apply, with the option to cite as few or as many as they think fit. "Forced" and "volunteered" answers differ. The first entails one answer from almost every respondent, the second the benefit of more "genuine" answers. In a policy area on which responses may be more prevalent than opinions, these differences of phrasing and structure can have an important bearing on the apparent substance of the answers. Third, most poll reports disclose the answers of all respondents, but not of subgroups. This makes it impossible to know how opinion differs across a population and how polarized it is between groups who tend to be united or opposed on other issues. Moreover, despite the existence of data archives in Britain, most of the polls cited are too recent to have been deposited in archives or processed by them for secondary analysis. It is therefore not yet feasible to look at the direct relationship between attitudes on one defense topic and attitudes on another, that is, to see to what extent a set of attitudes on defense and foreign relations "hangs together." Nonetheless, these real limitations do not preclude the drawing of clear conclusions about the British public, as the remainder of this chapter seeks to show.

Images of the Soviet Union

THREE INTRODUCTORY POINTS

Three features of the background to public opinion on the Soviet Union must be made at the outset. First, public attitudes are almost entirely at second hand. Almost nobody in Britain has personal or family experience of any aspect of the Soviet Union—unlike substantial numbers living in the Federal Republic of Germany (FRG), Austria, or Finland. The number of immigrants and refugees from the Eastern bloc is tiny: under one percent of the population. These small communities of Ukrainians, Poles, and Hungarians are not a serious political force; they have almost no impact on public opinion and only a toehold of influence on the political parties. Only they still have relatives in Eastern Europe; ties of kin between prewar refugees and immigrants from Eastern Europe and those they left behind are now fairly tenuous. In World War II, very few soldiers came into contact with the Soviet army or officialdom, and, of course, Great Britain has no experience of a Soviet military presence. Only four percent claim to have visited any country in East Europe (MORI 10/ 79), most of whom spent short vacations in the resorts of Yugoslavia and Bulgaria. The proportion of Russian speakers is minute. Thus British opinion about the Soviet Union is taken from secondary sources—largely the press and television—not from direct experience or knowledge.

Second, political forces sympathetic to the Soviet Union are weak. The Communist party (CP) has a membership of under 30,000, no members of Parliament, and only a handful of elected local councillors. Its daily newspaper, the *Morning Star*, has an estimated genuine circulation of about 60,000. The Communist party in Britain can no longer be relied upon to take a pro-Moscow stance (although it usually does); indeed there has recently been a small breakaway from the CP by members dissatisfied with its occasional deviation from Soviet orthodoxy. There are minorities within the Labour party and left-wing intellectual circles who are committedly pro-Soviet on issues of defense and foreign relations, but their numbers, influence, and status do not compare with that of their predecessors in the 1930s to 1950s. Even they, on the whole, adopt their position despite objections or scepticism about the Soviet political system, and not because of faith in it.

Third, cold war rhetoric has reentered and increasingly dominated public debate about East-West relations. Part of the Conservative government's so-called resolute approach has been its vocally resolute suspicion of the Soviet Union. Anglo-Soviet relations have been reduced to the necessary minimum of interchange, with a freeze on initiatives for improvement. This has been accompanied by vigorous, sometimes strident, anti-Soviet sentiments, upon which Margaret Thatcher has taken the lead, frequently against the advice of her Foreign Office (she earned the sobriquet of "Iron Lady" as a result of a speech in January 1976, in which she voiced doubts about détente and the prospective Helsinki conference and stressed the dangers of the Soviet military buildup). Like President Reagan, Prime Minister Thatcher regards the Soviet Union as an ideological as much as a military threat, as a danger not simply to Britain's interests but, as she constantly asserts, to "the British way of life." The government has been pragmatic about economic relationships with the USSR, siding with her West European partners against the United States on the issue of the gas pipeline. But it has been readier than the rest of Europe to take symbolic propaganda action against the USSR, notably in its boycott of the Moscow Olympics in 1980. This too was very much Margaret Thatcher's personal decision, taken despite its unpopularity among the ordinary public. Thus British public opinion has been given a much stronger dose of uncompromisingly anti-Soviet argument in the last few years than it had grown accustomed to.

GENERAL IMPRESSIONS OF THE USSR

Attitudes to specific aspects of East-West relations and Atlantic defense are formed against a backdrop of deep, widespread, and enduring distaste for the USSR. Hostility and suspicion appear to be entrenched in Britain's "collective consciousness," resembling and perhaps exceeding public antipathy to Napoleonic France. Only two percent "admire" the USSR and fewer than one half of one percent would like to live there (MORI 10/79). Positive admiration and potential emigration are exacting tests of a country's image, of course, but less demanding tests produce a similar picture. Only 14 percent hold a "very" or even "somewhat" favorable opinion of Russia; 74 percent do not (Gallup 3/82). A quasi open-ended question ("Which of these statements fits your ideas of the USSR?") revealed substantial proportions who volunteered that the Soviet Union is oppressive (49 percent), subject to "a lot of censorship" (51 percent) and overorganized and bureaucratic (50 percent). The only redeeming feature in an otherwise bleak view is a grudging acknowledgment of the place of national pride and endeavor in Soviet life; 58 percent describe Russians as "hardworking" (which, of course, has ambivalent connotations), 38 percent as "patriotic," and 25 percent as "proud."

The public's wary attitude toward the USSR displays a rocklike stability, apparently unaffected by the ebb and flow of East-West relations. For example, in 1966 only six percent "completely trusted" the USSR; nine years later a mere two percent did (ORC 6/66, Barker and Spencer 1975). In 1976, in a different survey, the weighted index of the British people's trust in the USSR (which can range from -1 to $+1$) was -0.61; in 1980 it was -0.67 (*Eurobarometer* 10/76, 10/80). Thus, the mass public is instinctively and, in the proper sense of the word, prejudicially suspicious of the USSR. How that is manifested in attitudes to particular facets of Soviet behavior is a separate matter.

PERCEPTIONS OF THE MILITARY BALANCE

In Britain there is now substantial, although far from universal, agreement that the balance of world power is tipped in favor of the USSR. The various polls and surveys phrase and structure their questions differently, but all show that for every person who regards the United States as the superior military power, between three and four pick the USSR. A substantial minority—between a fifth and a quarter say that power is evenly balanced between the two. Little distinction is made between nuclear and conventional forces (see Table 2.1). In late 1979, even larger numbers considered the Warsaw Pact countries superior to NATO countries in military forces (64 to 12 percent) than in nuclear weapons (54 to 15 percent); but by February 1983 the difference had virtually disappeared (55 to 17 percent, as against 54 to 15 percent). Perceptions of the USSR's nuclear weapons superiority have stayed the same over the past four years, despite the rapid growth of the antinuclear movement in response to the decision to deploy cruise and Pershing II missiles.

Not only does the majority see the USSR as the dominant military power but, it would appear, that dominance is expected to grow. In late 1982, 49 percent said they thought Russia's power would stay the same over the year 1983; 43 percent expected an increase, compared with only nine percent who foresaw a decline (Gallup 1982). The equivalent question was asked about the prospects for American power and the response was similar, except that slightly more (15 percent) anticipated a reduction in the United States' power. This pair of questions has, in fact, been asked annually for the past quarter-century. There has been little change in the answers over this long period (Table 2.2). In all but six of these years (1962–1965, 1972, 1981) the public has been more convinced that Russian power rather than American power would increase. The main shift of mood is the gradual contraction of the minority envisaging a decline in Russian power, and a compensating expansion in the proportion expecting it to remain the same. This may be interpreted as a final reconciliation on the part of the British public to the superpower status of the USSR.

Table 2.1   Perceptions of the balance of military power between NATO and Warsaw Pact countries (Gallup)

	Side with strongest *military* forces			Side with strongest *nuclear* forces		
	11/79	1/80	2/83	11/79	1/80	2/83
NATO	12	13	17	15	15	15
Both equal	3	6	7	6	8	9
Warsaw Pact	64	59	55	54	50	54
Don't know	21	22	20	25	26	21
Superiority of Warsaw Pact over NATO	52	46	38	39	35	39

A MILITARY THREAT?

It is one thing to acknowledge the military dominance of the USSR, another to interpret it as a *threat* to the West in general or Britain in particular. It could be perceived, more sympathetically, as a purely defensive strategy, adopted in automatic historical response to memories of the German invasion of 1941, or in reaction to a Western (or Chinese) military buildup. Almost half (44 percent) volunteered that the "USSR has built up its military power to defend itself from attack" (MORI 1/83).

A variety of surveys, however, reveal that the overwhelming majority see the USSR as a military threat to Britain and the rest of Europe (85 percent do, only eight percent do not), and substantial majorities see it as a political and scientific threat as well (see Table 2.3). There is even a slight majority (47 to 41 percent) who consider the USSR to be an economic threat, although what respondents had in mind is unclear (not, of course, cheap imports, cheap labor or investment, but control over oil or gold supplies perhaps, or, more likely, the belief that Soviet-inspired trade union militants sabotage and disrupt industrial production). More specifically, the USSR is seen as an aggressive, expansive power, as much a danger to poorer, developing countries as to the West. In January 1983, 59 percent volunteered that the USSR "wishes to extend its power over other countries," 44 percent that it "interferes in the politics of developing countries." Another poll (NOP 5/80), which asked a closed rather than open-ended question, found starker evidence of mistrust of Soviet military intentions: 81 percent agreed that "the Russians are deliberately trying to increase the number of countries under their control"; only 11 percent disagreed.

To portray the USSR as a threat is not necessarily to see it as the *only* threat to Britain's interests. Substantial minorities attribute to the United States the same threat to British and European interests as the majority

Table 2.2 Expectations about the power of the USSR and the United States

	(1) % predicting increase *minus* % predicting decline in power of US	(2) % predicting increase *minus* % predicting decline in power of USSR	(1)–(2) balance of expectations about power of US and USSR
1957	+ 3	+ 30	– 27
1958	+ 16	+ 20	– 4
1959	+ 18	+ 30	– 12
1960	+ 25	+ 36	– 11
1961	+ 23	+ 31	– 8
1962	+ 30	+ 4	+ 26
1963	+ 27	+ 23	+ 4
1964	+ 33	+ 24	+ 9
1965	+ 30	+ 20	+ 10
1966	+ 23	+ 27	– 4
1967	+ 13	+ 36	– 23
1968	+ 25	+ 40	– 15
1969	+ 23	+ 28	– 5
1970	+ 10	+ 33	– 23
1971	+ 1	+ 26	– 25
1972	+ 15	+ 8	+ 7
1973	+ 10	+ 22	– 12
1974	– 2	+ 34	+ 36
1975	+ 3	+ 32	– 29
1976	+ 23	+ 34	– 11
1977	+ 14	+ 30	– 16
1978	+ 8	+ 40	– 32
1979	+ 16	+ 35	– 19
1980	+ 34	+ 44	– 10
1981	+ 32	+ 23	+ 9
1982	+ 28	+ 34	– 6

Source: *Gallup Political Index* 268, December 1982

Note:
Question wording:
"Which of these do you think is likely to be true of 19... (next year): Russia (America) will increase her power in the world; Russian (American) power will decline?"

attribute to the USSR. For example, about a third claimed that the United States posed a political, economic, scientific, or military threat (Gallup 12/80, Table 2.3); 26 percent volunteered that the United States wishes to "extend its power over other countries"; 28 percent that "it interferes in the politics of developing countries." The USSR alarms the majority, but

Table 2.3   Perception of the threats posed to Britain and other European countries by the USSR and the United States (Gallup 1/80)

| | Does the USSR/US pose a threat in the | | | |
	military field?	political field?	scientific field?	economic field?
USSR:				
Yes	85	73	61	47
No	8	19	29	41
Don't know	6	8	10	12
US:				
Yes	35	29	36	33
No	54	62	51	53
Don't know	11	9	13	13
Balance of threat[a]	50	44	25	14

[a] Percentage seeing the USSR as a threat, *minus* percentage seeing the United States as a threat.

the United States alarms the minority (many of whom are the same people).

When surveys force respondents to say which of the two powers is the greater threat to peace, or to British interests, the USSR is always cited more often—but not conspicuously more often (see Table 2.4). For example, when asked to say which represented a greater threat to British security, 43 percent answered "the presence of Soviet missiles in Eastern Europe," but 29 percent said "the proposed installation of American missiles in Western Europe," and a further 28 percent were "don't knows"—an unusually large number, suggesting genuine uncertainty rather than apathy or ignorance on the part of many. A similar response emerged two years later (Gallup 2/83) when people were asked, "Which is more likely to start a nuclear attack in Europe, the United States or Russia?" The answers were as follows: Russia, 48 percent; United States, 28 percent; don't know, 24 percent (again, a high figure). It would be useful to have trend data on the question of which power is seen as the greater threat to peace, as I suspect that the gap between the two has narrowed. Unfortunately, no such data are available.

RELATIONSHIP WITH THE SOVIET UNION:
GOODWILL, TRUST, RELIABILITY

We have already seen that the level of general trust in the USSR is very low, but for many people "trust" in an abstract context boils down to little more than "like." And even among those to whom it denotes good faith, adherence to commitments, benevolence of intention, and so on, it would

Table 2.4   The USSR vs. the United States as a nuclear threat to British and European Security (Gallup)

Which represents the greater threat to the security of Britain?

	11/81
The presence of Soviet missiles in Eastern Europe	43
The proposed installation of American missiles in Western Europe	29
Don't know	28

Which is more likely to start a nuclear attack in Europe, the United States or Russia?

	2/83
Russia	48
United States	28
Don't know	24

not be inconsistent to combine general suspicion with trust on specific matters. One can trust one's enemies to keep a bargain without doubting that they remain enemies.

There is precious little evidence, however, that even grudging trust of this kind exists; there is little willingness to give Soviet good faith the benefit of the doubt (see Table 2.5). Over the past five years consistently three times as many say that Soviet advances "should be treated with suspicion" as believe that "Russia really wants to be friendly with the West." The absence of belief in Soviet sincerity, integrity, or good judgment is even more glaring in surveys that ask respondents to volunteer opinions rather than choose between proferred statements. In a February 1983 survey by Market and Opinion Research International only three percent volunteered that Soviet leaders "have sound judgment," five percent that the USSR "could be trusted to keep its word on disarmament," and nine percent that it "genuinely wants world peace." Good faith in the United States, however, is not much higher and has clearly fallen over the past two years. Sober scepticism bordering on deep cynicism informs popular attitudes to *both* superpowers, but especially the USSR.

The main conclusion to be drawn from the evidence so far is that, if attitudes on nuclear defense and the Atlantic Alliance have changed, this is not because of any softening of opinion about the Soviet Union. The Soviet image remains massively unfavorable in British eyes: The USSR is not seen as more benevolent either at home or in the world at large, there is no gullibility about its political system, and its military buildup is recognized and seen as a threat. However, the image of the Soviet Union is one thing; views on NATO's double-track decision and the United States' role in Britain's defense quite another. The first is only one component of

Table 2.5   Perceptions of trustworthiness and reliability of the United States and USSR (MORI)

	Percentage agreeing that statement applies to				Difference (US minus USSR)	
	US		USSR			
	10/81	1/83	10/81	1/83	10/81	1/83
Genuinely wants world peace	40	35	6	9	34	26
Can be trusted to keep its word on disarmament	22	16	5	5	17	11
Their leaders have sound judgment	14	9	6	3	8	6

the second. An unflattering near-consensus about the USSR is not inconsistent with a growing disagreement on Britain's defense strategy and international alliances. The next section deals with a second possible component in the dissensus: conflicting images of security.

Images of Security

FEAR OF WAR

Despite a recovery of moderate optimism about the immediate prospects of peace in the world, there undoubtedly remains a deep undercurrent of worry about nuclear war in Britain. Until very recently increasing numbers expected a nuclear war in the foreseeable future. Very few gave themselves any chance of survival. Despite the level of concern few people think anything can be done about it. Unilateral nuclear disarmament is rejected as a solution by the majority, demonstrations on behalf of unilateralism by an even larger majority. "Fatalistic awareness" may be a better description of the public mood than mere "worry." These conclusions are a simple summary of a variety of poll evidence. A more detailed commentary on some tables of evidence follows.

By the end of 1982 twice as many people in Britain were pessimistic (43 percent) as optimistic (21 percent) about the likelihood of international peace over the forthcoming year, and a large minority (36 percent) had no definite view (Gallup 12/82). Pessimists were not necessarily envisaging world war or nuclear conflict, but they did expect international disputes. This sober view of the world's immediate future is not particularly pessimistic by the standards of the last quarter-century. The identical question has been asked by Gallup at the end of every year since 1957. On only two occasions (1959 and 1963) have optimists outnumbered pessimists. The 22 percent majority of pessimists is about average for the whole

Table 2.6   Expectations about international peace over the next twelve months (Gallup)

| | The coming year will be: | | | |
	(1) Peaceful, more or less free of international disputes	(2) Troubled, with much international discord	No opinion	(1) minus (2)
12/70	23	45	32	− 22
12/71	16	61	23	− 45
12/72	25	55	20	− 30
12/73	20	61	18	− 41
12/74	14	69	17	− 55
12/75	26	53	21	− 27
12/76	24	47	29	− 23
12/77	33	33	34	0
12/78	16	45	39	− 29
12/79	7	69	24	− 62
12/80	10	64	26	− 54
12/81	15	55	29	− 40
12/82	21	43	36	− 22

quarter-century, and small compared with most years since 1970 (see Table 2.6). Indeed, since late 1979, immediately after the Soviet invasion of Afghanistan, when pessimism reached record levels (69 percent, as against a mere seven percent of optimists), there has been some recovery of optimism. This is corroborated by a different poll, which reported that the proportion of people thinking that prospects for world peace were improving had risen from 17 to 30 percent between April 1981 and January 1983, whereas the proportion of those thinking they were deteriorating had fallen from 65 to 40 percent (Marplan 4/81, 1/83).

The number expecting nuclear war has drifted upward since the autumn of 1980 (see Table 2.7). In February 1983, for the first time, pessimists outnumbered optimists. The contrast with April 1963, shortly after the Cuban missile crisis and after five years of activity by the Campaign for Nuclear Disarmament (CND), is very sharp: then only 16 percent expected a nuclear war and 59 percent did not. It would seem that the arguments of the antinuclear movement have at least succeeded in making many people, including those who do not support them, more concerned about the possibility of nuclear war, and that their arguments have carried more conviction than those of their parent organization, CND, a generation ago.

There has been a commensurate increase in worry: 56 percent are

Table 2.7   Expectation of nuclear war (Gallup)

	4/63	9/80	11/81	11/82	2/83
Yes, likely	16	39	42	38	49
No, not likely	59	45	42	44	36
Don't know	25	16	16	18	16
"Yes" minus "No"	−33	−6	0	−6	+7

Note:
Question wording:
"Do you think it is likely or not that there is ever going to be a nuclear war?"

"very" or "fairly" worried (25 and 31 percent, respectively) about "the chances of world war breaking out in which nuclear bombs are used" (Gallup 4/83). This is a slight drop from two months earlier (28 and 33 percent, respectively) but still markedly more than when the identical question was asked 19 years ago, and the proportion of worriers was 40 percent. In the last two or three years the British people have been more frightened by the possibility of a nuclear holocaust than ever before.

These questions make no reference to a time span. Some who worry may believe that nuclear war will come, but not for generations or centuries. Of those believing a nuclear war to be likely (49 percent), nearly a third could not predict when it would break out (Gallup 2/83). Among the remainder, 35 percent (or 17 percent of all respondents) expected it to come within ten years, 55 percent (or 27 percent of all respondents) within 20 years, that is, if not within their own lifetime then almost certainly within that of their children. In answer to NOP's question "How likely do you think it is that there will be a nuclear war *in your lifetime*?" (12/81 (italics added)), 38 percent thought it certain, very likely, or fairly likely, a figure close to the 42 percent recorded by Gallup a month later. However, some older respondents in NOP's survey may have replied "unlikely," knowing that their answer would be different if they had another 50 years to live: NOP found that 66 percent of those aged 55 and over, as against 32 percent of 18 to 24 year-olds, said a nuclear war was unlikely or certain not to occur.

People are even more pessimistic about the outbreak of another world war. NOP reports that in June 1980—six months after the Soviet invasion of Afghanistan—65 percent believed that there would be a World War III, 50 percent expecting it within 20 years. These proportions are higher than those claiming to foresee a nuclear war, because they include people who expect World War III to be fought by conventional weapons alone. However, the majority think that a new world war would be nuclear (46 to 31 percent, 16 percent saying it would be both nuclear and conventional).

People know what they are afraid of: they have no illusions about surviving a nuclear war. The proportions acknowledging that they would have no chance, or almost none, of living through it are overwhelming, and still increasing: 77 percent in September 1980 (Gallup), 76 percent in December 1981 (NOP), and again in February 1983 (Gallup). Many of the remainder are "don't knows," not optimists. People are slightly more sanguine about the chances of Britain as a nation surviving. About one in four (26 percent in September 1980 and 24 percent in February 1983) thought it would have at least a "fair chance;" only two percent gave Britain a "very good" chance. In the cases of both personal and national survival women, the young, and the working class were slightly more pessimistic than men, the old, and the middle classes, but the differences were always slender.

SALIENCE OF NATIONAL SECURITY

For a matter of public concern to become a political issue, it is not sufficient for large numbers of citizens to be worried. To be regarded as a subject of political debate and governmental decision, opinions on an issue must be represented and mobilized to action by a pressure group or, more frequently, by a political party. This has been the case with nuclear weapons and defense in Britain. Between 1979 and 1983, under the new Conservative government, the issue only rose to prominence in the public's mind in the final nine months; however, by the time of the 1983 election it was the second most salient issue and probably the most influential in changing people's vote. The trend in salience is presented in Table 2.8.

In the 1979 general election, defense was not an issue at all, being mentioned by only two percent of respondents and ranking fourteenth in importance. Its slow, fitful, and late rise to prominence correlates not with important events in the history of East-West relations or arms negotiations. Instead, it parallels the publicity given to the peace movement's campaign in Britain, notably the demonstration by women unilateralists at Greenham Common, but also the Labour party's adoption of unilateral nuclear disarmament in its election manifesto. The rapid movement of defense issues to the forefront of the 1983 election campaign was the result of the Labour leader, Michael Foot's long-held personal commitment to nuclear disarmament, of conspicuous strains within the Labour party's senior group over defense policy (in particular the future of Polaris), and of the decision of the Conservative government to make its differences with the Labour party over defense a major subject of the campaign.

This is perhaps the appropriate place to describe briefly the electoral impact of the defense issue in the 1983 election. There is no doubt that it did substantial damage to Labour's vote, to the benefit of both the Conservatives and the Liberal/Social Democratic alliance. This alliance is firmly antiunilateralist and pro-NATO, but opposed to the Trident pro-

Table 2.8   Salience of Defense (Gallup)

		Percentage mentioning defense as one of the two most urgent problems facing the country	Rank
1979	general election	2	14
	3rd quarter	a	b
	4th quarter	a	b
1980	1st quarter	a	b
	2nd quarter	3	12
	3rd quarter	3	10
	4th quarter	4	6
1981	1st quarter	1	8
	2nd quarter	6	4
	3rd quarter	6	6
	4th quarter	8	4
1982	1st quarter	6	4
	2nd quarter	5	5
	3rd quarter	5	6
	4th quarter	10	3
1983	1st quarter	15	3
	general election	38	2

Note:
Question wording:

"What would you say is the most urgent problem facing the country at the present time? And what would you say is the next most urgent problem?"

The question is asked every month. The figures given for each quarter are the mean across each of the three months.

a below two percent
b not applicable

gram. The two parties do not entirely see eye to eye on the future of Polaris or the conditions under which cruise missiles should be accepted on British soil.

Among those for whom it was an important issue, the Conservatives were preferred to Labour as the party for defense by a massive 54 percent majority. Voters switching from Labour since the previous election in 1979 were more likely to mention defense as an important issue (42 percent) than those sticking with Labour (33 percent). They also took markedly different views: 47 percent of Labour defectors, compared with only 24 percent of Labour loyalists, supported the siting of cruise missiles in Britain; 77 percent opposed the policy of renouncing Polaris regardless

Table 2.9   Views of the correct British response to three cases of Soviet aggression (NOP 10/81)

	What should Britain do if Russia and its allies launch		
	a *non*nuclear attack on Europe but *not* Britain	a *nuclear* attack on West Europe but *not* Britain	a *nuclear* attack on Britain
Launch a nuclear attack on Russia	6	28	62
Launch a nonnuclear attack on Russia	39	13	6
Not attack Russia	41	40	11
Don't know	14	19	22

of whether the USSR reduced its nuclear arms, compared with 59 percent of Labour loyalists. Those sticking with Labour did so despite Labour's defense policy; those deserting Labour did so, at least partly, because of the policy. Not since the war has defense played such a significant role in an election outcome.

FEASIBILITY AND ACCEPTANCE OF DEFENSE

The British public is anxious and increasingly pessimistic about the possible outbreak of nuclear war and readier than for many decades to vote for parties on the basis of their defense policies. But do they consider a defense of Britain—or Western Europe, for that matter—either practicable or justifiable? And, if so, what kind of defense: nuclear, conventional, or passive resistance?

What little evidence exists on this subject indicates a high level of acceptance of nuclear counterattack as a defensive posture. People were asked (NOP 10/81) what the government should do if it seemed likely that Russia would attack or invade Britain. Sixty percent replied, "defend Britain at all costs"; 26 percent, "hold out for the best terms"; and four percent, "surrender unconditionally" (ten percent did not know). Defending Britain at all costs turns out to mean precisely that: it includes a nuclear response to a Russian nuclear attack on Britain. Resort to such means won far less approval, however, when it came to defending Western Europe from Soviet aggression. The full flavor of British responses is set out in Table 2.9. Thus, in the case of Soviet aggression against Western Europe, excluding Britain, the single most popular response was for Britain not to engage in conflict with the Soviet Union, but there was still a slight majority fo some sort of counterattack, either nuclear or conven-

Table 2.10 Perceptions of whether it is better to resist or submit to Russian domination (Gallup 3/82)

	(1) Better to fight	(2) Better to be dominated	Don't know	(1) minus (2)
United States	83	6	11	77
Switzerland	77	8	15	69
Great Britain	75	12	13	63
Germany	74	19	7	55
France	57	13	30	44
Denmark	51	17	32	34
Belgium	45	14	41	31

Note:
Question wording:

"Some people say that war is now so horrible that it is better to accept Russian domination than to risk war. Others say that it would be better to fight in defense of Britain (United States, Switzerland, etc.) than to accept Russian domination. Which opinion is closer to your own?"

tional. In the case of a Soviet nuclear attack against Britain, on the other hand, 62 percent said they supported a nuclear counterattack, and only 11 percent wanted Britain to avoid further conflict.

Resistance against Soviet aggression appears to be much stronger in Britain than other European countries. In March 1982—before the Falklands war aroused national self-confidence—a cross-national survey (see Table 2.10) found that although readiness to resist Russian domination was slightly stronger in the United States than in Western Europe, within Europe it was greater in Britain than in France or, surprisingly, Germany. It was fractionally greater still in Switzerland, which is also unexpected, given its neutralist and pacific tradition. The weakest will to resist was found in Denmark and Belgium. This cannot be attributed entirely to their small size because potential resistance is very high in Switzerland, but Swiss terrain is, of course, much easier to defend or to use as a base for guerilla resistance (or, indeed, as protection in a nuclear aftermath) than Danish or Belgian terrain. Note that this question makes no explicit mention of *nuclear* attack, but stresses the horror of modern war, and so does offer the respondent a good reason for accepting Russian domination. Nonetheless, for every one British respondent willing to surrender, more than six preferred to fight. Nor can the robust response of the British be put down to nostalgic delusions of grandeur about their country's status or power in the world. Even at the triumphant culmination of the Falklands war, the public was realistic about Britain's place in the world: 71 percent agreed that it will become increasingly difficult to ignore the views of the rest of the world, and 64 percent agreed that the war showed that Britain needs the help of others, such as America and European countries (MORI 6/82). Eight months later, Gallup found that twice as many believed that Britain's influence in the world had fallen (46 percent) rather than risen (22 percent) over the previous two years, and a majority wanted Britain to be more like Sweden and Switzerland rather than a world power (35 percent). Nonetheless, there is little of the small nation "Soldier Schweik" tradition of resigned submission and passive resistance in the outlook of the British public.

NATIONAL SERVICE

Conscription was abolished almost a quarter of a century ago and civil defense is a voluntary and minority activity. Thus the great majority of the postwar generation has no experience of any kind of military service, and their attitudes toward national service as a form of security will not be based on direct personal knowledge. There is, in fact, no data on whether the public believes the presently constituted armed forces adequate to the task of defending Britain in case of attack, or on whether Britain would be more secure if national service were reintroduced. The restoration of conscription has not been raised in public as a serious policy option by any government and is therefore not a political issue in Britain.

However, two surveys asking differently formatted questions suggest that the response of young men and women to national service would, on balance, be positive, although not enthusiastic. In February 1983, Gallup asked, "Suppose the government decided that it was necessary to reintroduce compulsory military service for men. *Assuming* that you were the right age, how willing would you be to serve in the forces?" Over two-thirds of all men (68 percent) said they were very or fairly willing; 11 percent were not very willing; only 19 percent not at all willing—which does not mean that they would refuse. However, only a small majority (56 percent) of men aged 18 to 34 were very or fairly willing. Women were asked about their attitudes if they had a man of the right age in their family. The response was similar, although slightly less enthusiastic: 63 percent were very or fairly willing, 17 percent not very willing, 18 percent not at all.

Gallup's question did not mention the context in which national military service might be reintroduced; in particular, it contained no mention of war or national emergency. An earlier survey, however, referred to a conventional war and found a more widespread acceptance of military service among the young (NOP 6/80). Few of either sex would actually refuse to serve—and remember that many of the women in the sample will be mothers of young families—but many more would wait for a call-up rather than volunteer. Not unexpectedly, young men (18 to 24) were the

**Table 2.11 Willingness to serve in armed forces for respondents below age 35
(NOP 6/80)**

	Total	Men 18–24	Men 25–34	Women 18–24	Women 25–34
Volunteer to serve with the armed forces	28	40	30	21	21
Not volunteer, but *obey* a call-up to serve with the armed forces	54	44	59	63	53
Refuse to serve with the armed forces	10	8	4	12	16
Don't know	8	8	8	4	11

Note:
Question wording:

"In the event of a conventional (nonnuclear) war, would you *volunteer* to serve with the armed forces; not volunteer, but *obey* a call-up to serve with the armed forces; or *refuse* to serve with the armed forces?"

most likely to volunteer: the high youth unemployment rate will have been a factor here (see Table 2.11). The overall impression conforms to that given by questions on willingness to resist Soviet aggression. The overwhelming majority assume that foreign attack should be resisted by military means and that they would be involved in such resistance; radical pacifist dissent is confined to approximately one in ten.

THE PEACE MOVEMENT

The peace movement encompasses a variety of groups that have rapidly grown in support since late 1979, when NATO's double-track decision was taken. The majority of its active supporters are opposed to British possession of nuclear weapons of any description, whether independent or as part of Britain's NATO commitments, whether land- or sea-based. Most wish to see Britain withdraw from NATO, although this is a secondary consideration. A minority support a strengthening of conventional forces in exchange for a nonnuclear defense, but the majority are strongly opposed to the priority given to defense in public policy: to levels of defense expenditure, to the secrecy and centralization of defense policy-making and defense institutions, and to the culture of values and assumptions that accompanies concern about defense. The majority take little interest in a radical defense policy such as a network of citizen militias or a massive civil defense program. Indeed, most active supporters disparage

Table 2.12 Willingness to participate personally in protest against nuclear weapons (Gallup)

	9/80	11/80	11/82
Worried and willing to join demonstrations	7	10	9
Worried and willing to write to MP or newspaper	4	7	7
Worried but won't do anything about it	17	17	17
Worried but do not think anything can be done	37	38	39
Not worried	30	26	25
Don't know	5	3	3

civil defense as inescapably ineffective in a small, densely populated country such as Britain and as a smoke screen behind which successive British governments have hidden the impossibility of securing the survival of the mass population from a nuclear attack.

The main *target* of the peace movement, however, has been the installation of cruise missiles in Britain. The intended bases were the sites of mass demonstrations, many of them larger than any seen since the antibomb demonstrations of the late 1950s. The most publicized demonstrations of all were at the Greenham Common base, where for the last two and a half years a permanent camp of women has been protesting. The peace movement has massively succeeded in getting attention. In January 1983, a few weeks after a large women's demonstration at Greenham Common, 94 percent said that they had heard about the protest (MORI 1/83)—an astonishing penetration of an electorate of whom only 73 percent bothered to vote at the general election five months later. Moreover, it has succeeded in getting many more to reflect upon the issue: 49 percent said that it had made them think a lot or at least a little more about disarmament.

On balance, the British public's reaction to the peace movement's *aims* has been one of sympathetic scepticism; toward its more publicized methods, it has been less sympathetic and less convinced of their propriety or effectiveness. For example, among those worried by nuclear weapons— about three quarters of the public—fewer than one in four even claim that they are willing to engage in any form of protest, even the most minimal and entirely proper kinds such as writing to their MP or to the press. Only nine percent (11/82) claim to be willing to join a demonstration (which almost certainly exaggerates the true number). The majority (56 percent) say they are worried but will not, or believe they cannot, do anything

Table 2.13 Attitudes toward the peace movement and demonstrations

	MORI 1/83	MORI 4/83
More favorable	31	20
Less favorable	14	14
No difference	53	60
No opinion	2	4

Note:
Question wording:

"Has the protest made you more favorable or less favorable to the campaign to prevent cruise missiles being based in Britain or has it made no difference one way or another?"

	Gallup 11/81	Gallup 2/83	Gallup 4/83
Completely in agreement	23	18	14
To some extent in agreement	29	36	31
To some extent opposed	15	17	18
Completely opposed	24	23	33
Don't know	8	5	4

Note:
Question wording:

"Demonstrations against nuclear weapons have recently taken place in Britain and elsewhere in Europe; do you personally feel completely in agreement, to some extent in agreement, to some extent opposed, or completely opposed to these particular demonstrations?"

about it; fatalism reigns. On this there has been no movement of opinion between 1980 and 1982, which suggests that the televised coverage of the demonstrations has failed to persuade more people to become actively opposed to, as distinct from passively anxious about, nuclear weapons (see Table 2.12).

Nonetheless, active protest can influence the opinions of those who are unwilling to join in. The peace movement has, in fact, succeeded in turning more people against than in favor of cruise missiles—although only just and decreasingly so, as Table 2.13 reveals. Many of those saying "more" or "less" are probably people with long-committed opinions one way or another; the proportion of genuine converts will be small. The significant feature is the high, and rising, proportion who say that the demonstrations make no difference to their views.

The most likely reason for the recent small decline in the persuasiveness of the peace movement is that it has become less peaceful, and as publicity for its protests has grown, so too has popular unease with some of their methods. Table 2.13 shows that a slight majority (52 percent in November 1981 and 54 percent in February 1983—after the women's mass demonstration at Greenham Common in late 1982) were at least to some extent in agreement with the (then) entirely peaceful and respectable demonstrations. However, by April 1983 there was a sharp downturn of support. This was probably because of the widely televised direct action (sit-downs) and minor civil disobedience of the permanent camp of demonstrators, many of whom are radical feminists whose increasingly unkempt appearance will have alienated some segments of otherwise mildly sympathetic opinion. There was a marked fall in the proportion in complete agreement with the demonstrations (from 23 to 14 percent between November 1981 and April 1983) and an equivalent rise in the proportion in complete opposition (from 24 to 33 percent). Those with strong views, in other words, had turned decisively against the demonstrators over the eighteen-month period, and among all respondents what started as a slight majority in sympathy had turned into a slight majority in opposition.

An equally recent but more detailed survey (MORI 4/83) found stronger opposition to the antinuclear protests: Their tactics earned the approval of only a one-quarter minority, leaving the majority, if not all hostile, then at least uneasy or indifferent. Twenty nine percent approved of their tactics, 26 percent held a favorable opinion of them; 24 percent thought they contributed to peace. By contrast, 58 percent disapproved of their tactics, 54 percent held an unfavorable opinion of them; and as many as 70 percent thought their protests made no difference to peace (24 percent) or actually made peace more difficult to achieve (fully 46 percent said this).

We might summarize the data in this subsection as follows: a quarter of the British public—the same proportion that wants a nonnuclear defense strategy—approve of both the object and tactics of the peace movement. Another quarter sympathize with their broad aims and concerns but are sceptical about their methods and would not join them. Another 40 percent or so reject both their objectives and tactics and do not share their concerns, and the remaining ten percent have no views to speak of. That this latter figure is so small is testimony to the public impact of the peace movement, that their real support is no more than a quarter is testimony to its not insubstantial yet limited appeal.

Images of Deterrence

ACCEPTANCE OF DETERRENCE

The preceding section showed that a substantial majority in Britain say they would be prepared to use nuclear weapons in some circumstances, such as a countermove against a Russian nuclear attack; an overwhelming majority would choose vigorous and sustained resistance in preference to only limited action or unconditional surrender. This does not tell us, however, what the British public thinks would most deter the USSR from attacking in the first place.

There appears to be no evidence about British attitudes to theories of

Table 2.14 The armed forces Britain should adopt (Gallup)

	1/83	4/83
Rely on both nuclear weapons and a strong conventional nonnuclear force	54	51
Rely on nuclear weapons with only a small conventional nonnuclear force	9	10
Be strong in conventional, nonnuclear weapons, but no nuclear weapons	22	24
Have only a few or no weapons of any kind	8	9
Don't know	6	5

Note:
Question wording:

"Taking everything into account, including the cost, which of these comes closest to your view of what armed forces Britain should have to reduce the chances of war?"

conflict, aggression, and war, including the role of deterrence. Presumably no more than a small minority have settled convictions on such theoretical and abstract matters. However, a deeply embedded belief, especially among older generations who lived through World War II, stemming from Britain's failure to stop the continental spread of fascism in the 1930s, is that appeasement and inadequate defenses only encourage expansionist states to aggression. Among those old enough to remember, experiences of that war color their thinking about defense strategy now, with the USSR replacing Nazi Germany as Britain's main enemy. The pacifist tradition, rooted in Protestant Nonconformity and political radicalism, has survived but is very weak even among the churches and intelligentsia and virtually nonexistent in the rest of the population.

THE ROLE OF NUCLEAR WEAPONS

There exists a small amount of data on people's perception of the deterrent effects of nuclear weapons, and of the relative merits of conventional, as opposed to nuclear, weapons in preventing war. The most recent evidence is presented in Table 2.14, which is based on a somewhat clumsily conceived question that asks respondents to choose an optimal mixture of nuclear and conventional forces after taking considerations of both cost and deterrent effects into account. The factor of cost will have slightly reduced the proportion choosing a nuclear option; nonetheless, a clear majority (more than 60 percent) chose an explicitly nuclear defense strategy. Only one in five would rely on strong conventional forces exclusively, and only one in twelve would opt for quasi or real pacifism.

Table 2.15 Approval of unilateral nuclear disarmament (Gallup)

	9/80	11/81	11/82	1/83	4/83
Good idea	21	33	29	28	27
Bad idea	67	58	61	65	66
Don't know	12	9	10	6	7

The same picture emerges when a simpler, dichotomous question—whether to renounce or retain nuclear weapons—is put to respondents (see Table 2.15). The proportion opting for a nonnuclear defense was again between a quarter and a third. It rose from 21 to 33 percent during 1981—the year the antinuclear movement grew most in membership, but the year before its protests received most publicity—but since then has drifted down slightly to 27 percent (4/83). A trichotomous question asked by Marplan produced a lower level of support for a nonnuclear defense strategy. In answer to "Should Britain abandon nuclear weapons, no matter what other countries do, or maintain our (sic) current capability, or improve it by spending more money on nuclear weapons?" 21 percent replied "abandon nuclear weapons" in April 1981, and 23 percent in January 1983. These figures will have been slightly depressed by the emotive word abandon and by a question structure that places the maintenance of current nuclear capabilities in a middle category, the category that is most attractive to those without firm opinions. Nonetheless, there has been a real decline in support for unilateral nuclear disarmament: in the 1983 election campaign it had dropped to 16 percent (NOP 5/83), compared with 34 percent less than two years earlier (NOP 9/81).

However, a regularly asked question that focused specifically on the *deterrent* effect of nuclear weapons produced an apparently different response. By early 1983 only six percent more thought that the risk of nuclear attack on Britain decreased rather than increased as a result of their possession (Gallup 1/83). The proportion regarding nuclear weapons as a deterrent has consistently been lower than those approving of a nuclear defense for Britain (see Table 2.16). Closer scrutiny of the figures, however, shows that the discrepancy is more apparent than real. If the proportion believing nuclear weapons to have no effect on the likelihood of war is added to those regarding it as a deterrent, the difference almost disappears. Those seeing nuclear weapons on British soil as more likely to provoke than prevent nuclear war are always in the minority, albeit a substantial one of between a quarter and just over a third, the same size as the minority who opt for a nonnuclear defense strategy. It seems odd, nonetheless, that people who think that nuclear weapons have no effect on the prospects of war approve of spending money on a nuclear defense.

Table 2.16   Perception of the deterrent effect of British nuclear weapons (Gallup)

	9/80	9/81	11/81	11/82	1/83
Increases	26	26	31	28	35
No effect	27	27	22	24	17
Decreases	37	37	36	41	41
Don't know	20	10	10	7	7

Note:
Question wording:

"Do you think that the fact that Britain itself has nuclear weapons increases or decreases the risk of a nuclear attack on this country?"

Perhaps they take the view that the incidence and occasion of war is inherently unpredictable but that the retention of nuclear weapons allows Britain to deter follow-up attacks and prevent complete obliteration. Others in this category are probably "closet" don't knows (note how the "no effect" and "don't know" percentages decline in tandem over the period) who, perhaps, have a gut instinct in favor of strong defense without feeling able to predict the likely consequences.

AMERICAN NUCLEAR WEAPONS

Reaction to the likely deterrent effects of American or NATO weapons on British soil, however, is different; and this time the difference is not illusory or an artifact of question format. Forty-two percent think that having American nuclear missiles in Britain increases the chances of a nuclear attack, compared with 29 percent who think that they provide greater protection (see Table 2.17). A question on the effect of nuclear weapons without the tag of American as a prefix was not asked simultaneously, but three months earlier (Gallup 11/81) only 31 percent said that their presence made a nuclear attack more likely. Why the British should consider U.S. nuclear missiles more provocative than British nuclear missiles is not clear, given independent evidence of the high degree of trust felt by the British in Americans (for details, see Images of Allies). The puzzle is confounded by the fact that the question about the effect of American nuclear missiles was asked in three other European countries at the same time, and in each case narrow majorities thought that they acted as a deterrent rather than a provocation: 14 percent in Germany, eight percent in Denmark, and one percent in Belgium. Perhaps the British regard the United States as readier than Britain to initiate an attack against the USSR, perhaps the USSR is regarded as more likely to attack countries that are hosts to American, rather than natively owned, weapons. But neither of these explanations can account for the difference in

Table 2.17 Perception of deterrent effect of American forces in Britain (Gallup 2/82)

	US missiles	US troops
Increases chances of attack	42	25
Has no effect	24	46
Provides greater protection	29	24
Don't know	5	5

attitudes between Britain and the three other European countries. In the absence of better data one can only speculate, after making a note for reference in the next section, that accompanying British goodwill toward the United States are doubts among a large minority about the wisdom of relying on American missiles in Britain for the country's defense.

CRUISE MISSILES AND AMERICAN BASES IN BRITAIN

It is in the preceding context that one must assess the contradictory evidence about the British public's attitude to the implementation of NATO's double-track decision. Part of the apparent confusion stems from the timing and phrasing of opinion poll questions, but part of it reflects a real ambivalence, perhaps downright confusion, in the public mind. Opinion surveys ask one question at a time and do not require respondents to be consistent, even in the loosest sense, in their set of answers. There is nothing to discourage them from trying to square circles and to have the best of all possible worlds.

For two to three years before the 1983 election campaign, a majority had consistently opposed the siting of cruise missiles in Britain (Table 2.18). The level of opposition fluctuated, sometimes in response to contemporary events: immediately after the women's demonstration at Greenham Common in December 1982, for example, support for cruise missiles in Britain ebbed to its lowest point. It is also a function of question phrasing, as shown by the discrepancy between the MORI and Marplan polls, which were both conducted in January 1983. Marplan's question referred to "allowing the *Americans*" (not NATO) to base missiles on *British soil* [italics added], whereas MORI's question referred neither to Americans nor to British soil and was therefore the more neutrally worded of the two. Marplan's question probably induced a few waverers to disapprove. Nonetheless, the impact of question wording is slight in the context of the consistent evidence that, when asked whether they want cruise missiles in Britain, the majority of the British public, until very recently, said no.

During the 1983 election campaign, there was a marked turnaround of opinion: For the first time supporters of cruise missiles in Britain outnumbered opponents and by election day they made up 50 percent of the

Table 2.18 Attitude toward installation of cruise missiles in Britain

	Marplan 4/81	MORI 10/81	Gallup 10/82	MORI 1/83	Marplan 1/83	Gallup 2/83	NOP 5/83	Gallup 6/83
Approve	41	31	31	36	27	32	48	50
Disapprove	50	59	58	54	61	54	38	39
Don't know	9	10	11	10	12	13	14	10
Approve minus Disapprove	−9	−28	−27	−18	−34	−22	+10	+11

Note:
Question wording:

Marplan:
"Do you approve or disapprove of the government's decision to allow the Americans to base cruise missiles on British soil?"

MORI:
"I am going to read out some suggestions people have made regarding the defense policies of this country. Please tell me whether, on balance, you think Britain should or should not do each one...: Allow cruise missiles to be placed in Britain."

Gallup:
"Do you think Britain should or should not allow the new American-controlled nuclear cruise missiles to be based here?" (10/82, 2/83)
"Please say whether you think the (following) proposal is a very good idea, a fairly good idea, a fairly bad idea or a very bad idea: Allowing cruise missiles to be sited in Britain as part of the West's defense (6/83; approve = very good + fairly good idea, disapprove = very bad + fairly bad idea)

NOP:
"Please say whether you agree or disagree with the following statement: Britain should ban cruise missiles from being stationed in Britain."

electorate. This change of mood was due to the prominence of defense issues, but exactly why it occurred is difficult to say. Advocates of cruise missiles will wish to think that the public was converted once the supporting arguments were presented vigorously and the public had to give serious thought to the issue. Sceptics will claim that attitudes to cruise missiles were a by-product of prior partisanship and that as Conservative support consolidated and Labour support slumped so opinion on the missiles appeared to change. The objection to the latter argument, however, is that Conservative support did not *rise* during the campaign, but stayed steady. It was the Social Democratic Party's vote that went up, and its policy was opposed to cruise missiles. Moreover, examination of trends in opinion among supporters of the three parties shows that opposition to cruise missiles fell at a similar rate in all three groups. The sharp change in public attitudes was not simply a matter of the Conservative party persuading its usual supporters to toe the party line; the change occurred throughout the electorate.

Nonetheless, rejection remains very substantial. Why? Are they rejecting the missile because it is a Cruise, or because it is in some sense "American," or for another reason? There is no direct evidence, but contextual evidence casts strong doubt on the idea that the source of people's objection is the distinctive features of the weapon. Simultaneous surveys reveal, with equal consistency, that a majority in Britain approves of an independently British nuclear missile. At a time when only 36 percent supported the installation of cruise missiles, 59 percent agreed that Britain should have its own nuclear deterrent independent of America (MORI 1/83). It therefore does not appear to be horror at the destruction that can be wrought by cruise missiles that makes the British public reject them. Another clue to support this conclusion can be found in the supplementary question that followed upon Marplan's standard question on these missiles in January 1983: "One option would be to build cruise missile bases but not to bring nuclear weapons over from the United States for the time being. Would you approve or disapprove of this decision?" There was virtually no more support for this "compromise" policy (30 percent approval) than for straight deployment (27 percent approval). It is not the presence of nuclear missiles in Britain, therefore, that explains the majority's rejection of cruise missiles.

Is it, then, that these missiles are seen as American owned and controlled? The answer is yes—but not entirely. We already know that more people think American missiles in Britain will increase than decrease the chance of a Russian attack, and we have noticed that questions that mention cruise missiles' American connection elicit stronger opposition than questions that do not. Yet rejection of these missiles is not a product of simpleminded anti-Americanism. Evidence reported in this chapter reveals widespread goodwill toward the United States and faith in the United States as a highly dependable ally. Indeed, opposition to an American military presence is much weaker, as Table 2.19, setting out attitudes to American bases, shows. Once again, the message contained in the data is not entirely clear, probably because of question phrasing. Unlike NOP, Gallup refers to the continuation of *existing* U.S. bases (italics added), that is, invites respondents to evaluate the status quo rather than a new situation. What is clear, however, is that acceptance of a United States military presence in Britain has grown, not shrunk, over the past 18 months and that by February 1983 a solid majority was in favor. Acceptance of a nonnuclear American presence is even wider. A MORI poll (1/83) found that only 29 percent supported the closing down of all American military, naval, and air force bases in Britain, fully 63 percent did not.

Piecing together these bits of evidence suggests that if the British public thought collectively and sequentially about cruise missiles, its reasoning would be somewhat as follows: We recognize the value of the Atlantic Alliance. We have few doubts about the good intentions of the United States toward Britain's defense. We accept that nuclear weapons are a

Table 2.19 Attitude toward presence of United States military bases in Britain

	NOP 10/81	Gallup 10/82	NOP 10/82	Gallup 2/83	NOP 5/83
Approve	38	46	39	55	50
Disapprove	53	44	47	36	39
Don't know	9	10	14	9	10
Approve Minus Disapprove	−15	+2	−8	+19	+11

Question wording:

NOP:
"Should Britain continue to allow the United States to have missile bases in Britain or not?"

Gallup:
"Do you think Britain should or should not allow existing American nuclear bases in Britain to remain here?"

deterrent, especially to an aggressive and expansionist state such as the Soviet Union, and that their presence is a regrettable necessity. But we do not understand why additional nuclear weapons are now required. And we have severe misgivings about the fact that they will be under exclusive American control. Our confidence in the United States as a world power has been strained in recent years, especially by its apparent intransigence on disarmament. A strong case needs to be made before we are willing to accept cruise missiles, an even stronger case needs to be made for their remaining in exclusive American control.

Images of Allies

IMPORTANCE OF RELATIONS WITH THE UNITED STATES

The relationship between Britain and the United States intermittently flares up as a public issue, but it is not a burning topic of debate or subject to fierce party conflict. Inevitably the matter arises when the United States does not wholeheartedly endorse a British position, notably over sending troops to the Falklands or over cooperation with the USSR over the gas pipeline. But Britain has not known a period in which attitudes to the United States were the touchstone of partisan allegiance. There is no parallel with France in the Fourth and early Fifth Republic, with Italy in the 1950s, or Greece for most of the postwar period. The open-ended question on the most important problem facing Britain, which is regularly asked in the monthly polls, has never found as many as one percent citing it in their answers.

However, attitudes to the United States *are* the litmus test for factional allegiance within the Labour party. It is no exaggeration to say that anti-Americanism is the strongest and most prevalent component of the Labour left's thinking about defense and foreign policy—stronger even than opposition to the EEC—and the initial premise from which more specific positions derive. Among Labour's MPs, officials, and active members, Anglo-US relations are highly salient, the source of an irreconcilable division between left and right (almost all of Labour's defectors to the SDP were unashamed Atlanticists). These fierce internal divisions find a muffled echo within the Conservative party (see Haseler (1983) for a valuable summary of party positions on the Atlantic Alliance) but have not broken out among the wider electorate. There is public opposition to British accommodation of nuclear weapons, but this is neither confined to supporters of the Labour left nor couched in terms of anti-American sentiment; the main objection is to the presence of the weapons, not the fact that they are made or controlled by the United States.

Thus, Anglo-American relations are not a salient political issue in Britain. This is not to infer, of course, that a major alteration in the relationship, whether divergent or convergent, would not quickly propel it to the top of the political agenda, nor to deny that changing attitudes toward the United States are not involved in the growth of opposition to NATO's double-track decision.

ATTITUDES TOWARD THE UNITED STATES

The British public's view of the United States, in general and as an ally, displays four features that at first sight seem inconsistent. First, general attitudes of liking and trust are positive, but become lukewarm when directed to the performance and judgment of the United States government and of particular presidents. Second, attitudes have gradually become less favorable over the last decade. Third, opinion on the continuation of Britain's current relationship is ambivalent. But, fourth, the United States is still regarded as Britain's most redoubtable ally in a crisis, and there is negligible support for any serious severance of ties.

We turn first to the British people's general orientation to the United States. Diffuse goodwill is very strong (see Table 2.20). Asked their view about the *American people*, 70 percent said they were very or fairly trustworthy, only 18 percent that they were not (EB 10/80). The identical question was asked of the trustworthiness of 15 other peoples, and only the Swiss (trusted by 72 percent) and the Dutch (by 71 percent) were placed ahead (and then only just). This highly favorable image of the American people is not surprising, and too much should not be made of it. Respondents are usually benevolently disposed to the people (as distinct from the governments) of foreign powers, especially people with whom they share a common language and related culture and with whom, therefore, they are, or think they are, familiar. Comparison with attitudes

Table 2.20 Trust in other nations (EB 10/80)

	(1) Very trust worthy	(2) Fairly trust worthy	(3) Not particularly trust worthy	(4) Not at all trust worthy	Don't know	Balance of trust[a]
The Swiss	33	39	3	3	22	+66
The Dutch	30	41	4	3	22	+64
The Danes	25	41	3	3	28	+60
The Americans	24	46	12	6	12	+52
The Belgians	15	40	7	5	33	+43
The Luxemburgers	14	35	4	3	44	+42
The Germans	19	41	13	12	15	+35
The Irish	12	39	17	19	13	+15
The Portuguese	6	29	12	9	44	+14
The Greeks	7	30	15	13	35	+9
The Japanese	11	30	14	21	24	+6
The Chinese	8	33	15	20	24	+6
The Italians	4	35	22	16	23	+1
The Spanish	6	28	23	18	25	−7
The French	6	26	25	28	15	−21
The Russians	2	16	17	44	21	−43

[a] (1) + (2) − (3) − (4)

toward the United States (i.e., the government or state) is revealing. Asked to give their overall opinion, 46 percent said it was favorable (ten percent very, 36 percent fairly); 44 percent that it was unfavorable (13 percent very, 31 percent fairly), a positive balance of only two percent. Opinion was much more positive, on balance, in the five other countries in which the same question was simultaneously put (Gallup 2/82): Germany (+49 percent), Switzerland (+29 percent), Belgium (+27 percent), France (+23 percent) and Denmark (+ seven percent).

And the more a question focused on the capacities and motives of the United States government, the less enthusiastic the endorsement. The same survey (Gallup 2/82) asked, "How much confidence do you have in the United States to deal wisely with world problems?" Thirty five percent said a great deal or a fair amount, but 60 percent said not very much or even none at all—this emphatic latter reply coming from 21 percent. Asked whether their confidence in the ability of America to deal wisely with world problems had changed lately, 47 percent said it had gone down, and only five percent that it had gone up (for 43 percent it had remained the same (Gallup 4/82). It would appear that in Britain more

Table 2.21 Confidence in the United States as a world power (Gallup)

	1977	1978	1979	1980	1981	1982	1983
Very great	10	7	5	7	6	5	3
Considerable	38	30	23	26	24	22	21
Little	21	23	25	25	25	27	29
Very little	15	20	25	24	24	26	29
None at all (volunteered)	7	13	11	9	11	14	12
Don't know	10	13	12	10	9	6	6
Balance of confidence[a]	+26	+4	−11	−	−5	−13	−17
Gone up	22	11	7	10	14	6	4
Remained the same	53	57	51	49	43	48	43
Gone down	16	24	33	33	36	41	48
Don't know	10	8	10	8	7	5	5
Gone up minus gone down	+6	−13	−26	−23	−22	−35	−44

Note:
Question wording:

"How much confidence do you have in the ability of the United States to deal wisely with present world problems?"
"Has your confidence in the ability of America to deal with world problems tended to go up lately, go down, or remain about the same?"

This pair of questions was asked on between two and four occasions each year. The figures for each year are the mean.

[a] Percentage (very great + considerable) − (very little + none at all)

than in other European countries a marked distinction is drawn between the people and the government of the United States, between support for its values and doubts about its performance.

These last two questions have been frequently, although irregularly, asked since the mid-1970s. Table 2.21 shows the annual average trend. There are fluctuations, but the overall direction is clear: confidence in the United States as a superpower has drifted downward, as has also been summarized by Webb and Wybrow (1983). Between 1977, the first year of Jimmy Carter's presidency, and 1983, midway through Ronald Reagan's, the proportion expressing very great or considerable confidence was exactly halved, falling from 48 to 24 percent, and the proportion with very little confidence or none at all rose from 22 to 41 percent. Over these few years, therefore, the balance of confidence in the United States' capacity as a world power has shifted from clearly positive to clearly negative. In the eyes of the British the United States has lost credibility as an effective but safe world power.

This decline in confidence in the United States is recognized by

Table 2.22 Perception of closeness of relations between Britain and the United States (Gallup)

	4/82	6/82	11/82	1/83
Drawing closer together recently	42	50	20	21
No change	19	21	19	22
Getting further apart	31	23	53	49
Don't know	8	5	8	8

respondents. In 1977, the majority (53 percent) reported no change in their degree of confidence; of the rest, more said it had gone up (22 percent) than down (16 percent). By 1983, the position had markedly deteriorated. Those reporting a decline (48 percent) outnumbered those reporting no change (43 percent)—who will have included many closet don't knows—or a rise (a mere four percent) put together. Why respect has crumbled so fast is not exactly clear. Careful scrutiny of the timing of each survey in the timeseries reveals a sharp change of opinion for the worse soon after the Iranian seizure of the United States Embassy, but the averaged annual figures in Table 2.21 show a very steady erosion of confidence throughout Carter's and Reagan's terms of office. Perhaps a succession of disparate events—the economic recession in the United States, Reagan's less guarded comments on disarmament, and the various conflicts that the United States has tried but failed to stop (Afghanistan, El Salvador, Lebanon)—have cumulatively worked their way into the British public's image of the United States as a superpower. But this begs the question about the nature of this decline: does it reflect growing doubts about the power of the United States, or about the capacity of its recent Presidents to exercise it wisely? The distinction is probably unclear in many minds and no reliable data exist to disentangle the two, but I suspect that changing attitudes in Britain are a judgment of the United States political and diplomatic performance rather than its economic and military clout.

Hesitation about the United States' capacity as a world power has been accompanied recently by a dramatic change in the public's perception of Anglo-American relations (Table 2.22). By the end of the Falklands war (Gallup 6/82) more than twice as many believed that the two countries were drawing closer together than pulling further apart; since then the proportions have been reversed. Data prior to April 1982 do not exist, and it may be that attitudes have returned to normal after an exceptional phase during the Falklands war. Moreover, they may reflect expectations about an ideal and desirable degree of closeness—the "Special Relationship"— that are more ambitious than in most other West European countries, such that even slender differences between the two countries are sharply felt. The same point can be made of the juxtaposition of warmth toward

44   IVOR CREWE

American society and coolness toward recent United States governments: small disappointments are felt all the more keenly among old friends. As Webb and Wybrow (1983,52) conclude their review of recent Gallup data

> The British are more concerned with American political matters than they are with European ones, and that concern comes from their common language, common heritage, and common basic interests throughout the twentieth century. Consequently, the British approach the United States as one family member to another. Within a family speech is freer, attitudes are more open, and criticism is harsher. Such feelings arise from a sense of involvement with the United States, not distance.

ATTITUDES TOWARD NATO

There is a paucity of data on British attitudes toward NATO. What little exist suggest that opinions are based on hazy knowledge, especially about NATO's composition and constitution, that is the rights and obligations of member states. Although 92 percent claimed to have heard of NATO (Gallup 9/80) only slightly below a third knew what the acronym stands for (29 percent according to Gallup 9/80, 33 percent according to MORI 10/79). But a vague understanding of NATO's purpose appears to be sufficient for strong support of Britain's continued membership. Two independently conducted polls in October 1981 reported that only 12 (NOP) or nine percent (MORI) wanted Britain to leave NATO. In the more detailed of the two (MORI's) a further 18 percent wanted Britain to remain in NATO but to scale down its financial and military contribution; many of these respondents will have been more concerned about defense spending levels than the NATO connection (moreover, eight percent wanted to increase the contribution). By the 1983 general election only six percent supported Britain's withdrawal from NATO (NOP 5/83).

A more recent survey (Gallup 2/82) presented respondents with a more elaborate set of policy options, which produced a slightly weaker endorsement of Britain's current NATO commitment. The very structuring of the question was partly responsible. Six options were offered, of which three involved complete withdrawal (Table 2.23). These three combined received the support of 26 percent (11 percent for independent defense and no alliance, ten percent for a West European defense force unaligned to the United States, five percent for reducing the commitment to military defense and coming to an accommodation with the USSR). By contrast, 62 percent chose one of the three pro-NATO options, of whom 37 percent wished to continue as before, 20 percent wanted a unified West European defense force under European command but allied to the United States, and five percent wanted Britain to withdraw its military forces but remain in NATO for policy consultations. Here a technical point is necessary: many respondents do not have firm convictions about the details of defense policy. Elaborate questions of the kind just cited will elicit many random responses. These will be distributed evenly across the six answer

Table 2.23   The role of NATO in defense strategy options (Gallup 2/82)

Continue in the NATO alliance among the countries of Western Europe and the US and Canada	37
Establish within NATO a unified West European defense force under European command, but allied to the US	20
Withdraw our military forces from NATO but otherwise remain in NATO for things such as policy consultation	5
Establish an independent West European defense force under European command but not allied to the US	10
Rely on our own nation's defense forces without belonging to any military alliance	11
Reduce our emphasis on military defense and rely on greater accommodation with Russia	5
Don't know	12

Note:
Question wording:

"Thinking now of the protection of Britain against possible attack from the outside, which one of the statements listed comes closest to your own view on how Britain should provide for its security in the 1980s?"

categories. Thus the ratio of random to genuine responses will be the highest for those options receiving the smallest support and lowest for those receiving the highest support. This in turn means that real support for the two main pro-NATO options is probably a little higher than the figures suggest.

RELIANCE UPON NATO AND THE UNITED STATES

One reason for the high level of support for NATO is that both it and the United States are, according to a variety of polls, regarded as staunchly dependable. Faith in the United States' willingness to come to Britain's aid in an emergency is very strong. A Gallup poll in March 1981 asked, "In case of war, to what extent do you think we could trust ... as an ally?" mentioning nine possible allies, including France, West Germany, and Norway. Three answers were possible: a great deal, up to a point, and not at all. If we measure the trustworthiness of an ally by subtracting the percentage "not at all" from the percentage "a great deal," the United States emerges as far and away the most trusted ally (+55 percent), followed a long way behind by Norway (+27 percent) and Denmark (+23 percent). The scores for the two major powers in Europe were two percent for Germany and −36 percent for France. These figures are strongly correlated with the British public's degree of trust in foreign peoples,

Table 2.24   Reliability of the United States and NATO (Gallup 2/82)

	Confidence in	
	the US	NATO
A great deal	20	12
A fair amount	36	44
Not very much	28	25
None at all	12	10
Don't know	3	8

Question wording:

"If Britain's security was threatened by a Russian attack, how much confidence do you have in the United States to do whatever is necessary to defend Britain, even if this risked a direct attack against the United States itself?"
"How much confidence do you have in NATO's ability to defend Western Europe against attack?"

listed in Table 2.20, and thus suggest that faith in the United States as an ally arises not simply from a perception of its relative military strength but also from a belief in the trustworthiness of its people. It is worth noting that only seven percent were emphatic that the United States was not to be trusted at all a much lower number than those who wish to sever Britain's military links, especially in the form of nuclear bases, with the United States.

A more recent survey (Gallup 3/82) put the perceived reliability of the United States and NATO to a more exacting test: "If Britain's security was threatened by a Russian attack, how much confidence do you have in the United States to do *whatever is necessary* to defend Britain, *even if this risked a direct attack against the United States itself?*" (italics added). As Table 2.24 shows, the majority (56 percent) had considerable confidence in the United States' readiness to risk its own security for the sake of Britain, and only 12 percent were *convinced* that it would not. Faith in NATO's ability to defend Western Europe against attack showed an almost identical pattern: 56 percent were confident and only ten percent were clearly not. Thus the cause of any growing strain in Anglo-U.S. relations over defense does not lie in doubts about the United States' will or intentions.

Indeed, the source of strain, in the eyes of some, is not an absence of will on the part of the United States, but a reckless overabundance. We saw earlier that substantial segments of the public believe that the first move in a nuclear war is as likely to be American as Russian, that the United States holds equal responsibility with the USSR for the nuclear arms race, and that the presence of United States bases and cruise missiles increases rather than discourages the risk of attack on Britain. There is a thin line between the dependability of the United States and overdependence on the United States, but it is one that the public appears to recognize. Asked whether the foreign policy of Britain depends too much on the United States, 61 percent agreed and only 29 percent did not (Gallup 11/81). The catch in defense relations with the United States is that the same arrangements that ensure its reliability in a crisis are also seen to make a crisis more likely. The United States is a dependable defender of Britain, but also a reason why Britain needs defending. It is the alternative reactions to this conundrum that divide the minority of dissenters about the Atlantic Alliance from the majority of supporters.

The Attitudes of Different Social and Political Groups

INTRODUCTION

Before describing the differences of attitude about nuclear defense and the Atlantic Alliance among various social and political groups, it is worth reflecting briefly on what kinds of difference do or do not merit attention. There is, of course, an intrinsic if casual sociological interest in correlations between social groups and attitudes, but findings of such correlations often fail to serve any serious theoretical or practical purpose and as such border on the trivial. Moreover, statistical significance does not mean substantive significance: Attitudinal disparities of a few percentage points may signify more about the relative uniformity of opinion across social groups than about the minor differences between them. In the sections that follow we shall come across many group differences of this uninteresting kind.

To disentangle important from trivial group differences we need to keep three questions in mind. First, are the groups being compared on the same side or on opposing sides of the issue? Does the majority in each group take divergent or convergent positions? Do divisions of opinion run with or cut across social cleavages? Second, how big and how important (in the sense of being able to influence wider opinion) is the social group under scrutiny? It is often possible to identify social groups whose views are in marked contrast with the large majority of society, but this may be of little political significance. For example, a recent (self-selecting) sample survey of readers of *New Society*—a weekly popular social science magazine with a large readership among social workers—found a three to one majority *in favor* of unilateral nuclear disarmament, despite the three to one majority *against* unilateralism among the population at large (Lipsey 1980). But *New Society* readers, and indeed the wider group of whom they are typical, represent a tiny minority of British society with little influence on public opinion at large. Their opinions are of much more interest to those studying *New Society* readers than to those studying public opinion about defense and the Atlantic Alliance. Third, are the distinctive attitudes of a particular social group held because of the distinctive attributes of that group? It is always tempting, but not always correct, to assume that they are. For example, social class differences of opinion may occur only because of the well-known differences of party loyalty between classes and have nothing to do with the interests or consciousness of the classes; in other words, the correlation between social class and attitudes on defense may be "spurious." It is not always clear, moreover, quite what the distinctive attributes of a social category are. For example, differences of attitude between age categories could denote a "life cycle" or a "generational" phenomenon (or both): In the first case, the attitudes of young respondents would be expected to change as they grew older; in the second case they might persist throughout their lifetimes because they represent the outlook of a generation that shared the same formative experiences in youth. Unfortunately, there is no way of telling for sure whether an age-attitude correlation at a single point of time is a generational or life cycle phenomenon.

A note should be added about the availability and presentation of data in this section. A social and partisan breakdown of most of the attitudes reported in earlier sections (e.g., those in Gallup polls) is generally not available. What follows is predominantly drawn from the Marplan survey of January 1983, recent MORI and NOP polls, and the BBC/Gallup survey on the eve and day of the June 1983 general election. What the data lack in coverage they at least make up by being up-to-date. Separate tables containing breakdowns for each of sex, age, social class, and party preference are provided. Each lists almost all the questions for which a breakdown has been published, although where a question has been repeated the most recent example is given (there are generally insufficient data to follow trends within social groups over time). The percentages saying "don't know" are always omitted, even though these can systematically vary between groups, as will be noted in the accompanying commentary. Questions are listed in the same order in each table wherever possible, to enable easier comparisons between types of social group, for example, to compare class differences with partisan differences. The text that follows summarizes the main features of the tables.

ATTITUDINAL DIFFERENCES BETWEEN MEN AND WOMEN

The prominence of women in the protest movement against nuclear weapons, notably the women's camp at Greenham Common, makes it easy to assume that men and women adopt very different attitudes on issues of nuclear defense. Table 2.25 shows that attitudinal differences between men and women consistently take the same expected direction, with men adopting the more "hard-line" attitudes, but that these differences are very slender. Fewer than ten percentage points divide men and women in their answers to most questions. The majority of men and the majority of women take the same side on each question. There is no pitched battle of the sexes on defense.

The main features of Table 2.25 can be summarized as follows:

Almost without exception women are more likely than men to have no opinion on questions of defense and peace (the "don't know" percentages are omitted from the table, but readers can easily calculate them by subtracting the total percentage in each column from 100). This is not surprising; surveys have consistently found the same pattern for other social and political questions, but it is a warning against the assumption that defense and peace issues have more immediacy for women than for men. Here it is worth recording that at the 1983 general election more men (44 percent) than women (34 percent) mentioned defense and international peace as among the two most important issues affecting their vote (Gallup 6/83). This may have been because the election campaign turned on "the defense of Britain" rather than "policies for world peace."

Even if defense is a less salient electoral issue for women, it is women who are the more pessimistic and worried about the prospect of nuclear conflict. In January 1983, men were equally divided on whether the outlook for peace had improved or deteriorated over the previous year; among women there were almost twice as many pessimists (43 percent) as optimists (24 percent). Perhaps women are more averse to conflict, perhaps they are inclined to worry more, perhaps they are simply more realistic. They are certainly more realistic about the likelihood of their or Britain's surviving a nuclear attack—although the differences between men and women on this are small.

Women are only slightly more pacifist than men, but they are markedly less militaristic. For example, approval of *cuts* in defense expenditure is as low among women as men, but ten percent fewer of them support *increases* in defense spending. Similarly—and contrary to the common assumption—unilateral nuclear disarmament attracts barely more support from women (23 percent) than men (19 percent), but opposition to the enhancement of Britain's existing nuclear capabilities is more considerable among women than men. Perhaps women are more conscious of the cost of enhancing nuclear weapons and of the other things—education, the health service, and other social services—on which the money might have been spent. Whatever the reason, they have little of the grim enthusiasm for more nuclear weapons that can be found among a minority of men.

Attitudes to the construction of a new generation of nuclear weapons, as opposed to the destruction of existing weapons, display an identical pattern. Men and women alike reject in the same overwhelming numbers the Labour party's official policy of scrapping the Polaris fleet. On the other hand, there has consistently been more opposition among women than among men to the installation of cruise missiles or the buying of the new Trident missile system. But this opposition has taken the form of markedly lower proportions of women's than men's accepting the new missiles rather than markedly higher proportions rejecting them (the asymmetry being accounted for by the larger number of "don't knows"

Table 2.25 Attitudinal differences between men and women on various defense issues

	Men	Women	Difference (men minus women)
Prospects for world peace			
better than a year ago	36	24	+12
worse than a year ago	36	43	−7
(Marplan 1/83)			
Nuclear war between now and the year 2000			
very likely	9 ⎫ 28	8 ⎫ 33	+1 ⎫ −5
likely	19 ⎭	25 ⎭	−6 ⎭
not very likely	34 ⎫ 65	33 ⎫ 55	+1 ⎫ +10
very unlikely	31 ⎭	22 ⎭	+9 ⎭
(Marplan 1/83)			
Worried by nuclear weapons	58	72	−14
Not worried by nuclear weapons	39	23	+16
(Gallup 9/80)			
Respondent and family			
would not survive a nuclear attack	73	80	−7
would survive a nuclear attack	8	5	+3
(Gallup 9/80)			
Britain as a nation			
would not survive a nuclear attack	58	61	−3
would survive a nuclear attack	29	23	+6
(Gallup 9/80)			
Military spending in Britain should be			
increased	27	17	+10
held at present level	48	50	−2
cut	21	21	0
(Marplan 1/83)			
Who is to blame for current level and growth of nuclear weapons?			
Russia	17	18	−1
America	8	7	+1
Both equally	72	66	+6
(Marplan 1/83)			
Britain should			
abandon nuclear weapons unilaterally	19	23	−4
maintain current nuclear capability	57	60	−3
spend more on and improve nuclear capability	20	6	+14
(Marplan 1/83)			
Britain should get rid of all nuclear weapons even if other countries keep theirs			
Agree	24	22	+2
Disagree	73	71	+2
(MORI 1/83)			

Table 2.25 (Continued)

	Men	Women	Difference (men minus women)
On government's decision to allow the Americans to base cruise missiles on British soil, respondent			
Disapproves	55	67	−12
Approves	39	15	+24
(Marplan 1/83)			
Britain should allow cruise missiles to be based in Britain			
Disagree	49	58	−9
Agree	44	28	+16
(MORI 1/83)			
Allowing cruise missiles into Britain is			
a very bad idea	30 ⎱ 41	34 ⎱ 47	−4 ⎱ −6
a fairly bad idea	11 ⎰	13 ⎰	−2 ⎰
a fairly good idea	28 ⎱ 59	32 ⎱ 53	−4 ⎱ +6
a very good idea	31 ⎰	21 ⎰	+10 ⎰
(Gallup 6/83)			
On government's decision to purchase the Trident missile system to replace the Polaris fleet, respondent			
Disapproves	55	58	−3
Approves	35	16	+19
(Marplan 1/83)			
Giving up Polaris fleet irrespective of what other countries do is			
a very good idea	11 ⎱ 19	11 ⎱ 21	0 ⎱ −2
a fairly good idea	8 ⎰	10 ⎰	−2 ⎰
a fairly bad idea	13 ⎱ 81	19 ⎱ 79	−6 ⎱ +2
a very bad idea	68 ⎰	60 ⎰	+8 ⎰
(Gallup (6/83)			
Women's Greenham Common protest against basing of cruise missiles in Britain has made respondent			
more favorable to anticruise campaign	29	32	−3
no difference	56	50	+6
less favorable to anticruise campaign	13	14	−1
(MORI 1/83)			

among women). Note, however, that by the culmination of the 1983 general election campaign a majority among both men and women supported the installation of cruise missiles, testimony to the Conservative government's runaway victory in the argument over defense. As the very last figures in Table 2.25 show, the women's protest demonstrations at Greenham Common had no different an impact on women than on men among the wider public.

ATTITUDINAL DIFFERENCES BETWEEN THE AGE GROUPS

It is widely believed that one source of strain in the Atlantic Alliance is the emergence of a new generation, born after World War II, in some cases after the worst of the cold war, whose views are radically different from those of their parents' generation. This may or may not be true of the *political* classes in Britain—I suspect it is not—but it is certainly not true of the public at large. The fact that the majority of active campaigners for unilateral nuclear disarmament are young does not mean that the majority of the young favor the idea. On any issue the social composition of a protest movement has always been a poor guide to the social composition of public opinion.

Table 2.26 shows that there are indeed differences of opinion between age groups. The young, compared with the old, are more pessimistic about the possible outbreak of nuclear war and their chances of surviving it and more willing to cut defense expenditure, reject the cruise missile, cancel the new Trident missile system, scrap the Polaris fleet, and do without nuclear weapons of any kind. That these differences of view exist is not surprising, but that they are so small is. On only one of the 13 questions listed in Table 2.26 did the percentage difference between the under and over-45's exceed ten points. On every question the majority of the young took the same view as the majority of the old. This was also true (with one borderline exception on cruise missiles) of the very young—the under-25's—whose views barely differed from those of the 25 to 44 year olds. Among the ordinary public at least there is no generation gap to speak of on issues of nuclear defense and the Atlantic Alliance.

ATTITUDINAL DIFFERENCES AMONG THE SOCIAL CLASSES

Social class, as defined by occupational status, is the most important social basis of party allegiance in Britain, indeed the only such basis of any nationwide significance. Loyal supporters often follow their party's line on the major issues of the day. By extension one might therefore expect the social classes to take opposing, or at least markedly different, views on nuclear defense, in tandem with "their" parties. However, other factors work against this assumption. Defense is not an obvious "class issue" in the sense that the tax structure or welfare policies are. Nuclear bombs and invading armies do not discriminate among the classes. Particular class interests are only indirectly affected by defense policies, for example, by the potential trade-off between public spending on defense as against social services, and, at least in Britain, they are rarely mentioned by radical opponents of nuclear defense policies or by the Labour party. Moreover, the class-party link in the electorate has steadily attenuated over the past two decades and was particularly weak in the 1983 election (Sarlvik and Crewe 1983; Crewe 1983). And many people vote for a party despite of or in ignorance of its policies. As a result, surveys frequently find rather weak correlations between social class and issue positions.

This turns out to be true of nuclear defense. Table 2.27 shows that to know individuals' social classes tells one next to nothing about their attitudes on defense matters. Attitudinal differences between the social classes are even thinner than those between the age groups or between men and women. Moreover, the marginal class differences that occur do not follow as systematic a pattern as in the case of the sexes and age groups. For example, the working class (categories C2, D, and E) are more pessimistic about the likelihood of nuclear war but also slightly less worried about nuclear weapons; they are both more unilateralist and more expansionist in their attitude to nuclear weapons. This latter pattern hints at the existence of bipolar working class opinion, divided between traditional Labour loyalists adopting their party line on cruise missiles, Polaris, and defense spending generally and a "tough-minded, patriotic" working class (many of them Conservative voters) with hard-line views on the need to maintain or, if necessary, enhance Britain's nuclear capability. But, given the data available, this is conjecture, not established fact. What is certain is that British people do not respond to defense issues along class lines.

However, that is not quite the end of the matter. Social class is a slippery concept and can be defined differently. Education, as well as occupation, is a source of status, resources, and collective interest. Almost none of the published surveys break their results down by education, but the limited data available confirm the visible impression that it is the intelligentsia who are the most apprehensive and informed about nuclear defense issues and the most likely to take an antinuclear position. The majority (52 percent) of those whose education continued beyond the age of 19 believe that nuclear war is likely in their lifetime (NOP 10/81), compared with 38 percent of all respondents. The Gallup survey prior to the June 1983 election found that 31 percent of those without any tertiary education mentioned defense or international peace as one of the two most important issues affecting their vote; among those with some further education the figure was 47 percent; and among the university educated it was 51 percent. However, the substance of their opinions depended on what type of further education respondents had undergone. University graduates were the most radical: 31 percent supported the scrapping of Polaris and 43 percent described the installation of cruise missiles as a very bad idea. Among the electorate at large the figures were, respectively, 20

Table 2.26 Attitudinal differences between age groups on various defense issues

	15-24[a]	25-44	45-64	65 and older	Difference[b] (15-44 minus 45 and older)
Prospects for world peace					
better than a year ago	30	27	32	31	−2
worse than a year ago	48	44	33	36	+5
(Marplan 1/83)					
Nuclear war between now and the year 2000					
very likely	9	10	7	7	+2
likely	29 (36)	27 (37)	19 (26)	12 (19)	+11 (−13)
not very likely	32	34	31	36	0
very unlikely	19 (51)	22 (56)	34 (65)	28 (6∂)	−10 (−10)
(Marplan 1/83)					
Worried by nuclear weapons	62	67	67	66	−2
Not worried by nuclear weapons	36	30	29	28	+3
(Gallup 9/80)					
Respondent and family					
would not survive nuclear attack	74	83	78	65	+7
would survive a nuclear attack	5	7	6	7	−1
(Gallup 9/80)					
Britain as a nation					
would not survive a nuclear attack	63	60	61	52	+3
would survive a nuclear attack	20	28	26	29	−2
(Gallup 9/80)					
Military spending in Britain should be					
increased	21	22	21	21	+1
held at present level	44	49	51	53	−5
cut	30	22	20	14	+6
(Marplan 1/83)					
Who is to blame for current level and growth of nuclear weapons?					
Russia	16	15	18	26	−6
America	7	8	7	6	+1
Both equally	70	72	70	60	+5
(Marplan 1/83)					
Britain should					
abandon nuclear weapons unilaterally	24	23	17	21	+5
maintain current nuclear capability	55	56	65	56	−6
spend more on and improve nuclear capability	14	14	11	13	+2
(Marplan 1/83)					

Table 2.26 (Continued)

	15-24[a]	25-44	45-64	65 and older	Difference[b] (15-44 minus 45 and older)
On government's decision to allow the Americans to base cruise missiles on British soil, respondent					
Disapproves	64	66	57	58	+8
Approves	25	24	30	29	−5
(Marplan 1/83)					
Allowing cruise missiles into Britain is					
a very bad idea	33	34	29	29	+5
a fairly bad idea	17 50	14 48	11 40	7 36	+5 +9
a fairly good idea	31	30	30	29	+1
a very good idea	18 49	23 53	30 60	35 64	−10 −9
(Gallup 6/83)					
On government's decision to purchase the Trident missile system to replace the Polaris fleet, respondent					
Disapproves	65	58	53	52	+7
Approves	21	27	27	22	−1
(Marplan 1/83)					
Giving up Polaris fleet irrespective of what other countries do is					
a very good idea	9	13	10	11	+2
a fairly good idea	14 23	9 22	6 16	9 20	+3 +6
a fairly bad idea	23	17	14	11	+6
a very bad idea	53 76	61 78	70 84	69 80	−11 −5
(Gallup 6/83)					

Note:
[a] The youngest age category is 16-24 in the 9/80, and 18-22 in the 6/83 Gallup survey.
[b] As values in this column are computed weighting by proportions of age groups, they cannot be directly derived from the percentages reported for individual age groups.

Table 2.27 Attitudinal differences between the social classes on various defense issues

	AB[a]	C1[a]	C2[a]	DE[a]	Difference[b] (AB + C1) minus (C2 + DE)
Prospects for world peace					
better than a year ago	40	32	27	26	+8
worse than a year ago	28	36	44	43	−11
(Marplan 1/83)					
Nuclear war between now and the year 2000					
very likely	4	9	8	10	−3
likely	23	22	24	19	0
not very likely	37	33	33	32	+2
very unlikely	30	27	26	25	+2
(Marplan 1/83)					
Worried by nuclear weapons	68	69	63	65	+5
Not worried by nuclear weapons	30	28	33	30	−2
(Gallup 9/80)					
Respondent and family					
would not survive a nuclear attack	71	81	75	78	+1
would survive a nuclear attack	11	6	7	5	+2
(Gallup 9/80)					
Britain as a nation					
would not survive a nuclear attack	55	55	62	63	−7
would survive a nuclear attack	34	28	24	24	+6
(Gallup 9/80)					
Military spending in Britain should be					
increased	19	17	24	23	−6
held at present level	47	56	49	46	+6
cut	21	22	20	21	+1
(Marplan 1/83)					
Who is to blame for current level and growth of nuclear weapons?					
Russia	18	18	15	20	+1
America	7	8	7	7	+1
Both equally	70	70	72	64	+2
(Marplan 1/83)					
Britain should					
abandon nuclear weapons unilaterally	16	20	20	26	−5
maintain current nuclear capability	58	66	59	53	+7
spend more on and improve nuclear capability	14	11	14	14	−2
(Marplan 1/83)					

Table 2.27 (Continued)

	AB[a]	C1[a]	C2[a]	DE[a]	Difference[b] (AB + C1) minus (C2 + DE)
On government's decision to allow the Americans to base cruise missiles on British soil, respondent					
Disapproves	50	61	63	66	−8
Approves	34	27	26	23	+6
(Marplan 1/83)					
Allowing cruise missiles into Britain is					
a very bad idea	25	29	32	38	−8
a fairly bad idea	12 _37_	11 _40_	13 _45_	13 _51_	−1 _−9_
a fairly good idea	35	30	30	26	+4
a very good idea	29 _64_	29 _59_	25 _55_	23 _49_	+5 _+9_
(Gallup 6/83)					
On government's decision to purchase the Trident missile system to replace the Polaris fleet, respondent					
Disapproves	52	59	56	58	−1
Approves	27	22	28	23	−1
(Marplan 1/83)					
Giving up Polaris fleet irrespective of what other countries do					
a very good idea	9	10	12	14	−3
a fairly good idea	8 _17_	9 _19_	8 _20_	11 _25_	−1 _−4_
a fairly bad idea	17	15	15	16	+1
a very bad idea	66 _83_	64 _79_	68 _83_	59 _75_	+1 _+2_
(Gallup 6/83)					

Note:
[a] The social class categories are as follows:
AB: professional, managerial, administrative, self-employed
C1 : routine nonmanual, office workers
C2 : skilled manual workers, foremen
DE: semi- and unskilled manual workers, pensioners, welfare dependents
[b] As values in this column are computed weighting by proportions of classes, they cannot be directly derived from the percentages reported for individual classes.

and 32 percent. But others with a further education, at commercial or technical colleges, for example, were *more* pronuclear than electors as a whole. The university-educated constitute only 13 percent of those with some form of further education (and a mere six percent of the population). When all those with further education are compared with those without, differences of attitude disappear. The university-educated, in other words, are a special case: an intelligentsia of little numerical and thus electoral importance, but with an influence over the rest of society quite disproportionate to its size.

ATTITUDINAL DIFFERENCES BETWEEN CONSERVATIVE, LABOUR AND LIBERAL/SDP SUPPORTERS

We have good reason to expect attitudes on the Atlantic Alliance and nuclear defense to follow party lines. These issues were a matter of party conflict over the three years culminating in the general election in which they were second only to unemployment in importance to voters and the most prominent of all issues in the media coverage received. We should expect opinion to divide on partisan lines rather than on the basis of sex, age, or class for two reasons. First, only parties are mobilizing institutions, equipped and intended to educate their loyal supporters into a party line. Second, people cannot change their sex, age, or (except very slowly) their social class; they can and do change their party preferences, often in response to the parties' positions on the major issues, especially at an election in which they are called upon to make a definite choice between parties. It would be a peculiar kind of democracy in which public opinion on a major issue did not divide roughly along party lines.

Table 2.28 lists the many questions on defense for which a breakdown by respondents' party preference (as measured by voting intention) is known. A question-by-question description of the data is not possible in the space available, but the main features of the table can be summarized as follows:

As expected, party supporters differ in their opinions to a much more marked degree than the sexes, age groups, or social classes. In only three cases (worry about nuclear weapons, the perceived likelihood of personally surviving a nuclear attack, and government expenditure on civil defense) do Conservative and Labour supporters differ by less than ten percentage points. None of these cases is politically contentious. On every other question opinion differs typically by between 20 and 30 percentage points; by the general election differences reached 40 to 50 percentage points on the issues that most divided the parties. Compared with the sociodemographic differences, this seems very large. Yet complete party polarization of opinion would mean percentage point differences (on dichotomous questions) of 100; that is, all Conservatives would take one view, all Labour supporters the other. Table 2.28 shows that Britain is a

Table 2.28 Attitudinal differences among Conservative, Labour, and Liberal/SDP supporters on various defense issues

	Conservative	Labour	Liberal/SDP	Difference (Conservative minus Labour)
Prospects for world peace				
better than a year ago	39	23	22	+16
worse than a year ago	29	48	46	−19
(Marplan 1/83)				
Nuclear war between now and the year 2000				
very likely	3 ⎫21	15 ⎫38	9 ⎫33	−12 ⎫−17
likely	18 ⎭	23 ⎭	24 ⎭	−5 ⎭
not very likely	39 ⎫70	28 ⎫50	35 ⎫60	+11 ⎫+20
very unlikely	31 ⎭	22 ⎭	25 ⎭	+9 ⎭
(Marplan 1/83)				
Worried by nuclear weapons	60	69	71	−9
Not worried by nuclear weapons	36	28	24	+8
(Gallup 9/80)				
Respondent and family				
would not survive a nuclear attack	73	78	78	−5
would survive a nuclear attack	8	5	6	+3
(Gallup 9/80)				
Britain as a nation				
would not survive a nuclear attack	53	61	69	−8
would survive a nuclear attack	37	20	21	+17
(Gallup 9/80)				
Britain should				
reduce expenditure on defense	17	44	33	−27
not reduce expenditure on defense	81	47	62	+34
(MORI 10/81)				
The Government				
should spend less on defense	8	31	27	−23
is spending the right amount	40	33	31	+7
should spend more on defense	45	29	33	+16
(NOP 10/81)				
The Government				
should spend less on civil defense	13	20	19	−7
is spending the right amount	29	24	20	+5
should spend more on civil defense	46	48	47	−2
(NOP 10/81)				
Military spending in Britain should be				
cut	7	36	28	−29
held at present level	60	38	45	+22
increased	29	17	18	+12
(Marplan 1/83)				

Table 2.28 (Continued)

	Conser-vative	Labour	Liberal/SDP	Difference (Conservative minus Labour)
Government spending is				
too high on both nuclear and nonnuclear weapons	7	22	12	−15
too high on nuclear, about right on nonnuclear	13 30	24 64	23 54	−11 −34
too high on nuclear, too low on nonnuclear	10	18	19	−8
about right on both nuclear and nonnuclear	23	10	15	+13
	41	14	23	+27
about right on nuclear, too low on nonnuclear	18	4	8	+14
other combinations (MORI 1/83)	22	15	18	+7
Who is to blame for current level and growth of nuclear weapons?				
Russia	27	11	18	+16
America	4	10	11	−6
Both equally (Marplan 1/83)	63	73	68	−10
Britain should get rid of all nuclear weapons even if other countries keep theirs				
Agree	9	35	23	−26
Disagree (MORI 10/81)	86	56	69	+30
Britain should get rid of all nuclear weapons even if other countries keep theirs				
Agree	12	37	22	−25
Disagree (MORI 1/83)	87	58	74	+29
Britain should				
abandon nuclear weapons unilaterally	8	38	23	−30
maintain current nuclear capability	67	44	62	+23
spend more on and improve nuclear capability (Marplan 1/83)	19	10	10	+9
The suggestion that Britain should give up relying on nuclear weapons for defense whatever other countries decide				
a good idea	14	43	35	−29
a bad idea (Gallup 2/83)	82	48	56	+34

Table 2.28 (Continued)

	Conservative	Labour	Liberal/ SDP	Difference (Conservative minus Labour)
To reduce the chances of a war, and taking everything into account, including the cost, Britain should				
have only a few or no weapons of any kind	4	14	8	−10
	19	43	39	−24
be strong in conventional nonnuclear weapons but have no nuclear weapons	15	29	31	−14
rely on nuclear weapons with only a small conventional nonnuclear force	7	13	5	−6
	76	49	57	+27
rely on both nuclear weapons and a strong, conventional, nonnuclear force	69	36	52	+33
(Gallup 2/83)				
Britain should give up its nuclear arms even if other countries do not give up theirs				
Agree	5	33	14	−28
Disagree	91	59	82	+32
(NOP 5/83)				
Britain should withdraw completely from NATO	4	16	8	−12
(MORI 10/81)				
Britain's financial and military contribution to NATO should be				
reduced	13	20	19	−7
maintained at its present level	60	42	56	+18
increased	12	7	7	+5
(MORI 10/81)				
Britain should remain in NATO				
Disagree	3	12	1	−9
Agree	91	72	91	+9
(NOP 5/83)				
Should Britain allow American nuclear weapons to be based in Britain?				
No	36	72	63	−36
Yes	52	20	29	+32
(MORI 10/81)				
Should Britain continue to allow the US to have missile bases in Britain or not?				
No	26	64	58	−38
Yes	59	22	32	+37
(NOP 10/82)				

Table 2.28 (Continued)

	Conser-vative	Labour	Liberal/ SDP	Difference (Conservative minus Labour)
Britain should ban US nuclear bases from Britain				
Agree	20	63	48	−43
Disagree	70	29	42	+41
(NOP 5/83)				
On government's decision to allow the Americans to base cruise missiles on British soil, respondent				
Disapproves	44	79	69	−35
Approves	44	14	21	+30
(Marplan 1/83)				
Britain should allow cruise missiles to be based in Britain				
Disagree	35	69	64	−34
Agree	55	22	25	+33
(MORI 1/83)				
Britain should ban cruise missiles from being stationed in Britain				
Agree	20	59	53	−39
Disagree	67	28	37	+39
(NOP 5/83)				
Allowing cruise missiles into Britain is				
a very bad idea	9 ⎱ 17	62 ⎱ 75	38 ⎱ 55	−53 ⎱ −58
a fairly bad idea	8 ⎰	13 ⎰	17 ⎰	−5 ⎰
a fairly good idea	39 ⎱ 83	16 ⎱ 26	28 ⎱ 45	+23 ⎱ +57
a very good idea	44 ⎰	10 ⎰	17 ⎰	+34 ⎰
(Gallup 6/83)				
Britain should				
cancel Trident missile system	24	60	60	−36
buy Trident missile system	50	18	22	+32
(NOP 10/82)				
On government's decision to purchase the Trident missile system to replace the Polaris fleet, respondent				
Disapproves	38	71	69	−33
Approves	40	16	19	+24
(Marplan 1/83)				
Britain should build the Trident missile system to replace Polaris				
Disagree	16	46	48	−30
Agree	48	28	31	+20
(NOP 5/83)				

Table 2.28 (Continued)

	Conservative	Labour	Liberal/SDP	Difference (Conservative minus Labour)
Giving up Polaris fleet irrespective of what other countries do				
a very good idea	4	25	9	−21
a fairly good idea	4 } 8	15 } 40	12 } 21	−11 } −32
a fairly bad idea	11	18	20	−7
a very bad idea	81 } 92	42 } 60	59 } 79	+39 } +32
(Gallup 6/83)				
Women's Greenham Common protest against basing of cruise missiles in Britain has made respondent				
more favorable to anticruise campaign	20	45	35	−25
no difference	57	47	50	+10
less favorable to anticruise campaign	20	7	14	+13
(MORI 1/83)				

long way from that position. There are partisan differences but, with a few exceptions, these fall well short of partisan polarization.

Indeed, on most aspects of the Atlantic Alliance and nuclear defense the majority of Conservative and Labour (and Liberal/SDP) voters take the same, not the opposite, side. They agree, albeit in slightly different proportions, in their worry about nuclear weapons and the improbability of personal or national survival after nuclear attack and in the unlikelihood of a nuclear war by the end of the century. They agree in their even-handed blame of both superpowers for the escalation of nuclear arms. They agree on Britain's need for some sort of nuclear deterrent and so reject unilateral nuclear disarmament; they agree on Britain's continuing membership in NATO. The only matters on which they are unmistakeably divided, most Conservatives taking one side, most Labour supporters the opposite, is on whether to cut expenditure on nuclear defense, whether to allow the continuation of American bases in Britain, and whether to accept cruise missiles and purchase the new Trident system. These are, of course, among the issues on which recent party conflict has been most fierce.

The combination of Conservative and Labour supporters' views on issues on which a pro-NATO and anti-NATO position can be roughly defined is charted in Table 2.29. Views that split at least six to four (excluding "don't knows") are described as a clear majority for or against a position; those more evenly distributed are described as divided. The concentration of issues across the top row of Table 2.29 shows that on almost all aspects of the Atlantic Alliance and nuclear defense a clear majority of Conservatives take a pro-NATO position. Often the majority is overwhelming. Shortly before the 1983 election over 90 percent of

Table 2.29 Summary chart of relationship between Conservative and Labour
supporters' views on defense issues

Conservative supporters	Clear majority pro-NATO	Labour supporters Divided	Clear majority anti-NATO
	Continue member-ship of NATO	Maintain overall defense expenditure	Maintain nuclear defense expenditure
	Maintain civil defense expenditure	Unilateral nuclear disarmament	Purchase of Trident missile system
Clear majority pro-NATO	Maintain Polaris fleet	Persuasiveness of Greenham Common protest	Continuation of American bases in Britain
			Installation of cruise missiles (5/83 onwards)
Divided			Installation of cruise missiles (1980–2/83)
Clear majority anti-NATO			US and USSR equally to blame for nuclear arms escalation

Conservatives rejected unilateral nuclear disarmament and the scrapping of Polaris and supported Britain's continued membership of NATO; 89 percent wanted to maintain or increase defense expenditure; and 83 percent had come to accept the case for the installation of cruise missiles, after being much more evenly divided on the issue in 1981 and 1982. The only example of Conservatives taking an anti-NATO view is their perception of the United States as equally to blame with the USSR for the growth of nuclear weapons. This probably amounts to a belief that the United States could have done more by way of initiative and flexibility to advance the progress of disarmament talks and a perception of the obvious, namely NATO's response to the Soviet buildup of SS-20s.

The clustering of issues down the right-hand column of Table 2.29 indicates that a clear majority of Labour supporters took an anti-NATO line on many defense issues. But it would be mistaken to describe Labour voters as wholeheartedly or comprehensively anti-NATO. For one thing the anti-NATO majorities among Labour supporters are not as thorough-going as the pro-NATO majorities among Conservatives. For example, even at the end of the 1983 election campaign, when the Labour party had driven away a quarter of its usual support largely because of its defense policies, the remaining core of Labour voters rejected the purchase of Trident only by three to two, and 25 percent supported the installation of cruise missiles. Moreover, they were divided or took a pro-NATO position on many issues. On the question of defense spending, for example, although a clear majority wanted to see cuts in spending on nuclear weapons, a small majority supported the maintenance or increase of overall defense spending, including a clear majority for civil defense. On other issues Labour supporters are unequivocally pro-NATO even if this contradicts official party policy. By the time of the 1983 election only 12 percent of them rejected British membership of NATO, and the ending of the Polaris fleet was rejected by a three-to-two majority. A clear majority also renounced the arguments of the unilateral nuclear disarmament advocates, who had conquered the Labour party two years earlier. Opinion surveys have never recorded a majority of unilateral disarmament proponents Labour supporters, although they have always formed a substantial minority of at least a third, and over 40 percent at times. By the 1983 election, when support for Labour dipped to under 30 percent of voters (and barely over 20 percent of the electorate) Labour supporters renounced unilateral nuclear disarmament by 59 to 33 percent. Not only did Labour's defense policy lose it many erstwhile supporters; they were also repudiated by those who stayed loyal.

Supporters of the Liberal/SDP alliance—which took 26 percent of the vote in 1983, only two percent behind Labour—usually positioned themselves between supporters of the two established parties (although they were fractionally more worried and pessimistic about the future than others). On two issues, membership of NATO and retention of Polaris, they resembled Conservatives more than Labour supporters. Like Conservatives they supported both in overwhelming numbers, reflecting the staunchly pro-NATO position of the recently formed SDP (the Liberal party is somewhat more equivocal, especially over retention of Polaris, on which a substantial minority of activists dissent). On all other issues Liberal/SDP supporters were closer to Labour than Conservative voters in their views, partly because the two parties' policies on cruise missiles and Trident were similar, partly because many more were former Labour than former Conservative supporters.

The final feature to note about Table 2.29 is that the 1983 election campaign decisively shifted opinion, among supporters of all the parties, toward positions favorable to NATO and the Atlantic Alliance. The relatively favorable impact of the unilateralist anticruise-missiles demonstrations in early 1983 was obliterated by the campaigns of the Conservative government—and the Liberal/SDP alliance during the election. The specific issues of cruise missiles and Trident were smothered by the general question of whether Britain should have "strong" or "weak" defenses, which came to be synonymous with "nuclear" and "nonnuclear"; that question was resolved by the unity and conviction of the pronuclear parties, in contrast to the confusion and divisions within the Labour party.

Conclusion: Two and a Half Cheers for the Atlantic Alliance

If the state of the Atlantic Alliance depended exclusively on mass public opinion it would receive a clean bill of health. Somebody armed only with knowledge of British public opinion would deny that there was any crisis. Almost all the geopolitical and strategic premises on which the Alliance is based are accepted, often with large majorities, by the public. The Soviet Union, whose political system and society are near-to-universally rejected in Britain, is regarded as aggressive and expansionist, and as a clear potential threat (although not an immediate danger) to Britain and the West. Its professed good intentions on disarmament elicit a sceptical response. A large—but not overwhelming—majority accept the need for a nuclear defense, which is seen, on balance, as a deterrent more than a provocation. Unilateral nuclear disarmament is the conviction of a passionate and substantial minority—but always a minority nonetheless. There is a resigned awareness about the possibility of nuclear war and about the poor prospects of personal or national survival in such an event, but that is not the same as a fatalistic willingness to submit to nuclear blackmail: the public does, apparently, countenance a nuclear counterattack. Most of the practical implications of nuclear defense strategy for Britain are supported. The institutional foundations meet little resistance. Opposition to membership of NATO is negligible. The United States is the object of widespread if diffuse goodwill and regarded as by far and away Britain's most dependable ally, whose good intentions toward Britain's security are not in doubt. Its good judgment and effectiveness in global relations are another matter.

The weakest link in the chain of assumptions underlying the Atlantic Alliance is NATO's December 1979 double-track decision. In Britain it was immediately rejected by the opposition parties and precipitated the rapid revival of the almost defunct movement for unilateral nuclear disarmament. Throughout 1981 and 1982 a majority of the public opposed the installation of cruise missiles and the continuation of American nuclear bases in Britain. There were many reasons, but rejection of the Atlantic Alliance was not among them. Old-fashioned nationalism was one: There has consistently been majority support for the principle of an independent British nuclear deterrent. A second reason was that a convincing case for cruise missiles had not been made. Acceptance of existing nuclear weapons is one thing; embracing a new generation, and its cost, quite another. The need for deterrence was distinguished from adding an extra twist, as it was seen, to the spiral of nuclear weapons. None of these doubts, however, amounted to a principled rejection of the Atlantic Alliance.

The temptation to assume that a crisis was looming arose from the explicit and noisy opposition to NATO's double-track decision by many parties and movements in Western Europe. Britain participated in this response, without being at its center. The main opposition party, led since late 1980 by Michael Foot, a veteran peace campaigner and founder member of the original Campaign for Nuclear Disarmament, adopted unilateral nuclear disarmament as its official policy as a result of resolutions passed at a conference of local constituency and trade union delegates. Its new leader was also noted for his indifference to and ignorance of the United States. The revived nuclear disarmament movement grew very fast in 1980 and 1981 and was until recently impeccably respectable in methods and style, avoiding the disintegration into violence and radical left-wing politics that marked the tail end of its predecessor movement. In contrast public opinion was almost invisible and intangible, a reality not on the streets but only in opinion poll reports.

Yet public opinion, when aroused, is more decisive than protest movements. The 1983 general election was the first since the advent of nuclear weapons and the postwar Atlantic Alliance in which defense was a major issue. The electorate was offered a crystal-clear choice between the Labour party, which stood for the dismantling of Britain's nuclear defense, the ejection of American bases, and thus the abandonment of Britain's NATO commitments (although not its formal membership), and two other parties, one of them the Conservatives in government, which, despite differences, shared a staunch commitment to nuclear defense and the Atlantic Alliance. The Labour party went down to its worst defeat (in terms of votes) since 1918. It had paid the penalty for downgrading public opinion in favor of activist opinion and for confusing doubts about the case for new missiles with hostility to the Atlantic Alliance. The result was a stunning defeat for the antinuclear weapons movement. Except for the shouting (literally), the issue of cruise missiles had effectively been killed in Britain, even before the weapons were installed.

References

Barker, Paul, and Nick Spencer, "People and Power: A New Society Survey-I," *New Society* (29 May 1975): 527–531.

Crewe, Ivor, "Why Labour Lost the British Election," *Public Opinion* (June/July 1983): 7–9, 56–60.

Haseler, Stephen, "The Demise of Atlanticism: European Elites and NATO," *Public Opinion* (February/March 1983): 2–4, 52.

Lipsey, David, "What Do We Think About the Nuclear Threat?" *New Society* (25 September 1980).

Sarlvik, Bo, and Ivor Crewe, *Decade of Dealignment* (Cambridge: Cambridge University Press, 1983).

Taylor, Humphrey, and Timothy Raison, "Britain into Europe?-General Attitudes," *New Society* (16 June 1966): 6–8.

Webb, Norman L., and Robert J. Wybrow, "Friendly Persuasion: Advice from Britain," *Public Opinion* (February/March 1983): 13, 52.

Appendix A Opinion Poll Sources

National Opinion Polls (NOP)

NOP Political Social Economic Review no. 25, June 1980, pp. 8–10.
NOP Political Social Economic Review no. 34, December 1981, pp. 20–27.
NOP Political Social Economic Review no. 42, June 1983, pp. 15–20.

Market and Opinion Research International (MORI)

"Britain and the World About Us," research study for *NOW!*, October 1979.
"Nuclear Disarmament," opinion poll for BBC Radio 4 Reith Lectures, October 1981.
"World Nuclear Disarmament," *British Public Opinion*, May 1982.
"Defense," *British Public Opinion*, January 1983.
"Nuclear Weapons," *British Public Opinion*, April 1983.

Eurobarometers (EB)

No. 8, January 1978.
No. 13, June 1980.
No. 14, December 1980.

Gallup

The monthly surveys are reported in the *Gallup Political Index*. Questions of relevance will be found in a large number of them. But see in particular:

Index 241, September 1980 (survey for *New Society*).
Index 255, November 1981.
Index 256, December 1981 (survey for BVA).
Index 259, March 1982.
Index 270, February 1983.

Miscellaneous

Marplan, "Public Opinion on Defense and Nuclear Weapons," survey conducted for *The Guardian*, January 1983.
BBC/Gallup survey of British General Election, 9 June 1983.
Opinion Research Centre, June 1966.

3 France: Attachment to a Nonbinding Relationship

RENATA FRITSCH-BOURNAZEL

Introduction

The pacifist and antinuclear protests which presently exist in nearly all Western countries have once again revealed what one must call "the French paradox" (Willis 1982,151). During the 1960s, France was criticized because it withdrew from NATO's integrated military organization, but today it appears a model of stability within the Alliance. In equipping his country with an independent strategic force, de Gaulle was operating on the principle that there is no defense without responsibility. Master of her choices and responsible for her defense, France of the 1980s appears in a way as "a counter model which escapes the pacifist disease" of its European neighbors (Colard 1983,15).

There is no questioning of nuclear logic in France, at least as far as the national strategy of proportional deterrence ("du faible au fort") is concerned. There have been no great pacifist demonstrations tinged with anti-Americanism comparable to those that have taken place over the past few years in most other member countries of the Atlantic Alliance. National consensus on the objectives and the organization of French military posture seems rather large. Finally, the image of the USSR is today more negative than it is in most Western countries.

This "French uniqueness," which singularly contrasts with the weakening of consensus on defense that one sees in other member countries of NATO, has been the object of several analyses that will not be repeated here (Duroselle 1983; Moisi 1983; Gnessoto 1983). Our task will be to determine to what extent the reassuring image of France is confirmed or not, by the attitudes of the public at large (pays réel) as they appear in opinion polls.

One should certainly not exaggerate the significance of opinion polls that focus on military questions. The pollsters and their clients are not

The author wishes to thank her colleagues Roland Cayrol and Jean-Luc Parodi of the Centre d'Etude de la Vie Politique Française Contemporaine, as well as Professor Raoul Girardet of the Institut d'Etudes Politiques for their aid in deciphering the contradictory messages emanating from the public opinion polls analyzed in this chapter.

immune to preoccupations of the moment. France does not, contrary to countries like the Federal Republic of Germany and the United States, possess rigorously comparable time series data. Until the middle of the last decade, polls dealing with defense essentially posed questions concerning the "force de frappe" and military institutions. Since the late 1970s, one has begun to solicit opinion on the international balance of power, the risk of war, and the means of defense should conflict occur. Thus the analyst is forced to jump from one question to another, constantly confronting modifications in question formulation and the interruption of promising time series.

Furthermore, one can ask how much confidence the theoretician, and even more the politician or the decision maker, should place in the results of measurement that quantify the ephemeral. There have been, for example, very strong fluctuations in the results of different polls attempting to measure public opinion on the state of the East-West balance. During the same year, it is possible to conclude that various events, speeches, articles, or news programs have eroded public confidence, and that then this confidence has regained its normal level for the period in consideration as the effect of the news has receded or has been counterbalanced in the minds of the public. Under these conditions, it is wise to recall the remark of one participant at a 1980 colloquium on "La France face aux dangers de guerre": "To have courage means above all not to be discouraged by public opinion polls" (ENA 1981,212).

Nevertheless, a serious analysis of the evolution over the past decade of responses in France to a certain number of questions concerning defense allows one to present a number of clarifications that help better to define the contours of the "French countermodel." Within the limits posed by the fragmented nature of the available documentation, the analysis concentrates on four interrelated themes that in varying degrees, condition public perceptions on defense matters: the image of the potential adversary, of security and willingness to provide for defense, of nuclear deterrence, and of attitudes toward the Western Alliance.

Images of the Soviet Union

The evolution of French opinion vis-à-vis the Soviet Union over the last decade involves two successive phases. At the beginning of the presidency of Giscard d'Estaing, the Soviet Union attracted relatively favorable opinions whereas by the end of the 1970s, the negative responses became dominant (Duhamel and Parodi 1982; Le Gall 1980). This change of opinion seems to be explainable principally by assessments of whether the character of Soviet foreign policy was peaceful or not, and of the regime's policies on individual freedom at home. Yet the degradation of the Soviet image during recent years implies neither a total rejection of the country nor condemnation of a policy of cooperation with the East.

THE FAILURE OF THE SOVIET MODEL

In 1974, the Societé Française d'Enquêtes et de Sondages (SOFRES) made a study that showed an exceptionally positive opinion on the "Soviet experience" (SOFRES 3/74). The results were judged to be positive by a majority of respondents in the following fields: education, economic development, improvement in living standards, worker participation in enterprise management, and reduction in social inequalities. The majority judgment was negative, however, as far as the functioning of justice and respect of public and individual liberties were concerned. Positive opinions were more numerous for these last two points within the Communist electorate, whereas in the other areas, one observes a regular diminution of positive responses as one moves from left to right.

Six years later the majorities had been reversed (SOFRES 5/80 and 10/80). Whereas in 1974 positive perceptions of the French, though structured along the left-right axis, were a majority in all political groupings, in 1980 there were two distinct images of the Soviet system. On the one hand, one had the Communists, who assessed results positively in all areas except individual liberties, and on the other there were all the rest, Socialists included, who reached a negative judgment in all areas except education and health (these two questions were not asked in 1974).

The French, who judge without complacency the successes and failures of the USSR, in particular concerning public and individual freedoms (see Table 3.1) show the coherence of their attitudes when questioned on the evolution of these freedoms over the last decade. In 1974, a majority estimated that these freedoms were growing, and in 1980 the majority considered they were declining: in 1977, positive and negative assessments were roughly balanced. Even the Communist sympathizers themselves lost some of their convictions, as only 29 percent among them (vs. 66 in 1974) had the impression of an improvement.

Table 3.1   Level of political freedom in the Soviet Union

	Increasing			Decreasing			No change		
	1974	1977	1980	1974	1977	1980	1974	1977	1980
All	46	30	18	13	14	21	21	28	32
PC	66	39	29	11	14	12	4	14	29
PS	48	36	20	13	15	26	22	26	30
RI-UDF	46	21	14	19	17	21	23	39	39
UDR-RPR	37	27	23	15	18	24	27	35	39
NSP	37	21	—	9	8	18	19	26	28

Source: Duhamel and Parodi, (1982):174.

This evolution of opinion seems to reflect well "the Gulag effect," that is to say, the discovery by the French of the repressive character of the Soviet system through the *Gulag Archipelago* of Solzhenitsyn, which became widely available to them in 1974 (Duhamel and Parodi 1982,173). This phenomenon is somewhat paradoxical in the sense that the French finally recognized the reality of Soviet workcamps under Brezhnev, whereas those of Stalin clearly would have merited even greater attention. Nevertheless, it was in fact during the reign of Leonid Brezhnev that an audience for Soviet dissidents developed in the West. At the same time, France is the country where the intellectuals, having believed more than others in revolution, have also felt most strongly the shock of Solzhenitsyn and the dissidents of the East (Hassner 1980,521). This revelation helped nourish the rejection of the Soviet model by making socialism in the East a new field for study.

It became evident notably that one could demand the defense of human rights and freedoms without being left-wing and even be against certain forms of totalitarianism of the revolutionary left. This recognition is quite clearly reflected in a study carried out in October 1981 confirming the negative judgment in the area of political freedoms that appeared at the end of the 1970s (*La Croix* 10/81). Only two percent of the French (but 11 percent of the Communists) considered that the USSR respected human rights; it was placed second only to Iran among the countries that least respect these rights.

THE SOVIET THREAT

The decline of the USSR as an ideological model during the 1970s developed in parallel with a profoundly deteriorated image of the Soviet Union as a "power committed to peace" and, therefore, the transformation of its role in French political life. Often used by the right as a tool for fending off the left, the Soviet Union has in a way now been devalued: it has ceased to be an element in internal ideological battles and has returned to being a geopolitical factor (Colombani 1982).

As a sign of the times, "Prospects of Soviet Power in the 1980s," published in 1979–1980 under the auspices of the International Institute for Strategic Studies (IISS) in London, was translated into French under the title "The Soviet Threat" (IISS 1982). "The Kabul effect," followed by the events in Poland, put an end to a rather long period dominated by "the spirit of détente." The idea that this spirit is dangerous in that it leads one to lower one's guard, and that France itself is threatened, has gained wide acceptance. François Mitterrand himself contributed to this development by being the first to emphasize the danger there would be for France if the Soviets continued to deploy the SS-20 and the United States failed to install its Pershing-IIs. He had, before being elected, contributed to making the French Socialist party a spearhead of resistance against Soviet influence within the Socialist International.

Table 3.2   Soviet commitment to peace

	5/75 Yes	No	5/80 Yes	No	Change Yes
All	58	19	24	46	−34
PC	77	9	49	21	−28
PS	68	17	29	47	−39
UDF	55	26	19	65	−40
RPR	58	25	13	67	−45

Source: Duhamel and Parodi (1982):175.

At the level of public opinion, the effect of the Soviet intervention in Afghanistan, however, was not decisive. The French population did not wait for pictures of Soviet tanks in Kabul to perceive the expansionist temptations of the Soviet Union; the deterioration of the peaceful image of the Soviets was largely underway before 1979 (Duhamel and Parodi 1982,178). Although one study in 1975 showed that the USSR was considered as peace-loving by the majority of those polled (in all categories), five years later the USSR, on the contrary, was considered as not being sincerely committed to peace by majorities in all categories (of sex, age, social class, and party preference) except the Communists (SOFRES 5/75 and 5/80).

In 1975, the USSR benefited simultaneously from an image of being devoted to détente and from the negative image of the Americans who were just getting out of Vietnam. In fact, during May 1975, when 58 percent of the French considered that the Soviets were sincerely committed to peace, there were only 43 percent who judged the United States similarly. Two years later, however, when questioned this time about the sincerity of the Soviet attachment to "the politics of peaceful coexistence and détente," the French were already more sceptical (SOFRES 6/77). 28 percent (vs. 56 in 1975) considered that the USSR was "sincerely committed" to the idea; 34 percent (vs. 15 percent in 1975) had the opposite opinion. This drop occurred for all categories of respondents, but it grew stronger from left to right on the political spectrum. In 1980, as the intervention in Afghanistan was added to Soviet advances in Africa during the previous years, the reversal was even more pronounced. Only 24 percent thought "that the Soviet Union is sincerely committed to peace," whereas 46 percent (21 percent of the Communist electorate vs. nine percent in 1975) now had an aggressive image of the Soviets (see Table 3.2).

The collapse of Soviet ideological attraction and of its peaceful image in France coincided with the emergence of perceptions free from illusion and centered on the military dimension of Soviet power. In April 1976, when questioned about the respective power of the United States and the Soviet Union, 40 percent of the French mentioned the United States "as the world's most powerful country", 24 percent chose the USSR (*Sondages* 1976,69). In the eyes of the French public, the United States remained number one in the fields of technical and scientific innovation (60 percent), medical research (59 percent), and clearly less so for its military power (43 percent).

In November 1980, the responses on the East-West balance of military forces were clearly different (SOFRES 10/80). Nearly one year after the NATO double-track decision on Euromissiles and the intervention in Afghanistan by the Red Army, 41 percent of the French seemed convinced that "the Eastern countries are presently the most powerful militarily"; only 11 percent felt this was true for the West, whereas 31 percent considered that in terms of nuclear megatonnage, tanks, aircraft carriers, or submarines, there was a general equilibrium between East and West.

On the eve of the 1981 presidential election, this slippage of opinion toward a pessimistic view of the East-West balance was confirmed (BVA 2/81). Forty-eight percent of the French thought that Soviet influence had increased in the world over the previous decade whereas 31 percent responded in the affirmative for the United States. The same poll indicated that 51 percent believed "the military power of the Communist countries was greater than that of the Western countries," only 14 percent felt the West was superior, and 13 percent saw an equilibrium.

From a list of 11 countries offered in November 1981, 47 percent of the French judged the USSR as threatening world peace "most at the present time" (SOFRES 11/81). When the question was limited to the USSR, the United States, and China, and after the declaration of martial law in Poland, 63 percent of the French considered the USSR as the greatest threat to peace (against ten percent for China and the United States, respectively) (BVA 1/81).

FRANCO-SOVIET RELATIONS

When taken as an ensemble, the various public opinion polls produce a certain coherence in the French image of the Soviet Union: perception of military power supremacy, deterioration of the Soviet model, fear of a threat to peace for which that country would be responsible. These certainties, however, are accompanied by a number of questions and ambiguities when it comes to choosing an appropriate diplomacy. French opinion, to which the Soviet Union appears as uncommitted to peace and as militarily superior to the West, nonetheless does not wish the return of the cold war.

Along with an exceptionally positive perception of the "Soviet experience" and of the Soviet commitment "to the policy of coexistence and détente" (49 percent), the SOFRES survey of 1974 also showed a very

Table 3.3   Judgment of French policy toward the Soviet Union (SOFRES)

	3/80 (i)	5/80 (ii)	10/80 (iii)
Too conciliatory	21	24	23
Not conciliatory enough	12	8	5
As it should be	42	37	51
No opinion	25	31	21

Note:

(i) Question wording: "After the intervention of the Soviet army in Afghanistan, do you think that the French government has adopted a position toward the USSR which is: too conciliatory, not conciliatory enough, or as it should be?"

(ii) Question wording: "In its international policy, do you feel the French Government's position toward the Soviet Union is ...?"

(iii) Question wording: "Do you think that in relations between France and the Soviet Union, President Giscard d'Estaing has been ...?"

clear majority of the French as favorable toward Franco-Soviet cooperation (SOFRES 3/74). To the question "Do you think it is normal or not normal that a capitalistic country such as France considers cooperation with the Soviet Union as an important goal of its foreign policy?" 64 percent of the French responded that it was "normal" and only 17 percent contested this point of view. On the eve of Leonid Brezhnev's trip to France in June 1977, this score improved even more in spite of the deterioration of the Soviet image that was visible at the same moment (SOFRES 6/77). In fact, 88 percent of the French considered that it was "rather a good thing that France maintains good relations with the Soviet Union," whereas only a tiny minority of three percent considered it to be "rather a bad thing."

This result may be surprising because it coincided with the swing of opinion reflecting growing mistrust of Soviet objectives triggered by their adventures in Africa, and increasing disenchantment with the record of "socialism" inside the Soviet Union. But these results were confirmed just after the Soviet intervention in Afghanistan when, asked on three separate occasions in 1980 to judge the policy of Valéry Giscard d'Estaing vis-à-vis the Soviet Union, a majority of the French declared their support, responding that the French government was neither "too conciliatory", nor "not conciliatory enough" but "as it should be" (see Table 3.3). The percentage of those satisfied passed from 42 percent in March 1980 (see Table 3.4) to 51 percent in October 1980, after having experienced a moment of doubt in May, however, with 37 percent approval and an elevated percentage (31 percent) of no opinion (Le Gall 1980,50).

In fact, during this year of crisis, the French mistrusted the Soviets but still considered that one should not necessarily abandon détente whatever

Table 3.4   Judgment of French policy toward the Soviet Union by party preference
(SOFRES 5/80)

	Too conciliatory	Not conciliatory enough	As it should be	No opinion
Total	24	8	37	31
Party preference				
PC	13	22	37	28
PS	24	8	36	32
UDF	26	4	48	22
RPR	40	7	33	20
Without preference	18	6	27	49

Source: Le Gall 1980:50

its failures might be. This explains their massive approval of President Giscard d'Estaing's visit to Warsaw to meet with Leonid Brezhnev (SOFRES 5/80); 66 percent of the French considered that "he acted correctly," 12 percent that "he should not have done it." It is to be noted that on this aspect of foreign policy, the sympathizers with the Socialists (67 percent) and Giscardians (81 percent) did not have positions that differed significantly from those of the Communists (64 percent) or Gaullists (63 percent). Five months later, there were still 68 percent of the French who considered "that a compromise must be sought at any price with the Soviet Union in order to save détente," whereas 14 percent thought that France should show more firmness toward the Soviet Union (SOFRES 10/80).

The "sharpening" of French foreign policy under President Mitterrand did not have an immediate effect on public opinion. In October 1981, 55 percent of the French wanted the country for the near future "to maintain its policy of détente toward the USSR," 20 percent wanted it "accentuated" and only 13 percent wanted it abandoned (IFRES 10/81). Only progressively did popular French commitment to détente give way to a certain indifference toward the USSR.

In September 1982, only 15 percent of the French accorded importance to the search for dialogue with the USSR "to assure the future security of the West," whereas 33 percent of the Germans favored active policy toward the East (LH/AI 9/82). It is true that the arrival of François Mitterrand in power brought "a cure of disintoxication" (Tatu 1982) to Franco-Soviet relations that was not interrupted until February 1983 with the first official visit to the Soviet Union of Foreign Minister Claude Cheysson. The purpose was not only to force people to forget the Warsaw encounter (for which the new president criticized his predecessor vigorously) but also to show the new firmness of Paris toward the situation in Afghanistan and Poland, as well as toward the balance of power in Europe.

Even if the French no longer believe, since the second half of the 1970s, that the USSR is "sincerely committed to peace," and even if they seem to be aware of a change in the military balance in favor of the East, they nevertheless have no illusions about the role or weight of any given attitude or sanction toward the Soviet government. In the Harris poll of September 1982, only eight percent worried about having too conciliatory an attitude toward the Soviet Union, and at the strategic level, the Soviet threat was considered as secondary in comparison with the dual and equal responsibility of the two superpowers for the disorder of the world (LH/AI 9/82). In the end, a great number of the French seem inclined to believe that relations with the Soviet bloc should not be simplistically reduced into a triple war—economic, politico-ideological, military—when the dangers that threaten peace are multiple and diffuse (*Le Monde* 6 June 1983).

Images of Security

On 12 and 13 June 1980, the Association of Former Students of the Ecole Nationale d'Administration organized a colloquium to discuss "France confronting the threat of war." By choosing this theme, the organizers explained, "our association was neither hawkish nor alarmist. It recognized a concern in public opinion" (ENA 1981,11). At the same moment, not far away, the Institut Français des Relations Internationales and the Institut d'Histoire des Relations Internationales Contemporaines had chosen to explore the theme "Crises and wars in the twentieth century: analogies and differences" to analyze whether "a Third World War is more possible today than before" (IFRI 1981,7). In both cases, one pointed to the fact that, in the international situation marked by the double crises of Afghanistan and Iran, politicians and the media had for the first time pronounced the word war instead of talking about crisis or tension.

Was this simply alarmism or did the world situation justify a fundamental change of attitude? Did the concern among the experts and political leaders also exist in the opinions of the public at large? In any case, the double colloquium of June 1980 catalyzed a true avalanche of polls concerning the dangers of war, the first being that of the ENA.

FEAR OF WAR

In May 1980, 75 percent of the French considered that "the present international situation carries the risk of a world war" ("very great" 28 percent, "medium" 47 percent), whereas only 16 percent saw the risk as low or nonexistent (IFOP 5/80). The risk of war was evaluated in roughly the same way in the various sectors of society defined according to social characteristics. There were, however, many more workers (34 percent) than farmers (12 percent) who consider the risk to be very great.

Table 3.5 Willingness to risk a nuclear war

| | (IFOP 5/80) (i) | | (LH/IIG 4/83) (ii) | |
	USSR	US	USSR	West
Yes	39	28	32	13
No	38	43	53	73
No opinion	23	29	15	14

Note:

(i) Question wording: "Do you think that today the USSR has or has not the desire to widen its influence and penetration into different regions of the world? And the United States? And do you think the desire could lead the USSR to run the risk of world war? And the United States?"

(ii) Question wording: "Do you believe the Soviet Union/the West is capable of risking a nuclear war in order to enlarge its zone of influence?"

Whatever their party affiliations, the French did not believe in the innocence of either of the superpowers. To a question concerning probable factors leading to war, they answered (in order): the world economic crisis (77 percent), Soviet initiatives in the world (74 percent), Third World tensions (71 percent), and finally, American initiatives in the world (64 percent). It is remarkable that 67 percent of the Communist electorate thought that Soviet initiatives were "very" or "rather" important as factors that could produce war, and that 66 percent of the UDF and 63 percent of the RPR electors had the same judgment toward the American initiatives. The USSR and the United States are nevertheless not exactly horses of the same color for the French. If with a very slight majority (39 vs. 38 percent) they judged that the Soviets were willing to risk a world war, they do not consider (43 vs. 28 percent) that this applies to the Americans.

Three years later, despite the prominence given to the Soviet threat in the meantime by politicians and the media, the fear of a nuclear war caused by the Soviet Union seems to have weakened in public opinion (Table 3.5): 32 percent of the French thought that the Soviets could "take the initiative to start nuclear war in order to widen their zone of influence," whereas 53 percent did not (this percentage reached 73 percent among Communist sympathizers and 61 percent among the Socialists compared to 42 percent for the RPR and 45 percent for the UDF) (LH/ IIG 5/83).

Even if the poll of May 1980 is very clearly colored by the existence of a crisis and a more accentuated pessimism toward the possibility of war, it nevertheless reveals a profound tendency that only gets stronger during the following period: the obsession of French opinion with the economic crisis and the damage it causes. In the middle of diplomatic and military tensions, the French had chosen the world economic crisis as the principal

Table 3.6   Priority concerns of the French (LH/AI)

	9/82	3/83	Change
Threat of war	42	34	−8
Energy crisis	22	15	−7
Inflation	50	48	−2
Insufficient defense methods	5	6	+1
Unemployment	69	70	+1
Social inequalities	22	24	+2
Law and order and security of the public	33	32	−1
Nuclear weapons	18	19	+1
Public overspending	18	21	+3
Government mediocrity	18	14	−4
No opinion	1	1	=

factor that could ignite a war (77 percent). In September 1982, of all the threats that weighed on France, it was not the risk of world war that caused greatest concern (LH/AI 9/82). It was unemployment (69 percent) and the loss of purchasing power via inflation (50 percent) that surpassed by quite a margin the other sources of concern for those interviewed. Forty-five percent of the French directly blamed American monetary policy, skyrocketing interest rates, and the rise of the dollar for present international tensions, whereas only 21 percent pointed to the USSR and its growing military potential.

The priority thus given to the problems of "internal security" (Table 3.6) does not, however, mean that the population shows no anxiety about its "external security" (Flynn 1983,224–5): In the September 1982 poll, the fear of war ranked third among the preoccupations (42 percent). But this same poll also showed that France, along with the United States, remained the country where nuclear arms were least feared: only 18 percent in fact express such anxiety in the two countries, compared to 32 percent in the FRG and 49 percent in the Netherlands. A second international poll commissioned by the Atlantic Institute for International Affairs on the eve of the Williamsburg Economic Summit confirmed that the French appear much more worried about economic threats than about war (the latter preoccupation having decreased tangibly during the six-month interval between the two polls) (LH/AI 3/83).

ECONOMY AND DEFENSE

The coincidence of a less dramatic perception of the threat of war with growing economic preoccupations evidently raises the problem of national consensus over military expenditures. During a colloquium organized in June 1977 by the journal *Défense Nationale* on the theme "public opinion and defense," one of the speakers noted that the public "is satisfied with what exists and is not too eager to ask questions about the need for continuous adaptation of our defense in a world which is changing" (Le Theule 1977,46). From the above list of major concerns of the French, it is apparent, in fact, that the fear of war is not linked in France to a feeling that the means of defense are lacking. Only five percent worry about their insufficiency and only 18 percent see an East-West military equilibrium as a priority "for the security of the West."

Moreover, the importance of economic concerns reappears when a connection is drawn between arms expenditures and the country's economic growth. In a poll about nuclear war (August 1982), 53 percent of the French agreed that expenditures on military research and arms development were "necessary to technological innovation and economic growth (creation of jobs, exports)," whereas 35 percent had the contrary opinion (LHF 8/82). Although it is true that economic conditions during this period of recession and underemployment weighed very heavily, it is nevertheless to be noted that the young, although sensitive to constant threat of unemployment, disagreed (52 percent) with this statement.

The distinction made between defense and the threat of war was particularly clear in the responses to one precise question on the utility of French nuclear forces. Although 37 percent of those questioned considered that "they protect France from war," 44 percent thought that "they serve no purpose because if they were used against a great power, France would in return be wiped off the map," and 12 percent dreaded the fatal consequences (because we have them, we will be obliged to use them one day). This question brought out the greatest divergence between men and women: 46 percent of men considered nuclear arms as capable of keeping France out of war; 63 percent of women expressed an opposing view. They were joined by the young (69 percent unfavorable opinion among 18 to 24 year olds). One must, however, try to avoid exaggerating such poll results. The responses of those who were questioned—as will also be seen in other public opinion polls on defense issues—reveal an ignorance on the logic of deterrence rather than a questioning of the necessity of French strategic nuclear forces.

At the same time, it is perhaps over the cost of the nuclear arsenal that the current consensus on defense matters could crack. In a poll dealing with disarmament issues in October 1982, 40 percent of the French considered "the current development of the French nuclear arsenal" as "economic waste" (30 percent) or a "threat to peace" (ten percent) (LHF 10/82). This attitude was particularly present among women; the age group between 18 to 24, those sympathizing with the ecologists and Communists; and the workers, representing all the way from 46 to 73 percent of opinion in these groups. Sixty-one percent of the French were rather favorable to the idea of reducing military expenditures and "developing other means of defense based on nonviolent methods"; 23 percent opposed this view. Women (68 percent), those between 18 and 24 years

(70 percent), those between 25 and 34 years (65 percent), and even those between 35 and 49 years (66 percent) showed clearly greater-than-average interest, as well as the *cadres moyens* and employees (69 percent), workers (64 percent), supporters of the ecologists (86 percent), Socialists (74 percent), and Communists (70 percent). More importantly, in all categories of the population, the percentage of "rather favorable" opinions toward reduction of military spending was greater than 50 percent, with the only exception being those supporting the RPR (48 percent).

The poll on war and peace commissioned by Marie-France Garaud seems to confirm this discrepancy between threat perception and defense-mindedness (LH/IIG 5/83). Although considering that the peace we know today is "a rather precarious peace" (55 percent), a majority of French public opinion (62 percent) refused additional sacrifices to finance an increase in the defense budget. The situation, however, is more encouraging when people are asked not for money but for some of their time for the defense of their country; 54 percent of the French would then be available to "devote voluntarily a few days per year for defense," this percentage being higher only in Great Britain (57 percent) and in the United States (79 percent).

PACIFISM AND DISARMAMENT

While intimately tied to the economic worries of the French, the aspiration to reduce military spending does not, however, seem to signify that the pacifist theses on disarmament are gaining ground. Only ten percent of the people questioned about defense and nonviolence in October 1982 thought that a country "can begin disarming if it creates a defense based on nonviolent means"; four percent thought that unilateral disarmament would be contagious (LHF 10/82). "No general disarmament is nor will ever be possible" was supported by 44 percent of the French. This figure is higher among *cadres supérieurs*, industrial executives, and those from the *professions liberales* on one side, and among the sympathizers of the RPR and the UDF on the other. In all categories, it represented at least one-third of the responses. One year earlier, in a poll on pacifism, 51 percent of the French thought that presently "a general agreement on arms reduction between East and West constitutes an unrealistic objective," whereas 30 percent believed in such a possibility (SOFRES 11/81).

To this scepticism about the real possibilities to work for a less dangerous world, one must add that the "peace movement" has historically been equated with the Communists; in France, this plays a dissuasive role in the eyes of a great part of the population (Gnesotto 1983). The absence of militant pacifism, which is the specific characteristic of the French countermodel, is not, however, synonymous with a disapproval of the pacifist demonstrations that have swept through Europe during the last few years.

Questioned in the fall of 1981, at the moment of the great demonstrations in Bonn (200,000 people), London (175,000), Rome (200,000),

Table 3.7   Support for pacifist demonstrations (IFOP 11/81)

	All	Opposition	Majority
Approve completely	31	23	41
Approve rather	24	26	24
Disapprove rather	13	15	11
Disapprove completely	12	18	13
No answer	20	18	11

Madrid (400,000) and Amsterdam (300,000), 55 percent of the French approved (31 percent totally, 24 percent rather), and disapproval only reached 25 percent (IFOP 11/81). Those under 35 were most favorable (63 percent) but were closely followed by those between 35 and 49 years (62 percent). In spite of the very firm attitude of the government on this question, 65 percent of the electorate supporting the government approved "totally" (41 percent) or "rather" (24 percent) "the pacifist demonstrations which are now taking place in Europe."

One year later there were still 55 percent (vs. 24 percent) of the French who declared themselves "rather favorable" to those who "struggle in the associations working for disarmament"; 45 percent (vs. 35 percent) were "rather favorable toward those who participate in public demonstrations against the arms race" (58 percent among the 25 to 34 age group; 55 percent among the 18 to 24 year-olds, and, respectively, 71, 67, and 51 percent among the Ecologists, Communists and Socialists) (LHF 10/82). But these results should, of course, be interpreted with prudence because France is not directly concerned by the Euromissile controversy that is largely at the origin of the antinuclear dispute inside the Atlantic Alliance (see Tables 3.7 and 3.8).

The data from this poll, moreover, permit one to observe that the French hardly seem ready to associate themselves actively with the current movement for disarmament. When people were asked if "personally" or "eventually" they would agree to protest against the arms race, only 15 percent said they would be ready to "participate in a public demonstration," and 16 percent would "refuse to pay that part of your taxes corresponding to military spending." Similarly, the very high percentage of no opinion (which reaches 40 percent) signifies quite clearly the general indifference of public opinion to militant pacifism.

It is true that, as France did not participate in the NATO double-track decision, French public opinion finds itself rather outside of the major controversies concerning the strategic negotiations between the two superpowers. In an overarmed world, France in effect needs the means to defend itself, and its strategic nuclear forces could not be reorganized before the moment when the two blocs had reached an agreement on

Table 3.8   Support for those who demonstrate, by political preference (LHF 10/82)

	All	PC	PS	UDF	RPR	Ecologists
Rather favorable	45	67	51	38	31	71
Rather opposed	35	20	32	46	54	15
No opinion	20	13	17	16	15	14

mutual reductions. On this point the national consensus even includes the pro-Communist peace movement, which carefully avoids calling into question the special status from which France benefits within the Atlantic Alliance.

Images of Deterrence

France has chosen for itself a strategy of proportional deterrence that, according to military officials, is and will remain "the best guarantee of our defense and national independence" in a strategic environment marked simultaneously by "the constancy of the Soviet effort" and "American uncertainties." At the same time, because of its geo-strategic situation, the ensemble of the values it shares, and its democratic institutions, France "shows its solidarity with the Western world and is closely concerned with the security of its European partners" (Hernu 1982).

THE CHOICE OF FRANCE

Even if French policy reflects its double political-strategic status, "a continental nuclear power and a European power loyal to its neighbors" (Poirier 1983,8), it does not seem that these two aspects are interrelated in the same way in the eyes of the public. All the governments of the Fifth Republic have spoken more strongly about national defense than Western security; whenever questions related to deterrence are formulated in a European or Atlantic rather than in a national context, misunderstandings are to be expected. According to the results of the international poll commissioned by the Atlantic Institute for International Affairs in September 1982, 98 percent of the French believed their strategic nuclear force "does not play an essential role," and for 95 percent not even "an effective role" in defending Western interests (LH/AI 9/82). The likely explanation, as expressed by Alfred Grosser in his commentary on the poll, probably resides in the fact that, on this question, the link is not formed between "the West" and "the French" (Grosser 1982).

It would seem that the political debate on defense in France has long been governed by internal political considerations, with the parties defining their positions vis-à-vis government policy in terms of their position

Table 3.9   Attitudes toward the French nuclear deterrent

	LHF 9/77 (i)	SOFRES 3/80 (i)	LHF 6/81 (ii)	SOFRES 4/83 (iii)
Very positive	12) 49	15) 50	72	27) 66
Rather positive	37)	35)		39)
Rather negative	19) 38	20) 35	15	13) 20
Very negative	19)	15)		7)
No opinion	13	15	13	14

Note:

(i) Question wording: "Are you favorable, rather favorable, rather opposed, or very opposed to the French nuclear deterrent, that is, the force de frappe?"

(ii) Question wording: "In your opinion, should France continue to have nuclear deterrent forces?"

(iii) Question wording: "Do you think that the existence of nuclear deterrent forces for France is something: very positive, rather positive, rather negative, or very negative?"

either within or outside of the majority. Thus it required about fifteen years before all political parties came to adhere to the concept of nuclear deterrence and accepted that the French nuclear arsenal contributed to the maintenance of peace.

Ever since the parties of the present majority embraced nuclear deterrence, all polls give a majority of favorable responses to maintaining the strategic nuclear forces (see Table 3.9). There is even a perceptible increase in positive responses during the last few years, which attests to a remarkable continuity in spite of the changes in government. Majority support is henceforth to be found in all political "families," all social categories, and even in all age groups.

The results of the 1981 poll, carried out just after the presidential elections, reflect a particularly large consensus, without major distinction along party lines, as 62 percent of the Communist sympathizers (vs. 46 percent in 1980) approved of the historic choices of Gaullism. It is probable that the left's massive approval of nuclear deterrent forces has been facilitated greatly by its new governmental responsibilities after having been out of power so long.

Hesitations appear, concerning the cost of this military tool, but even during an economically difficult period, more than one French citizen out of two (52 percent) considers the current modernization of French nuclear armament (Table 3.10) as either "normal" (27 percent) or "an indispensable condition for the grandeur and progress of the country" (25 percent) (LHF 10/81). The older the respondent, the greater the support for this thesis; the support is also greater among the sympathizers of the previous majority (69 and 68 percent of positive responses among the RPR and UDF vs. 49 and 33 percent among the PS and PCF).

Table 3.10   Judgment on current French nuclear modernization (LHF 10/82)

A threat to peace	10
Economic waste	30
A normal development	27
Indispensable for the growth and progress of France	25
No opinion	8

THE ROLE OF NUCLEAR ARMS

Although more difficult to evaluate through opinion polls, attitudes on the role of nuclear arms nevertheless reveal certain gray zones that may cast into doubt the reality of "the collective education of the French on deterrence" (Huntzinger 1982,41). This notion was expressed at a colloquium on "commitment to defense and security in Europe," organized jointly in June 1982, by the Comité d'Etudes de Défense Nationale and the Fondation Pour les Etudes de Défense Nationale to explain the uniqueness of France when compared with the pacifist tendencies inside the European left. Even if it is undoubtably true that the embracing of French strategic nuclear forces by the PS and PCF protects France from the antinuclear movement in the West, ignorance of the logic of deterrence seems, nevertheless, a widely spread phenomenon among the French as well as among their neighbors.

The poll carried out in 1980 for the colloquium of the ENA gives some elements of information on this subject (IFOP 5/80). These results have to be interpreted with caution, of course, as they represent only an instantaneous photograph of an opinion that can evolve very rapidly, even if other later polls seem to confirm the general trend of 1980 (Girardet 1982,74).

French opinion seems to have only an approximate knowledge of the international environment and of the threats that can weigh on national independence. More than half of those polled (58 percent) thought that the threat of using nuclear arms, the essence of deterrence, should not be employed, not even "in a case where France was on the point of being invaded." This refusal was massive and concerns the entire electorate: the PC (66 vs. 26 percent), the PS (67 vs. 24 percent), the UDF (46 vs. 43 percent), and the RPR (46 vs. 41 percent). A great difference of appreciation according to sex is nevertheless to be noted: 37 percent of men would favor threatening the use of nuclear arms to prevent the invasion of France, but only 22 percent of women. Three people out of four of those interviewed opposed the principle of the French president using nuclear arms. Finally, two-thirds of the French thought that a president of the republic who would threaten to use these arms would be disapproved by public opinion and, in such a case, would be faced with extreme

Table 3.11   The recourse to nuclear arms (IFOP 5/80)

Agree	29
Disagree	58
No opinion	13

opposition. Violent reactions are particularly predicted by the Communists (51 percent), Socialists (40 percent), and the young (see Table 3.11).

The French refuse to think about an eventual conflict, are not familiar with modern strategic concepts, and compensate by placing disproportionate hope in hypothetical resistance. Even if they refuse war and consider (64 vs. 22 percent) that "everything should be sacrificed to maintain peace," the French in large numbers (32 percent) declare that they would go underground (45 percent of the Communists and 34 percent of the Socialists) if the national territory were occupied. Sixty-two percent of them think that the United States would intervene militarily to save Western Europe in such a situation. The RPR, UDF, and the Socialists are overwhelmingly persuaded of this (between 64 and 70 percent), as are the Communists (59 percent).

Here one finds strategic notions inspired by the Second World War with, in addition, a certain tendency to search for a way out in the old French tradition of resistance. One can, however, ask whether the conditions of modern war would once again allow France "to assure its defense by relying on an elite which, once again, declares itself ready to participate tomorrow in the resistance of yesterday" (ENA 1981,190). Whatever the case, no study, carried out "cold", i.e. in the abstract, is capable of indicating in which direction public opinion would move—paralysis out of fear or the crystalizing of a willingness for resistance—in the case of *crise majeure*, in the face of imminently perceived peril.

THE EUROMISSILES

More than any other weapons system, the "Soviet" and "American" Euromissiles pose the problem of the relationship between the political-

Table 3.12   Confidence in different means of defense (LHF 10/82)

Classic conventional army	28
Armed resistance by the whole population, planned in advance	20
Nuclear strike force	18
Nonviolent resistance by the whole population, planned in advance (strikes, demonstrations, civil disobedience)	17
No opinion	17

military force posture of France and that of its allies. François Mitterrand was recognized well before his election for the interest he showed in this question, interest that contrasted with the silence of his predecessor on the subject of the NATO double-track decision in December 1979 (David and Halleman 1981). The French signature of the Williamsburg declaration on security on 29 May 1983 only confirmed France's position since summer 1981, that is, the approval of the principle to deploy the American Euromissiles in case the Soviet-American negotiations in Geneva fail. Nevertheless, for the first time France, which was not directly involved in the decision in question, associated itself with an expression of collective solidarity destined to reinforce Atlantic cohesion.

Until now most observers believe that public opinion has followed official policy on this point. France, in fact, has not experienced spectacular pacifist demonstrations against the Pershings, similar to those of the FRG, the Netherlands or Great Britain. The Fête pour la Paix in Vincennes organized on 19 June 1983 by the Communist party and the Conféderation Générale du Travail (Communist-dominated trade union), under the auspices of "Appel des Cent," did indeed attract 250,000 to 300,000 persons (80,000 according to the police, 500,000 according to the organizers). But the success of this meeting is not enough to prove that war is perceived as a real risk today in France, embedded in a policy against which people should mobilize themselves (Jarreau 1983).

If the installation of the new NATO missiles is considered by an important fraction of public opinion in the concerned countries as a first step toward armed confrontation, this question is not posed with the same sense of urgency in France. Moreover, in a poll published on the eve of the demonstrations in Vincennes, the French recognized by an overwhelming majority (four out of five) that they are particularly poorly informed about the installation of the American missiles in Europe (LHF 5/83). Those between the ages of 18 and 34 consider themselves even more poorly informed (84 percent) than the population in general. The French politically close to the Communist party (24 percent) and to the UDF (21 percent) consider themselves slightly better informed than those to the RPR (18 percent) and the Socialist party (16 percent).

At the same time, the French who declare themselves against the installation of the Pershings, "even if the USSR maintains its SS-20 missiles," are more numerous than would have been expected (44 percent). This figure goes up to 51 percent for those between the ages of 18 and 34. The percentage of those favorable to deployment does not reach over 34 percent for the French as a whole and 32 percent for those between the ages of 18 and 34. The French are also numerous (50 vs. 35 percent) in their approval of the pacifist demonstrations. Those between the ages of 18 and 34 are clearly even more favorable than their elders toward the pacifist demonstrations (59 percent) but practically the same degree of approval can be found among the Socialists (58 percent). Furthermore, 47 percent of the Socialists (which is considerable, given the clear position taken by the president of the republic) prefer negotiations at any price, and 71

Table 3.13   The Pershing II and France (LHF 5/83)

	All	PC	PS	UDF	RPR	Ecologists
France should install Pershing on her territory under the control of the Atlantic Alliance.	10	10	7	18	16	6
France should install Pershing on her territory under the exclusive control of the French government.	35	16	36	41	45	31
France should refuse to install Pershing on her territory.	35	63	38	26	22	50
No opinion	20	11	19	15	17	13

percent of the Communists have the same opinion. But the sympathizers of the opposition (the UDF and RPR) are relatively numerous in their support of the same point of view (35 and 38 percent), which is even more surprising.

This poll brings well into light one of the major difficulties that confront the analyst. That portion of the public that is not informed on military questions and does not try to inform itself or does not have an opinion should not be underestimated. At the same time, among those who answer other than "don't know," there are without doubt some individuals who prefer to choose a category at random rather than admit that they "don't know" or that they "do not have an opinion."

The same type of question concerning the degree of real popular comprehension of very complex matters becomes evident when reading the results of the poll commissioned by the International Institute of Geopolitics last spring (LHF/IIG 5/83). According to this poll, 45 percent of the French would, in fact, be in favor of "a French decision to install Pershing missiles on its territory," whereas 35 percent were against and 20 percent were without opinion (Tables 3.13 and 3.14). Among the favorable responses, ten percent would go as far as leaving the control of these arms to the United States, whereas 35 percent would prefer a French finger on the button. Only the Communist sympathizers would feel hostile to this solution (63 percent), and 43 percent of the Socialists were in favor of it.

Images of Allies

The foreign policy of the Fifth Republic has for a long time been built around the idea of preserving or establishing independence vis-à-vis France's primary ally and, as a result, the most violent transatlantic antagonisms have been Franco-American (Grosser 1978,438). With the coming of the left to power, the threat against the position of France is no longer perceived as a global challenge coming exclusively from the United

Table 3.14   The Pershing II and Europe (LHF 5/83)

	All French	18 to 34 year-olds
If the USSR maintains its SS-20's, the United States should install Pershing in order to retain equal forces and to assure peace in Europe.	34	32
Even if the USSR maintains its SS-20's, the United States should renounce Pershing, which is a danger to peace, and negotiate with the USSR	44	51
No opinion	22	17

States but is equally found in the negative impact that the increase in Soviet power exercises on the margin of diplomatic-strategic maneuver of Paris.

Since François Mitterrand, freshly elected to the presidency, addressed head on for the first time the question of American interest rates and the erratic fluctuations of the dollar at the Ottawa summit in July 1981, the subjects of friction between Paris and Washington have remained numerous, whether they concerned the economic sanctions against the USSR, the measures taken by the American administration against several European companies under contract with both the Soviet Union and American subsidiaries, or the reform of the international monetary system. At the same time, one can observe a reconciliation in the French and American analyses of Soviet policy toward the West and of the necessity for defense. Solidarity with the allies has been presented as an indispensable complement to national independence. What has lagged behind is the general public. Either by traditional scepticism vis-à-vis the United States or by general indifference when confronting the notion of "the West," it shows above all proof of remarkable lack of enthusiasm toward the possibility of firm commitment that would limit the freedom of decision in France.

In the end, the majority of the public has remained very close to the attitude expressed almost 20 years ago in a response to a questionnaire on the future of the Alliance: "Flirtation, yes; liaison, perhaps; marriage, no" (Deutsch 1967,83).

THE IMAGE OF THE UNITED STATES

For about ten years the image of the United States in France has experienced important fluctuations, linked on one hand to the general evolution of East-West relations, and on the other to America's misfortunes in the Watergate affair, the Vietnam War, or the hostage problem with Iran. Nonetheless, contrary to what one can observe concerning the image of the USSR during this period, there have been no spectacular

Table 3.15   Confidence in President Carter (LHF 11/77)

	All	PC	PS	PR	RPR
Very confident	6	4	6	7	7
Rather confident	40	32	45	47	47
Little confidence	17	23	21	16	21
No confidence at all	8	18	9	7	8
No opinion	29	23	19	23	17

reversals of tendencies. Rather one finds moments of irritation against a backdrop of general scepticism toward the ally on the other side of the Atlantic.

In May 1975, just after the fall of the Thieu regime in Saigon, 43 percent of the French believed, looking at the balance sheet of the last 30 years, "that the United States is sincerely committed to peace," 32 percent having an opposite opinion, and 25 percent no opinion. Among those who consider that the United States is "not sincerely committed to peace," one finds 59 percent Communists, 37 percent Socialists, and 39 percent of those between the ages 18 and 24. One must remember that, at the same time, 58 percent of the French thought that "the USSR is sincerely committed to peace" (see Table 3.2). During the same period, only 33 percent of the French said they felt confident in "the capacity of the United States to treat in a reasonable way current problems of the world," 58 percent lacked confidence, and 60 percent believed that America's rhetoric and action too often differed from one another (IFOP 4/76).

Five years later, 43 percent (vs. 28 percent) of the French were certain that the United States would not run the risk of a world war, but 50 percent (vs. 30) still had an "imperial" image of the United States (with

Table 3.16   Statesmen as a threat to peace (IFOP 11/81)

	All	Electors from the Opposition	Majority
Leonid Brezhnev			
— A threat to peace	38	48	40
— Not a threat to peace	27	26	36
— No answer	35	26	24
Ronald Reagan			
— A threat to peace	34	21	47
— Not a threat to peace	36	54	33
— No answer	30	25	20

only one electorate, the UDF (34 vs. 44 percent), not believing in American imperialism) (IFOP 5/80). And in October 1981, President Reagan followed closely on the heels of Leonid Brezhnev when the French were asked which political leaders, in their declarations or policies, posed a "threat to peace" (38 vs. 34 percent of responses) (IFOP 11/81). In November 1977, 46 percent of the French were "very" (six percent) or "rather" (40 percent) confident of President Carter "in case of a world crisis" (Table 3.15). In 1981, the leaders of the two superpowers came, however, far behind Ayatollah Khomeiny and Colonel Khadafi in the hit parade of "the most dangerous statesmen for world peace." The high percentage of no opinions in these two polls is also noteworthy (Table 3.16).

THE ECONOMIC CHALLENGE

A prudent, reserved attitude toward America thus forms an integral part of the "countermodel" that immunizes the French against the effect of the confidence crisis that seems regularly to burden the relations of the other European Allies with the United States. As there have never been many illusions about the convergence of Franco-American interests, there is less risk of disappointment.

"France and the United States," remarked Foreign Minister Jean Sauvagnargues in the beginning of the Giscard presidency, "have interests which are not contradictory but which rarely are identical" (*Le Monde* 26 October 1984). This statement retains its validity during the period of economic disputes that are at the heart of the problems between France and the United States during the presidency of Mitterrand. Right after the elections in 1981, two American scholars predicted that conflicts with Socialist France would probably not arise with regard to NATO but in the field of economic relations (Harrison and Serfaty 1981,48). A public opinion poll carried out in September 1981 (IFOP 9/81), and largely confirmed by the international study on Euro-American differences of September 1982, show the pertinence of this analysis (LH/AI 9/82).

In September 1981, 43 percent of the French were more afraid of "the United States and its monetary policy" than "the USSR and its defense policy" (Table 3.17). Sixty-six percent of the Communists and 53 percent of the Socialists shared this opinion and the Soviet danger comes out ahead only among supporters of the UDF (39 percent). One year later, 45 percent of the French considered "American interest rates and the role of the dollar" as responsible for current international tensions. This opinion was very widely entrenched among the leftist electorate (51 percent of the Communists and 54 percent of the Socialists) but was also to be found among the UDF (43 percent) and the RPR (44 percent). The results of this last poll (Table 3.18) also showed that the mobilization campaign of the government begun at the time of the Ottowa summit in May 1981 on the theme of economic threat had been a success because France was the only

Table 3.17   Primary threats to France (IFOP 9/81)

	All	PC	PS/MRG	RPR	UDF
The US and their monetary policies	43	66	53	38	30
The USSR and their defense policies	24	7	18	32	39
Japan and their economic policies	16	14	20	19	19
No answer	17	13	9	11	12

country, among the Western countries allied with the United States, to stress so clearly economic factors rather than military sources of tension.

PATTERNS OF A "SPECIAL RELATIONSHIP"

French public opinion shows proof of a certain coherence because on the eve of the Williamsburg summit 41 percent of the French did not have confidence in the United States "playing the role of a leader among the Western countries" in the field of economics, whereas the majority was confident in the field of science and technology (63 percent) and in the military field (48 percent) (BVA 5/83).

The last figure seems to indicate a relative improvement in the image of the United States, leader of the Atlantic Alliance, which can also be found in other opinion polls. According to the February 1983 poll on the Alliance carried out for the Institut International de Geopolitique, nearly two-thirds of those interviewed felt reassured by French membership in the Alliance and less than one-fourth considered it a source of concern (Gallup 2/83). Nevertheless, 40 percent of those polled were unable or unwilling to answer a question on "which of its true allies France can really count on," and nearly one-third did not know whether "membership in the Atlantic Alliance increases or decreases our chances to be drawn into war." Those responding also reflect the existence of considerable uncertainty: 34 percent thought that membership in the Alliance increased the risk of a fatal involvement, whereas 36 percent had the contrary opinion. Company directors, *cadres supérieurs*, and those of the *professions liberales* had a higher than average perception of risk in being an ally, whereas farmers showed more confidence toward the Alliance.

One can, however, question the real significance of opinion on these issues. Not only can two contradictory opinions easily be expressed simultaneously but, above all, it is always very uncomfortable to gauge the extent to which opinion is mobilizable, the intensity with which opinions are held, in short, their impact on attitudes and behavior. What should one emphasize? People's support for basic principles or their shrinking from the realities that flow from those principles?

Thus, as soon as more concrete judgment is to be made, the perception

Table 3.18   Primary sources of international tension (LHF 9/82)

	All	PC	PS	UDF	RPR
American interest rates and the role of the dollar	45	51	54	43	44
Growth of Soviet military potential	21	13	18	24	30
Insufficient European unity	26	17	28	39	30
No opinion	17	22	14	15	9

Note: Totals add up to more than 100 percent because of multiple responses (9 possible choices).

of the role of the Atlantic Alliance in French public opinion becomes extremely vague. Basically, the doubts over the credibility of the American nuclear guarantee, which were at the root of the decision by General de Gaulle to withdraw from NATO's integrated military organization, seem largely to be shared by the French. This has been reinforced by the growing scepticism of some of their European neighbors toward "the American friend," which supplies a supplementary ex post facto justification for the French choices of the 1960s.

In a study carried out in January 1979, on the eve of the first direct European parliamentary elections, only 19 percent of the French thought that the best solution for France was "to participate in a military alliance between the countries of Western Europe and the United States"; 30 percent chose a position of absolute neutrality; 28 percent preferred the solution of "a military alliance among the countries of Europe, but independent from the United States"; two percent wished to "participate in an alliance with the Soviet Union" (LHF 1/79) (see Table 3.19). The alliance with America was chosen by only 17 percent of the Socialists and eight percent of the Communists, but was preferred by the Gaullists (34 percent) and the UDF (29 percent). When this question was posed "hot" (two months after the Soviet troops entered Afghanistan), the option in favor of neutrality received as much as 36 percent of the responses, whereas the choice in favor of an alliance with the United States increased by 2 points, even among the Communists (SOFRES 2/80).

It was the search for "a third alternative" that prevailed very clearly during this crisis situation; 51 percent of the French thought that "France must remain loyal to the United States but also deal with the Soviet Union to keep intact the possibilities for détente between East and West," whereas only nine percent thought that France "should very clearly declare its solidarity with the United States" (four percent preferring "solidarity with the Soviet Union"). It is noteworthy that the Soviet intervention seriously shook the certainties among the Communists, only 17 percent of whom chose solidarity with the USSR, whereas six percent

Table 3.19   Which alliance for France?

	LHF 1/79	All SOFRES 2/80	PC	Party preference SOFRES 2/80 PS	UDF	RPR
Participate in a military alliance between the countries of Western Europe and the US	19	21	10	19	31	32
Participate in a military alliance between the countries of Western Europe but independent of the US	28	28	19	37	33	23
Participate in an alliance with the USSR	2	1	3	2	–	–
Not participate in any alliance, taking a position of absolute neutrality	30	36	55	34	27	33
No opinion	21	14	13	8	9	12

chose the United States, and 37 percent wished to preserve the chances of détente. In the Socialist left, ten percent declared their solidarity with the United States and 52 percent chose détente, whereas with the RPR one finds, in spite of 56 percent being committed to détente, 19 percent who chose the traditional Gaullist attitude: priority for Western solidarity in times of serious international crisis.

Two years later, right after the declaration of martial law in Poland and in the context of an extremely firm official policy concerning the aggravation of the Soviet threat, 55 percent of the French thought "that considering the international situation at the moment, a country is obliged to choose its camp between the two superpowers, the USSR and the United States" (IFRES 2/82). Even if there are only six percent "no opinion" for this question, the percentage grew to 48 percent when people were asked to choose "personally" their camp. Of the two questions, the necessity of choice is better accepted among the sympathizers of the opposition (71 and 86 percent of the responses) than in the majority (43 and 48 percent) (see Table 3.20).

The particularity of the French attitudes toward the problems of the Western Alliance is most clearly demonstrated not by the opinions but by those not expressed. First, there are those who choose "don't know" systematically and openly from the categories proposed by the pollsters. But should one not also add to this group those who are practically never counted, that is, those who refuse by lack of interest in problems of defense to participate in the polling game?

These results are in no way contradictory to the attitudes of 1980, insofar as the particularly high number of "no responses" when a personal

Table 3.20   The necessity for a country to choose sides? (IFRES 2/82)

	Majority	Opposition	Global
Yes	43	71	55
No	51	23	39
No opinion	6	6	6

And which side would you yourself choose?

	Majority	Opposition	Global
US	48	86	63
USSR	4	–	3
No opinion	48	14	34

engagement is to be made seems to express an unwillingness to choose between the two camps. This attitude finds its corollary in the disabused, even negative judgment that the French place on "the manner in which the United States assumes its role in the defense of Western interests." In September 1982, only four and five percent of those polled judged this role "essential" and "effective," whereas 22 and 18 percent qualified it as "interfering" and "arrogant" (LHF/AI 9/82). It is significant that 30 percent of those interviewed were incapable of defining, in concrete terms, the role of the United States. Moreover, the reproaches of being interfering and arrogant were overrepresented among the Communists (22 and 26 percent) and the Socialists (27 and 22 percent), whereas the parties of the previous majority found this role, above all, "insufficient" (20 percent for the UDF and 25 percent for the RPR). It is noteworthy that in the same poll, 46 percent of the Germans considered the role of the United States "essential" and 22 percent "effective," whereas 27 percent of the Americans judged themselves above all "inconsistent" in their relations with the Europeans.

This fundamental pessimism, however, does not prevent a clear majority of the French from thinking that, in case of serious difficulties, the United States would, after all, come to their aid. In 1980, 64 percent of those polled (vs. 14 percent) thought that "if the Soviet Union tried to occupy Western Europe, the United States would intervene to defend it" (IFOP 5/80). Two years later (see Tables 3.21 and 3.22), they were even more convinced (80 vs. 11 percent) that "the Americans would intervene if Europe was in difficulty" (BVA 1/81). One should note, however, that these responses are ambiguous because it is not stated precisely by which means the United States would deliver Europe from the threat; further, it should be remembered that in a poll of January 1982, 41 percent of the French thought that "in case of war between the USSR and Europe," the USSR would emerge as the winner.

Table 3.21   Confidence in US commitment to defend Europe

	IFOP 5/80 (i)	BVA 1/82 (ii)
Yes	64	80
No	14	11
Don't know	22	9

Note:
(i) Question wording: "If the USSR attempted to occupy Western Europe, do you believe the United States would intervene in Europe's defense?"

(ii) Question wording: "Do you think that the Americans would intervene if Europe was in difficulty?"

How does one measure in such a question the real magnitude of divergence between a rationally expressed point of view and the uncertainties of behavior? How does one capture the opinion of the population at large when this is laid out in the form of a multifaceted, fluid, and constantly changing complex of prejudices, beliefs, stereotypes, loyalties, or repulsions?

In summary, the opinion polls carried out in France on the problems of the Atlantic Alliance, fewer than in other European countries for historical reasons, show simultaneously a certain fidelity to "a nonbinding relationship" and symptoms of "disengagement" (Grapin 1982). Probably the international poll of Gallup (March 1982) expressed best this ambivalence. At a general level, 54 percent of the French said they had a "very favorable" (five percent) or "rather favorable" (49 percent) opinion of the United States. This percentage falls to 40 percent when it is a question of the capacity of the United States to "act with judgment in world affairs." As to the question of whether one could "trust NATO to defend Western Europe against an eventual attack," there were only five percent who expressed "very great confidence," whereas the figure of no opinion went up to 23 percent (vs. 13 and 14 percent for the two previous questions); those showing distrust (38 percent) were for all practical purposes equal to those who have confidence.

These uncertainties about military alliances can be found again in the responses to questions on the role of nuclear arms. At all times, moreover, opinion polls have revealed this ambiguous attitude of the French toward the United States and the Allies, and even that party lines strangely break down when it comes to designating the friends of France. The attitudes are clearer at the levels of the image of enemies, and partisan sympathies are again evident in appreciation of the dangers confronting France. At the same time, the threat is not perceived by French public opinion as being exclusively military nor as a unique result of Soviet activities (particularly in the Third World) (Fontaine 1983). It is equally, if not even more,

Table 3.22   Judgment of US role in defending Western interests (LHF 9/82)

	All	PC	PS	UDF	RPR
Essential	4	—	1	4	11
Effective	5	—	4	8	9
Arrogant	18	26	22	14	17
Naive	4	3	3	3	6
Adequate	10	4	10	16	11
Inconsistent	14	12	18	12	10
Insufficient	17	19	19	20	25
Interfering	22	22	27	14	19
No opinion	30	20	25	26	23

Note: Totals add up to more than 100 percent because of multiple responses.

economic and thus linked to the image of the American ally. One can hardly be surprised, under these conditions, to find that attitudes toward security issues are diffuse and multifaceted, as are the dangers that France confronts.

Conclusions

An opinion poll is usually no more than a reflection of the information offered by the press and the audio-visual media. It takes into account events and themes that the media have made public. It is the echo of an echo. The risk is thus great that one exaggerates out of proportion the sensitivity of the people being polled, in particular when interviewing them about fields, such as national security, that hardly affect their everyday life.

Over the past ten years, according to a military expert on defense-related polls, changes both internal and external to the army have combined to raise the image of the military and to reinforce support for defense policy (Thieblemont 1983). In spite of that, the French still remain indifferent or sceptical about certain aspects that concern the activities and capacity of the military or the understanding of deterrence strategy. In 1982, he concluded, "the military tool is accepted. But it is to be feared that the confidence in this tool does not reach the level of its acceptance."

As to the perception of the risks of conflict, it is probable that the possibility of war is more present in the minds of the French than it was ten years ago. But they speak about it abstractly as if it were a distant phenomenon and the great majority do not imagine seriously that they could be touched by this tragedy. International events, of course, prove to the French that they live in a dangerous world. But dangerous for whom?

More often than not for others. The French are rather the spectators of international conflicts on which they comment but, concretely, they do not perceive a risk of either a conventional or nuclear war that would be capable of disturbing their everyday life. As a result, they are not very prepared to mobilize themselves on the themes of "peace" or "defense of the country."

The USSR is presently perceived as a hostile power by the majority of the population, but here as well, one must point again to the limited vision of public opinion. The USSR "frightens," but to answer that it "threatens world peace" does not imply necessarily that a majority of the French feel directly concerned, at the national or the European level, by the Soviet threat. In the general context of increasing talk about war, the French are relatively unconcerned. If they express themselves about a threat, they say that it may come from the Soviet Union or, more generally, from confrontation between the superpowers, but they also point to the Middle East and South West Asia, where permanent instability reigns.

Finally, the identified tendencies in the declared attitudes toward conflict situations or invasion of national territory provide an equal number of uncertainties. Information offered by the polls on peoples' intentions to defend themselves or on international loyalties are heterogeneous and to analyze them is tricky. So it is prudent not to draw definitive conclusions on the state of public opinion, which, concerning a particular topic, reacts to an imaginary future and not to present constraints.

It is thus confirmed that the French population in its ensemble is not demanding major modifications of the military strategy that has been adopted during the Fifth Republic. In the context of the public's general anxiety vis-à-vis economic threats, the formulation and legitimization of security policy becomes, nevertheless, more and more difficult. The recognition of the economic crisis and acceptance of demands for austerity can, in fact, create in certain social categories an image of the army as a "money waster."

Nothing remains permanent, however, and it cannot be excluded in the future that the rejection of the excesses of modernization, which seems to be a characteristic of the "successor generation," will not create doubts about nuclear strategy within a portion of the French youth (Szabo 1983,224). At the present moment, one is reduced to speculation on this point, as on many others as well, this being even more true because the elections of 1981 have somewhat upset traditional political cleavages.

It remains to be seen what will happen in case the Communist party, which is increasingly reticent to support the government in its military policy, would align itself openly with Soviet theses. Coming after other signals, such as the abstention of Communist deputies on Article 1 of the military programs law (under the pretext of its summary formulation, in fact because the text denominates the USSR as the only adversary) and the refusal to approve the entry of Spain into NATO, the differences between the Socialists and the Communists over the Euromissiles, and whether

French forces should be "taken into account" in the Geneva negotiations indicate, in any case, that in an international context that witnesses increasing tensions, the consensus of the left on security questions will become more and more precarious (Tatu 1983).

References

Colard, Daniel, "Les mouvements pacifistes européens," *Documents* 2 (1983): 3–16.

Colombani, Jean-Marie, "De l'effet goulag à l'effet Kaboul," *Le Monde*, 13 November 1982.

"Comment les Français apprécient-ils leur défense?" *Défense nationale* (August-September 1977): 21–72.

La Croix, 21 October 1981.

David, Dominique and Guy-Philippe Halleman, "Les partis politiques français et les euromissiles," *Défense nationale* (February 1981): 67–84.

Deutsch, Karl W. et al., *France, Germany and the Western Alliance. A Study of Elite Attitudes on European Integration and World Politics* (New York: Charles Scribner's Sons, 1967).

Duhamel, Olivier and Jean-Luc Parodi, "Images du communisme. 1. La dégradation de l'image de l'Union soviétique," *Pouvoirs* 21 (1982): 169–180.

Duroselle, Jean-Baptiste, "Les précédents historiques: pacifisme des années 30 et neutralisme des années 50," in Pierre Lellouche, ed., *Pacifisme et dissuasion* (Paris: Institut Français des Relations Internationales, 1983) Pp. 241–252.

ENA (Ecole Nationale d'Administration), *La France face aux dangers de guerre* (Paris: Conti-Fayolle, 1981).

Flynn, Gregory, "Opinions publiques et mouvements pacifistes," in Pierre Lellouche, ed., *Pacifisme et dissuasion* (Paris: Institut Français des Relations Internationales, 1983) Pp. 223–238.

Fontaine, André, "Quelles armes contre la guerre?" *Le Monde*, 18 June 1983.

Le Gall, Gérard, "Les Français: un bilan 'globalement nègatif' des pays Socialistes," *Revue politique et parlementaire* (December 1980): 40–51.

Girardet, Raoul, "Tradition nationaliste et tentation neutraliste en France, aujourd'hui", in *Pacifisme et neutralisme en Europe* (Paris: Association Française pour la Communauté Atlantique, 1982) Pp. 53–64.

Gnessoto, Nicole, "La France, fille ainée de l'Alliance?" in Pierre Lellouche, ed., *Pacifisme et dissuasion* (Paris: Institut Français des Relations Internationales, 1983) Pp. 267–284.

Grapin, Jacqueline, *Le Point*, 15 March 1982.

Grosser, Alfred, "Il n'existe pas d'Europe homogène" *Le Matin*, 25 October 1982.

Grosser, Alfred, *Les Occidentaux. Les pays d'Europe et les Etats-Unis depuis la guerre* (Paris: Fayard, 1978).

Harrison, Michael M. and Simon Serfaty, *A Socialist France and Western Security* (Washington D.C./Bologna: SAIS, 1981).

Hassner, Pierre, "Prosaïque et puissante. L'U.R.S.S. vue d'Europe occidentale," *Commentaire* 8 (Winter 1979–1980): 520–528.

Hernu, Charles, "Face à la logique des blocs, une France indépendante et solidaire," *Défense nationale* (December 1982): 7–21.

Huntzinger, Jacques, "L'esprit de défense en France," *Défense nationale* (December 1982): 37–43.

IFRI (Institut Français des Relations Internationales), *Crises et guerres au XXe Siècle: analogies et différences* (Paris: IFRI, 1981).

IISS (International Institute for Strategic Studies), *La menace soviétique* (Paris: Berger-Levrault, 1982).

Jarreau, Patrick, "Un terrain de mobilisation pour le PCF," *Le Monde*, 21 June 1983.

"Mentalités collectives et relations internationales," *Relations Internationales* 2 (November 1974): 322p.

Moisi, Dominique, "Les limites du consensus," in Pierre Lellouche, ed., *Pacifisme et dissuasion* (Paris: Institut Français des Relations Internationales, 1983) Pp. 253–266.

Poirier, Lucien, "La greffe," *Défense nationale* (April 1983): 5–32.

"Images des Etats Unis en 76," *Sondages* 3–4 (1976): 68–72.

Szabo, Stephen F., ed., *The Successor Generation, International Perspectives of Postwar Europeans* (London: Butterworths, 1983).

Tatu, Michel, "Ambiguités à gauche et à droite. La France et les euromissiles," *Le Monde*, 23 June 1983.

Tatu, Michel, "La fin d'une 'cure de désintoxication," *Le Monde*, 25 December 1982.

Le Theule, Joël, "L'opinion publique, le Parlement et la défense," *Défense nationale* (August/September 1977): 29–46.

Thieblemont, Lieutenant-Colonel André, "1973–1983: les Français, l'Armée et la Defense," *Armées d'aujourd'hui* (January/February 1983): 8–11.

Willis, F. Roy, *The French Paradox: Understanding Contemporary France* (Stanford, Ca.: Hoover Institution Press, 1982).

Appendix B
Sources of Data

BVA:	Brulé-Ville Associés
IFOP:	Institut Français d'Opinion Publique
IFRES:	Institut Français de Recherches Economiques et Sociales
LHF:	Louis Harris France
LH/AI:	Louis Harris / Atlantic Institute
LH/IIG	Louis Harris / Institut International de Géopolitique
SOFRES:	Société Française d'Enquêtes et de Sondages

Acronyms

PC:	Parti Communiste
PS:	Parti Socialiste
UDF:	Union pour la Démocratie Française
RPR:	Rassemblement pour la République

4 The Federal Republic of Germany: Much Ado About (Almost) Nothing

HANS RATTINGER

Introduction

Complaints that West German foreign policy in general and national security policy in particular have more often than not taken place within a vacuum of societal attention, interest, information, and discussion are as old as the Federal Republic itself. Compared to the United States, it has indeed been difficult to identify, on the *elite level*, a national strategic community extending beyond the professional military, a few selected decision makers, and journalists who permanently and competently would have scrutinized ongoing security issues, from weapons procurement to Alliance strategy, with visible feedbacks into the decision process and with enlightening and mobilizing functions for the general public. This abstinence can be explained by the history of the FRG's defense contribution, by its position within the Western Alliance, and by the initial preoccupation of its political elites with economic growth and the division of Germany, but explanation obviously does not get rid of what is being explained.

Involvement of the *general public* in foreign policy and security issues has been seemingly unpredictable, paradoxical, and inconsistent. Sudden surges of attention to specific problems have been paralleled or followed by long lulls of concern with other issues. Rearmament and a possible nuclear role for the FRG were widely debated in the 1950s, but dramatic shifts in the superpower military balance and in NATO strategy were largely ignored in the 1960s. The new *Ostpolitik* after 1969 received considerable emotional support—quite unlike simultaneous arms control

This study would have been impossible without the data provided by Contest-Census, the Federal Ministry of Defense, the Federal Office for Press and Information, Forschungsgruppe Wahlen, Institut fuer Demoskopie, Social Science Research Institute of the Federal Armed Forces, Social Science Research Institute of the Konrad-Adenauer-Foundation, and the Central Archive for Empirical Social Research. These institutions do not bear any responsibility for the interpretations presented here, but their cooperation is greatly appreciated.

Petra Gossler and Petra Heinlein have served as research assistants for this project.

efforts like MFR and SALT, components of an American "Ostpolitik" that was a precondition for the German efforts to promote détente.

However, behind these "hiccups" of public opinion one can discern systematic patterns. For all practical purposes, national security and foreign affairs are fairly remote from most people's everyday knowledge, experience, and concerns. In view of the low personal salience of the issue area, people lack the incentives to collect, store, and analyze systematically information related to these areas. Under these conditions a temporary mobilization or polarization of public opinion over issues of national security will, almost invariably, be characterized by a series of distinctive features. First, it will focus on general, rather than on specific or technical, problems since the cognitive requirements for a sophisticated debate over details are lacking. Second, it takes highly motivated and knowledgeable minority groups of "opinion leaders" to catalyze mobilization. Third, as catalyzing a public discussion and bringing issues from the periphery of public opinion to the center of the political debate does not dramatically increase the general public's information or information-seeking behavior, public responses will be dominated by emotions, sympathies, and anti-pathies, rather than by well-informed judgment. A corollary is, of course, that which does not lend itself to emotional treatment never comes to the forefront of public opinion on foreign affairs and defense.

If these general notions of the role of international politics in public opinion are correct, then the German experience well into the late 1970s is not at all unusual, but conforms to expectations as well as to what we have seen in other nations. Judging from the presentation in the media, however, something dramatic has happened to the West German public's attitudes toward national security within the last few years. It is hard to give a specific date for this alleged change. The heat and style of discussions over the "immoral neutron bomb" certainly mark quite a departure from times when nuclear warheads could be deployed in the FRG or withdrawn without much public attention. Then came, of course, NATO's December 1979 decision that created the specter of new nuclear missiles in Europe for many residents of the continent. Thereafter, many observers and decision makers, European and particularly American, have expressed considerable concern over the development of public senti-ments that they see as moving toward pacifism and neutralism, toward a potentially dangerous erosion of mass support for the Western Alliance in general and for nuclear deterrence and related military measures in particular. This concern carries with it deep implications regarding the process of legitimizing defense and military strategy in Western democra-cies. At the same time, it addresses the very practical necessity of designing and pursuing defense and security policies that promise to be effective according to established military and strategic criteria, while simultaneously taking into account new realities of the social context surrounding national security—provided there are such "new realities."

This precisely is the point where the analytic effort of this paper will be focused. There is ample reason to doubt that we have a comprehensive and adequate understanding of the scope and extent of the alleged dramatic changes in West German public opinion. There can be no doubt that within small, but very active and vociferous, groups in the FRG a wholesale erosion of support for NATO and for established ways of providing for security has indeed taken place, that the United States, not the USSR, is seen as the primary threat to peace. There also can be no doubt that segments of the media, of the churches, of some unions, and of some parties have served as resounding "echo chambers" for the themes of these activist groups of the peace movement. The campaign for the March 1983 parliamentary elections was even dubbed the "missile campaign," as the appropriate position of the FRG on the implementation of the double-track decision had finally become an issue of partisan dispute. The final outcome of the election, together with some other considerations indicates, however, that the center of gravity of "new realities" in the FRG may thus far have remained confined to less numerous but very outspoken groups of opinion leaders.

The most important of these considerations is that the missile issue is not one that should lend itself easily to the mobilization of mass opinion, since it involves myriads of technological and strategic details. It is not a vital but simple problem like "should we join NATO?" or "should we have better relations with the East?" Because it is so complex, the emotional content of the issue does predominate. If the problem is personally very salient, rejection of new missiles may structure other attitudes; for example, it may lead to a rejection of NATO. If it is not, dissonance between endorsing NATO and disliking missiles may be tolerable or not even be perceived. The crucial dividing line, then, may not be between the ones liking or disliking missiles (most people dislike them, of course), but between the ones for whom this sentiment is highly salient or personally rather unimportant. The key problem before us in attempting to arrive at a comprehensive picture of recent developments and changes in public opinion on national security in the FRG, therefore, is to avoid jumping to far-reaching conclusions on the demise of the foreign policy consensus from some isolated survey results. Before lamenting or advocating drastic action, it is mandatory to try to ascertain to what extent and why decision makers actually have to deal with new realities in the field of defense-related mass political attitudes.

This chapter will do so in three steps. First, a descriptive overview of public opinion on various components of images of the Soviet Union, of national security, of deterrence, and of the Allies will be presented. It will stress developments over time and contain critical discussions of the available survey items, of what one can and cannot conclude from them. Included will also be an analysis of the consistency of attitudes between the various themes within each image cluster. This historical treatment of the trends in public opinion over the 1970s is required in order to put the current situation into perspective. The second main section will consist of a modest attempt to evaluate the interrelationship of attitudes among the four main themes that have just been mentioned. In the third part, finally, the impact of a few potential determinants of national security attitudes will be examined, including individuals' positions in the social structure and their partisan affiliations.

It is critical to bear in mind certain theoretical and methodological caveats because their practical implications will be encountered again and again below. Unlike Schoessler and Weede in their impressive book on *West German Elite Views on National Security and Foreign Policy Issues* (1978), we will be dealing with mass opinion. What is everyday fare to the political and military elites they have surveyed can easily be enigmatic to most randomly selected individuals. A survey item that taps previous or ongoing reflection on familiar substance in an elite survey may easily overtax the average respondent. Personal salience of, and information on, the subject matter to be surveyed, therefore, are of vital importance for a reasonable assessment of public opinion on security. Unfortunately, both these dimensions are often included when surveys are made or reported. People are asked whether they welcome President Reagan's decision to build Enhanced Radiation Weapons (ERWs), they are not asked before whether they know what ERWs are. People get asked which part of the double-track decision they prefer; they are not asked in advance to what extent they care about which part is implemented. Because of these omissions we know less than we should on the personal importance of various components of security policy and almost nothing on the degree of knowledge or ignorance of these matters in the mass public. Furthermore, reactive measurement applied in this way is bound to produce "nonattitudes," responses that sound and look like judgments, evaluations, expectations but that have not been there before the survey and, most likely, will not be there afterwards. What is worse, if these dimensions are not ascertained in the original interviews, it is extremely hard *post festum* to separate random responses from meaningful ones.

In order to realize the magnitude of these difficulties, it is necessary to have a look at the types of items on security and defense that are typically surveyed. Generally speaking, they fall into five broad classes. First, there are questions designed to measure individuals' evaluations of the importance of political objectives, among them economic or social goals, national security, and many others, for themselves and for the FRG as a whole. General policy objectives tend to belong to the class of so-called valence issues: most people agree they are acceptable ones, that unemployment and inflation should be reduced, economic growth furthered, old-age-pensions guaranteed, the environment should be protected, crime reduced, peace preserved, and national security and independence protected. These issues become politically relevant when people disagree on the rank order of their salience and on which parties, coalitions, or candidates are most capable to implement them.

The second and third groups of defense-related attitudes fall into the class of "position issues." People disagree on what should be done. The second class of security attitudes deals with second-order goals, with the implications of the usually consensual feeling that national security, survival, and independence are good things. Does this imply defense within NATO, European defense collaboration, purely national defense or deterrence, neutralism, or attempts to substitute military security by negotiations and political détente; or does it require a stronger emphasis on nuclear deterrence as opposed to conventional capabilities? In the third class, we have dispute on the appropriate strategies to realize these second-order goals. Do we need more or less military manpower or weapons; what is the adequate level of defense spending, should there be a draft; do we require particular weapon systems like Pershing IIs or ERWs, what should be the guidelines for arms control negotiations, and so on?

The fourth class of defense opinions contains judgments of facts, present, future, or hypothetical. Who is or is going to be militarily superior? What are the size of the threat and the likelihood of war? What is war going to look like? Who is likely to win? Is the United States going to honor her commitments?

The fifth class, finally, comprises affective orientations toward actors, both internally and internationally; toward the armed forces or the peace movement; toward NATO, the Allies, or the Soviet Union and other Warsaw Pact countries. Are these actors evaluated as necessary, friendly, reliable, compromising, peaceful, and so on? If other nations are the objects of such evaluations we find ourselves in the realm of national stereotypes and prejudices.

The extent to which reactive measurement can produce valid and reliable findings on opinions on security varies sharply across these five classes. The smallest problems are probably encountered with evaluations of actors. National stereotypes are widespread, and even without extensive previous reasoning many respondents are in a position to state whether a given stimulus evokes positive, indifferent, or negative feelings in them. Difficulties become somewhat larger with the first class of judgments on salience. Most people are able to rank-order very general political objectives according to their personal importance, but most people will also be unable to differentiate between personal importance and salience for the nation as a whole. If national security, compared to others, is perceived as a less pressing problem for oneself and for society, this has far-reaching implications for the assessment of attitudes in the other three classes.

If salience is comparatively low, information will be so, too. Asking people with little interest and little knowledge for their opinions on what national security policy should look like, what steps would be appropriate to pursue it, and what are the basic parameters of the security environment, is likely to evoke "non-attitudes" (Converse 1970, Achen 1975). Specifically this means that we have to expect high proportions of refusals and "don't knows" and concentration of responses in ambiguous categories, if they are provided. Moreover, sizeable effects of instruments, notably question wording, will be likely. It makes a lot of difference for respondents who don't think a lot about these things whether you ask them about "strategic systems" or about "nuclear missiles." Finally, blatant contradictions between responses to different items will occur if we survey issue areas sufficiently remote from the respondents. People will, for example, opt for the necessity of a strong conventional defense but name military spending as the field in which government expenditures should be cut first; or they will simultaneously agree with the double-track decision and with the demand not to deploy any new missiles in Europe. It is only exaggerating slightly to say that adding high complexity of issues to respondents' low concern and information enables pollsters to project a wide variety of attitudes onto large indifferent segments of the population.

This, of course, is a potentially very dangerous situation, in which everyone can pick—or even produce—the evidence in support of a position. To ascertain, with a reasonable degree of confidence, whether what we are currently witnessing is a surge of interest and information or of alienation and emotion in regard to national security affairs, therefore, is of crucial importance for an adequate assessment of the fundamental societal conditions under which decision makers will have to act in the future. As should have become obvious, such an enterprise has to be a critique of methods at least as much as a narrative of findings. As yet no systematic and rigorous study of the development and the dynamics of the cognitive and affective dimensions of defense-related mass opinion in the FRG is available. Summarizing empirical data for the FRG can thus only be a first step toward evaluating the type and range of conclusions they permit.

Lest this be misunderstood, existing public opinion data can and must be taken seriously. It must, however, be examined less cavalierly than is frequently the case. Only then can meaningful conclusions be reached concerning what can be said and above all what cannot be said about the evolution of public attitudes on national security policy. To this effort we now turn.

Salience of National Security

According to the theoretical considerations presented in the introduction, salience of national security issues should be a crucial variable for an adequate assessment of public opinion on these matters. Three aspects of salience must be differentiated: importance of the issue for the FRG as a whole, personal importance, and level of personal interest and information.

In a multitude of surveys respondents have been asked what they believe to be the most important political problems for the FRG. There are two basic question formats. In the first, people can name as many problems as they want to. In the second, they are to name the most important problem, then the one they rank second in importance, then the one they rank third (sometimes this is continued beyond third rank). The first format allows multiple responses, the second format invites them. Therefore, the data in Table 4.1 are not strictly comparable, because the second format evokes less salient nominations from respondents who, with the first format, would come up with just one problem.

Table 4.1 nevertheless conveys a clear and consistent picture. As in most modern democracies, economic and domestic issues are seen as most important tasks for the political system. Their preponderance was less notable in the late 1960s and early 1970s, when the economic situation of the FRG was still rather rosy, but after 1973 economic and domestic policies regularly received more than 80 percent of the nominations for most important problems.

Furthermore, it would be mistaken to conclude from Table 4.1 that the West German public during the earlier years devoted its "surplus" attention (that not absorbed by economic matters) to foreign affairs. Ostpolitik, reunification, problems of Berlin, and FRG-GDR relations are very peculiar aspects of West German politics, highly interrelated with internal politics and not a normal component of foreign policy—according to official doctrine and also to mass perceptions. The high importance ascribed to this issue area well into the early 1970s is no indication at all that public opinion was looking "outward." It is rather a particular component of preoccupation with German politics.

Nominations of foreign policy issues in the strict sense as most important problems for the FRG have declined steadily over the 1970s. Among them maintaining peace has always played the most prominent role, but with the same downward trend over the 1970s. After the first term of Willy Brandt as chancellor, preservation of peace seems to have been taken for granted by many of those who a few years earlier had thought this to be a very pressing problem. Only in the early 1980s has the salience of the preservation of peace increased somewhat in surveys, but not dramatically (nine percent of overall responses in 1982). Matters relating to defense, national security, NATO, the Bundeswehr, or to European integration or foreign policy in general, have never been selected as most important problems for the FRG by more than very small fractions of the population. Unfortunately, the cross-national poll done for the Atlantic Institute in September 1982 (frequently referred to in other chapters of this book) is not directly comparable to Table 4.1. In that study, salience of issues was surveyed in a close-ended format, and the ten stimuli provided for choice seem to have caused responses to deviate from what is usually observed with open-ended questions. "Nuclear weapons" and "excessive government spending," for example, received ten and 12 percent of overall responses, respectively, but both items are seldom volunteered if no list to choose from is provided.

An overwhelming majority of West Germans thus views "bread and butter" issues as the most important ones for the country: a strong, stable, and growing economy; low unemployment and inflation; functioning

Table 4.1 What are the most important political problems for the FRG today?

	IfD	IfD	ZA 426-7	IfD	IfD	SFK	SFK	IfD	SFK	SFK	IfD	SFK	SFK	ZA 823	SFK	FGW	CC
	1/68a	1/69a	9/69b	1/70a	1/71a	1/72b	3/72b	5/72a	10/72b	1/73b	6/73a	10/73b	11/75b	10/76b	11/76b	11/80b	2/82b
Economic situation	43	25	44	38	45	45	51	37	51	47	47	55	73	58	61	54	54
German politics	7	11	23	14	20	36	33	23	36	37	15	31	21	34	32	29	26
Ostpolitik, Berlin, reunification, GDR	29	33	15	25	15	10	9	26	6	8	27	4	3	2	4	6	2
Maintaining peace	13	15	7	11	8	3	3	5	4	4	3	4	0	2	1	3	9
Foreign policy in general	0	1	3	2	3	3	2	1	2	3	2	3	1	2	1	6	5
European community	3	2	2	2	1	0	0	0	0	0	3	0	0	0	0	0	1
Defense, national security, NATO, Bundeswehr	0	2	1	1	0	1	0	0	0	0	0	0	0	0	0	0	1
Others	5	10	5	7	7	1	2	9	1	1	3	3	2	2	1	2	3

aMultiple responses; percentages of overall responses
bPercentages of responses for up to three problems per respondent

social services and social security, and so forth. In the "German politics" category that ranks second we also find concerns such as law and order, liberalization of laws, transportation, housing, education, and environment. The "German problem" has lost very much of its importance as perceived by the mass public, and foreign policy in general, peace, security, and defense in particular, are comparatively marginal problems for the nation in the views of most people. The events of late 1979, however, have led to some increase of concern with national security (Figure 4.1).

Regarding personal salience, things look very much the same. In contrast to the open-ended measurement of importance for the FRG, personal salience is usually ascertained by presenting respondents with a list of items they have to scale according to importance for themselves. As the lists of items and the forms of scales differ from survey to survey, strict longitudinal comparisons are hard to perform.

In spite of this methodological caveat, Table 4.2 shows with sufficient clarity that defense and national security by no means top the list of personal concerns. With some variations over time in rank (that are easily accounted for by macroeconomic developments and political events in the FRG), inflation, unemployment, and old-age pensions are the personally most salient issues with very high percentages of "very important" ratings and very high average scale scores. A somewhat less important cluster of items comprises law and order, style of government, education, protection of the environment, and taxation.

Foreign policy problems generally rank lowest for most respondents; they are described as personally "very important" by 20 to 40 percent of the samples—as opposed to usually well above 70 percent for the top group of economic issues. There are no discernible systematic longitudinal fluctuations in the personal salience of these items. There is, however, a major instrument effect on the importance ascribed to military security (bottom row of Table 4.2). In September 1969 and in September 1980 the item was "protection against Russian attack"; in January 1972, it was "strengthening NATO"; in September 1972, "military security." "Military security" without any specific reference to the Western Alliance or to the threat from the East obviously is personally least important, whereas a reminder by the wording of the stimulus that it is about protection against an attack significantly increases its personal salience. This implies two things. First, most respondents cannot have a very solid and cognitively well-founded and differentiated image of national security if variations in the wording of stimuli have such a sizeable effect on the evaluation of personal salience. Second, it is probably possible to manipulate the ranking of policy goals according to personal importance to a considerable extent by appropriately choosing stimuli.

This point can be further illustrated by another strong effect of question wording on ratings of personal salience that can be observed if "national

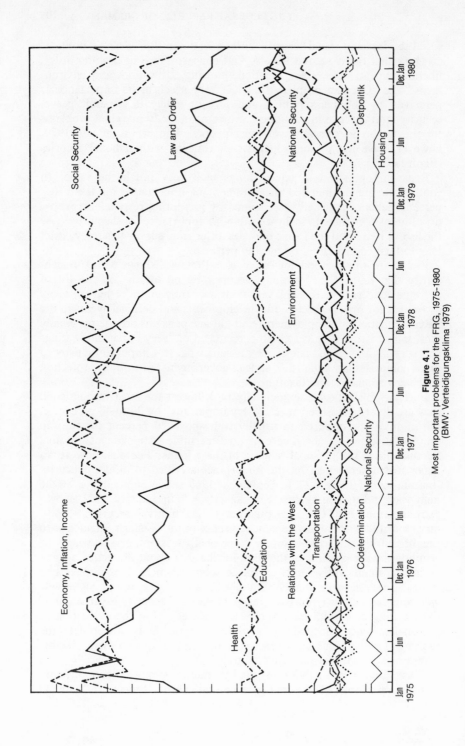

Figure 4.1
Most important problems for the FRG, 1975–1980
(BMV: Verteidigungsklima 1979)

security," "defense," and so on, are replaced by "peace" in close-ended questions. Infas (Monatsberichte) monthly has respondents choose the three personally most important aspects of life from a list containing six items: social security, law and order, peace, local living conditions, economic prosperity, and industrial democracy. Already in 1976, peace received about one-sixth of nominations as being among the personally most important aspects, a rating that the more military items related to the preservation of peace never did receive in open-ended question formats (see, for example, Table 4.2). Whereas for four of these items almost no changes occurred from the mid-1970s to early 1983 (industrial democracy about five percent, economic prosperity about 20 percent, local living conditions about ten percent, and social security about 25 percent), the percentage of nominations of peace rose to around 25 percent; those of law and order fell by almost ten percentage points to about 12 percent. Because of the fixed set of stimuli, the personal salience of peace is certainly exaggerated in these data, but peace is obviously nevertheless evaluated as personally much more salient than concrete military measures to preserve it, and it has come to be rated as personally far more salient than it was several years ago. This corresponds, of course, to the recent trend that can be observed in the final column of Table 4.1 on the importance of the preservation of peace for the country as a whole.

Our finding of rather low personal salience of foreign policy in general and national security in particular for the mass public in the FRG from the early 1970s to the present is corroborated by a number of scattered survey items that are not directly comparable in a longitudinal fashion. In a 1974 survey (ZA 757) people were required to select the personally most and least important political goals out of a list of eight items. "Strong defense" was most important for the smallest group (six percent) and was most frequently picked as least important (21 percent). In 1976 IfD presented respondents with a long list of problems, asking them to indicate about which they were personally "very worried." The most frightening items were unemployment (90 percent), inflation (84 percent), terrorism (48 percent), and crime (39 percent). National security ranked very low as a personal concern: too many Western compromises vis-à-vis the East (rank 9, 23 percent), Russian military superiority (rank 10, 22 percent), the Bundeswehr not being strong enough (rank 31, six percent); Europe and the United Stated drifting apart (rank 32, five percent). One year later IfD made respondents pick three "wishes" out of a list of ten goals according to personal satisfaction with their attainment. Although reducing unemployment and stopping inflation were selected by 71 and 61 percent, respectively, only 16 percent of the "wishes" referred to "better relations with the East," 15 percent to "more security against the Russians."

In another 1976 survey (ZA 823) people were asked what they were most afraid of concerning the future of the FRG and their personal future. On the future of the FRG, 34 percent said they had no fears; of those who had fears, 44 percent named economic difficulties, 27 percent parties and

Table 4.2 Personal importance of problems (Rank Order)

	ZA 426-7 9/69	SFK 1/72	ZA 839-42 9/72	ZA 823 9/76	FGW 2/80	FGW 6/80	FGW 9/80	FGW 2/83
Number of Ranks	15[b]	12[c]	16[d]	7[d]	7[d]	11[d]	11[b]	9[d]
Inflation	1(9.0)	1(2.8)	1(83)	2(81)	2(75)	2(70)	3(8.8)	4(53)
Unemployment, job security	a	2(2.8)	a	1(82)	1(81)	1(76)	1(9.0)	1(88)
Old-age pensions	2(8.5)	a	3(64)	a	3(70)	3(69)	2(8.8)	2(64)
Taxes	4(7.6)	a	6(52)	a	a	a	6(7.8)	a
Law and order	a	a	2(64)	3(59)	4(56)	5(56)	a	6(41)
Moral government	3(8.2)	a	a	a	a	a	4(8.2)	a
Environmental protection	a	a	7(45)	a	5(51)	6(51)	7(7.6)	5(48)
Education	6(7.2)	a	8(37)	4(50)	a	7(43)	8(7.5)	a
Reunification	7(7.1)	10(1.3)	a	a	a	a	10(7.1)	a
Relations with the West, US	8(7.0)	a	10(29)	a	6(41)	8(37)	9(7.4)	7(27)
Relations with the East, USSR	9(6.4)	5(2.1)	9(29)	7(23)	7(33)	10(29)	11(6.6)	9(23)
Military security, strengthening NATO, protection against USSR attack	5(7.3)	8(1.8)	13(19)	a	a	a	5(8.0)	a

[a] Not surveyed
[b] In brackets: average score on scale from 0 (no personal importance) to 10 (highest personal importance).
[c] In brackets: average score on scale from −3 (unimportant) to +3 (important).
[d] In brackets: percentage "very important"

ideologies, 24 percent a foreign threat, and seven percent other fears. Forty percent had no fears regarding their personal future; of the other respondents, 53 percent were most afraid of personal economic trouble, insufficient old-age pensions, and poverty; 31 percent of illness, aging, and dying; ten percent of war; and four percent each were most afraid of communism, radicalism, and other threats. What is remarkable about these data is the extent to which foreign threat is seen as personally very remote. One-quarter of respondents who have fears about the future of the

Table 4.3 What political events from the past twelve months do you remember (SFK)?

	3/72	10/72	10/73	11/75	11/76
Economic policy	12	2	10	30	15
German politics	22	59	20	27	37
Ostpolitik	52	31	13	20	22
International affairs in general, UN	11	7	7	12	17
Middle East	1	0	30	4	1
Energy problems	0	0	7	1	0
Vietnam	1	0	3	1	1
Watergate	0	0	7	3	2
NATO, national security, Bundeswehr	0	0	1	0	0
Others	1	0	1	2	4

Note: Open-ended questions; percentages of responses for collapsed issue areas from up
to three events per respondent

FRG do so because of foreign threat, but that fear for the FRG as a whole does not affect private fears; only one-tenth of private fears are due to the threat of war. In other words, there is some threat of war, but that is for the state, not the individual, to worry about.

Data on the level of information on national security and on the extent to which individuals follow these issues in the media would be very helpful as indicators of personal salience. Unfortunately, little recent material is available. During 1972 to 1976, SFK inquired five times what political events respondents remembered from the past twelve months. As is evident from Table 4.3, economics, German politics, and Ostpolitik commanded most attention (with 80 percent of responses or more). Problems of NATO, of national security, and of the Bundeswehr were outside people's attention screen. Events in international affairs in general were remembered to a limited extent, but it took dramatic things such as the Middle East war and the oil embargo to push them to the foreground. Once these events were past, they soon disappeared from people's consciousness.

In the October 1979 "Verteidigungsklima" survey for the Federal Ministry of Defense, respondents were presented with eight items tapping their information on security affairs. What is NATO; what is the Warsaw Pact; who is secretary of defense; what are the three services of the Bundeswehr and how many soldiers does it have; what do *SALT II* and *enlisted soldier* mean; who would decide on the use of nuclear weapons on FRG territory in case of war? Although the multiple choices presented to the sample were almost ridiculously biased in favor of correct responses (e.g., Is NATO the economic council of the European Community, the Atomic Energy Commission, or the Western defense alliance?), only 15 percent could be classified as very well-informed (seven or more correct answers), 14 percent as well-informed (five or six correct answers). NATO and the Warsaw Pact were correctly identified by 91 percent and 89 percent, respectively, the secretary of defense by 87 percent, the three services by 76 percent, SALT II by 59 percent. Seventy-two percent knew the meaning of *enlisted soldier*, 38 percent the size of the Bundeswehr, and only 35 percent chose the United States president as the authority for nuclear use. It is not hard to imagine what results would have looked like with open-ended questions!

In the same survey, people were also asked whether they were interested in TV or newspaper reporting on defense issues or the Bundeswehr. Forty-eight percent said so for TV, 43 percent for newspaper reporting. If these figures appear high, indicating the widespread desire to collect relevant information, it must be remembered that experience shows people will claim interest in anything, unless they are forced to set priorities—just as any political problem is at least "important" to many people. One has to set these figures against the actual level of information that has just been described and against the frequency of conversations about defense issues that was also surveyed. Only eight percent of respondents indicated them to be "permanent" or "frequent" topics for themselves, 26 percent reported "occasional" conversations on security, 38 percent said they talked "seldom"; 26 percent "never" about these things. These figures seem to mirror much more closely actual personal concerns, and they are corroborated by PIB data from May 1981, when 22 percent said they held "strong" interest in national security affairs, 43 percent claimed "average" interest (whatever that may mean), and 32 percent openly admitted little or no interest at all.

This information is not very recent, of course, so one might argue that things would look much different today with all the debates on the NATO double-track decision and strategy. This does not seem to be so, as we will see later in connection with the deployment of new missiles. Times that feel turbulent while you live through them often look quiet in retrospect.

Table 4.4   Which side is militarily superior in your opinion, NATO (West) or Warsaw Pact (East)?

	IfD 3/73	SOWI 12/77	SOWI 10/79	SOWI 2/80	FGW 5/81	FGW 5/82	FGW 5/83
NATO	7 (9)	13 (17)	11 (13)	10 (12)	10 (10)	9 (9)	11
Both equal	24 (30)	30 (39)	31 (37)	36 (42)	38 (38)	36 (36)	42
Warsaw Pact	48 (61)	34 (44)	42 (50)	39 (46)	51 (52)	54 (55)	47
DK, NA	21	23	16	15	1	1	—

Note: In brackets: percentages without DK (don't know), NA (not applicable)

The years from 1972 to 1979 have not been all that dull in terms of NATO problems, arms control, and so on. Very many people did not notice these things then, and, judging from the salience readings in Tables 4.1 and 4.2, very many people may nowadays be only marginally aware of current discussions over security and defense and may attribute only limited importance to them, both personally and for the FRG as a whole. This will have to be remembered throughout the remainder of this report, as we may frequently be talking about judgments and attitudes that have little cognitive foundation and about which most respondents themselves do not feel very strongly.

Images of the Soviet Union

PERCEPTIONS OF THE MILITARY BALANCE

Perceptions of the military balance between East and West have not undergone substantial changes over the 1970s. In May 1983, almost one-half of West Germans saw the Warsaw Pact as militarily superior, about 40 percent perceived both blocs as equally powerful, and only one-tenth of respondents ascribed military predominance to NATO (Table 4.4).

This overall picture has been broken down by Zoll (1982,53) for 1979/ 1980 evaluations of various components of the total balance. Most respondents saw the Warsaw Pact as superior in regard to numbers of military personnel and of weapons. A majority of Germans viewed both sides to be equal in terms of morale and combat readiness of soldiers, defense willingness of the populations, and training of troops. NATO was judged superior only in quality of weapons. Zoll's analysis demonstrates beyond reasonable doubt that the global evaluations of the East-West military balance in Table 4.4 mirror perceptions of numerical conventional force ratios.

The pessimistic assessment of Western military strength vis-à-vis the East in the FRG is, moreover, strongly associated with a secular trend of decreasing belief in the long-run predominance of the United States against the USSR (see Table 4.5). When asked in 1953, which of the two superpowers would be more powerful "in 50 years" (for all practical purposes a survey synonym for "in the long-range future"), almost one-half of West Germans gave no response; of those who did, almost two-thirds opted for the United States. By the end of the 1960s, the level of no response had gone down considerably, and responses divided evenly between "United States," "both equal," and "USSR." By the mid-1970s, uncertainty on this issue had dropped further, the USSR being predicted as more powerful by half of those giving meaningful responses, the United States being chosen by less than one-fifth. One cannot but conclude that Western military inferiority is perceived in the FRG as an existing condition of national security that will remain and probably become even more accentuated over the years because of a continuing realignment in the superpower military balance.

This "fatalistic" projection of the future does not imply, however, that Eastern military superiority is regarded as harmless or as easily acceptable. In the September 1982 Atlantic Institute survey, the "Soviet military buildup" was chosen as being among the factors contributing to current international tensions by 55 percent of West Germans (21 percent of total choices). In May 1981 (according to a PIB survey), only eight percent of West Germans found it acceptable to live with Eastern military superiority, 71 percent advocated military equilibrium, and 16 percent called for Western superiority. On the other hand, in the Atlantic Institute study, the salience of the East-West balance was not rated outstandingly high. When asked which of seven issues were most important to the future security of Western countries, 53 percent of Germans chose U.S.-European cooperation; the East-West military balance, European economic cooperation, continued dialogue with the USSR, and arms control negotiations each were mentioned by percentages in the mid-30s; Western European defense collaboration and better relations with the Third World were referred to by only 26 percent and 21 percent, respectively.

Even if it may appear so at first glance, there really is little contradiction between these findings. The PIB question evokes notions of some kind of ideal world in which parity naturally would prevail, as it does not require respondents to endorse specific efforts or sacrifices for parity. Who would like to accept inferiority in an abstract sense? But who would like to do something about it? Inferiority of the West is perceived as a fact of life, it is perceived as here to stay, it is perceived as increasing international tension. But reducing the Eastern military edge in order to provide greater security is not more important than détente and arms control; it is less important than good transatlantic relations. The extent to which military inferiority is regarded as unpleasant, but not as of vital importance, certainly is related to the extent to which it is seen to constitute an imminent threat—to which we next turn.

THE MILITARY THREAT

Assessments of the military threat to the FRG over the 1970s appear to have changed as little as perceptions of the military balance. If one compares the 1981 to the 1969 or 1971 data in Table 4.6, each shows that about one-third of West Germans have considered the USSR and the Warsaw Pact as a military threat, and about two-thirds have not. Dramatic changes, however, have taken place over the 1950s and 1960s. In 1952, more than 80 percent thought the East to constitute a threat, a figure that was down to one half by the mid-1960s and then increased sizeably after the 1968 Warsaw Pact intervention in Czechoslovakia. This event did not have lasting effects, and the subsequent "détente level" of relatively low threat perception only recently seems to have increased somewhat, as is shown by data from Forschungsgruppe Wahlen (FGW) of May 1982 and May 1983. This appears to conform to the increase in perceptions of Warsaw Pact superiority in the early 1980s (Table 4.4) and has been

Table 4.5   Who is going to be more powerful in 50 years, United States or USSR (IfD)?

	8/53	5/66	1/69	3/73	5/75
US	32 (62)	25 (43)	21 (34)	14 (21)	13 (18)
Both equal	9 (17)	16 (25)	21 (34)	21 (31)	22 (31)
USSR	11 (21)	21 (32)	20 (32)	32 (48)	37 (51)
DK, NA	48	35	38	33	28

Note: In brackets: percentages without DK, NA

foreshadowed by FGW data from September 1980 on respondents' evaluations of the change in threat over the past five years. At that time, 48 percent said the military threat to the FRG had grown, 43 percent said it had remained the same, and only eight percent believed it had decreased.

Table 4.6 illustrates another feature, however, that should be a very strong warning against careless interpretation of survey findings on threat perceptions. The SOWI data from 1979 and 1980 clearly demonstrate an impressive effect of survey instruments, of question wording. Unlike IfD and FGW, SOWI provided an intermediate category of "not so *serious* threat" and accentuated the extreme category by calling it "serious threat." The consequences are obvious: the level of no response goes down just as the extreme categories of "serious threat" and "no threat" do; the ambiguous category "not so serious threat" at the same time contains almost one half of meaningful responses. If this category is omitted, these respondents are scattered all over the other three categories. If it is included, on the other hand, it is most likely a very attractive response with which many people feel comfortable, especially if they don't think or know a lot about a threat from the East. This sizeable instrument effect in security-related items indicates the difficulty of assessing precisely the extent to which Germans currently feel threatened by the East. The perception of threat is, however, anything but overwhelming.

Another reasonable measure of comparatively low threat perception in the FRG is available from the October 1979 Verteidigungsklima survey performed for the Federal Ministry of Defense. Respondents were presented with four explanations of Soviet armaments and required to indicate agreement or disagreement. The most popular explanation (80 percent agreement) was that Soviet military power was necessary to hold the Warsaw Pact together: 76 percent agreed that the Soviet Union wanted to be prepared against attacks, 46 percent agreed that Soviet armaments were caused by the feeling of being threatened by the West. The lowest share of respondents (42 percent) accepted the view that the Soviet military buildup is due to aggressive intentions. The public obviously does not infer intentions from the capabilities it perceives.

Table 4.6: Do you think that the USSR (East) is a threat to us or don't you think so?

	IfD 7/52	IfD 3/58	IfD 11/64	IfD 11/68	IfD 9/69	IfD 4/71	SOWI 2/80	SOWI 5/81	FGW 5/81	FGW 5/82	FGW 5/83
Serious threat	66(81)	51(65)	39(51)	54(63)	32(37)	28(38)	10(12)	14(16)	36(37)	44(44)	44(47)
Not so serious threat							41(48)	42(47)			
No threat	15(19)	27(35)	37(49)	32(37)	55(63)	46(62)	35(44)	33(37)	62(63)	55(56)	49(53)
DK, NA	19	22	24	14	13	26	14	11	2	1	8

Note: In brackets: percentages without DK, NA

RELATIONS WITH THE SOVIET UNION

Comparatively little recent survey evidence is available on perceptions of general East-West relations. According to an FGW survey of October 1981, 46 percent of West Germans considered relations between the FRG and the USSR to be good, and 54 percent described them as bad. This conforms closely to previous expectations. In December 1977, October 1979, and February 1980, SOWI surveyed expectations of possible future changes in East-West relations. In 1977, 60 percent of respondents expected no change, the remaining responses were divided equally between improvement and deterioration. In October 1979, 52 percent expected no change, 32 percent saw future improvements, and only 16 percent predicted worse relations. In early 1980, however, after the December 1979 decision of NATO and after Afghanistan and the Iranian hostage crisis, 47 percent expected no change, 41 percent, deterioration; and only 12 percent, improvements of relations.

This is, of course, consistent with the data presented above. In the beginning of the 1980s, the strains in East-West relations show up in West German public opinion. General relations with the East are evaluated as bad and as getting worse, there are more references to military threat and to Warsaw Pact superiority. A large majority of Germans in fact agrees as to what should be done about this. In October 1981, 56 percent were in favor of extending relations between the FRG and the USSR, 29 percent believed they should stay the same, and only 16 percent said they should be reduced. For a plurality of Germans the most important aspect of relations with the East is the preservation of peace (41 percent, according to a FGW survey of October 1981). Economic collaboration follows closely as the most important aspect for 36 percent of respondents. Human rights in the Eastern countries (16 percent), sports (five percent), and cultural exchange (two percent) are the most important aspects for minorities only. With this list of priorities, extending and improving relations with the USSR is a strategy that seems obvious to many Germans. Their détente-mindedness vis-à-vis the East also clearly shows in CC data from February 1982, when 67 percent—and 28 percent partially—agreed that détente should be continued in spite of some setbacks. In the same study, only 21 percent agreed (42 percent partially) that as a result of the events in Poland economic aid to the East should be discontinued; agreement with the notion that increasing economic ties to the East could be dangerous was even lower.

GOODWILL AND COOPERATION

It is significant to note that this desire is not paralleled by a very optimistic view of the Soviet Union. The USSR is seen as militarily superior by a majority of Germans who also doubt her goodwill to come to acceptable terms with the West. This judgment has become less frequent over the

Table 4.7   Does the USSR have the goodwill to come to terms with the West (IfD)?

	4/59	4/65	4/66	4/70	6/71	7/74	2/77	1/80	7/81
Yes	17(23)	23(29)	26(33)	33(42)	34(40)	29(35)	27(31)	16(19)	36(43)
No	57(77)	56(71)	54(67)	46(58)	50(60)	55(65)	60(69)	70(81)	48(57)
DK, NA	26	21	20	21	16	16	13	14	16

Note: In brackets: percentages without DK, NA

1960s, but over the 1970s still more than 60 percent of respondents have regularly expressed such doubts (Table 4.7). In January 1980, confidence in Soviet goodwill even reached an extremely low point with 19 percent of respondents. By July 1981, considerable recovery seems to have taken place, even though two-thirds of respondents in an October 1981 FGW survey said they would not expect Soviet reliability as a business partner in case of political crisis.

Considerable suspicion vis-à-vis the USSR is also obvious in CC and PIB surveys from February 1982 and May 1982, respectively. In the first study, 50 percent of respondents agreed (41 percent partially) that Soviet policies are a threat to peace. In the second survey, 73 percent attributed the motive of striving for military superiority to the USSR (50 percent to the United States); 18 percent said the Soviet Union was aiming at equilibrium (42 percent for the United States); and only tiny fractions held that either superpower was ready to accept inferiority. Sixty-five percent agreed that the USSR was trying to split the FRG apart from the West, and 77 percent said the Soviet Union had not forsaken her goal of worldwide revolution. At the same time, however, the image of the Soviet Union was not all black and white: 64 percent attributed to the USSR some concern about international reputation and cooperation, and even 80 percent held her to be interested in good economic relations with the West. This is by no means a contradiction: The USSR is seen as willing to

Table 4.8   Relations between the FRG and the USSR and Soviet reliability (FGW 10/81)

Relations should be	Relations are		Soviets are reliable as business partners in case of political crisis	
	Good	Bad	Yes	No
Extended	63	50	75	46
Kept the same	30	27	17	34
Reduced	7	23	7	20

cooperate for purely selfish (economic) reasons, but her underlying long-range motives and policies are essentially judged as rather sinister by sizeable majorities.

It is probably not overstretching the available data if one concludes that most out of the majority of West Germans who think East-West relations to be bad would blame the East for this state of affairs. Likewise it seems possible to summarize that images of the Soviet Union held in the FRG have been fairly stable since the early 1970s, but subject to some rapid shifts due to spectacular international events such as the invasions in Czechoslovakia and Afghanistan, the effects of which have tended to fade away after some time.

INTERRELATIONS BETWEEN ITEMS

One would expect perception of a Soviet military threat to be a function of the perception of the military balance, and this is indeed the case to a significant degree. In May 1981 (FGW) 37 percent of those surveyed felt the East to be militarily threatening. Among those who viewed both sides as equally strong, the figure was 25 percent, only 20 percent among those who perceived Western military superiority, but 49 percent of those who evaluated the East as stronger. Similarly, in October 1979 (BMV) 20 percent of those who said the Warsaw Pact had increased its armaments evaluated the military threat to the FRG as high, whereas only seven percent of those who viewed Warsaw Pact armaments as having remained the same shared this judgment. In the same survey, 17 percent (23 percent) of those who attributed defensive (offensive) intentions to Eastern armament increases evaluated the military threat as high. These latter two associations are clearly visible but not very strong.

Threat perception has marked effects on the perceptions of East-West relations. Also in October 1979, of those who saw the military threat as high 77 percent evaluated East-West relations as rather hostile, 16 percent as in between, and only five percent as rather friendly. Among those with low threat perceptions the figures were 20, 61, and 16 percent, respectively. In addition, 41 percent of respondents in the first group expected relations to deteriorate, 37 percent expected them to stay the same, and only 11 percent projected improvements. In the latter group these percentages were 12, 54, and 18 percent.

Judgments on East-West relations also are strongly influenced by perceptions of Soviet reliability. In October 1981 (FGW) 64 percent of those respondents who said one could rely on the Soviet Union as a business partner in case of political crisis evaluated relations between the FRG and the Soviet Union as good, the same percentage of those disagreeing on Soviet reliability said relations were bad. Evaluations of East-West relations and of Soviet reliability, in turn, are both associated with attitudes on whether FRG-USSR relations should be extended or reduced (Table 4.8).

Table 4.9   Do you think we have to expect another World War or do you think nobody
            will take that risk (IfD)?

	9/61	1/63	2/64	2/65	6/67	12/75	9/83
Have to expect World War	46(51)	42(46)	35(38)	41(46)	38(41)	29(32)	24(36)
No	45(49)	49(54)	56(62)	48(54)	54(59)	63(68)	42(64)
DK, NA	9	9	9	11	8	8	34

Note: In brackets: percentages without DK, NA

In sum, separate indicators of images of the Soviet Union are consistently interrelated without any apparent contradictions in overall public
opinion. However, associations are not sufficiently strong to claim a very
tight pattern of attitudes at the individual level where numerous nonobvious combinations of judgments occur. In May 1981, for example, roughly
one-fourth of total respondents recorded a military edge in favor of the
East and, at the same time, said they saw no military threat.

Images of Security

FEAR OF WAR

The fear of another World War in the FRG shows a secular downward
trend from the early 1960s to the mid-1970s. In December 1975 more than
two-thirds of respondents agreed that nobody would take the risk of
another World War (Table 4.9). This time series by IfD is continued by
SOWI data from 1977 to 1980, in which more than 80 percent said that the
threat of East-West war in Europe was "rather limited" (Table 4.10).
These two sets of data are, of course, not directly comparable. SOWI by
its choice of response categories invited respondents to select "rather
limited threat of war" as a highly ambiguous reply. The stimuli of "World
War" vs. "East-West war in Europe" also may have evoked very different
fears. In view of the different question wording, it is virtually impossible
to judge whether the discrepancies between Tables 4.9 and 4.10 are due to
instrument effects or whether there is, in fact, a paradox in public opinion
in the FRG: where military conflict in Europe is seen as less likely than
World War, in other words where the global situation is perceived as more
dangerous but, surprisingly, largely decoupled from the threat of war in
Europe.

Consistent with what has been said on perceptions of threat and of the
military balance, the perception of the threat of war also seems to have
grown in the early 1980s. Direct measurements are not available, but in

Table 4.10   Is the threat of war between East and West in Europe rather great or rather limited (SOWI)?

	12/77	10/79	2/80
Rather great	11(13)	9(11)	14(16)
Rather limited	74(87)	73(89)	72(84)
DK, NA	15	18	14

Note: In brackets: percentages without DK, NA

October 1981 and May 1982 and 1983 FGW asked whether peace in Europe had become more or less secure over the past year (Table 4.11). In the first survey, 27 percent of the sample replied that nothing had changed, and 67 percent said that peace had become less secure. In the second and third surveys, the corresponding figures were 39 percent (56) and 57 percent (38), respectively. There is no straightforward interpretation of the sizeable increase of "no change" responses from 1981 to 1983, the parallel decline of perceptions of peace having become less secure over the past year. Maybe many people in 1983 believed that the stability of peace had not changed because they thought it had deteriorated so much previously. On the other hand, this item may have tapped judgments of the current situation rather than of the dynamics of the threat, indicating that more alarmist threat perceptions of 1981 and 1982 had given way to more optimistic attitudes.

However this may be, if one sees peace as more in jeopardy than earlier then logically war is more threatening. Interestingly, this seems to result from a rather general impression of the overall international situation and does not stem from a belief that particular crises would escalate into war. In January 1980, when FGW asked whether respondents believed the Soviet invasion of Afghanistan would lead to superpower war, 78 percent said they did not think so.

Table 4.11   Has peace in Europe over the past year become more or less secure, or has nothing changed (FGW)?

	10/81	5/82	5/83
More secure	6	3	6
Nothing changed	27	39	56
Less secure	67	57	38
DK, NA	0	1	0

Table 4.12   In case of aggression by the East, do you think defense — together with the allies — would be possible or not?

	IfD 9/60	IfD 9/71	IfD 3/76	SOWI 12/77	IfD 9/79	SOWI 10/79	SOWI 2/80	BMV 6/80	IfD 5/81
Defense possible	19(34)	27(42)	26(48)	38(40)	27(47)	33(41)	33(38)	28(35)	25(39)
Defense question-able				46(48)		34(42)	40(47)	36(46)	
Defense impossible	37(66)	37(58)	28(52)	12(13)	31(53)	14(17)	13(15)	14(18)	41(61)
DK, NA	44	36	46	5	42	19	14	21	34

Note: In brackets: percentages without DK, NA

FEASIBILITY OF DEFENSE

Judgments whether the West could defend itself against aggression by the East illustrate some of the points that have been made in the section on salience of national security (Table 4.12). How are people to know? If one looks at the IfD data one gets the impression that between one-third and almost one-half of respondents believe they cannot evaluate this, and among the others there is a solid majority rejecting the feasibility of defense all over the 1970s. The SOWI data tell a much different story. "No responses" are much less frequent, just as are responses in the two unambiguous categories. Does this mean that most people think they can say anything meaningful on this question, and that most view the feasibility of defense as somewhere between absolute certainty and absolute impossibility? Probably not. The ambiguous "defense is questionable" category attracts respondents who either feel uncomfortable with the two extreme positions or who do not know for sure but do not want to say so (maybe to please the interviewer).

This is not to argue that there may be a better or "correct" instrument, but only to point out again the problem of instrument effects. Even more than with threat perception, these seem to occur when one polls images of hypothetical futures in issue areas that are not very salient to respondents and on which their information is not terribly good. From a substantive point of view, it does not make sense to have, at almost the same time, an absolute majority or only between 10 percent and 20 percent of meaningful responses claiming impossibility of defense, especially if we have no yardstick by which to assess what is "correct."

Evaluation of defensive capability seems to be particularly subject to such effects of question wording, as is illustrated by another interesting

Table 4.13   What is more important, defending democracy — even if this involves a
nuclear war — or avoiding war — even if this means living under a
communist government (IfD)?

	5/55	4/56	3/59	7/60	12/75	3/76	2/79	5/81	7/81
Defending democracy	33(48)	35(51)	32(49)	30(44)	25(34)	28(35)	23(31)	27(36)	30(40)
Avoiding war	36(52)	34(49)	33(51)	38(56)	49(66)	52(65)	52(69)	48(64)	45(60)
DK, NA	31	31	35	32	26	20	25	25	25

Note: In brackets: percentages without DK, NA

example from the early 1970s. In April 1971, IfD inquired whether respondents thought the fighting power of the Bundeswehr to have decreased over the past couple of years. In a split-half sample design, the time-horizon for comparison for half of the respondents was defined as "since Helmut Schmidt has been Secretary of Defense." Without mention of Schmidt, 47 percent said the fighting power of the Bundeswehr had gone down, in the other subsample only 22 percent agreed. If an issue is so elusive, remote, and hypothetical, respondents will jump to the clues they are given.

ACCEPTANCE OF DEFENSE

Since the 1950s, IfD has been intermittently posing a "red or dead" question, asking respondents to choose between defending democracy (even if this would involve nuclear war) and avoiding war (even if this would mean living under a communist regime) (Table 4.13). From 20 to 35 percent of samples have always refused this choice. Among nonrefusers both alternatives were about equally popular in the 1950s, but over the 1970s, the scales were permanently in favor of avoiding war (60 percent and more). As both options are heavily "loaded" with affective content ("nuclear war" vs. "communist regime"), it is very hard to interpret this item in terms of the degree to which different modes of a national security policy based upon military defense are accepted or tolerated in West German public opinion. All one can tell with some confidence is that there have been no major changes in recent years in the degree to which war avoidance dominates preferences, although military defense—at the price of nuclear war—seems to be considered somewhat more inevitable in the early 1980s, conforming to perceptions of threat, the military balance, and the danger of war.

A far better insight into the complexities of the acceptance of military defense in public opinion is gained from three survey items employed by

SOWI in 1977, 1979, and 1980. Respondents were asked to indicate whether or not the FRG should militarily resist an attack on its territory, whether or not the FRG should be militarily defended against attack if war would be primarily fought on her territory, whether or not she should be militarily defended against attack if this would involve using nuclear weapons on her territory. Findings from all three points in time do not differ much. About one-fifth of respondents gave no reply. Of the others, about three quarters advocated military defense by the FRG against attack. This dropped to around 60 percent if fighting would occur mainly on FRG territory, and only about one-fifth supported defense if it involved nuclear war on FRG territory.

This poses the question of what the "red or dead" item or the SOWI instruments actually measure. There seems to be an enormous effect of question wording. Resisting foreign attack, if isolated from specific scenarios, appears as something many people can agree upon as a necessary course of action. This consensus falters if military resistance is to take place predominantly "at home." If it would involve nuclear war, the majority opts *against* military defense, and if nuclear war would occur "at home," the majority against military defense is even slightly stronger than the majority *for* military resistance as a general principle.

There are various possible interpretations of this pattern of public opinion. A majority of people, for instance, may accept conventional military forces in a defensive role—with very little enthusiasm for fighting on FRG territory, of course—but might refuse to conceive of a war-fighting role for nuclear weapons, which would be exclusively seen as deterrent devices. Their use in case of conflict, a breakdown of deterrence, would make military resistance unattractive and unacceptable.

This interpretation may, however, assume too much sophistication on the part of the mass public. There may in fact be no elaborate thinking on the acceptability of various types of defensive military action. Survey stimuli alone may create the observed complexity. People may in general agree with "defense" against attack, because the term carries positive connotations. Their agreement may dwindle simply to the extent that "defense" is connected to more and more unpleasant additional information. There may be other interpretations as well, but the two outlined here suffice to demonstrate the possibility for wildly diverging conclusions. The first interpretation would tell us that West German public opinion accepts conventional defense and nuclear deterrence but not nuclear war as a means of defense. The latter interpretation would tell us that we simply know very little about the acceptance of military defense in the FRG and that what we elicit from respondents to a significant degree depends on the stimuli used. As realistic scenarios for employing military force for countering aggression against the FRG all involve sufficiently unappealing details, military defense is thus likely to be rejected as soon as one provides those details. Without them it will be endorsed.

It is not possible here to demonstrate which interpretation is closer to reality. What this clearly does demonstrate is the difficulty one has in arriving at any meaningful conclusions on the acceptance of defense in the FRG from available survey data. A further question that cannot be pursued here is the extent to which acceptance of military defense by public opinion actually would even matter in case of conflict.

Another illustration of the complexity of public acceptance of military defense comes from PIB and CC data from May 1981 and February 1982. CC surveyed agreement with various strategies to preserve peace. For the sake of this goal, only five percent of respondents were willing to terminate German membership in NATO "under all circumstances" (16 percent, "maybe," 78 percent, "never"). Also a mere five percent (15, "maybe") said they would accept living in a socialist country, 33 percent (51, "maybe") would tolerate a lower standard of living; and 39 percent (38, "maybe") claimed to be willing to accept efforts to maintain the military balance, even by Western buildup if it had to be. This reads like rather solid support for military defense. However, in the same study, only ten percent (26 "maybe") accepted risks to their own lives in order to preserve peace, and 57 preferred unilateral disarmament or arms control negotiations without Western INF deployment over increases of Western military power. The May 1981 PIB study shows, moreover, that détente was evaluated as far more important (90 percent) than concrete measures to increase Western defensive capacity, like the issue of INF deployment (56 percent, "important"). Again, the conclusion is that military defense is endorsed by public opinion much more easily as an abstract principle than in its burdensome practice, and that it has no chance if it is up against more "civilized" concepts such as negotiations and détente.

DEFENSE SPENDING

Believing that the FRG should be defended militarily against foreign attack does not make people fond of military spending. In an October 1980 FGW survey, one-fifth of respondents avoided commenting on the size of the defense budget; of the remainder, 46 percent said it was just right, ten percent said it was too low, and 44 percent too high. Two more recent surveys from February and November 1982 yielded even less support for defense spending (Table 4.14), with far more than half of responses in favor of moderate to strong reductions.

In an October 1979 survey by SOWI only one-tenth of the sample showed a willingness to pay a special tax for maintaining the fighting power of the Bundeswehr. When asked in the same study where the government could make expenditure cuts for that purpose, only foreign aid appeared as a tolerable source of additional revenues to more than 50 percent of respondents. These results were confirmed by an FGW survey of April 1981 in which respondents were asked for their opinion about where government spending should be reduced: 61 percent called for cuts in government salaries, 54 percent in defense, 53 percent in foreign aid, 31

Table 4.14 Self-placement on seven-point scale on size of defense budget

		Defense budget should be							
		strongly reduced 1	2	3	4	5	6	strongly increased 7	DK, NA
ZA 1160	2/82	18(20)	14(15)	18(20)	26(28)	10(11)	4(4)	2(2)	6
ABI*	12/82	33(34)	13(14)	16(17)	23(24)	6 (6)	3(3)	2(2)	4

Note: In brackets: percentages without DK, NA

*Survey conducted for Arnold-Bergstraesser-Institut, Freiburg im Breisgau

percent in subsidies to agriculture, 23 percent in social services and security, 19 percent in science and research. This ranking was very closely reproduced by a February 1982 CC study, and it obviously corresponds to evaluations of the salience of national security for individuals and for the country. It is not among the top priorities, so the volume of military outlays is viewed very critically.

THE BUNDESWEHR

Curiously, there are few recent survey findings on mass attitudes vis-à-vis the Bundeswehr. What is available supports what has just been said on the connection between the low salience of national security and the desire to see military spending reduced.

In three SOWI surveys from 1977 to 1980 people were required to evaluate the importance of the Bundeswehr for the FRG (Table 4.15). That fewer than ten percent described it as "unimportant" in all three studies should not be read as an indication of widespread enthusiasm about the armed forces. The question wording is a good example of the point made earlier: if people are asked for judgments on importance, almost everything tends to be important or even very important to large majorities, as they do not have to make trade-offs. As soon as they are forced to do so (e.g. via spending alternatives), more meaningful ranking according to salience emerges, as could be seen in the previous section.

Careful analysis of the data in Table 4.15 also leads to a confirmation of our earlier analysis. When one compares the percentages of "very important" responses to top priority items in Table 4.2, the differences are striking; the latter received percentages of 70 percent up to 90 percent or more. One can thus assume that the concentration in Table 4.15 of responses in the "important" category shows that the importance of the Bundeswehr for the FRG was in fact *not* evaluated as particularly high by respondents in these studies. Had there been a whole battery of items for comparison, this would have been immediately obvious. But even so this

Table 4.15   How important do you consider the Bundeswehr to be for our country?

	SOWI 12/77	SOWI 10/79	SOWI 2/80	BMV 6/80
Very important	22(22)	25(27)	34(36)	32(36)
Important	52(53)	45(49)	45(47)	43(48)
Neither/nor	18(18)	14(15)	11(12)	9(10)
Unimportant	7 (7)	8 (9)	6 (6)	6 (7)
DK, NA	2	8	5	10

Note: In brackets: percentages without DK, NA

interpretation is clearly in line with previous comments: the armed forces are not seen as extremely important for the country, so it is logical to perceive part of the financial burden they constitute as dispensable.

On the surface, one can suspect a paradox in the juxtaposition of these attitudes toward the Bundeswehr with the high endorsement of military defense against foreign attack. Various explanations can be offered. First, if the threat is perceived as low, the Bundeswehr can be less important in spite of the necessity to resist militarily when attacked. Second, plausible scenarios for military defense in which the Bundeswehr could play a meaningful role may not be perceived. Finally, the whole issue of security, defense, and of the role of the Bundeswehr in it may simply be so remote and low in salience that attitudinal inconsistencies do not matter.

THE PEACE MOVEMENT

There are not very many data on attitudes toward the peace movement in the Federal Republic. A May 1983 survey by FGW does provide, however, some recent data. It was evaluated as "necessary" by 47 percent of the sample, as "superfluous" by 24 percent, and as "detrimental" by seven percent. Twenty-three percent said they did not care about it. Interviewed one month later by FGW on what actions out of a list of five they would participate if new missiles were to be deployed in the area where they lived, petitions were chosen by 60 percent, demonstrations by 28 percent, blockades of military installations by seven percent, illegal demonstrations by six percent, and, finally, damaging military facilities by one percent of respondents. When asked about the proximity of the peace movement to political parties in October 1981 (FGW), nine percent of respondents avoided any judgment and 38 percent saw no linkages between parties and the peace movement. Fourteen percent said it was closest to the Social Democrats, 12 percent to the Greens, and four percent saw it equally close to both these parties. Four percent regarded the peace movement as closest to the Christian Democrats, three percent to the Communists, and one percent to the Liberals. Three percent responded that the peace movement was equally affiliated with all parties, and 11 percent saw it closest to other than the listed parties (there are no other parties).

These numbers are hard to interpret. One can say with some confidence, however, that the figures on the necessity of the peace movement and on possible participation in demonstrations are greatly inflated. The goal of the movement implied by its name draws excess sympathies—just as with environmentalists—and the indication of a general willingness to become active does not commit respondents in any way. On the partisan proximity of the movement there is considerable insecurity: fewer than 40 percent of respondents identify it with existing parties. This corresponds, of course, to the very heterogeneous nature of the peace movement in the FRG.

INTERRELATIONS BETWEEN ITEMS

In the second section of this chapter, salience of national security items in the FRG has been dealt with separately, because of the critical role of this variable. For the sake of convenience, we will from now on treat salience as a component of images of security, as it logically is. Therefore, within this subsection we will first look at the interrelations among indicators of interest, information, and salience of national security, then at their associations with other measurements pertinent to this cluster. In October 1979 (BMV), 24 percent of those who named national security as a top-priority political goal evaluated the Bundeswehr as "very important," 62 percent as "important." Among the overwhelming majority (86 percent), who gave low salience to national security, the corresponding numbers were 17 and 60 percent. This is not much of a difference, so judgments on the importance of the armed forces are not to a significant degree determined by the perceived salience of security affairs.

The association between interest in media reports on national security and the level of knowledge of these matters is somewhat closer. In the same survey, 22 percent of those who said they were interested in such reports were very well-informed and 15 percent well informed. For those without interest these figures were only ten and 12 percent; 61 as opposed to 78 percent had a low level of information. Table 4.16 reveals quite clearly, moreover, that perceived salience of national security is much more closely related to interest than to level of information. Those who view national security and the armed forces as more important tend to be only somewhat better informed, but they are much more interested and have a lot more conversations on security issues. The causal structure seems to be like this: personal salience of national security has a strong direct effect on interest and little direct effect upon information. Only if high personal salience *and* personal interest coincide is the level of information increased significantly.

Table 4.16 Salience of national security, level of information, and interest
(BMV 10/79)

	Top priority of national security		Armed forces		
	Yes	No	Very Important	Important	Less Important
Information on defense					
Very good	18	12	18	14	16
Good	17	13	13	15	11
Deficient	66	73	67	73	71
Correct responses on who is to authorize use of nuclear weapons	33	35	40	34	35
Interest in media reports on defense					
Yes	50	34	54	36	20
No	50	66	46	64	80
Conversations on defense					
Often	14	8	19	7	5
Occasionally	34	24	30	28	18
Seldom	31	40	33	41	37
Never	21	28	18	24	40

Unlike the fear of war, for which no systematic relations could be detected, evaluations of the feasibility and acceptability of military defense are in fact associated with attitudes toward the armed forces and with information and interest. This is not the case, however, for the perceived salience of national security. Table 4.17 shows what these associations look like: those who hold the Bundeswehr to be very important, or have more information, or are more interested in security issues tend to entertain stronger beliefs that the FRG could be defended militarily and tend to be somewhat more willing actually to defend the country, even if presented with very unattractive scenarios. Most of these intergroup differences are by no means dramatic, however.

As to defense spending, there is some evidence from February 1982 (ZA 1160) that high perceived salience of national security leads to more favorable attitudes vis-à-vis military expenditures. For those respondents who said that strong defense was their personally most important political concern, the average position on a seven-point scale on military expenditures ranging from "strong reduction" (1) to "strong increases" (7) was 4.1 (i.e., almost exactly in the center indeterminate category). All other respondents had an average score of 3.1, which illustrates the widespread desire to reduce military expenditures that has been described above.

Table 4.17   Importance of armed forces, information, interest, and feasibility and acceptance of military defense (BMV 10/79)

	FRG could be defended militarily	FRG should be defended militarily		
		in general	if war on FRG soil	if nuclear war on FRG soil
Bundeswehr is				
Very important	47	79	77	41
Important	38	58	58	22
Less important	21	27	25	11
Information on defense				
Very good	41	67	62	27
Good	32	54	60	21
Deficient	36	53	52	22
Interest in media reports on defense				
Yes	42	68	62	27
No	33	48	50	21

Note: Percentages of agreement with column stimulus within row categories

Finally, there are some recent data (FGW 5/83) on the relationship between perceptions of the stability of peace and attitudes toward the peace movement. It is less popular (41 percent, "necessary") among those who see no recent change in the security of peace. These respondents also are most "indifferent" (28 percent, 25 percent "superfluous", six percent, "detrimental") about the peace movement. If peace is seen as having become less secure (almost no respondents called it more secure), the peace movement tends to be evaluated far more positively (57 percent, "necessary"); "indifference" (17 percent) and mild or strong rejections (20 and six percent, respectively) are less frequent. Perceptions of the stability of peace also have some impact on the inclination to participate in peace movement activities that is higher for those who see less security.

Images of Deterrence

ACCEPTANCE OF DETERRENCE AND OF NUCLEAR WEAPONS

We have seen that attitudes toward military defense in the FRG are very ambiguous. It is endorsed in principle, but not in practice. Therefore it does not come as a surprise that preventing foreign attack by deterrence receives solid support (Table 4.18). From the mid-1970s to the early 1980s about 70 percent of those who replied considered deterrence to be the best

Table 4.18 Do you agree that an attack by the East can best be prevented by deterrence, if the West has sufficient armaments (IfD)?

	2/76	1/78	9/79	3/81	7/81	12/81
Agree	58(72)	58(73)	55(72)	50(67)	53(71)	50(68)
Disagree	23(28)	22(27)	21(28)	25(33)	22(29)	24(32)
DK, NA	19	20	24	25	25	26

Note: In brackets: percentages without DK, NA

way to prevent aggression. Unfortunately, however, the IfD instrument is both insufficiently differentiated and actually confusing. The reference to "sufficient armaments" makes it hard to decide whether nuclear deterrence ("by punishment") or deterrence by conventional parity or sufficiency ("by denial") is being evaluated by respondents. However, if one bears in mind our earlier findings, it seems plausible that for most respondents the key term here will be "deterrence," and not "sufficient armaments."

The support by the majority of West Germans for preventing war through deterrence is for "pure deterrence," however, and does not include acceptance of the complex notion that one must have a capability of fighting a war in order actually to prevent fighting. This is the conclusion one must draw from comparing Table 4.18 with the previously demonstrated absence of widespread support for actually defending the FRG. It would require very sophisticated measuring devices—that may easily overtax most respondents' level of information—to assess more precisely the degree of acceptance of various competing deterrent strategies.

What one can say, however, is that in spite of the great abstract endorsement of deterrence, nuclear weapons are viewed rather critically in the FRG. In April 1983 (FGW), two-thirds of respondents said they felt threatened by nuclear weapons in general, that is more than usually say so about the Soviet Union (see Table 4.6). In the same survey, people were interviewed about whether they believed nuclear armaments to be acceptable for Christians. Only nine percent agreed unconditionally, 44 percent held nuclear arms to be acceptable for defensive purposes only, and 47 percent entirely ruled out any compatibility between nuclear weaponry and Christianity. Interestingly, this latter view was most strongly shared by people without any religion (62 percent) and Christians with lowest church attendance (57 percent). These findings, again, leave one wondering what conclusions public opinion surveys on these matters really do permit. Nuclear weapons, after all, are the key instrument of deterrence. Still, the latter is accepted much more readily if it is not related to the "ugly" term *nuclear weapons*. One is tempted to speculate how low

Table 4.19   Do you think the double-track decision to be a good one (IfD)?

	5/81	7/81	8/81	9/81	1/82	12/82	8/83
Yes	53(73)	52(71)	49(65)	50(69)	52(70)	51(67)	49(68)
No	20(27)	21(29)	26(35)	22(31)	22(30)	25(33)	23(32)
DK, NA	27	27	25	28	26	24	28

Note: In brackets: percentages without DK, NA

support for deterrence could drop if some more "ugly" information were tied to it in survey stimuli.

NEW MISSILES IN EUROPE

Data on the West German public's level of information about NATO's double-track decision are not very recent, but they still must be reported in order to put the subsequent description of attitudes into perspective. In May (July) 1981, 63 percent (77) had heard or read about the NATO decision, according to PIB. From the same source we learn, however, that awareness did not imply precise knowledge of the substance of this decision. Faced with an open-ended question on what it is about, in May (July) 1981, 48 percent (41) said they could not tell. Only nine percent in May (11 in July) correctly described the December 1979 decision. Most of the wrong responses (almost one-third of the total) characterized this decision as aiming for unilateral Western armaments buildup. Most likely the level of information will have increased somewhat in the meantime, but as this information was polled more than a year and a half after the initial decision had set off the public debate there is reason to doubt that such changes could be dramatic.

In the past several years quite a number of survey studies on the public's reaction to the NATO decision have been performed. Since 1981, IfD has repeatedly polled attitudes toward this decision after presenting its contents to respondents in a simplified version. While about one-quarter of samples consistently refused any judgment, more than two-thirds of evaluations were in favor of the double-track decision, indicating widespread support of parallel negotiations and missile deployments (Table 4.19).

Similar results from PIB are available for May and July 1981. Adjusting for the level of no responses, 68 percent agreed that the NATO decision was the right thing to do, since the USSR would not be willing to negotiate without threats of Western INF deployment, 57 percent did not endorse the view that the West was strong enough and INF deployment, therefore, was unnecessary. At the same time, there was majority opposition (55 percent) against INF without parallel negotiations, and a rather favorable response toward Eastern moratorium initiatives (63 percent in favor). All these distributions, however, should be seen in the light of 62 percent agreement that these defense issues are so complex they should be left to experts because the average citizen could not judge them.

In the same survey, agreement with the double-track decision was significantly lower if the stimulus did not tie the prospect of deployment to the need to force the USSR to the negotiating table. A narrow majority (52 percent) believed that the greater part of the German population expected INF deployment to be inevitable. Regarding the perceived preferences of a series of political actors, some selected results deserve being mentioned: The United States was perceived as extremely favorable toward INF, Chancellor Schmidt only slightly less so; Schmidt's party, the SPD, was seen as rejecting them by a clear majority.

August 1983 data from IfD show even more clearly how an appropriate choice of question wording can reduce—or even reverse—anti-INF majorities. Respondents were asked whether they were in favor of or opposed to Pershing II deployment, if "Soviet SS-20s would continue to be targeted on Western Europe". With 23 percent undecided, 37 percent favored, and 40 percent opposed deployment. When presented with a choice between deployment and the FRG's leaving NATO, 46 percent chose missiles, 22 percent would abandon the Alliance, and 32 percent did not respond. In the same survey, 50 percent said that currently there was no INF balance between East and West (only 13 percent believed this to be the case), and 59 percent (24 percent) replied that such an INF balance is (not) necessary. At the same time, however, 46 percent advocated unilateralism in arms control; 37 percent were opposed (in July 1981 figures had been 33 and 47 percent, respectively).

Findings by FGW stand in stark opposition to what has just been reported. Inquiring how the West should proceed with the double-track decision, FGW found in May 1981 that 67 percent of its sample favored immediate negotiations without any Western deployments, 25 percent favored immediate negotiations with simultaneous Western arming to achieve parity, and only six percent favored NATO INF deployments without negotiations.

These are obvious effects of question wording. If you ask for attitudes on the NATO decision or mention SS-20s, as IfD did, positive sentiments vis-à-vis NATO or fear of Soviet missiles produce positive evaluations of United States INF, as a direct choice between the two tracks implied by this decision is not required. If it is required, an overwhelming majority emerges for the negotiating track and against deployment, which logically implies comparatively low support for the NATO decision as it was taken. This is also evident from a February (May) 1983 survey by FGW, in which 55 percent (50) of respondents agreed with the demand not to deploy any new missiles in the FRG, no matter what the East would do. The smaller majority against deployment (compared to the 67 percent in May 1981) is most likely again due to an instrument effect, as the side condition "regardless of Eastern behavior" loads the stimulus in favor of disagreement. Without its inclusion, resistance to new missiles would have scored much higher, according to the FGW instrument. It does not come as a big surprise that in a very recent study by FGW (June 1983) opposition against new missiles *in the respondent's area* ran at 79 percent.

Let us now have a look at the perceptions of motivations of the superpowers to pursue INF arms control and at expectations and preferences of the German public regarding the future of these talks. In July 1981 (PIB), about 30 percent of respondents felt unable to evaluate superpower interest in INF limitations; of those who passed a judgment, about 70 percent held each superpower to be interested in such accords. In the same study the largest part of the sample (46 percent, with eight percent giving no response) expected failure of arms control negotiations over INF and a subsequent arms race; 37 percent predicted an agreement between the United States and the USSR that would be coupled with some Western INF deployment. Only nine percent expected reductions of Soviet missiles to an extent that would allow the United States to refrain from stationing INF in Europe. Recent data by FGW (July 1983) is not directly comparable, as here respondents were asked whether they expected deployment of new missiles in the FRG *this year*. Sixty-two percent answered that they expect this to happen, and 37 percent replied in the negative—suggesting a remarkably high proportion of optimists still believing in timely success of negotiations.

We have already seen that recent FGW data showed substantial opposition against new missiles in the FRG in summer 1983. This opposition emerged even stronger when people were asked what course of action they would prefer if the Geneva talks would fail to produce agreement until fall 1983. In July 1983 (September 1983, after the downing of the Korean airliner by the Soviets), 76 (65) percent of the sample preferred continuing negotiations without INF deployment; 20 (31) percent opted for continuing negotiations with parallel deployment; while only three percent called for discontinuing talks and stationing missiles. This information is to be interpreted with great caution, however. The three alternatives presented to respondents do not embrace the possibility that negotiations not only do not lead to agreement but prove entirely futile and are aborted, so there would be no arena for continuing talks. One can be very sure that under such conditions the pattern of responses would look totally different.

ENHANCED RADIATION WARHEADS

Two other recent survey items concerning enhanced radiation weapons (ERWs) confirm the above pattern of attitudes toward Western nuclear capabilities. In August 1981, FGW polled attitudes toward President

Reagan's decision to build ERWs and on whether the FRG should consent to the stationing of ERWs on her territory. With very few refusals, 62 percent of the sample disapproved of the decision to proceed with ERWs, and 69 percent said the FRG should refuse to have them deployed here. This is not at all surprising: defense and deterrence are accepted as general principles, but when it comes to specific scenarios, sacrifices, measures to increase military capabilities, or to particular weapon systems, enthusiasm is very low, especially with nuclear weapons that have been the object of mainly critical and highly publicized debates.

INTERRELATIONS BETWEEN ITEMS

Some of the interrelations between items that have been descriptively analyzed in this section appear as moderately strong and substantively interesting. Feeling threatened by nuclear weapons and evaluating them as acceptable for Christians "hang together" as follows (FGW 4/83): almost two-thirds of those who feel threatened by these arms reject them as incompatible with Christian standards, whereas more than 80 percent of those who feel no such threat judge them as either unconditionally (19 percent) acceptable for Christians or at least in a defensive framework (62 percent).

Among items on INF talks or deployment, several patterns deserve being mentioned: Of those who supported the demand by no means to station Western INF, 88 percent favored continuing negotiations without deployment in case no timely agreement should be achieved. Of those who rejected the first position, only 54 percent favored the same approach toward possible failure of the Geneva talks (FGW 5/83). Not surprisingly, among those who would not agree to missile deployment in their area, 86 percent favored continuing negotiations without deployment, 78 percent of those who would bear with stationing new missiles close to their residence opted for introducing Western INF should negotiations not be satisfactorily completed by the end of 1983 (FGW 6/83). It also conforms to expectations that those who resist INF deployment even if no agreement should be completed by a large majority (82 percent) call for a referendum on stationing these missiles; whereas all others reject this introduction of direct democracy into national security policy by an almost equally strong margin (FGW 7/83).

A final association that can be reported here is between agreement with the decision to build ERW and with possible ERW deployment in the FRG (FGW 8/81). The figures show such a high correlation that one could almost talk about multiple measurement of the same underlying attitude. Seventy percent of those who agree with the ERW decision would also go along with deployment in the FRG. Ninety-four percent of those who disapprove of the ERW decision would oppose deployment here. Only 15 percent of the total sample have held inconsistent views.

Images of Allies

RELATIONS WITH THE UNITED STATES

The last of the four main themes of this descriptive overview begins with evaluations of the relations between the FRG and the United States. According to Table 4.20, there was no decrease during the 1970s in the extent to which collaboration with the United States was regarded as more important than with the USSR. Quite the contrary: although in 1973 there was an absolute majority for equally close relations with both superpowers, through the late 1970s and until 1981 supporters of closer ties with the United States outnumbered those in favor of equally close relations. Moreover, in February 1982 (CC), 43 percent fully and 41 percent partially agreed that cooperation and friendship with the United States should play a bigger role in German foreign policy.

By 1983, however, something had clearly transpired. The majority of meaningful responses had shifted back to favoring an equally close relationship with both superpowers. When one compares the recent IfD data with those of May 1981, the change is in fact quite significant. This decline in the importance attached to closer collaboration with the United States is confirmed by the most recent Atlantic Institute survey (11/83). In response to the question on what was most important for future Western security, a full 19 percent drop occurred since the autumn 1982 (from 53 to 34 percent) in those who chose effective cooperation between Europe and the United States. Ranking first in the 1983 survey was continued dialogue with the Soviets (up from 33 to 42 percent of respondents). It is difficult to determine how temporary or permanent a shift this is and what its causes are. But given the consistent negative image of the Soviet Union described earlier, the origin of the shift must lie in a German loss of confidence in the United States and probably in current American policies. The magnitude of the shift should not be overdrawn, but it is nevertheless real.

In July 1980 the most important aspect of relations between the FRG and the United States for West Germans was the economic one, according to FGW (50 percent). Mutual support and military cooperation followed behind (27 and 17 percent, respectively). Sports (four percent) and recognition of United States leadership (three percent) were considered of minor importance. What makes collaboration with the United States desirable for West Germans is predominantly cooperation in the fields of economy and security.

Relations between the United States and the FRG were evaluated as good by 67 percent of respondents in August 1981 and by 75 percent (59) in May (August) 1982, according to FGW. Evaluations of this kind are really hard to make for average respondents, so the high volatility of this data and their susceptibility to short-term fluctuations are not unusual.

Table 4.20 Should we, in the future, strive for closer collaboration with the United States or the USSR (IfD)?

	5/73	10/77	9/78	1/80	5/81	7/81	12/81	1/83	3/83	4/83	6/83
US	36(39)	49(55)	51(58)	49(53)	56(63)	50(56)	45(52)	39(43)	40(44)	42(47)	42(46)
Equally close	54(58)	38(43)	36(41)	41(45)	32(36)	37(42)	41(47)	51(56)	49(54)	46(52)	47(52)
USSR	3 (3)	2 (2)	1 (1)	2 (2)	1 (1)	2 (2)	1 (1)	1 (1)	1 (1)	1 (1)	2 (2)
DK, NA	7	11	12	8	11	11	13	9	10	11	9

Note: In brackets: percentages without DK, NA

Table 4.21 In what direction have relations between the FRG and the US changed "recently" (IfD)/"since Reagan took office" (FGW)?

	IfD 3/73	FGW 8/81	FGW 5/82
Improved	10(11)	9	5 (5)
Remained the same	50(57)	49	51(52)
Deteriorated	27(31)	42	43(43)
DK, NA	13	0	1

Note: In brackets: percentages without DK, NA

People probably make such judgments in reaction to current news, so most likely the low August 1982 rating was produced by U.S. action against European firms involved in the pipeline deal with the USSR. All in all, however, this degree of satisfaction with bilateral relations may to some extent explain why the personal and "national" salience of good relations with the United States ranks so low in Tables 4.1 and 4.2.

Many more people have perceived a deterioration rather than an improvement in U.S.-FRG relations at various points during the past decade (see Table 4.21) but this is not contradictory with two-thirds of respondents describing relations as "good." First, there seems to be some kind of "negativity bias" in this instrument, as is shown by the IfD measurements from 1973, because difficulties and strains in transatlantic relations naturally receive far more media attention than smooth cooperation. Second, reference to President Reagan in the FGW question probably reinforced that bias. In February 1982, the U.S. president's foreign policy vis-à-vis the East was regarded as too hard-line and as a danger to détente by 43 percent of a CC sample; 39 percent partially agreed to this view. Thus, it is probable that the perception of deterioration is exagger-

Table 4.22 Generally speaking, do you like the Americans (IfD)?

	12/57	4/61	7/62	5/65	1/67	5/73	3/75
Yes	39(47)	51(61)	54(61)	58(64)	47(54)	48(54)	42(49)
In between	20(24)	17(20)	17(19)	13(14)	16(18)	17(19)	21(25)
No	24(29)	16(19)	18(20)	19(21)	24(28)	24(27)	21(25)
DK, NA	17	16	11	10	13	11	16

Note: In brackets: percentages without DK, NA

ated in Table 4.21. This suspicion is supported by SOWI data from October 1979 and February 1980, in which more than two-thirds of those expressing an opinion expected U.S.-FRG relations to stay the same, about one-fifth expected improvements, and one-tenth deterioration. The former two expectations were disappointed, but not to the degree apparently indicated by Table 4.21.

On the actual and desired style of relations between the FRG and the United States little survey information is available. In 1972 SFK presented a sample with the statement that the freedom of action for the FRG was so little one could almost describe her as a U.S. satellite and asked for the extent of agreement or disagreement on a scale (from $+3$ to -3). For the 87 percent of respondents who made a judgment the mean scale score was exactly zero (agreement was exactly balanced by disagreement). In August 1981, and again in May 1982, FGW presented samples with the choice whether in case of disagreement the FRG should adopt United States views or decide according to her own interests. Only about one-quarter of respondents were in favor of adopting United States policies, whereas three-quarters thought the FRG should follow her own interests. This, by the way, stands in remarkable contrast to Schoessler and Weede's (1978,60) findings for West German elites, in which, 63 percent of the sample endorsed the notion that "minors" within alliances should accept superpower guidance. In summary, close relations with the United States are seen as very desirable by a large majority of West Germans who also view relations as quite satisfactory, although levels of confidence appear to have dropped. Above all, and this may be related to the drop in confidence, there is a decided rejection of any political subordination of the FRG—as people of almost any nation would.

ATTITUDES TOWARD THE UNITED STATES

Underlying the desire for close cooperation are favorable attitudes vis-à-vis the United States and widespread convictions about her indispensability for the security of Europe. Table 4.22, which unfortunately only runs through 1975, shows the longitudinally stable positive stereotype of America in West Germany. This series is continued by a PIB thermometer of feelings (from -5 to $+5$) about the United States The mean score in 1979 was 1.9, in April 1980 it was 2.0, and in February 1982 it was 1.6; so there really was no significant change in images of the United States since the mid-1970s. Table 4.23 clearly demonstrates that the support for the presence of American troops in Europe has not faltered since the Berlin crises. In the early years of NATO a withdrawal of United States troops would have been quite popular; nowadays it would be regretted by four out of five people who comment on the issue. For the past twenty years, little disagreement over the importance of American security guarantees and of their symbolic representation by troops in Europe has been discernible in survey data.

Table 4.23 If the United States were to pull their troops out of Europe, would you welcome or regret this (IfD)?

	7/56	1/57	12/57	6/62	4/69	5/70	5/73	6/76	8/78	9/79	9/81
Welcome	51(71)	33(49)	34(50)	12(17)	17(23)	22(30)	23(34)	15(22)	17(23)	11(15)	17(22)
Regret	22(30)	34(51)	34(50)	59(83)	56(77)	51(70)	45(66)	54(78)	57(77)	60(85)	59(78)
DK, NA	27	33	32	29	27	27	32	31	26	29	24

Note: In brackets: percentages without DK, NA

Table 4.24   Does NATO have more advantages or more disadvantages for the FRG (IfD)?

	11/55	4/59	8/63	9/71	9/79	5/81	12/81
More advantages	20(71)	35(88)	33(87)	47(82)	48(87)	55(80)	50(82)
More disadvantages	8(29)	5(12)	5(13)	10(18)	7(13)	14(20)	11(18)
DK, NA	72	60	62	43	45	31	39

Note: In brackets: percentages without DK, NA

ATTITUDES TOWARD NATO

Up to the 1980s, NATO has always been evaluated by large majorities as having more advantages than disadvantages for the FRG (Table 4.24), even though insecurity of judgment has been rather high, mainly due to low (but growing) information on what NATO is. That an alliance is seen as yielding more advantages than disadvantages does not necessarily imply, however, that one prefers this alliance to other (e.g., nonaligned) security policies. Unfortunately, the IfD series on neutralism vs. the Western Alliance only extends up to 1975 (Table 4.25). It contains far lower levels of no response than Table 4.24 and shows considerably smaller enthusiasm for NATO than for American troops in Europe, with no obvious longitudinal trend. This discrepancy between regret about hypothetical American troop withdrawal and comparatively high popularity of neutralism could to some extent be explained by question wording, as in Table 4.25 German ties to NATO and the United States are juxtaposed to "neutrality," a concept that does not exclusively bear negative connotations. If withdrawal of American troops from Europe

Table 4.25   Should the FRG continue its alliance with the West (America) or try to be neutral (IfD)?

	12/55	9/61	9/65	5/69	5/73	9/74	2/75
Western Alliance	43(60)	40(49)	46(55)	44(54)	41(49)	51(57)	48(57)
Neutral	29(40)	42(51)	37(45)	38(46)	42(51)	38(43)	36(43)
DK, NA	28	18	17	18	17	11	16

Note: In brackets: percentages without DK, NA

Table 4.26   Agreement with statements on NATO (IfD)

	1/69	9/71	3/76
NATO has brought Western countries closer together	51	51	53
NATO is not strong enough to defend Europe against agression	39	28	31
NATO nations disagree too much	33	24	31
Without NATO we would have been attacked already	32	32	35
Russians are afraid of NATO defense	28	29	28
NATO has too little influence over member nations	25	15	21
NATO's main benefits go to US	19	18	18

were linked to some positive alternative, regret would probably also be much lower.

Even though the IfD series stops in 1975, some more recent evidence is available, although not directly comparable. Data reported by Just and Muelhens (1981) on the FRG trying to maintain good relations with the United States vs. the USSR vs. aspiring for neutrality show very clearly that in 1980 and 1981 somewhat lower proportions of respondents opted for neutrality than throughout the 1950s and 1960s. A report for the United States International Communications Agency (Shaffer 1981) demonstrated that—faced with a direct choice between staying in NATO and the FRG becoming neutral—in February 1982; 70 percent were in favor of continued NATO membership, 13 percent in favor of neutrality, and 17 percent did not reply. Even though they do not contain explicit references to neutrality, the following data also corroborate NATO's outstanding acceptance in the FRG until now. In May 1981 (PIB), 69 percent advocated continuing membership in the present form, only 13 percent called for reducing German ties to NATO, and 18 percent refused to commit themselves. Two years later, in May 1983, 89 percent said that NATO is necessary to preserve peace in Europe; only ten percent disagreed (FGW). The same survey shows that 83 percent of respondents held German membership in NATO to be a "good thing," seven percent did not think so, and ten percent did not care. In August 1983 (IfD), with 19 percent undecided, 72 percent favored continuing FRG membership in NATO; only nine percent wanted to get out. The prevalent motivations for endorsing NATO can be clearly read from Table 4.26. NATO is accepted for the FRG because it serves to promote collaboration among Western nations and because of its peace-keeping and deterrent roles. It was mainly criticized for a lack of strength. Yet as we have seen earlier, there is very little willingness to support activities by the FRG to do anything about this. There also was some criticism of NATO members disagreeing too much and of the alliance's inability to reduce dissonance. On the whole, however, agreement with positive statements on NATO was

Table 4.27   To what extent could we rely upon the United States in case of conflict (SOWI)?

	12/77	10/79	2/80
Totally	24(25)	20(22)	21(23)
Very much	43(45)	36(39)	38(41)
Somewhat	27(28)	32(34)	32(34)
Not at all	3 (3)	5 (5)	3 (3)
DK, NA	4	7	7

Note: In brackets: percentages without DK, NA

stronger and has increased, and acceptance of negative statements has decreased over the period covered in Table 4.26.

RELIABILITY OF NATO AND THE UNITED STATES

Predominantly positive evaluations of NATO and of the United States among sizeable majorities of West Germans would logically be very implausible if they were not backed by a belief in the reliability of the allies in critical situations. In 1977 through 1980, SOWI three times surveyed mass opinion on the extent to which the FRG could rely upon NATO and the United States in case of conflict (Tables 4.27 and 4.28). These data show that virtually no distinction was being made between NATO as a whole and the United States; the reliability of the latter was obviously seen as the key necessary and sufficient ingredient in the reliability of the former. There were surprisingly few refusals to make this judgment, and complete treachery was expected only by negligible portions of samples. Expectations of rather low ("somewhat") reliability of the allies increased slightly between 1977 and 1980, up to around one-third of respondents, with all remaining persons believing that the FRG in case of conflict could rely on NATO and the United States "totally" or at least "very much."

According to PIB, in March 1981, 72 percent said they believed the United States would come to the assistance of the FRG and West Berlin in times of crisis; only 12 percent disagreed; and 16 percent refused to answer. Three out of four of those who believed in United States assistance said the United States would behave that way in any case, the others believed the United States would do so only if threatened themselves. In February 1982, again according to PIB, belief in the reliability of United States guarantees in crisis was even higher, at 78 percent. In August 1983 (IfD) 62 percent expected the United States to resist Soviet aggression against the FRG, 19 percent did not believe so, and the remainder were undecided.

Table 4.28   To what extent could we rely upon NATO in case of conflict (SOWI)?

	12/77	10/79	2/80
Totally	27(28)	20(22)	18(20)
Very much	43(44)	39(42)	39(42)
Somewhat	24(25)	30(32)	30(33)
Not at all	4 (4)	4 (4)	4 (4)
DK, NA	3	7	8

Note: In brackets: percentages without DK, NA

DECISION MAKING IN NATO

We have already seen above that positive evaluations of and favorable attitudes vis-à-vis the United States have gone along with a clear rejection of subordination. Similarly, majority endorsement of NATO does not involve widespread acceptance of United States leadership in the alliance. This is amply demonstrated by two items from FGW surveys. In the context of the decision to build ERWs respondents were interviewed in August 1981 as to whether this type of decision should be taken by NATO or by the United States alone. With almost everyone responding, 83 percent opted for a NATO decision. One might assume this implies that part of the resistance to the decision taken by President Reagan was due to its perceived unilateral character and that opposition would have been smaller if the federal government had been obliged internally to defend an alliance decision like the one of December 1979. This point should not be exaggerated, however. Much of the support for a decision by NATO probably stems from the hope that it would have looked different. It is indeed very hard to disentangle pro-NATO and antinuclear sentiments in these responses.

In February 1980, respondents were asked what relations between Western Europe and the United States should look like. Not surprisingly, 65 percent demanded equal rights for both sides, only 13 percent preferred U.S. leadership, and 22 percent advocated political independence of Western Europe from the United States. Mass support for NATO in the FRG thus is intimately linked to the general notion that the alliance has to accommodate the interests of all participating nations.

INTERRELATIONS AMONG ITEMS

Most of the patterns that can be reported here refer to evaluations of the relations between the United States and the FRG. In May 1982, 83 percent of those who judged these relations as bad said they had deteriorated since President Reagan took office; among those who evaluated them as good, 63 percent said they had registered no changes since then (FGW). The percentage of those describing U.S.-FRG relations as good declined from 86 percent to 68 percent as one moved from a very positive to a very negative evaluation of the U.S. president; the percentage reporting a recent deterioration in relations rose in parallel from 25 to 65 percent. Obviously the highly abstract judgment on bilateral relations in general and their dynamics is heavily colored by sentiments about people that are easier to evaluate.

This relationship seems to be even stronger for people's position on the issue of whether in case of disagreement the FRG should pursue her own interests or adopt U.S. views. People who evaluated Reagan very positively favored adopting U.S. policies by a 71 to 28 percent majority, whereas very negative ratings for Reagan produced 87 percent in favor of following FRG interests. Another set of cross-tabulations from an August 1981 FGW survey does not yield any additional insight, as its emphasis was on the issue of who should make decisions such as the one on ERW in the future. As an overwhelming majority of respondents (85 percent) was in favor of NATO, rather than U.S. decisions, there logically can be only little variation within the categories of other variables subsumed under this theme.

Patterns of Public Opinion on National Security

INTRODUCTION

After describing the development of public opinion on national security in the Federal Republic in recent years, we now want to look at some structures that can be detected within these attitudes. In this section we will investigate the interrelations of opinions on individual items among the four general themes addressed in this study. In the subsequent final section the attitudes that have been described will be broken down according to respondents' position in the social structure and their partisan affiliations.

In this enterprise we have to be aware of some methodological and substantive limitations. First, the number of associations that could be reported is potentially enormous, so we have to be selective, occasionally choosing just one or two indicators from each of the four major themes for assessing interrelations. Second, for quite a number of combinations of items no data at all are available, as the two items have never appeared together in one survey. Third, for the same reason, it is not possible to construct indices for various dimensions of public opinion on defense—for example, information, salience, consistency of attitudes, or optimism—that could then be related to each other, to possible causal variables, or to individual national security items.

For such a hierarchical causal analysis to be feasible, all relevant measurements would have to be available for one and the same sample of respondents instead of being scattered over a multitude of surveys. The most recent major single survey covering a great number of relevant aspects of national security attitudes is from October 1979. Its results have been analyzed with a reasonable degree of sophistication by Raeder (1982). This study is too old, however, to evaluate developments over the past few years, its original data set was not accessible (only cross-tabulations were available), and national security attitudes since 1979 had to be collected from two dozen or so separate surveys. The above, combined with what follows, might thus be the most extensive review of patterns of public opinion on national security in the FRG, but it must fall short of perfection. Only bivariate relationships are presented (e.g., whether perception of a foreign threat increases the willingness to accept new nuclear weapons in Europe), but no controls could be performed. It is impossible, therefore, to ascertain whether this association between threat perception and acceptance of new missiles is stronger with men or women, with the better or the less educated, with CDU/CSU or SPD followers, with those for whom national security is more or less salient, and so on.

IMAGES OF SECURITY AND OF THE SOVIET UNION

We will first examine the associations between perceptions of the military balance and the military threat on the one hand and evaluations of the stability of peace, the danger of war, and salience of national security, information, and interest on the other. For those who perceived military parity in May 1982 (FGW), evaluations of the stability of peace were almost equally divided between "no change" and "less stability." Interestingly, those who judged either the East or the West as superior had rather similar response patterns, with roughly one third reporting "no change" and two-thirds reporting less stability of peace.

Between perceived military threat and danger of war we find a very close association. Fifty-three percent of respondents with perceptions of high threat perceived a high danger of war (BMV 10/79), 39 percent saw this danger to be low, eight percent did not know or did not answer. Respondents who evaluated the military threat as low predominantly also held the danger of war to be small (71 percent); only seven percent reported high danger of war, and 22 percent did not commit themselves.

In the same survey, there was no relationship at all between threat perception and judgments on the importance of national security as a political goal for the FRG. Remaining associations with indicators of salience, information, and interest are summarized in Table 4.29. High threat perceptions went along with somewhat higher evaluations of the importance of the armed forces and with more interest in national security affairs but were unrelated to the level of information. Of course, it is impossible here to say anything definitive on the direction of causality: Do people regard the Bundeswehr as more important and devote some attention to these questions because they feel the military threat to be high, or vice versa?

For October 1980 we have some evidence on the impact of threat

Table 4.29   The military threat and the importance of armed forces, information, and interest (BMV 10/79)

	Military threat High	Low
Budeswehr is		
Very important	33	15
Important	52	64
Less important	15	20
Information on defense		
Very good	17	17
Good	13	14
Deficient	69	69
Correct responses on who is to authorize use of nuclear weapons	32	36
Interest in media reports on defense		
Yes	51	43
No	49	57

perception on attitudes toward the defense budget (FGW). For those respondents who said the threat had decreased, a large majority (77 percent) evaluated defense spending as excessive, 16 percent said it was just right, and only seven percent regarded it as too small. Among those who perceived the threat as having remained unchanged, 49 percent rejected military spending as too high. 46 percent were content, and six percent pleaded for more. Of those who thought the military threat to have grown, 35 percent regarded defense spending as exaggerated, 51 percent were satisfied, and 14 percent said it was too low.

In the October 1979 BMV survey, threat perception had a nonobvious relationship with opinions on the feasibility and acceptability of military defense. Those who regarded the military threat as high had a stronger tendency to advocate military defense against attack, even if this would involve nuclear war on FRG territory. On the other hand, these respondents at the same time were more sceptical of the chances for success of Western defense against Eastern attack. Thirty-two percent said such an attack could not be repelled, a view that was shared by only 10 percent of those who perceived the military threat as low. One possible interpretation for this pattern is that high threat perception may be more an outgrowth of a "pessimistic" attitude toward national security (just like scepticism about the feasibility of defense) than the product of gathering and analyzing relevant information. This is supported by the zero relationship between threat perception and the level of information.

Perceptions of the military balance in this survey were only weakly

Table 4.30 Soviet armaments and the salience of national security, information, and interest (BMV 10/79)

| | Soviet armaments have | | Soviet armaments are due to | |
	grown	not grown	offensive motives	defensive motives
Bundeswehr is				
Very important	21	7	24	18
Important	63	50	61	65
Less important	16	24	16	17
National security is a top political priority				
Yes	15	11	14	14
No	85	89	86	86
Information on defense				
Very good	19	7	14	16
Good	14	13	16	16
Deficient	67	80	70	68
Interest in media reports on defense				
Yes	41	24	40	39
No	59	76	60	61

related to measures of salience and of interest; there was no relationship at all with the level of information. Those who regarded the East as militarily superior held the Bundeswehr to be somewhat more important and gave slightly higher priority to national security as a political objective for the FRG. Those who saw rough military parity had the lowest level of interest in defense matters. Table 4.30 reveals that perceptions of whether Soviet military capabilities have grown or not were much more important, but that the motivations ascribed to the Soviet military buildup were virtually unrelated to images of security. If Soviet capability was seen to have increased over the past years, the Bundeswehr was judged as more important, and these respondents were significantly more interested in defense and had more knowledge of these things.

Associations between perceptions of East-West relations and images of security are available from several surveys. From an October 1981 FGW survey we learn that people who evaluated bilateral USSR-FRG relations as bad were much more likely to see peace in Europe as having become less secure. Surprisingly, this latter perception was not associated with a stronger desire to extend bilateral relations; people obviously did not believe this to be an appropriate strategy for increasing the stability of peace. This finding is similar to those in Table 4.28: there does not seem to

Table 4.31   Perceptions of the military balance and of the military threat and positions toward INF deployment (FGW 5/83)

| | Who is superior? | | | Military threat? | |
	East	Both equal	West	Yes	No
Continue negotiations, no INF deployment	66	76	78	70	74
Continue negotiations and deploy INF	29	22	19	27	24
Deploy INF, discontinue negotiations	4	3	2	3	1

be an instrumental concept of East-West relations; rather there are optimists and pessimists. The former think relations are good and should be improved, the latter view them as bad and are not enthusiastic about improvements.

In the October 1979 BMV survey, all associations between perceptions and expectations of East-West relations and the indicators of salience, interest and information were practically zero, the only exception being that people who expected these relations to deteriorate more often than others felt the Bundeswehr to be very important. Finally, there is a report from FGW of October 1981 indicating that attitudes vis-à-vis the peace movement had very little to do with perceptions of East-West relations.

IMAGES OF DETERRENCE AND OF THE SOVIET UNION

In this section, there are some interesting findings from a May 1983 study that are described in Table 4.31. When faced with alternatives on how to proceed if the Geneva talks failed to produce agreement, only a negligible share of the sample opted for INF deployments without continuing arms control negotiations. The other two alternatives, continuing negotiations without deployment or a parallel approach, were chosen in systematic covariation with perceptions of the military balance and of the military threat, the direction of patterns being as expected. As in the previous subsection, perception of the military balance again emerges as a more potent predictor of other defense-related attitudes than threat perception.

However, even among those who perceived Eastern superiority and a military threat, we find two-thirds majorities in favor of negotiations only. As almost half of respondents saw the East to be superior, more than 30 percent of the total sample at the same time said the East was ahead in military power and that there should be no Western deployment of INF. It would require the assumption that we do not want to make—that NATO deployment is indispensable in order to compensate for Eastern superiority to describe these respondents' attitudes as contradictory or illogical. We prefer the interpretation that here we have the typical situation of more general and more specific defense attitudes falling apart for people for whom these things are not terribly important. When asked generally about the military threat or the military balance, people respond on the basis of very general feelings, whatever their factual or cognitive foundation might be. When asked specifically about new missiles, most people reject them, many probably not even being aware that the two issues may be related. Only with a minority do attitudes on the one dimension have an impact on those on the other, and this minority produces the aggregate relationship visible in Table 4.31. Such a pattern clearly would be inconceivable with very salient items. One could never observe large majorities of those who think unemployment to be a major evil opposing concrete measures to cope with it.

IMAGES OF THE SOVIET UNION AND OF THE ALLIES

On the relationship between images of the Soviet Union and of the allies little evidence is available. In the October 1979 BMV survey, threat perception had no effect at all on evaluations of the reliability of NATO and of the United States. In May 1983 (FGW), on the other hand, perceptions of the military balance and of the necessity of NATO clearly were related. If the East was viewed as superior, NATO was rated as indispensable by 95 percent; if both sides were viewed as equally strong, this percentage was 87 percent—still high, but definitely lower.

Data by FGW from June 1980 suggest that evaluations of the importance of good relations with the West or with the East run highly parallel. As the bulk of responses falls into the "very important" or "important" category there can hardly be any widespread pattern of stressing relations with one side at the expense of the other. Rather there are those for whom good external relations of the FRG, whether with the East or with the allies, are very important, and those for whom all international relations are personally of minor concern. Finally, in July 1980 (also FGW) respondents who named the preservation of peace as the most important aspect of East-West relations were somewhat more likely to identify military cooperation or mutual support as the most important aspect of relations with the United States than those who selected other areas of East-West relations (economic, cultural, or sports exchange, or human rights) as most salient (52 percent as against 36 percent).

IMAGES OF SECURITY AND OF DETERRENCE

From a survey performed by FGW in May 1983, we can learn how images of security and of deterrence are currently associated in the FRG. Among those for whom the stability of peace in Europe was perceived as having remained the same over the past year, only 46 percent agreed with the position not to deploy any new missiles in the country, no matter what the

East would do; however among those who believed that peace had become less secure, this percentage was 60 percent. Similarly, only 70 percent in the first group and 77 percent in the second group preferred to continue negotiations without missile deployment if the Geneva negotiations should fail to succeed before the end of 1983. This clearly shows that, apart from possible instrumental considerations, all these attitudes on peace and new missiles to a certain extent reflect a dimension of public anxiety that increases resistance to nuclear weapons as peace is perceived as being endangered. Data from the same study also show quite clearly that the peace movement in the FRG was evaluated far more positively by respondents who wanted arms control negotiations to be continued without INF deployment than by those who were willing to station these weapons should no timely agreement be found.

IMAGES OF SECURITY AND OF THE ALLIES

A similar pattern to that in the previous section can be observed between perceptions of peace and evaluations of the Western Alliance. Ninety-three percent of those people who believed that nothing had changed as to the stability of peace, and only 83 percent of those who said peace had become less secure, held NATO to be necessary (FGW 5/83). Again, this is not a paradox, as it may seem at first glance, but the product of a minority strongly believing at the same time that war is imminent and that our familiar way of trying to prevent it in the framework of military alliance should be abandoned.

In an October 1979 BMV survey, the data on perceived reliability of the United States and of NATO and on trust in the United States are almost identical, so only figures on reliability of NATO are reproduced in Table 4.32. Obviously, the level of information on defense matters and the evaluation of the priority of national security were virtually unrelated to judgments on the reliability of the Western alliance. People with higher interest in national security, on the other hand, rated the reliability of NATO slightly above average. Finally, the higher respondents judged the importance of the armed forces, the more likely they were to have confidence in NATO.

IMAGES OF DETERRENCE AND OF THE ALLIES

Not surprisingly, evaluations of NATO are to a considerable degree related to opinions as to what the West should do if there would be no agreement in Geneva. As in May 1983 (FGW) almost three out of four respondents were in favor of continuing talks without missile deployment, there can be no dramatic associations, but what can be observed is strong enough: 70 percent of supporters of NATO preferred continuing negotiations over alternatives that would imply stationing missiles in the FRG; among those who thought NATO to be unnecessary this proportion was 91 percent.

Table 4.32 Salience of national security, information, and interest and reliability of NATO (BMV 10/79)

	In case of conflict we could rely upon NATO			
	completely	to a large extent	to a limited extent	not at all
Bundeswehr is				
Very important	48	36	14	2
Important	23	56	20	1
Less important	7	37	46	9
National security is a top political priority				
Yes	29	47	21	3
No	24	48	25	3
Information on defense				
Very good	27	46	24	3
Good	23	48	24	4
Deficient	25	48	24	3
Interest in media reports on defense				
Yes	33	44	21	2
No	21	49	26	3

Attitudes on ERWs in a study by FGW in August 1981 were in a remarkable way connected to perceptions of bilateral relations between the FRG and the United States. In general, agreement with the decision to build ERWs was about ten percent above agreement with their possible deployment in the FRG. Both these approval rates were unrelated to the perception of the current quality of bilateral relations as such. If people were asked about the development of bilateral relations since President Reagan was elected, however, the connection with their responses on ERWs was very close. Respondents who saw recent improvements of relations were considerably more favorable of these weapons in general and of their deployment in the FRG than those who saw no change or a deterioration. This pattern was even more dramatic with respect to direct evaluations of the U.S. president. It is therefore probably fair to say that these attitudes on specific weapon systems reflect general pro- and anti-American sentiments fueled by opinions about the current U.S. leadership rather than calculations of these systems' relative merits or disadvantages.

Opinions on ERWs furthermore were linked to attitudes on what relations between the partners of the Western alliance should look like. Table 4.33 documents that if the United States, rather than NATO, was regarded as being in charge of decisions of this kind, approval of ERWs tended to be higher. Similarly, in the same survey 66 percent of those

Table 4.33 Evaluations of FRG-US relations and attitudes on ERW (FGW 8/81)

	FRG-US relations		FRG-US relations since President Reagan was elected			Evaluation of President Reagan					Who should decide on ERW	
	Bad	Good	Deteriorated	Remained	Improved	−2	−1	±1	+1	+2	NATO	US alone
Building ERW												
Agreement	36	40	32	40	61	9	14	25	53	76	35	57
Disagreement	64	60	68	60	39	91	86	75	47	24	65	43
ERW deployment in FRG												
Agreement	30	31	22	26	49	10	12	21	41	60	25	34
Disagreement	70	69	78	74	51	90	88	79	59	40	75	66

respondents who said that in case of disagreement the FRG should adopt U.S. views agreed to the stationing of ERWs, opposition to these warheads among those who wanted the Federal Republic to pursue her own interests ran at 81 percent. Summarily this could be interpreted as follows: general acceptance of the Western alliance is very high but support erodes quickly if conflicts of interest are presented to respondents. If this conflict takes the form of announcing the possibility of introducing additional nuclear weapons not very much of this support survives.

SUMMARY OF PATTERNS OF PUBLIC OPINION ON NATIONAL SECURITY

As has been stated in the introduction to this section, the multitude of associations between individual survey items presented here could not be selected according to substantive criteria but had to be accepted according to availability. What conclusions do they allow?

First, most of the non-zero relationships that could be reported are as one would expect. However, in many cases measures that should or could be related in fact are unrelated. Even if there is covariation, it often is rather weak in the aggregate. This can mean only one thing, of course: that in some people's attitudes there is a clear-cut structure, although in many others' there is none. In many cross-tabulations off-diagonal responses prevail. Consistency among defense-related attitudes at the individual level is not particularly high, which, in turn, is another indicator of low personal salience.

Second, even though we have not been able—because of the particularities of the available data base—to simplify the complex picture of numerous indicators by reducing them to a smaller number of dimensions, one can probably claim that such a solution still would have to be multidimensional. Raeder's (1982) optimism-pessimism dimension, which is derived from threat perception, expectations of East-West relations, and personal salience of national security, appears as too simple. Salience and cognitions should be kept apart, and affective components, such as pro- or antimilitary or American feelings, seem to be important, as is indicated by the effect of evaluations of the current American president. Let us now turn to the question of whether the associations between defense attitudes and nondefense variables may be stronger than the ones among national security items themselves.

Nondefense Correlates of Public Opinion on National Security

IMAGES OF THE SOVIET UNION

Table 4.34 reveals that there is some variation of images of the Soviet Union among the categories of various variables indicating people's posi-

Table 4.34   Images of the Soviet Union and social structure (FGW 5/83)

| | Who is superior | | | Military threat | |
	East	Both equal	West	Yes	No
Sex					
Men	44	44	11	45	55
Women	49	40	10	51	49
Age					
18–24	40	46	13	47	53
25–29	35	55	8	47	53
30–39	42	44	14	51	49
40–49	52	36	11	44	56
50–59	46	44	10	49	51
60–	52	39	9	49	51
Education[a]					
Low	54	38	7	45	55
Medium	48	42	10	45	55
High	41	44	14	53	47
Size of city					
– 5,000	52	36	12	44	56
5,000– 20,000	44	46	10	49	51
20,000–100,000	50	42	8	47	53
100,000–	43	42	14	49	51
Church attendance					
Often	54	38	7	53	47
Now and then	47	42	11	45	55
Seldom, never	44	45	11	48	52
Total	47	42	11	48	52

[a] Low: Hauptschule only; high: at least Mittlere Reife

tion in the social structure, but that this variation is not dramatic. Women in the May 1983 FGW survey were somewhat more "pessimistic" in evaluating the military balance and the military threat than men. Those with better education more often regarded the West as militarily superior and the military threat as high. Frequent church attendance, as a measure of intensity of religious feeling, was related to higher perception of threat and of Eastern superiority.

Perceptions of the military balance differed somewhat with the size of the place of residence; in rural towns and villages the East was judged superior by more respondents than in major cities. With respect to the age of respondents, there was little variation in perceptions of the military

158   HANS RATTINGER

Table 4.35   Images of the Soviet Union and party preference (FGW 5/83)

| | | Who is superior | | Military threat | |
	East	Both equal	West	Yes	No
SPD	41	49	10	44	56
CDU/CSU	52	37	10	46	54
FDP	41	47	12	58	42
Green party	24	52	24	77	23

threat. Those between 25 and 29 held the most "optimistic" views of the military balance. Respondents younger than 30 were below average in perceiving Eastern superiority but at the same time held "normal" threat perceptions. The former observation may be a function of "political generations" (these people went through their politically formative years between the late 1960s and the mid-1970s, the era of détente), but this concept fails to explain why the youngest age groups tended to evaluate Eastern military superiority less than others while having average threat perception. Some light can be shed on this result, however, by looking at the distributions according to party preference.

From Table 4.35 we learn that perceptions of threat and of the military balance are much more closely related to party preference than to social structure. Adherents of the CDU/CSU were most "pessimistic" about Soviet superiority, followers of the SPD and the FDP were below average in reporting Eastern superiority, and three out of four sympathizers of the Green party denied Eastern military superiority. The ranking of followers of the three established parties on threat perception was not the same, potential SPD voters feeling roughly the same threat as potential CDU/CSU voters. Adherents of the Green party, on the other hand, had by far the strongest perception of threat. For these people the measure of military threat was not—as with all other respondents—almost exclusively related to the power of the East. They were very likely to see a military threat, but not necessarily one attached to Eastern military superiority and rather reflecting a more general fear of war in spite of the predominant perception of parity. The high percentage of followers of the Green party in the youngest age groups thus explains the discrepancy between perceptions of the military balance and of threat recorded in Table 4.34.

IMAGES OF SECURITY

The survey results that have been incorporated in to Table 4.36 indicate that men and women did not differ in their perceptions of the stability of peace in Europe or in the personal importance attached to protection against an Eastern attack. Women, however, viewed good relations of the

Table 4.36 Images of security and social structure

	Peace in Europe in past year (FGW 5/83)		Personal importance of protection against Russian attack (FGW 9/80)[a]	Percentage good relations with the East very important (FGW 2/83)	Position toward defense spending (ABI 12/82)[b]	The peace movement is (FGW 5/83)			
	Less secure	More secure, no change				necessary	superfluous	detrimental	don't care
Sex									
Men	36	64	7.6	21	3.0	48	23	9	20
Women	39	61	7.7	26	2.5	46	24	5	26
Age									
18–24	41	59	7.0	20	2.3	61	18	3	19
29–29	43	57	6.2	22	2.7	69	11	6	14
30–39	45	55	7.5	22	2.6	52	17	7	23
40–49	34	66	7.8	23	2.8	45	25	8	22
50–59	29	72	7.7	26	2.9	40	26	8	27
60–	37	63	8.4	25	2.8	35	32	7	27
Education									
Low	34	65	8.3	26	2.6	36	24	7	33
Medium	37	64	7.8	23	2.8	44	26	7	24
High	41	58	7.2	23	2.7	57	21	6	16
Size of city									
– 5,000	35	65	7.9	12	2.9	48	24	4	25
5,000– 20,000	31	69	8.0	21	2.3	40	28	7	26
20,000–100,000	39	61	7.5	24	2.9	49	25	4	22
100,000–	42	58	7.4	29	2.6	49	19	11	21
Church attendance									
Often	32	68	8.0	21	2.8	36	30	8	26
Now and then	36	63	7.7	23	2.7	44	25	6	26
Seldom, never	40	60	7.6	23	2.7	54	19	7	19
Total	38	62	7.7	23	2.7	47	24	7	23

[a] Average score on scale from 0 (no personal importance) to 10 (highest personal importance)
[b] Average score on scale from 1 (should be strongly reduced) to 7 (should be strongly increased)

FRG with the East as somewhat more important, were more in favor of reducing military spending, and were more indifferent toward the peace movement.

In the various age groups we again see the youngest two groupings as deviating from average attitudes. The youngest respondents expressed stronger feelings that peace in Europe had become less stable recently, a finding that supports what has been said above on their level of anxiety and fear that did not stem from widespread perceptions of an Eastern threat but from more general notions of the political and military insecurity of the current world. At the same time, the younger respondents were the ones most "optimistic" about the Eastern bloc. Conforming to perceptions of the military balance (Table 4.34), protection against Eastern attack was least important to people between 18 and 29 years of age. The personal salience of good relations with the East increases only slightly with age. The same trend is visible in attitudes toward defense spending, but here the youngest age bracket set itself apart more clearly from the others by advocating, on the average, rather sizeable reductions. Not surprisingly, the youngest were fondest of the peace movement; two thirds rated it as "necessary," and only one-third of the oldest respondents did so. Indifference increased somewhat, while rejections of the peace movement rose with age from 21 to 39 percent.

Correlates of education can be detected in attitudes toward the peace movement and toward the importance of protection against Russian attack. Respondents with low formal education attributed much more importance to military protection and were far less convinced of the necessity of the peace movement. If one combines high education with youth—a combination typical of sympathizers of the Green party—this is the group of people to whom the peace movement appeals most. The same two indicators of images of security also co-vary with urbanization and religious practice; in addition, good relations with the East are deemed much more important by respondents from cities than from villages. People from the countryside and/or with close ties to their church are far more worried about protection against a Russian attack than city dwellers and/or less religious respondents; support for the peace movement is highest among people with weak ties to their church.

Again, the relationship between images of security and party preference is much closer than the one between these images and positions in the social structure. On most indicators in Table 4.37 the followers of the Green party deviate even more strongly from adherents of the three established parties than on the images of the Soviet Union in Table 4.35. An overwhelming majority of Green voters viewed peace in Europe as having become less secure. At this point we can also demonstrate the reason for the strong aggregate decline of perceptions of peace having become less secure from May 1982 to May 1983 that has been reported in Table 4.11. Most of this change is due to the attitudes of CDU/SCU followers, 58 percent of whom in spring 1982 believed peace to have

Table 4.37 Images of security and party preference

	Peace in Europe in past year (FGW 5/83)		Personal importance of protection against Russian attack (FGW 9/80)a	Percentage good relations with the East very important (FGW 2/83)	Position toward defense spending (ABI 12/82)b	The peace movement is (FGW 5/83)			
	Less secure	More secure, no change				necessary	superfluous	detrimental	don't care
SPD	45	55	7.3	26	2.3	58	17	2	23
CDU/CSU	27	73	8.3	21	3.1	35	30	11	25
FDP	42	58	7.4	18	3.0	57	18	7	18
Green Party	73	27	4.8	18	1.6	93	4	0	3

a,bCompare Table 4.36.

become less secure; in spring 1983, this figure had dropped to 27 percent. Obviously, threat perception is a function of whether the composition of government conforms to one's wishes at least as much as it is a function of what is going on in international politics.

Sympathizers of the Green party also gave very low priority to military protection, which was evaluated as most important by sympathizers of the Christian parties. The salience of good relations with the East was not a very partisan issue, even though it ranked highest, as one should expect, for Social Democratic voters. Positions toward defense spending, on the other hand, varied widely even between adherents of the three established parties. Those who intended to vote for either of the current government parties on the average were in favor of small reductions. Followers of the Green party desired very deep cuts in the military budget, of course, and Social Democratic voters ranked in between. Finally, attitudes vis-à-vis the peace movement are distributed roughly as one should expect, Green voters being enthusiastic, CDU/CSU voters being very sceptical, with FDP and SPD leaners being in between.

IMAGES OF DETERRENCE

From Table 4.38 some associations between images of deterrence and respondents' position in the social structure emerge. Opposition against ERWs, either in general or on FRG territory, was strongest in the youngest age group and weakest in the middle-aged group (30 to 39 years). Women were significantly less willing than men to accept new nuclear weapons in the FRG, either in the framework of NATO's December 1979 decision or in the context of the modernization of TNF. An absolute majority among men refused to support the demand to deploy no new missiles in the FRG regardless of Soviet behavior, although almost two-thirds of the women endorsed that position. Nearly half of the surveyed men agreed with the American president's decision to build ERWs, but more than two-thirds of the women disapproved of this decision.

Women in spring and summer of 1983 also were less inclined than men to concede compatibility between Christian values and nuclear arms, to accept new missiles in the area where they lived, or to deploy INF in case of failure of the Geneva negotiations, in these attitudes women were closest to the youngest respondents. Acceptance of nuclear weapons increased somewhat with education and with intensity of religious practice. As has already been mentioned, those with little tie to their church most strongly believed nuclear weaponry to be incompatible with Christian faith.

If one separately examines these attitudes for the adherents of the various parties, however, one finds far more significant discrepancies than between the two sexes (Table 4.39). Naturally, very few of those who intended to vote for the Green party agreed to any new nuclear weapons. But even among those leaning toward the SPD and the FDP there were

Table 4.38 Images of deterrence and social structure (FGW)

| | Agreement with demand not to deploy any new missiles in FRG 2/83 | Agreement with decision to build ERW 8/81 | Agreement with ERW deployment in FRG 8/81 | For Christians nuclear weapons are: 4/83 | | | Acceptance of deployment of new missiles in respondent's area 6/83 | What to do if no agreement in Geneva? | | |
				Acceptable	Acceptable for defense only	Not acceptable		Continue negotiations, no deployment of INF	Continue negotiations, deployment of INF 7/83	Deploy INF, discontinue negotiations
Sex										
Men	47	46	36	12	46	42	31	72	25	3
Women	62	32	26	7	42	51	14	80	17	3
Age										
18–24	59	29	26	6	36	58	18	85	13	2
25–29	57	37	34	7	27	65	21	86	12	2
30–39	57	45	36	5	47	48	28	74	20	6
40–49	51	36	31	14	47	39	23	72	24	4
50–59	53	34	27	13	49	38	21	74	25	1
60–	57	42	30	8	47	45	19	73	23	4
Education										
Low	61	35	24	4	46	50	12	80	16	4
Medium	53	43	34	11	46	42	25	75	22	3
High	54	34	29	10	39	51	22	75	21	3
Size of city										
– 5,000	51	42	32	5	57	38	20	76	20	4
5,000– 20,000	59	46	35	8	46	46	22	71	25	4
20,000–100,000	58	32	27	10	48	42	29	78	18	4
100,000–	53	34	28	11	36	53	17	79	19	2
Church attendance										
Often	48	43	36	9	52	39	23	66	30	4
Now and then	56	38	29	10	50	40	20	76	21	3
Seldom, never	59	38	31	9	34	57	23	82	15	3
Total	55	38	31	9	44	47	21	76	21	3

Table 4.39 Images of deterrence and party preference (FGW)

| | Agreement with demand not to deploy any new missiles in FRG 2/83 | Agreement with decision to build ERW 8/81 | Agreement with ERW deployment in FRG 8/81 | For Christians nuclear weapons are: 4/83 | | | Acceptance of deployment of new missiles in respondent's area 6/83 | What to do if no agreement in Geneva? | | |
				Acceptable	Acceptable for defense only	Not acceptable		Continue negotiations, no deployment of INF	Continue negotiations, deployment of INF 7/83	Deploy INF, discontinue negotiations
SPD	66	28	21	7	37	56	10	87	11	1
CDU/CSU	40	54	42	14	54	33	35	62	33	5
FDP	66	20	21	12	53	35	23	71	22	7
Green party	73	13	10	1	14	85	3	96	4	0

two-thirds—or even larger—majorities against new nuclear missiles in the FRG, against building ERWs, or against deploying them in the Federal Republic. Surprisingly, followers of these two parties were rather similar in these attitudes both in fall 1981 and in 1983. The electorate of the liberal party in the 1983 election without any doubt had been very much different from previous elections and had become most similar to that part of the electorate leaning toward the CDU/CSU, as also was evident in Table 4.37 with regard to positions on the defense budget. Considering the rejection of missile deployment in the FRG, however, the old SPD-FDP coalition was still visible in 1983, at least on the part of the electorate. Those who said they intended to vote for the CDU/CSU, on the other hand, by their very different opinions seemed to justify the "missile party" (*Raketenpartei*) charge brought against these parties by the SPD during the recent campaign: 60 percent would not endorse the demand to refuse any new missiles in the FRG under all circumstances, 54 percent agreed to the building of ERWs, 42 percent said they would even agree to their deployment in the FRG, 35 percent stated support for stationing new missiles in the area where they live, and 38 percent advocated INF deployment if the Geneva negotiations should fail.

IMAGES OF ALLIES

In 1982 and 1983, women were very close to men in their attitudes on NATO and on U.S.-German relations. While urbanization likewise had little to do with evaluations of NATO and the United States, some consistent patterns can be observed in Table 4.40 of positive images of U.S.-FRG relations and the Western Alliance becoming more frequent with age and strength of respondents' religious convictions and less frequent with better education. These associations are clearly visible but far from being dramatic.

Compared to previous tables, most interrelations between images of the allies and party preference (Table 4.41) are not very strong; still they are much stronger than with social structure. Followers of the two parties then supporting the government of Helmut Schmidt and those who leaned toward the CDU/CSU in August 1982 rated bilateral U.S.-FRG relations almost equally, sympathizers of the Green party most frequently perceived them to be bad. CDU/CSU voters most likely regarded strained relations with the United States as an indication of the German government's failure to avoid frictions and thus were most inclined to have the Federal Republic follow U.S. leadership. Green voters, on the other hand, probably saw problems in bilateral relations predominantly as the outcome of U.S. foreign policy, so they joined supporters of the government coalition in rejecting the adoption of U.S. positions by the FRG in case of disagreement. For the supporters of the coalition parties SPD and FDP this rejection did not follow from similar perceptions of a bad climate of relations for which the United States was to blame, but from the judgment

Table 4.40   Images of the allies and social structure (FGW)

	Relations between US and FRG are Good / Bad 8/82		In case of disagreement FRG should adopt US positions / decide according to own interests 5/82		NATO is necessary / not necessary 5/83	
	Good	Bad	adopt US positions	decide according to own interests	necessary	not necessary
Sex						
Men	58	42	31	69	91	9
Women	59	41	27	73	89	11
Age						
18–24	49	51	30	70	82	18
25–29	57	43	26	74	85	15
30–39	60	40	26	74	90	10
40–49	61	39	27	73	92	8
50–59	58	42	35	65	90	10
60–	62	38	31	69	93	7
Education						
Low	60	40	28	72	92	8
Medium	61	39	33	67	92	8
High	55	45	26	74	86	14
Size of city						
– 5,000	64	36	24	76	90	10
5,000– 20,000	59	41	42	58	93	7
20,000–100,000	55	45	25	75	89	11
100,000–	59	41	26	74	88	12
Church attendance						
Often	61	39	35	65	96	4
Now and then	59	41	32	68	91	9
Seldom, never	57	43	24	76	87	13
Total	59	41	29	71	90	10

that bilateral affairs were quite satisfactory, so there was no need for subordination in order to improve them.

Attitudes on NATO, finally, were most polarized along partisan lines in spring 1983. While almost identical overwhelming majorities of CDU/CSU and FDP adherents regarded NATO as necessary for the FRG, SPD followers were significantly less enthusiastic, and Green voters were least convinced of the alliance's indispensability. It should be stressed, however, that even in this latter group, which was most critical of NATO, a majority of respondents judged the alliance as necessary. Rejection of new nuclear weapons (see Table 4.39) for more than half of the sympathizers of the Green party was *not* equivalent to rejection of the Western Alliance.

Table 4.41   Images of the allies and party preference (FGW)

	Relations between US and FRG are Good / Bad 8/82		In case of disagreement FRG should adopt US positions / decide according to own interests 5/82		NATO is necessary / not necessary 5/83	
SPD	59	41	24	76	86	14
CDU/CSU	61	39	39	61	96	4
FDP	66	34	18	82	95	6
Green party	44	56	21	79	56	43

Conclusion

After presenting such a multitude of descriptive findings and associations among attitudes, an extended critical summary and final evaluation of results is required. Let us begin by repeating that the data base was far from satisfactory. Available survey items on security issues have turned out to be scattered over a multitude of studies, and on several relevant topics we have no measurements at all from the past couple of years. The lack of comprehensive recent investigations of the subject stands in strange contrast to frequent allegations of dramatic changes in the mass support for Western defense in the FRG. National security issues still are marginal in most public opinion surveys in this country. Our evidence would suggest that this may somehow correspond to respondents' evaluations.

In the descriptive portions of this chapter, much contradictory and inconclusive evidence was presented but we have not been able to identify major dramatic shifts in national security attitudes in the early 1980s. In their affective orientations toward the actors of security policy, large majorities of West Germans are still sceptical and critical of the USSR and friendly toward the Western Alliance and the United States. The latter are both evaluated as reliable and as necessary for security. This sympathy is restricted to a defensive and peaceful alliance that does not constitute a dangerous commitment. As long as this perception prevails, tendencies toward neutralism are blocked off by fears of losing American friendship and support. This has already been described as the fundamental situation in the FRG in the 1950s by Deutsch and Edinger (1959,23f.). Their analysis appears to remain valid.

Perceptions of the factual framework of national security and expectations of hypothetical futures seem to follow closely spectacular and well publicized events in the international arena, again with no really dramatic changes over the past few years. Dissent within the Western Alliance and the deterioration of East-West relations, proclaimed by many as the ultimate failure of détente, have had very predictable effects on public opinion in the FRG. The relations of the FRG with both superpowers are seen as somewhat worse than they used to be. The East is perceived as somewhat more superior and threatening, war as somewhat more likely, and defense as more difficult. In view of the information input into public opinion all other trends would be very surprising indeed.

These changes in perceptions have not been sufficiently strong, however, to effect any realignment in the importance ascribed to national security issues for the FRG as a whole and for individuals. Assessments of salience are hardly straightforward, but generally speaking there seem to be many more pressing concerns. This, of course, is a function of discontent. If things within an issue area are going satisfactorily it will be considered less important than others. National security issues are less salient than others partly because they are so remote to individuals, but partly also because many people are willing to tolerate security policy as it is and tend to view it as sufficiently successful. Unfortunately, we have not been able to present very much longitudinal evidence on the general public's level of information on these matters. The data we have indicate it is rather low.

The key contradictions among the attitudes we have reviewed occur between higher order and lower order national security instruments. Defense and deterrence are widely accepted as very general principles, especially if deterrence is conceptually related to the prevention of war and thus benefits from the universal desire for peace. As soon as it comes to the operational implications of these principles, however, opposition exceeds support. The feasibility of defense and specific scenarios are evaluated critically, and there is little enthusiasm about defense preparations, military expenditures, or nuclear weapons.

If contemplated in isolation, these measurements of public opinion could be construed as supporting the notion of a wholesale erosion of the national security consensus in the FRG. Anyone who would jump to this conclusion, however, must first consider what else one should expect. One can argue for a number of reasons that the apparent contradiction between levels of support is only normal. As matters of national security are not very salient concerns, it is cognitively very easy to judge stimuli according to the emotional associations they evoke without recognizing or considering contradictions. Deterrence and defense are sufficiently abstract notions to be endorsed in the framework of positive feelings about national sovereignty, independence, and self-determination. The specifics of these notions are rejected, however, as these global objectives are perceived as existing, which in turn allows people to rate national security low in salience. Thus, if deterrence is seen as useful and as working satisfactorily, support for measures to maintain this state of affairs can be very low. Psychological repression seems to work that way.

The decrease in support for defense that one might be tempted to read into our data of the past few years is probably more apparent than real, but comparable earlier data simply is not available as there was no political incentive to poll such attitudes. The rise of the peace movement and the extensive reflection of its concerns in the media have introduced items on the apparent issues of the day into surveys on which there is no strictly comparable evidence from earlier years. This is a universal feature of commercial surveys, and it can lead to dramatic exaggerations of changes in public opinion, if, for example, current rejection of INF is compared to the general acceptance of NATO in the 1960s or 1970s. In the past few years survey items have tended to go beyond the very general national security attitudes polled earlier and to focus on specific issues of budgets and weapons. It is very likely that responses to those specific stimuli would not have been much different had they been presented to respondents in the past. Nuclear weapons, or more particularly nuclear weapons in the FRG or to be exploded on her territory, have always been very unpopular in this country if one asked the appropriate questions (cf. Deutsch and Edinger 1959,27).

As there are no directly comparable longitudinal data we cannot tell for sure whether attitudes on specific issues of Western strategy have in fact become somewhat less favorable in recent years or not. If this should have been the case, however, there could be a very plausible explanation. As is well known, nuclear strategy as the key element of Western deterrence for a long time has received diverging interpretations in Western Europe and in the United States. The version presented to the public in the FRG by leading political figures and the media usually has been one extending the basic notion of "massive retaliation," stressing the key role of American strategic nuclear weapons and downplaying the importance of conventional forces. Conventional strength even tended to get interpreted as dysfunctional, as weakening the linkage of American central systems to the security of Europe. Escalation into the general nuclear exchange was described as the primary vehicle to guarantee security: "Either they (the East) leave us alone or we all perish"—so they will leave us alone. As threatening mutual annihilation is the business of the United States, rejecting improvements or increases of the West German defense contribution is consistent with this image of security. Accepting deterrence in this version meant that one could stop thinking or worrying about war and was not oneself primarily responsible for deterrence. In 1979 former Secretary of Defense Apel said in a radio interview, "Especially with respect to nuclear weapons we should kick the habit of imagining their (actual) use. Whatever we do militarily in general and in the field of nuclear armament in particular is but a part of a deterrence policy" (Yost and Glad 1982).

In recent years the interpretation of flexible response prevailing in the United States has gradually penetrated the West German debate. Its war-fighting components, "if they start a war they will with high probability lose," cannot easily be reconciled with the notions of deterrence cherished in the FRG. Dissonance can take various forms. A mild one is the feeling that endorsing deterrence as a general principle does *not* mean one is allowed to stop thinking about and preparing for war. The emotional response can be increased rejection of concrete manifestations of military defense in general and of nuclear weapons in particular. The stronger form of dissonance confuses the war-fighting interpretation of deterrent strategy with the desire actually to prepare and fight conventional and/or nuclear wars under appropriate circumstances.

This is not the place to investigate what events, what type of rhetoric by whom, or whose mistakes in enlightening and educating the West German public are to blame. There can be little doubt, however, that the public in the FRG, as in other countries, has recently been exposed to information and debates on the security of the alliance that are at variance with previous beliefs. If underneath the continuing majority support for the general notions of deterrence and defense the attitudes toward their practical requirements and toward the peace movement should have changed, this is most likely primarily due to this exposure. For a small but vociferous minority, the reaction has not been confined to those less salient attitudes on how best to provide for deterrence and defense but has extended to rejection of the Western alliance as a whole and of established approaches to national security. This pattern is characteristic of part of the peace movement, to which these things are of central concern, and lends itself to broad media coverage producing exaggerated laments about the waning of the national security consensus. For the majority, the implications of war-fighting notions of deterrent strategy are equally unpleasant and may reduce support for military spending, nuclear weapons, etc. but are not salient enough to effect widespread and dramatic alterations in the general images of national security.

We have seen that public opinion on national security in West Germany co-varies quite strongly with individuals' party preference, much stronger than with their position in the social system. This immediately presents us with a puzzle, of course, that refers back to some of the questions raised in the introduction: what is the cause and what is the effect, attitudes on national security issues or party preference?

From all established knowledge of electoral research and sociology it is safe to conclude that opinions on national security determine political behavior only for a very small fraction of the electorate. Compared to long-lasting partisan identifications and candidate orientations, issue positions generally have the lowest impact on voter choice. This is particularly true for foreign policy issues in general, and in view of the low salience of national security that has been described above it must be so for the attitudes we have been examining. It is inconceivable that more than very small minorities behave politically as they do *because* of their insights, beliefs, or positions on national security. These, however, are people that require the party they have previously been associated with to conform to their preferences on national security; if it fails to do so they will turn to someone else. This pattern certainly is descriptive of the behavior of some Green voters, and some activities of the Social Democrats over the recent years can be interpreted as attempts to prevent this from happening.

But how about the overwhelming majority of those whose political behavior is not determined by national security attitudes? Are their opinions on these matters simply products of their partisan attachment; do they only reproduce what their party tells them as they lack independent yardsticks to arrive at evaluations of their own? This is a plausible alternative interpretation of the co-variation between national security attitudes and party preferences, but not the only one. This co-variation also could be largely spurious if political behavior is determined by more or less consistent patterns of political cognitions and affective orientations vis-à-vis problems outside the area of national security that at the same time influence opinions on defense. Such patterns could be called "conservative," "liberal," "socialist," "progressive," "materialist," "nonconformist," "revolutionary," and so forth, each term denoting a specific combination of various dimensions of basic political orientations as well as its antecedents in social structure, socialization, and so on. These clusters can very likely be responsible for maintaining partisan affiliations, once acquired, but also for shaping attitudes on "new" issues that are brought in line with existing ones. For those people for whom this interpretation is valid, party preference and national security attitudes obviously have to co-vary, but there is no causal relationship. They vote for the party closest to their cluster of basic orientations and take opinions in the less salient field of national security that feel consistent with these orientations. Regarding these voters, parties to a certain extent have to follow public opinion, in order to avoid creating inconsistencies. On the other hand, they can utilize their publicized stand on particular issues to hold their supporters together by assuring them that they can feel "at home" with them even on issues other than the fundamental ones that constitute the initial allegiance.

Yet if one allows for the possibility of parties "educating" their clients on issues, particularly less salient ones, one has to take the other possibility seriously: that partisan preferences can influence issue positions. The boundary line to the second interpretation is rather ill-defined of course. There may be people who have derived their national security attitudes from their more general political convictions but are willing to be convinced by the party they feel comfortable with that these general convictions go along better with different positions on these particular matters. There might be others who derive no discernible original national security attitudes of their own and wait to be "educated." If the parties face this challenge and play their role in the formation of political will, as the West German Federal Constitution tells them to do, correlations between party loyalties and opinions on national security have to be found for these segments of the electorate as well, but they will be causal rather than spurious correlations. These individuals will not hold firmly based views on defense and security, but will tend to reproduce what the political elites they trust feed into the echo chamber of public opinion. Parties then would not be stimulated and guided by public opinion, but would direct it themselves.

Naturally, these three classes are ideal-types, and it is difficult to tell for sure for a given individual or group of individuals to which they belong. Transition over time between these categories can occur, just as people, at the same time, might belong to one class with regard to one set of issues and to another class regarding other issues. One might, for example, find people who, for whatever reasons, have strong personal convictions about the necessity of close political and military cooperation between the United States and the FRG, but have never independently thought about the nuclear threshold. Even though the lines separating the three classes are obscure, it is evident that they have a lot to do with the personal salience of the issues at stake. This insight enables us to state with some confidence what the current situation in the FRG looks like, in spite of the virtual absence of any serious recent social-psychological research attempting to assess why and under what conditions particular defense related attitudes appear in which individuals, why and for whom they become more or less salient, what the preconditions for such processes are in terms of political socialization, and why particular issues shoot to the foreground of public opinion or are taken up by elites. Even preliminary answers to these questions would require considerable research efforts, but for now we have to do with the available evidence.

This evidence tells us that the salience of national security affairs for most people in the FRG has been low and still is low. Therefore, the portions falling into the first two classes, those for whom security is an overriding concern, and those who have at least some independent concepts and notions of their own to enter into a dialogue with the elites, even though they might not feel very strongly about these issues, are most likely rather small. This has two obvious consequences for a concluding judgment on what is going on today in the Federal Republic.

First, studies that survey highly specific attitudes in the field we are dealing with are bound to produce many findings that closely follow party lines, as only few people feel so strongly about the issues that they opt for the party closest to their views, while very many of the others know so little and/or have such a low level of concern that in their responses they rely on inputs supplied by sources they trust. Second, what we are currently witnessing to a large extent is an elite problem with two facets: those few for whom national security is of paramount importance either always were attached to the party they regarded as best according to these criteria or they have switched their allegiance, possibly to the Green party.

The great majority, for whom these matters are way down in a list of much more pressing priorities, does not face this problem of having to translate marginally important views into political action. This majority is exposed to debates going on between competing elites that are designed to stabilize and motivate the respective groups of followers and that receive extensive media coverage. These elite controversies so far have changed very little the salience of security policy for the mass public, but they have made people aware that national security is another additional dimension of the polarization between the parties. But this awareness does not have significant political effects. A large majority of people nowadays realize that parties disagree on these issues, they realize the positions taken by the political elites they trust, and to a large extent they accept and reproduce these positions, so there is disagreement at the level of public opinion as well. But most of this disagreement would not take its current partisan shape, much of it would not even be there without the stimulation by debates among elites for whom these matters are of utmost importance. Ironically, these debates were initiated by the parties—responding to minority protest—because some mistakenly assumed that defense issues were sufficiently salient to be suitable for a profitable polarization of party images. The May 1983 elections have shattered this belief. In short, what we are witnessing is not mass protest against established national security policy but a combination of minority protest and the dynamics of political mass communication. As is generally the case for the social context of foreign policy, it is more important to study what is going on within activist groups—be they within or outside the established parties—than to stare at public opinion because the former shapes the latter much more strongly than vice versa.

References

Achen, Christopher H., "Mass Political Attitudes and the Survey Response," *American Political Science Review* 69 (1975): 1218–1231.

Boutwell, Jeffrey, "Politics and the Peace Movement in West Germany," *International Security* 7 (1983): 72–92.

Converse, Philip E., "Attitudes and Non-Attitudes" in E. R. Tufte, ed., *The Quantitative Analysis of Social Problems* (Reading, Mass.: Addison Wesley Publishing Company, 1970) Pp. 168–169.

Deutsch, Karl W., and Lewis J. Edinger, *Germany Rejoins the Powers* (New York: Octogon, 1973).

Just, Dieter and Peter C. Muehlens, "Zur Wechselbeziehung von Politik und Demoskopie," *Aus Politik und Zeitgeschichte* 32 (1981): 63–68.

Raeder, Hans-Georg, "Meinungsbildung und Meinungsaenderung zur Sicherheitspolitik unter dem Einfluss politischer Ereignisse," in R. Zoll, ed., *Sicherheit und Militaer* (Opladen: Westdeutscher Verlag, 1982) Pp. 66–119.

Russett, Bruce M., and Donald R. Deluca, "Theater Nuclear Forces: Public Opinion in Western Europe," *Political Science Quarterly* 98 (1983): 179–196.

Schoessler, Dietmar, and Erich Weede, *West German Elite Views on National Security and Foreign Policy Issues* (Koenigstein: Atheneum, 1978).

Shaffer, Stephen M., *West European Public Opinion on Key Security Issues, 1981–1982* (Washington, D.C.: U.S. International Communications Agency, R-10-82, 1982).

Siegmann, Heinrich, *Sicherheitspolitik im Wandel der Elitemeinungen: Umfrageergebnisse der letzten zwanzig Fahre* (Berlin: Wissenschaftszentrum, IIVG/dp 83/115, 1983).

Yost, David S., "West German Party Politics and Theater Nuclear Modernization Since 1977," *Armed Forces and Society* 8 (1982): 525–560.

Zoll, Ralf, "Sicherheitspolitik und Streitkraefte im Spiegel oeffentlicher Meinungen in den Vereinigten Staaten von Amerika und der Bundesrepublik Deutschland," in R. Zoll, ed., *Sicherheit und Militaer* (Opladen: Westdeutscher Verlag, 1982) Pp. 33–65.

Appendix C Sources

In the tables months and years of surveys are generally given together with acronyms denoting sources. Sources of data reported in this study are as follows:

BMV: Data from surveys conducted for the Federal Ministry of Defense (*Bundesministerium der Verteidigung*) within its "Verteidigungsklima" series. These data have been taken from reports supplied by BMV.

CC: Data from surveys conducted by Contest-Census, Frankfurt, directly provided by CC.

FGW: Data from the regular ZDF-Politbarometer surveys conducted by Forschungsgruppe Wahlen, Mannheim. These data have either been taken from tables supplied by FGW or (for 1980) computed from the original FGW-datasets.

IfD: Data from surveys conducted by Institut fuer Demoskopie, Allensbach. This data has been taken from IfD's *Jahrbuch der Oeffentlichen Meinung (later Allensbacher Jahrbuch der Demoskopie)*. Several more recent results have been directly provided by IfD.

PIB: Data from surveys conducted for the Federal Office for Press and Information (*Presse-und Informationsamt der Bundesregierung*). These data have been taken from reports supplied by PIB.

SFK: Data from surveys conducted for Sozialwissenschaftliches Forschungsinstitut der Konrad-Adenauer-Stiftung, St. Augustin. These data have been computed from the original SFK-datasets.

SOWI: Data from surveys conducted for Sozialwissenschaftliches Institut der Bundeswehr, Munich. Unless otherwise indicated, these data have been taken from tables in Zoll (1982).

ZA: Data from surveys conducted by various contractors for various customers, supplied through Zentralarchiv fuer empirische Sozialforschung, Cologne. Surveys are identified by the studynumber assigned to them by the Central Archive. These data have been computed from the original data sets.

5 *Public Opinion and Atlantic Defense in Italy*

SERGIO A. ROSSI

Introduction

For the last four or five years, Italy has not been spared the wave of popular criticism of national security and defense priorities that has been unleashed by the NATO double-track decision of December 1979. In many Italian cities, we have witnessed familiar scenes of antinuclear protest and peace demonstrations staged by various organizations, from leftist political parties to Catholic movements. However, there is a striking difference between the situation in Italy and that in other European countries, notably West Germany, the Netherlands, and Belgium, where the pacifist and antinuclear movement has had a serious impact on government attitudes and policies. It is widely acknowledged that the pacifist movement in Italy, although it has received considerable attention by the media and certain support from some political quarters, has failed to reach a "critical mass," that is, the intensity and the political weight necessary to affect the government's foreign and defense policy.

The principal reasons for this failure are twofold. On the one hand, the Italian peace movement lacks genuine cultural roots; its behavior and objectives are often perceivéd as imported or borrowed from foreign models and experiences. On the other hand, the movement's credibility has been diminished by its growing internal politicization and the struggle between Radicals and Communists over its control (Rossi and Ilari 1983).

The ineffectiveness of the Italian peace movement in its activities against the deployment of Euromissiles in Sicily help to underline two salient features of the Italian situation: the still largely elitist nature of foreign and defense policy, even on issues crucial for the future of the country, and the weak interdependence between popular and political consensus on these issues. The elitist nature of Italian defense and foreign policy is best symbolized by the two most crucial choices of the postwar period, the decisions to join NATO and to participate in the foundation of the EEC. These were taken by a small group of dedicated politicians and diplomats, preempting the consensus of a still uncertain parliament and of a public opinion rather divided during the cold war period, not least because of the presence of a strong Communist party. Moreover, the public at large seems unlikely to demand a change in this. A survey

Table 5.1 Public interest in international politics by sex and age (DXSO 5/83)

	Total	Men	Women	18-34	35-54	Over 54
		Sex			Age	
Great or moderate interest	35	48	23	41	35	31
Little or no interest	63	51	75	58	64	67
No opinion	2	1	2	1	2	2

conducted in spring 1983 by the Doxa Institute, the best known public opinion research institute in Italy, with a sample of almost 2,000 individuals, showed that only 35 percent of Italians have great or moderate interest in international politics, whereas 63 percent have little or no interest. The percentage of interest, as is shown in Tables 5.1 and 5.2, is somewhat higher for men and for young people (age 18 to 34). It reaches a remarkable 61 percent for people with high school or university degrees, and 63 percent for people belonging to the upper and upper middle class. Conversely, interest is close to the national average for people with average education (junior high school) or belonging to the middle class.

The "elite" character of those who follow foreign policy issues more closely is confirmed by the breakdown of interest in foreign affairs by political affiliation (Table 5.3). The highest degree of interest in international politics is registered by the Radicals and Proletarian Democrats (66 percent) on the left of the political spectrum, and by the Republicans and Liberals (60 percent) on the center right. All these parties are small political formations and have images of being elitist or vanguard parties due to their intellectual activism and quality of leadership. Conversely, interest in international politics is significantly lower for followers of all the mass parties, the Communists (39 percent), the Socialists (36 percent), and the Christian Democrats (29 percent).

Table 5.2 Public interest in international politics by education and social class (DXSO 5/83)

	High School or University	Junior High School	Elementary Schooling or none	Upper Upper Middle	Middle	Lower Lower Middle
	Education			Social Class		
Great or moderate interest	61	40	22	63	41	33
Little or no interest	39	59	75	37	58	75
No opinion	—	1	3	—	1	2

Table 5.3   Public interest in international politics by political affiliation (DXSO 5/83)

	PCI Commu- nists	PSI Social- ists	DC Chris- tian Demo- crats	PR-PDUP Radical and Extreme Left	MSI Right	PRI-PLI Repub- licans and Lib- erals	PSDI Social Demo- crats	No party iden- tifi- cation
Great or moderate interest	39	36	29	66	36	60	40	29
Little or no interest	59	63	70	34	65	40	61	68
No opinion	2	1	1	–	–	–	–	2

Can one safely assume, therefore, that the impact of Italian public opinion on decision making in foreign and defense policy is negligible? Certainly this has been the case in the past, as Bechelloni (1967) points out in one of the few essays written on this subject. One is tempted to give more or less the same evaluation for the present, at least judging from the most recent Italian general elections held on 26 June 1983. In the campaign, defense and foreign policy issues, especially the problem of Euromissiles, were shrewdly held in the background and drowned under dominant economic and social questions. With the partial exception of the Communists, there existed a tacit agreement among the main political parties that this should be so. This was done as was confirmed to this author by more than one candidate in order not to scare or overload an electorate already highly confused by other issues of Italian politics.

Still, there is some merit in being reluctant to proclaim a rather weak interdependence between popular opinion and political consensus. Although it is almost impossible, because of the paucity of data and research, to assess the dynamics and extent of this interrelationship with a reasonable degree of confidence, there is little doubt that the weight and influence of public opinion in Italy has increased, especially in the last decade or two. The concept of "public opinion" remains today rather vague and abstract even in the minds of opinion leaders and opinion makers, as was shown by a recent survey among the chief editors of the most influential Italian daily newspapers and weeklies. Nevertheless, there is a common feeling, expressed by Piero Ottone, former editor in chief of *Il Corriere della Sera*, that public opinion in Italy "is able to influence how the State is run to a lesser extent than in any other democratic country, but it is evolving quickly, and the day is not far away when it will succeed in making its voice heard."[1]

[1]*identikit di un Fantasma* "Nuova Società," 26 febbraio 1983, p. 49.

At least some preconditions for such an evolution are present: according to a December 1982 survey by ISEGI (an organization of publishers of daily newspapers), average weekly newspaper circulation has increased by 4.2 million over the last seven years, while the population above age 15 has increased over the same period by only 3.1 million. Moreover, there is the impact of television, not only of the three national programs, but also of the private networks. Some of them now have nationwide broadcasts, and over the last two years they have competed successfully for quality of programs, including foreign news and special features. One example is the controversial NBC series on *The Defense of the United States*. If the readership of newspapers and the audience of television as well as the general coverage of international and defense issues by the media have expanded, this evolution has also been stimulated by the more active foreign policy pursued by the Italian government within NATO and in the Mediterranean and Middle East over the last four years. Its landmarks range from the double-track decision to the treaty guaranteeing Malta's neutrality and to the participation in the multinational peace-keeping force in Lebanon. At the same time, the receptiveness of the population to security issues has also improved, with the "democratization" of the educational system in the last two decades following the 1962 law requiring mandatory schooling until age 14 and with the university reform of the late seventies. With open admission to all university departments being granted to all students having completed five years of high school, the number of university students in Italy rose from about 250,000 in 1960 to over one million in 1978–1979. Today about 30 percent of young people in the 25 to 34 age group have received a university education.

Thus the basis for more adequate information and education of Italian public opinion on international and security issues has been improved, at least to a certain extent. Much remains to be done, however, in terms of introducing enough courses and seminars on strategic studies, international politics, and national security at the university level. Moreover, this does not necessarily imply that these new opportunities have been exploited by the population in order to attain a better knowledge of defense and security issues.

A better degree of information and understanding does not automatically translate into popular support for the course adopted by the political elite. On the contrary, there is strong suspicion that the effect, at least in the short run, might well take the opposite direction, especially on crucial issues of defense and national security, which have always been controversial even among experts. These suspicions or fears of what a "democratized public opinion" actually might mean are reflected in the justification offered by politicians for trying to keep the issue of cruise missile deployment away from the electoral debate. Thus Italy is in an awkward situation, where political elites are not only reluctant but sometimes not even aware of the need to make available information and, above all, to offer political leadership on security issues as the easiest way to further popular consensus.

This chapter attempts to provide additional insight into some of the issues raised thus far. It describes the attitudes and perceptions of Italian public opinion toward the four main themes of this volume: the Soviet Union, security, deterrence, and the Allies. In the first part of the chapter, we will describe attitudes and also try to analyze the evolution of these perceptions over a relatively extended period of time, depending on the availability of data. In the second part we will try to relate, to the extent possible, opinions expressed on the four main themes to social class, age, education, interest or participation in politics, and party identification of respondents. This will allow us to point out important differences between positions of the general public and those of particular social groups. In the third and concluding section, a brief analysis of consistency among opinions related to the main four themes is also included.

Finally, a brief comment about sources and data is in order. There are many shortcomings and gaps in the availability of relevant data and sources, partially due to the situation of relative indifference to foreign and defense issues that has been described. Throughout the whole postwar period until recently, specific surveys and opinion polls on these types of issues have been remarkably few, and it is noteworthy that most have been conducted on behalf of the United States Information Agency. We are indebted to this agency for having made available to us these data, many of them previously unpublished. In the last three years, more frequent opinion polls on international and defense issues were commissioned by media that have felt the need to probe this particular field. We were able to use the data from the two international surveys organized by the Atlantic Institute for International Affairs and Louis Harris in 1982 and 1983, which were sponsored in Italy by *Il Sole 24 Ore*. Finally, for detailed data on public opinion by social groups (reported mainly in the second part of this chapter) we relied heavily on a survey conducted by Doxa in April and May 1983 on behalf of *Il Sole 24 Ore*.

Images of the Soviet Union

PERCEPTIONS OF THE MILITARY BALANCE

In Western Europe the common reference made to the "Soviet threat" tends to encompass indiscriminately various existing conceptions of the Soviet Union as an adversary. Such an excessively generic evaluation carries substantial risks of misunderstanding. It would be necessary to elaborate in more detail popular perception of the political, military, and economic factors embodied in what is called the Soviet threat and also to clarify the correlations among these factors, in order to gain a better impression of what underlying popular images of the Soviet Union really are. Unfortunately, our data only permit us to begin the process.

In October 1981, 41 percent of Italians considered the United States and the USSR roughly equal in total military strength, while 24 percent thought the United States were ahead, and 29 percent believed the USSR

Table 5.4   Italian perception of the US-USSR military balance (DXUS)

	11/69	4/77	5/81	7/81	10/81
US ahead	44	22	20	21	24
USSR ahead	13	17	28	27	29
About equal	25	34	45	44	41
No opinion	18	27	7	8	6

superior. As shown in Table 5.4, this marks an important change in Italian public perceptions from a decade earlier. A gradual erosion of American global military superiority is clearly seen, although the policies of the Reagan administration, with their accent on increased defense spending (widely reported in the media), do appear to have influenced these judgments. There has been a steady increase in the number of those who feel the growth of Soviet military power has produced Soviet superiority (from 13 percent in 1969 to 17 percent in 1977 to 29 percent at the end of 1981). But the evolution of the military balance has not been generally interpreted by many Italians as a transition from American to Soviet superiority. Most believe that the changing balance has evolved to a condition of rough global parity. When asked about the possible evolution of the balance over the next five years, Italian opinion showed 25 percent believing in a return to United States military superiority, 14 percent believing in a transition to Soviet superiority, and 44 percent persuaded that essential parity would continue.

Perceptions of the evolution of the Soviet-American nuclear balance parallel the general trends just described, as is shown in Table 5.5. The decade 1972–1982 has witnessed a belief in the growing reality of Soviet nuclear forces, that the U.S. nuclear arsenal has actually decreased or at least remained stable, and that the result has been a situation of parity. An approximately equal percentage of respondents believes in the existence of parity in both nuclear and overall weapons. People also expect a situation of nuclear parity to continue over the next five years (43 percent in April 1982), while the chances of attaining superiority by either the United States or the USSR are almost evenly split (20 against 19 percent).

Table 5.5   Italian perception of nuclear strength US vs. USSR (DXUS)

	6/72	3/77	4/82
US ahead	31	25	18
USSR ahead	12	17	32
About equal	29	37	42
No opinion	28	22	8

When asked in October 1981 for judgments of the European theater balance, 22 percent of Italians perceived the United States ahead in nuclear forces, 32 percent believed in Soviet nuclear superiority, and 39 percent perceived a situation of parity. In the same poll, 27 percent of respondents indicated that the United States was superior in conventional forces in Europe, 32 percent indicated Soviet conventional superiority in Europe, while those who perceived parity decreased from 39 to 30 percent (DXUS 10/81). Finally, when asked to express personal preferences about the global balance of forces, 29 percent of those polled preferred the United States to be stronger than the USSR, and only three percent wanted Soviet military superiority; the overwhelming majority (64 percent) supported the maintenance of parity. While substantially in favor of overall East-West equality, the Italians clearly leave no doubt about their pro-American sentiments.

THE MILITARY THREAT

The available data clearly show that Italian public opinion considers it a Soviet objective to shift further the balance of power. In October 1981, 82 percent of Italians indicated the attainment of military superiority over the United States to be the principal aim of Soviet foreign policy, while only 13 percent thought the Soviet aim to be the attainment of military parity with the United States (DXUS). Equally clear, according to more recent data, is a perception that the scope of Soviet influence in the world is increasing (37 percent) rather than declining (six percent) (DXLS 5/83). Moreover, these same data indicate the Italians do not seem to minimize the possibility that the Soviet Union might start a nuclear war to extend its area of influence: 40 percent think such an initiative possible, 36 percent not, and 24 percent remain uncertain. Despite the fragmented nature of these data, when taken together, there can be little doubt that the Italian public does not evaluate Soviet power as benign. These data may reflect the increasing attention given by the media to the issue of intermediate nuclear forces in Europe and the increase in Soviet SS-20 missiles.

On the other hand, fear of a Soviet attack against Europe has been consistently low in Italy. In July 1981 only 21 percent of Italians thought that the USSR would be prepared to launch an attack against Western Europe in the next five years, while 70 percent considered this possibility either unlikely or not at all likely. In April 1982 there was a slight increase in the number of respondents who thought a Soviet attack possible (23 percent vs. 69 percent). It is interesting to note that in March 1981, 21 percent of Italian respondents believed that the Soviet Union could interfere with Western access to Middle East oil, while 28 percent saw no great risk, and 36 percent saw no risk at all. But it is difficult to assess the real significance of these data, because they are sparse and drawn from different surveys.

Table 5.6   In favor of constraining improvement of East-West relations (DXUS 3/81)

Soviets invade Poland	35
Soviets interfere with access to Middle East oil	29
Soviets refuse to remove forces from Afghanistan	17
Soviets exert severe political pressure on West Europe	16
Soviets invade China	9
Soviets support military conflicts in Africa	8
Soviets supply military aid to antigovernment forces in Latin America	8
Soviets do none of these	7
Don't know	20

RELATIONS WITH THE SOVIET UNION

In March 1981, Italians were asked which events would cause them to favor Italy suspending further efforts to improve East-West relations. In the list offered, several events that later materialized were included. The results are given in Table 5.6.

The imposition of martial law in Poland gave rise to a series of additional surveys on Italian public attitudes on appropriate policies to be pursued. In April 1982, people were asked what attitude Italy should take in its trade relations with the USSR. Seven percent of those polled favored increasing these relations, 25 percent preferred a decrease, and the majority (58 percent) were in favor of maintaining trade relations with the Soviets at the existing level (DXUS). On the issue of high-technology trade with the East, one found a preference for the continuation of sales to the Soviets (Table 5.7).

Nevertheless, the Italian public was not ready to make special concessions, such as low-interest loans and credits, in order to promote trade with the USSR: 28 percent was in favor of special concessions but 60 percent was against (DXUS 4/82). The Italian public generally favored continuation of the Siberian natural gas pipeline to Western Europe (64 percent in favor of the pipeline, and only 28 percent against) and even

Table 5.7   Restrictions on selling high technology to USSR (DXUS)

	6/81	4/82
Strongly agree	16	15
Somewhat agree	22 38	27 42
Somewhat disagree	29	28
Strongly disagree	18 47	18 46
Don't know	14	12

Table 5.8   Effects on Italy of Soviet gas purchase (DXUS)

	6/81	4/82
Makes Italy vulnerable	37	37
Will moderate Soviet actions	15	21
Not much effect either way	30	23
Don't know	19	19

considered that it would help overcome present economic difficulties if trade relations with the USSR and the other East European countries were increased: 48 percent agree, 28 percent disagree, and 31 percent don't know (LHIA 5/83).

Other data add some contours to this picture. For instance, when asked whether buying energy products and raw materials from the USSR was more likely to make Italy vulnerable to Soviet political pressures, or was more likely to result in Italy having a moderating influence on Soviet actions, respondents did not show excessive confidence in the Soviets (Table 5.8).

When confronted with the choice of Italy making the best trading deals it could with the Soviets, even if it harmed relations with the United States, or coordinating Italian trade policy with the United States, even if it meant trading less with the USSR, Italian opinion was almost evenly split (Table 5.9). There is thus a certain ambiguity when the political dimension of trade is introduced. A utilitarian mood and spirit of national independence seems to prevail over the attachment to the Atlantic bond, but with a sizeable margin of uncertainty that could significantly change the picture during a moment of real need for choice.

It is difficult to draw definite conclusions about Italian attitudes on preferred policies toward the Soviet Union. As might be expected, the data embody a certain ambivalence. This may be ascribable both to the general volatility of public opinion and to the difficulty to ascertain its orientation with great accuracy where detailed questions of policy are explored. In general, however, it seems clear that despite their perception

Table 5.9   Italian autonomy in Soviet trade policy vs. coordination with the US (DXUS)

	6/81	4/82
It is better to:		
– make the best deal with the USSR	45	41
– coordinate trade policy toward the USSR with the US	35	39
Depends on type of trade	9	12
Don't know	11	9

of a shifting balance, Italians consider that trading relations with the Soviet Union should be maintained.

GOODWILL AND RELIABILITY OF THE SOVIET UNION

It is worthwhile putting these data into perspective by comparing them with results (unfortunately not homogeneous) from public opinion surveys taken in the fifties and in the sixties (Bechelloni 1967). Unlike in some of the other countries studied in this book, it is clear that the general image of the Soviet Union has improved in Italian public opinion, especially during the détente process of the sixties and the early seventies. Recent international behavior of the Soviet Union (such as the Afghan crisis or the shooting down of a South Korean airliner) has damaged its image in Italian and Western European opinion, but it is uncertain how permanent this will be.

The long-term trend in the attitude of Italian public opinion toward the Soviet Union is given in Table 5.10. A generally unfavorable orientation is fairly persistent. A decade after the end of World War II, in the cold war atmosphere of the early fifties, unfavorable opinion of the USSR among the Italians prevailed by 30 percent over those who had a favorable opinion of the Soviets. The Hungarian crisis added considerably to this feeling, so that by November 1956 the negative image reached a peak of 60 percent. The speed with which the impact of events dissipates is demonstrated by the fact that the balance of unfavorable opinion toward the USSR dropped to 34 percent in 1957 and to only 14 percent in 1958. Continuing this trend, in 1959 the Soviets scored for the first time a majority of favorable opinion among the Italians (two percent), probably due to the impact of the first Soviet successes in the conquest of space.

Between 1960 and 1972 negative opinion of the USSR again prevailed, with unfavorable peaks ranging from seven to 20 percent. In 1973 the negative difference narrowed to a mere one percent, and in 1978 a favorable balance of five percent surfaced (highly or rather favorable 49 percent, unfavorable 44 percent, no opinion seven percent). Clearly, the East-West détente process was yielding its results also at the public-opinion level. Eventually, in the early eighties, the abrupt shift in Soviet foreign policy underlined by the invasion of Afghanistan and other initiatives connected with the nuclear balance of intermediate forces in Europe, not to speak of the Polish crisis, led to a dramatic shift in Italian public opinion back to the negative judgments of earlier periods. In October 1981 those who had a favorable opinion of the USSR dropped to 21 percent, while those unfavorable climbed to 73 percent.

A few months later, in February 1982, positive opinion dwindled further to 13 percent, but negative opinion had also decreased somewhat from 73 to 68 percent (DXUS). The beginning of a limited recovery of the Soviet image was probably in the cards, with people thinking less of

Table 5.10   Evolution of the Soviet image in Italian public opinion (DXUS)
             (favorable minus unfavorable responses)

10/54	−30	
12/55	−29	
11/56	−60	Soviet intervention in Hungary
11/57	−34	
10/58	−14	
12/59	+ 2	Soviet successes in space
7/60	−19	
7/61	− 7	
6/62	−20	
2/63	−15	
3/64	−15	
7/65	−19	
11/69	− 9	Salt II Treaty and
4/72	− 8	East-West détente
4/73	− 1	
10/78	+ 5	
10/81	−52	Soviet invasion of Afghanistan
2/82	−55	Polish crisis, INF
4/83	−43	Andropovean leadership (DXSO)

Afghanistan and worrying less about the Polish situation. With the advent
of the new Andropov leadership in fall 1982, the hope for some internal
reforms (especially of the economy) and renewed negotiations on arms
control may have grown. At least this could be the reading of the
improvement in the negative balance of opinion from − 55 to − 43 over
the last year, according to data of May 1983. They are from a different
survey but conducted by the same polling institute, and they also predate
the incident with the South Korean airliner in September 1983.

The image of the USSR in Italian public opinion is undoubtedly linked
to what may be described as the perceived degree of goodwill and
reliability of the Soviets. In April 1982, for instance, only 11 percent of
Italians thought that the policy of the Kremlin was intended to promote
peace, while 76 percent thought that it pushed instead toward war. But
whatever opinion the Italians may have of a country such as the USSR,
which is still rather unknown in its complex reality, it cannot be said that
the Italians do not have a certain degree of respect for the Soviet Union,
although this respect has been subject to considerable variations.

As we can see from Table 5.11, the overall respect for the USSR during
the last fifteen years has never registered a percentage below 25 percent.
On the other hand, the lack of respect for the USSR in Italian public
opinion has never dropped below 50 percent during the same period, and

Table 5.11   Degree of respect in Italy for the Soviet Union (DXUS)

	7/65	11/69	4/72	10/81
Great respect	6	11	9	4
Moderate respect	20	17	32	21
Little respect	23	30	33	40
Almost no respect	27	24	21	31
No opinion	24	17	6	4

even increased to 71 percent in 1981. Most interesting is that the percentage of those Italians who had no opinion or were uncertain dropped heavily in the meantime, adding to the majority of negative opinion.

Another indication of the general attitude of the Italian public toward the Soviet Union comes from a recent poll conducted for *Il Sole 24 Ore* (DOXA 6/83). The degree of confidence in the Soviet political system was rather low (1.34) if compared with other political systems, such as in France (1.70), Germany (1.97), the United States (1.99) and, surprisingly, in Italy (2.09). The same index for Poland was 1.17. The index ranges from a minimum of one, or no confidence, to a maximum of four, and one cannot help but note that the Italian public generally has little confidence in any political system. Perhaps most interesting is the extent to which the shadow of the USSR varies with the political persuasion of the respondent. Confidence in the Soviet political system ranks fourth in the opinion of Italian Communists, just after Italy, France, and Germany, but drops considerably in the opinion of followers of all the other parties from Socialists to Christian Democrats and to the lay group.

In conclusion, it can be stated that the general attitude of Italian public opinion toward the USSR has been rather negative. Politically speaking, Italians have not shown too high a degree of confidence in the goodwill and reliability of the Soviet Union, with the remarkable and constant exception of economic and business relations. Major events such as the intervention in Afghanistan have always brought forth a stronger negative judgment of the Soviets, but the pattern has been one that demonstrates a consistent tendency toward improvement once memories begin to fade. This is in contrast to the perceptions of a shifting military balance and a certain increased perception of threat, and in contrast to the more across-the-board deterioration of the Soviet image that one finds in other countries of the Alliance.

Images of Security

FEAR OF WAR

Today more than ever, the boundaries between national or internal, personal or physical, security seem to lose any well-defined contours:

Table 5.12 Major concerns for Italians (LHAI)

	10/82	5/83	Variation
Unemployment	61	67	+6
Crime	62	61	−1
Threat of war	42	44	+2
Inflation	46	43	−3
Nuclear weapons	21	33	+12
Social injustice	25	27	+2
Poor political leadership	26	27	+1
The energy crisis	22	23	−1
Excessive Government spending	16	21	+5
Inadequate defense	7	6	−1

Note: Multiple answers were possible

multidimensional threats to the security of both individuals and nations generate perceptions of a bewilderingly complex threat environment in which military threats are only one element, and perhaps not even the most important one.

A survey of May 1983 (Table 5.12) indicated that 44 percent of Italians consider the threat of war one of their greatest concerns for themselves and their country. It is significant that the threat of war ranks third in a list of ten major concerns in Italy, just after unemployment (67 percent) and crime (61 percent), and before inflation (43 percent), (LHAI).

The high saliency of the threat of war seems to be connected to a high level of dissatisfaction with the general situation of Italian security: 59 percent of those polled considered Italian security as fragile and only 29 percent as fairly stable (DXLS 5/83). However, the majority of Italians polled do not consider a new world war "probable" in the next decade (DXEB 12/82), indicating that concern about the threat of war and its probability are decoupled to some degree. More specifically, perceptions of the probability of military conflict seem to be much more responsive to perceptions of the international environment at each point in time than the more generalized concerns regarding "threat of war" or the state of Italian security. Thus Table 5.13 shows that this kind of perception was very strong during the cold war (57 percent in 1953), decreased sharply in the sixties and the seventies, increased again in 1980 to 32 percent (crisis of détente and NATO decision on nuclear weapons in Europe), and shrunk to 14 percent by the end of 1982. At the same time, it appears that the fear of war has grown over the past year. According to LHAI data, over 50% of those polled in October 1983 responded that the threat of war was of major concern, up from 42% a year earlier.

Regarding specific threat perceptions, a survey taken in March 1981 (DXUS) indicated that 60 percent of Italians feared above all the

188   SERGIO A. ROSSI

Table 5.13   Probability of a new world war in the next decade (DXEB 12/82)
(Percentage "likely")

11/53	57
1/63	6
4/71	13
11/71	14
4/80	32
10/81	18
10/82	14

possibility of a cut-off of Middle Eastern oil; 51 percent feared increased tension between the two superpowers; 22 percent a possible Soviet intervention in Poland; 17 percent a long-term buildup of Soviet military forces; eight percent increased competition with the United States and Japan; seven percent Soviet military presence of Afghanistan; only five percent feared the threat of economic demands by developing countries.

SALIENCE AND ACCEPTANCE OF NATIONAL DEFENSE

As we have already seen, only six percent of Italians consider an inadequate defense posture as one of the major concerns for their country (Table 5.12), and only 12 percent believe that independence and national sovereignty are indispensable for real peace. These attitudes have remained relatively stable over a long period. In this context, according to DXUS data of July 1981, 45 percent of Italians thought that the best policy for their country's security would be to begin arms control negotiations with the USSR as soon as possible and not try first to strengthen NATO's nuclear forces; 14 percent thought it better to seek to strengthen NATO before beginning arms control negotiations with the USSR, and 26 percent were in favor of simultaneously seeking to strengthen NATO's nuclear forces and beginning arms control negotiations (DXUS). Moreover, 50 percent of Italians were opposed to giving more active attention to national defense. In another survey of March 1981, only 22 percent were

Table 5.14   Italian attitudes toward defense spending (DXUS)

	10/80	3/81	4/82
Increase defense spending	10	16	16
Decrease defense spending	39	43	46
Keep at present level	36	36	34
Don't know	19	6	4

in favor of improving national defense to strengthen NATO; 60 percent favored increasing arms control efforts; only seven percent favored strengthening Italy's defense, as well as greater arms control efforts (DXUS).

In sum, these data indicate a rather low public acceptance of national defense efforts in Italy. However, according to the same poll in 1981, 68 percent of Italians supported military resistance against a Soviet conventional attack, and 39 percent against a nuclear attack. At the same time, 29 percent considered military resistance against a conventional attack useless and 49 percent against a nuclear attack. A crucial factor in conditioning Italian public opinion on national security seems to be the public image of the Italian military. As indicated by unpublished surveys conducted by the Ministry of Defense, many Italians seem to perceive their armed forces as having a rather low level of competence. This may be also borne out by the discrepancy between support for national defense efforts (generally low) and support for European-wide defense efforts: according to some polls up to 37 percent of Italians supported a strengthening of European defense.

ATTITUDES ON DEFENSE SPENDING

Quite naturally, these attitudes carry over into the question of defense spending. Thus, polls show an increase from 39 to 46 percent of the respondents supporting reductions in defense spending while support for greater defense outlays fluctuated from 1980 to 1982 between ten and 16 percent. The growing economic worries seemed to have contributed also to reducing the percentage of those who were uncertain from 19 to four percent (Table 5.14). In addition, one poll shows that 68 percent of its respondents were convinced that present economic problems could be overcome if the government would cut defense spending to improve social services.

As already indicated, cultural factors as well as economic and social considerations heavily influence Italian attitudes toward defense spending. There seems to be a generalized perception that defense money is wasted and spent more on "image-enhancing" activities of the military than on improving operational capabilities. In addition, distrust of the military hierarchy and the perception of mismanagement and corruption seem to contribute to the low public willingness to support defense spending and national defense.

Images of Deterrence

ACCEPTANCE OF DETERRENCE

The growth of organized protest against nuclear weapons in the West has been one of the main factors leading experts and politicians to take a hard look at current NATO strategy and to evaluate, for instance, the necessary political, economic and technological conditions that would allow a shift away from early reliance on nuclear use and greater reliance on conventional forces. In this process it is certainly critical for policy makers to understand the true extent to which the way the West provides itself with security is considered more threatening than the Soviet Union.

It is difficult in Italy to find any survey that deals directly with the general acceptance of deterrence by the public at large. A rough indication of the Italian attitude toward the present international situation, where mutual deterrence is provided by two opposing politico-military blocs, can be found in the Makno survey of February 1983 already mentioned. When asked whether it was possible to think of an international political situation without the two blocs (pro-American and pro-Soviet), 39 percent responded that it would be desirable, but not possible; 27 percent considered it undesirable because the blocs are the only guarantee of peace; 18 percent felt it was possible; 14 percent did not know. Positive acceptance of the present situation was thus not very high. But if we add the number of Italians who reluctantly believe that there is no other choice, the result is a total of 66 percent who accept in one way or another the international system of today.

Conversely, 18 percent of Italians do not accept this situation, and the refusal of the concept of blocs (and of deterrence?) is highest among those between 15 and 19 years of age (27 percent). Only 17 percent of them show a positive acceptance of blocs, and 36 percent show a reluctant acceptance, totaling 53 percent. The percentage of uncertainty is relatively high in all age groups.

ROLE OF NUCLEAR WEAPONS

From November 1982 to May 1983, the percentage of Italians who considered nuclear weapons one of the major concerns for their country increased by 12 percent, from 21 to 33 percent (LHIA). Concern for nuclear weapons is higher among young people under 24, middle-class individuals, and Socialists (37 percent in all three groups) and highest among Communists (41 percent). This considerable growth of concern about nuclear weapons seems to follow, although with a certain delay, a general trend in Western European opinion.

Moreover, roughly the same number of Italians favored unilateral nuclear disarmament of their national territory as opposed it (47 to 49 percent); a rather large 31 percent of Italians favored U.S. unilateral disarmament, although 63 percent were opposed (DXUS 7/81). Finally, although there has been some fluctuation of opinion, and the 1983 data in Table 5.15 is not strictly comparable to the 1981/1982 data, the percentage of respondents against any use of nuclear weapons is quite high. It is difficult to say with any certainty what the reasons for the fluctuation are or whether opposition to nuclear use is going to stabilize at a higher level.

Table 5.15 Italian attitudes toward use of nuclear weapons

	DXUS 7/81	DXUS 10/81	DXUS 4/82	LHAI 10/83
NATO should not use nuclear weapons of any kind under any circumstances	42	55	38	47
NATO should use nuclear weapons only if the USSR uses them first in attacking Western Europe	38	31	42	28
NATO should use nuclear weapons to defend itself if a Soviet attack by conventional forces threatens to overwhelm NATO forces	12	10	14	5
Don't know	7	4	6	20

But it is significant that on only one occasion (4/83) were those opposing any use of nuclear weapons outweighed by those accepting nuclear use under either of the other scenarios offered.

NEW MISSILES IN EUROPE

In July 1981, 40 percent of Italians opposed Intermediate Nuclear Forces (INF) deployment in Western Europe (and also on their national territory). In October of the same year, after the indication in mid-August that Comiso (Sicily) would be a future base for 112 NATO cruise missiles, this percentage rose to 50 percent. It decreased to 44 percent in April 1982, but by April 1983 was up to 54 percent. At the same time, as Table 5.16 shows, 35 to 40 percent of Italians have been consistently in favor of a conditional INF deployment (that is, linked to arms control negotiations with the USSR), and around ten percent have favored unconditional INF deployment. This divided opinion on INF was confirmed by an October 1981 poll in which 49 percent of respondents had confidence in a likely success of INF negotiations between the United States and the USSR in Geneva (in about two years time), 40 percent were sceptical, and 11 percent were uncertain (DXUS).

An important aspect, however, is that roughly half of Italian respondents have consistently shown confidence in INF deterrence, believing that INF deployment in Europe will help to prevent a Soviet attack (see Table 5.17), whereas roughly one-third have believed, on the contrary, that INF will make an attack more likely.

The high percentage of uncertainty (19 percent) has led pollsters to test the degree of information existing on the INF issue. The results shown in Table 5.18 give a good idea of the extent to which there is real confusion or lack of knowledge of the factual situation (the situation was even worse in Germany and Britain). The rather poor information levels on strategic

Table 5.16   Support for INF deployment in Europe (DXUS)

	3/81	7/81	10/81	4/82	7/82	4/83
Unconditional opposition	54	40	50	44	45	54
Accept only if arms talks with USSR have failed	21	27	25	30	31	25
Accept only if there are arms talks with USSR at the same time	12	15	13	10	10	10
Accept without first insisting on arms talks	6	10	9	8	9	7
Don't know	7	8	4	7	–	–

issues in Italy and the equally poor success of the government and the mass media in adequately informing the public seem evident. This low level of information on politico-military affairs, in spite of the increasing availability of data and news, would indicate that people simply don't care very much about these issues. This is confirmed by data showing that international politics ranked 15th in a list of 21 subjects that the Italians follow in the various media (DXSO 5/83). In the same survey, the first three places were taken by news on health and medicine, problems of youth, and social services.

Hostility toward INF deployment, however, does not seem to depend on the degree of information, as shown in Tables 5.19 and 5.20. When questions were preceded by the information that the USSR had 450 nuclear warheads on SS-20 medium-range missiles targeted against Western Europe, although NATO did not have anything of this kind targeted against Soviet territory, acceptance of INF deployment only rose from 35 to 42 percent, and opposition did not decrease significantly (from 60 to 51 percent). Although of low but perhaps increasing saliency, nuclear missiles in Europe thus remain an issue of emotion, linked to a generic fear of nuclear weapons and to a reluctance to accept the hard logic of nuclear deterrence.

As it is shown in Table 5.20, opposition to INF deployment in Italy increased from 48 percent in July 1981 to 52 percent in April 1982, even

Table 5.17   Perception of INF deterrence (DXUS)

	7/81	10/81	4/82
INF in Europe:			
Help to prevent a Soviet attack	52	47	48
Make attack more likely	29	37	33
Don't know	19	16	19

Table 5.18   Italian awareness of INF capabilities of USSR and NATO (DXUS)

	7/81	10/81	4/82
Both USSR, NATO have INF in Europe	47	45	48
NATO has INF, USSR does not	20	14	17
Neither USSR nor NATO have INF	6	6	7
USSR has INF in Europe, NATO does not	27	35	28

when the questions included the information cited. Hostility toward INF thus seems ascribable to a certain prevailing political and psychological attitude. Judging from Table 5.21, however, opposition to INF did not seem linked to anti-Americanism, because only 39 percent of those opposing INF had an unfavorable opinion of the United States. Furthermore, at roughly the same time, 56 percent of Italians had confidence in U.S. proposals for INF reduction at the Geneva negotiations (against 26 percent who had no confidence), and confidence in Soviet INF proposals was only 22 percent (DXUS 2/82).

But it must be reiterated that the data on Italian attitudes toward nuclear weapons are far less than satisfactory, given the absence of in-depth surveys on the key psychological and political motivations.

Public opposition to INF deployment in Italy decreased slightly during 1983, as can be seen from two Makno Institute surveys, the last one conducted after the first three months of the new Socialist-led government elected in June 1983 (Table 5.22). The questions are not comparable to those used by Doxa (Table 5.16), so the absolute differences should presumably be attributed to question wording. The trend, however, is what interests us here. Some observers have ascribed this evolution to the careful handling of the INF issue by Socialist Prime Minister Bettino Craxi, one example being his exchange of personal letters with both President Reagan and CPSU Secretary General Andropov. Also

Table 5.19   Effect on INF support of information on Soviet capabilities (DXUS 10/81)

	Version with information	Version without information
Favor	42	35
Oppose	51	60
Don't know	6	5

Question wording: "Do you favor or oppose having new nuclear missiles that can reach the Soviet Union stationed in Italy?"

Table 5.20   Evolution in Italy of support for deployment, version with information
(DXUS)

	7/81	10/81	4/82
Favor	45	42	41
Oppose	48	51	52
Don't know	8	6	8

interesting in these two polls was their focus on the issue of control. Although one cannot be sure, they seem to indicate that public support for INF would probably not be higher if the systems involved a double-key. Nevertheless, even when this option was offered to respondents, opposition was still somewhat higher than in the Doxa surveys, which focus on the link between deployment and arms control.

ENHANCED RADIATION WARHEADS (ERWs)

Italian opposition to introducing the ERW (neutron bomb) in Europe is certainly stronger than to INF, and also the awareness of ERW is quite high. Table 5.23 shows that Italians informed by interviewers that U.S. production of neutron weapons "was intended to prevent a tank attack in Europe, since they are designed to be used against attacking enemy tanks and soldiers, not against enemy cities and civilians" registered 68 percent opposition to deployment, which rose to 74 percent when no "information" preceded the question.

When the degree of information on ERW was probed more clearly, those aware of the U.S. decision to produce still had a rather poor knowledge of ERW capabilities. In October 1981, 45 percent thought that neutron weapons were to be used mainly against civilian population and enemy cities, 34 percent did not know, and only 21 percent knew that ERWs were mainly for attacking enemy tanks and soldiers (DXUS).

Table 5.21   General opinion of the US by attitude on INF deployment in Italy
(DXUS 10/82)

	Favor INF deployment in Italy	Oppose INF deployment in Italy	No opinion
General opinion of the US			
Favorable	83	58	64
Unfavorable	14	39	27
No opinion	3	3	9

Table 5.22   Attitude toward INF deployment in Sicily, related to a double-key system (Makno-Panorama)

	4/83	10/83	North West	North East	Centre	South Islands
Unconditional opponents	60	58	55	52	62	61
Conditional supporters if INF are placed under Italian control (dual-key system)	16	19	19	30	16	16
	30	32	35	41	31	29
Unconditional supporters	14	14	16	12	15	14
Don't know	8	8	9	6	7	9
No answer	2	1	1	0	0	1

Awareness of the difference between ERWs and other nuclear weapons was slightly better. Thirty-two percent knew that ERWs kill people with less destruction by heat and blast, but 11 percent believed ERWs to be more destructive and powerful; only two percent saw them as less destructive, and 19 percent believed there was no difference.

Hostility to deployment of the ERWs in Italy was even higher. Seventy-eight percent of Italians were against and 17 percent in favor. A majority (55 percent) thought that having such weapons would increase the likelihood that conventional battles would become nuclear wars. Only 14 percent believed the contrary, while 20 percent thought that there would be no effect (DXUS 2/82). Paradoxically, although Italians perceive the ERWs as likely to accelerate escalation in conflicts, they nevertheless believe in its deterrent effect. In case of deployment, 45 percent thought

Table 5.23   Italian attitudes toward US production of ERW (DXUS 2/82)

	Version with information	Version without information
Of those aware (64 percent):		
Favor	28	21
Oppose	68	74
Don't know	3	5
Of those opposed, when told US will not deploy ERW in Europe:		
Favor	31	
Oppose	64	
Don't know	5	

Table 5.24   Desirability of US leadership (DXUS)

	3/81		4/81	
Very desirable	23	64	20	62
Fairly desirable	41		42	
Not very desirable	17	26	19	29
Not at all desirable	9		10	
Don't know	10		10	

that the ERWs would help prevent a Soviet attack on Western Europe, while 36 percent thought the ERWs would make attack more likely, and 19 percent were uncertain.

Images of Allies

IMPORTANCE OF U.S. LEADERSHIP

The growing strains among the members of the Atlantic Alliance and the often differing views between Europeans and Americans on important political and strategic issues have also affected Italian public opinion, especially in its perceptions of the United States and NATO.

The importance attached in Italy to relations with the United States has been gauged by a number of indirect poll questions. For example, over 60 percent of those polled in 1981 considered firm U.S. leadership in world affairs desirable (Table 5.24). At the same time, when one probed somewhat deeper, only 33 percent of Italians desired close coordination of Italian foreign policy with the United States, and 47 percent did not consider this a requirement for Italy (DXUS 6/82). Relations with the United States are thus considered very important by Italian public opinion; there is a preferential relationship, but not to the extent of binding Italy's political choices.

ATTITUDES TOWARD THE UNITED STATES

The majority of Italians have a favorable opinion of the United States (see Table 5.25), although in the last five years a process of erosion has reduced

Table 5.25   Italian opinion of the United States (DXUS)

	10/78	10/81	2/82	3/82	4/82
Very/fairly favorable	79	67	63	62	65
Very/fairly unfavorable	15	28	21	19	25
Don't know	5	5	16	19	10

Table 5.26   Long term evolution of Italian opinion about the US (DXUS)

	Very good or good	Neither good nor bad	Opinion about the US Bad or very bad	No opinion	Difference good-bad opinion
1954	59	16	10	15	+49
1955	67	15	6	12	+61
1956	73	12	6	9	+67
1957	70	12	9	9	+61
1958	67	12	14	7	+53
1959	71	13	5	11	+66
1960	58	18	6	18	+52
1961	59	20	6	15	+53
1962	64	14	3	19	+61
1963	71	12	3	14	+68
1964	76	9	2	13	+74
1965	65	12	3	20	+62
1969	57	21	5	17	+52
1972	68	21	8	3	+60
1973	66	20	9	5	+57
1976	41	35	16	9	+25
1981	52	38	9	1	+41

this percentage from 79 to 65 percent. If we examine the long-term evolution of Italian opinion about the United States (in Table 5.26, starting in 1954), we find that until 1973 the generally favorable opinion oscillated between a minimum of 57 percent and a maximum of 76 percent; hostility ranged from two to 14 percent, neutrality from nine to 21 percent, and uncertainty from three to 20 percent. The difference between favorable and unfavorable opinions has maintained a large margin, from +49 to a peak of +74 percentage points.

The influence of political events on this evolution is rather evident: the Vietnam War and the Watergate scandal produced by 1976 an all-time post-war low of only 41 percent having a favorable opinion of the United States, with 16 percent expressing hostility and 35 percent a neutral attitude. Since 1977–1978, however, a modest recover of the U.S. image in Italy has taken place (the data in Table 5.25 give roughly the same balance of favorable and unfavorable opinion as the 1981 data in Table 5.26). The erosion thus seems to have been arrested and opinion to have stabilized in the early 1980s.

Confidence in U.S. capability to handle world affairs responsibly decreased considerably in the last ten years (as Table 5.27 shows, from 71 to 55 percent). The erosion of U.S. credibility is underlined by the fact that the loss of confidence has only partially produced increased uncertainty

Table 5.27   Italian confidence in US handling of world problems (DXUS)

	3/72	4/73	10/81	3/82	4/83
Great deal/fair	71	69	61	53	55
Not very much/not at all	23	23	35	28	34
No opinion	6	8	4	19	11

(from six to 11 percent) but rather a lack of confidence (up from 23 to 34 percent).

The political perceptions that underlie this trend are quite visible. In April 1982, 43 percent of Italians thought that, on balance, U.S. policies and actions during the past year had done more to promote peace, while 44 percent thought that they had more likely increased the risk of war (DXUS). By the same token, a few months earlier, in October 1981, over 74 percent of Italians thought that the primary objective of the United States was to attain military superiority over the USSR, against only 20 percent believing in U.S. commitment to military equality with the Soviets.

Perceptions of a militaristic trend in U.S. policy during the first year of the Reagan administration were evident in Italian public opinion, irrespective of U.S. motivations for such a policy. But whatever opinion the Italians may have of the U.S. foreign and domestic policy, expressions of "respect" for the United States are always fairly high. We see in Table 5.28 that on this question roughly 75 percent still express themselves positively, although the former "great respect" has been largely replaced by "fair respect," while the total percentage of "no respect" has increased from seven to 22 percent (mainly due to the gradual dwindling in the percentage of those uncertain, from 19 to three percent, over sixteen years).

ATTITUDES TOWARD NATO

When asked whether NATO is essential to their country's defense, a clear majority of Italians have answered in the affirmative, as is shown in Table

Table 5.28   Italian respect for the US (DXUS)

	6/65		11/69		4/72		10/81	
Great	43	74	32	71	27	80	23	75
Considerable	31		39		53		52	
Little	5	7	14	18	13	17	15	22
Very little	2		4		4		7	
No opinion	19		11		4		3	

Table 5.29   How essential is NATO for Italian security (DXUS)

	10/80	3/81
NATO is essential	54	62
NATO is not essential	25	27
Don't know	13	11

5.29. These data are not strictly comparable, because in 1980 this question was posed only to those who were aware of NATO's role (i.e., 80 percent of those polled), whereas in 1981 everybody was asked the same question. There may, nevertheless, even be a slight increase in perceptions of NATO's essential role for Italian security. Equally stable among Italians seem to be judgments on the importance of belonging to NATO (Table 5.30).

If a pro-NATO attitude generally prevails, opinions on what Italy should do to provide for its security in the best way are more differentiated (DXUS). In March 1981, 30 percent of Italians preferred staying in NATO; 25 percent wanted NATO changed so that Western Europe had more say in return for paying more of the costs; 16 percent had no specific opinion; 15 percent preferred to establish an independent Western European defense force not allied to the United States; 12 percent wanted Italy to withdraw her military forces from NATO but remain within the Alliance's political arrangements (more or less like France); finally, two percent wished to rely on accommodating the interests of the Soviet Union. These results are supported by the more recent, though different survey published by *Il Sole 24 Ore* on 15 June 1983 (DOXA). Here 31 percent of Italians (almost the same as in 1981) wanted to continue membership of NATO; 17 percent wanted to establish a Western European defense force within the NATO framework and 11 percent independent from the United States; seven percent wanted to rely on Italy's own national defense; five percent wanted to withdraw altogether from NATO, and 26 percent expressed no opinion.

RELIANCE UPON NATO AND THE UNITED STATES

If the general attitude of Italians toward NATO is relatively positive, the same can be said of the confidence in NATO's ability to *prevent* a Soviet

Table 5.30   Desirability of belonging to NATO (DXUS)

	3/81	7/81	4/82
Better to belong	60	49	59
Better to get out	30	42	34
Don't know	9	8	7

Table 5.31　Confidence in NATO defense (DOXA)

	7/81	4/82
Great/fair confidence	56	50
Not much/none	34	26
Don't know	9	24

attack against Western Europe (64 percent confident, 27 percent sceptical, and nine percent uncertain (DXUS 3/81)) as well as (though slightly diminishing) the confidence in NATO's ability to *defend* against such an attack (Table 5.31).

On the other hand, according to a survey published by *La Stampa* on 31 May 1983, 29 percent of Italians thought that NATO countries were in an aggressive mood (i.e., that they are prepared to start a nuclear war to extend their international influence), 46 percent of Italians didn't accept this proposition; 29 percent were uncertain (DXLS). On NATO decision making, a majority (54 percent against 29 percent) considered Italy to be excessively dominated by the United States (DXUS 5/82). Nevertheless, despite their opposition to U.S. hegemony, Italians demonstrated a surprisingly high confidence in U.S. willingness to defend Italy (Table 5.32).

NEUTRALISM AND PACIFISM

In July 1981, 31 percent of Italians thought that their governemnt should side with the United States in disputes between the United States and the USSR if important Italian interests were involved. Sixty-five percent preferred instead to stay out of such disputes, with only three percent having no opinion. This indirect index of neutrality should probably be tempered, given that the notion of a dispute between the two superpowers always raises some fear of a possible escalation into nuclear war.

As shown in Table 5.30, being confronted with the direct question of belonging to NATO or getting out and becoming a neutral country, produced a majority of respondents which preferred to remain in NATO. A survey taken at the beginning of 1983 by the Makno Institute, although not directly comparable, gave a lower percentage both of those wanting to stay with NATO (44 percent) and of those favoring neutrality (32 percent). In this survey, five percent wanted to join the Soviet bloc, and there was a relatively higher percentage of no opinion (15 percent).

The interesting aspect in the Makno survey is that support for neutralism seemed to be stronger among young people in the 20 to 24 age group (41 percent) and decreased with age, dropping below the national average starting with the 45 to 55 age group (25 percent). Yet teenagers were among the least neutralist (28 percent) and also less pro-NATO (36

Table 5.32 Confidence in US willingness to defend Italy (DXUS)

	7/81	4/82
Great/fair confidence	54	56
Not much/none	40	39
Don't know	6	5

percent) than all other age groups. The percentage of those with no opinion remained remarkably close to the average of 15 percent in all age groups but differed markedly between men (five percent) and women (25 percent). Generally, men had stronger opinions and a higher percentage of both pro-NATO (51 percent) and neutralist (35 percent) tendencies than women (37 percent pro-NATO and 30 percent neutralist).

The percentages of neutralism in both the 1982 and 1983 surveys are quite close to the percentage of Italians who consider that military force should never be used under any circumstance (see Images of Security), which may indicate a rather substantial bloc of "unconditional pacifists". Unfortunately, this evidence is only circumstantial as the surveys available did not ask the same questions and there is no possibility to correlate responses. The pacifists remain a minority when it is a question of using military force to respond to a direct attack on Italy by the USSR, but the number who favor a military reaction drops significantly if another NATO country is attacked, indicating relatively little support for collective security arrangements within NATO.

Correlates of Opinion

In this section we shall try to relate the general opinions expressed on the four main themes to particular background variables: sex, age, education, social class, and political persuasion. The availability of data varies considerably and is often inadequate, especially on images of the Soviet Union. Thus the following offers a highly selective and incomplete picture.

THE SOVIET UNION

An interesting aspect of the Italian image of the Soviet Union relates to the peculiar position of the Italian Communist Party (PCI) and to general preferences regarding the present and future evolution of political and ideological ties between the PCI and the USSR. In 1976, PCI General Secretary Enrico Berlinguer officially stated that NATO could act as a "shield" for the development of a separate road to socialism free from Soviet interference. Since then, attitudes toward this PCI position supply

Table 5.33   Desirability of closer ties between the PCI and the USSR by political affiliation (DXSO 5/83)

| | Ties between the PCI and the USSR have to be | | | |
	Increased	Decreased	Kept at present level	Don't know
PCI (Communists)	18	30	36	16
PSI (Socialists)	13	48	19	20
PRS/PSDI/PLI (Lay Parties)	2	49	27	22
DC (Christian Democrats)	8	44	23	26
PR/PDUP (Leftist Parties)	13	52	35	–
Total	13	37	29	21

a useful index, not only of the PCI standing in Italian opinion but also of the desirability of a certain type of relations with the USSR.

In June 1983, Italians were asked whether, in the wake of recent events in Poland and the official disavowal of Soviet policy by the PCI, they thought the PCI still had to go a long way before being fully accepted in the Western system. Preference was to be expressed on the kind of ties with the USSR the PCI should have: closer, less close, or just as they are now. As shown in Table 5.33, more than one-third of PCI supporters accepted the present state of relations with the Soviet Union. But 30 percent asked to decrease ties further, 18 percent wanted to increase ties with the USSR, and 16 percent were uncertain. The majority of suppor-

Table 5.34   Confidence in the Soviet political system by political affiliation (DXSO 5/83)

	PCI Communists	PR-PDUP Radical and extreme left	PSI Socialists	PSDI Social Democrats	PRI-PLI Republicans and liberals	DC Christian Democrats	MSI Right	No party identification
Great confidence	8	6	4	2	2	1	3	2
Moderate confidence	27	17	14	7	5	5	5	8
Little confidence	23	20	35	27	30	21	16	24
None/Almost none	16	51	33	45	57	47	65	27
Don't know	24	6	15	20	7	26	11	39

Table 5.35   Confidence in the Soviet political system by education and social class (DXSO 5/83)

	Education			Social Class		
	High School or University	Junior High School	Elementary Schooling or none	Upper Upper Middle	Middle	Lower Lower Middle
Great confidence	3	3	4	3	3	4
Moderate confidence	12	11	13	12	13	11
Little confidence	31	28	22	31	29	21
None/Almost none	44	40	27	46	35	30
Don't know	11	17	35	8	20	34

ters of all other parties preferred a decrease of ties between the PCI and the USSR.

Other detailed indications from the same survey can be found on the degree of confidence in the Soviet political system revealed by the Italians. The picture contained in Tables 5.34, 5.35, and 5.36 can be summarized as follows. The degree of positive confidence in the Soviet political system is constantly low (about 15 percent) and does not depend on age, sex, education, or social status, but rather on political affiliation. Here confidence is highest among Communists (35 percent) and Radicals and Proletarian Democrats (23 percent); it is near the average among Socialists (18 percent) and lowest among Christian Democrats (seven percent) and Lay Parties (seven percent for Republicans and Liberals). Significantly, uncertainty is highest among the Communists (24 percent) and the Christian Democrats (26 percent), probably because they are both large parties with several internal currents and groups harboring varying intensities of political activism, and also because both are mass parties with a lower than average level of education among adherents. But the

Table 5.36   Confidence in the Soviet political system by sex and age (DXSO 5/83)

		Sex		Age		
	Total	Men	Women	18–24	35–54	54+
Great confidence	3	4	3	4	2	5
Moderate confidence	12	14	11	13	13	11
Little confidence	25	30	21	30	28	18
None/Almost none	34	37	31	34	31	37
Don't know	25	16	35	20	26	30

importance of political affiliation is clear also from the fact that the highest degree of uncertainty, almost 40 percent, occurred among those who did not indicate a party preference.

Lack of confidence in the Soviet system averaged 59 percent, was higher among men and for young people (64 percent in the 18 to 34 age group), and increased markedly with education and social status. The percentage reaches a peak of 75 percent for highly educated and upper or upper-middle class Italians. Although we have no time series data, the tendencies visible here are clear enough and undoubtedly describe some of the main factors that determine popular Italian images of the USSR.

SECURITY

In March 1981, 71 percent of Italians with university education, 69 percent of those holding high school diplomas, 44 percent of those with junior high school education, and 45 percent of those with primary education stated they followed with great or at least moderate interest news concerning defense issues. Although these data are perhaps too optimistic, they do seem to confirm that both information and attention are a function of education levels. Considering the esoteric nature of these issues, this is not surprising and is likely to be the case in all Western countries. Unfortunately this only shows that those who generally pay more attention to defense problems are better educated, and we have no data on the real amount of attention paid by this public to defense issues.

As we have seen, the position of Italian public opinion on defense expenditure is negative. In 1981, 16 percent were in favor of its increase, 46 percent wanted it to decrease, and 34 percent preferred to keep defense expenditures stable. The percentages among those with a university education (students or people holding degrees) were 16 percent in favor of increasing defense expenditures, 39 percent for reductions, 37 percent for maintaining present levels, and eight percent uncertain. The share of those who supported an increase of military expenditure was the same as the national average, the percentage of those in favor of reduction was lower, and that in favor of maintenance of the status quo was higher.

By themselves, these data tell us relatively little. But if we break this group down according to age, we get a somewhat more interesting picture. Education may be an important determinant of interest, but among the highly educated it is age that is clearly a major factor affecting attitudes. Younger people with university education are close to the national average in favoring decreases in spending or in maintaining current levels, and have a significantly higher level of uncertainty. With age, one finds a steady increase in support for increased spending and less opposition to military expenditures generally. It is clear that older Italians with university education shift the national average in favor of defense. But the opposition to defense cannot be attributed simply to radical university

Table 5.37   Attitudes toward defense expenditures of those with university education
by age (DXUS 3/81)

	Students	−34	35–44	45–54	55+	Total
Increase	12	13	15	19	22	16
Decrease	47	47	40	36	27	39
Maintain current levels	31	34	39	36	43	37
Uncertain	10	7	5	9	7	8

students. The rest of the answer must lie elsewhere, presumably with
political preference, although these data were not available (Table 5.37).

A slightly different pattern emerges when we turn to arms control issues
(Table 5.38). It was pointed out earlier that the Italian public would prefer
to improve security by means of successful arms control negotiations (60
percent) rather than by strengthening NATO (22 percent). If we look
again at those with university education, we find the young deviating more
visibly from the national average, favoring international negotiations and
being much less willing to strengthen NATO. In this case, one can in fact
argue that the youth may be a driving force in promoting arms control,
but it should not be overlooked that a majority of all age groups prefer
arms control to strengthened defense efforts.

DETERRENCE

We have earlier described the position of Italian public opinion regarding
the deployment of new INF missiles in Europe. In the March 1981-April
1982 period, the installation of Euromissiles was opposed by between 40
and 54 percent of Italians and supported, at least conditionally, by
between 39 and 52 percent. During the same period, the installation of the
missiles *in Italy* was supported by between 45 and 41 percent and opposed
by between 48 and 52 percent. In the absence of specific preliminary
information about the current nuclear balance in Europe, the percentage
in favor of new missiles dropped to 35 and that opposed rose to 60 percent.

Table 5.38   Preferences on arms control vs. NATO of Italians with university education
by age (DXUS 6/82)

	Born in the fifties	Born in the forties	Born before the forties
Strengthen NATO	10	27	27
Promote arms control negotiations	85	61	54

Table 5.39   Attitudes toward INF deployment among educated Italians by age
              (DXUS 3/81)

	University students	−34	People holding degrees 35–44	45–54	55+	Average
In favor	20	22	30	42	53	34
Against	71	69	58	48	34	55
Uncertain	9	9	12	10	13	11

When we note the effect of information and specific question wording on responses, this indicates that the issue of deterrence and nuclear weapons is one where attitudes are heavily influenced by emotional content. Preferences reflect a certain influence of "myths" that have nothing to do with the real issues involved (Flynn 1983). In such cases, it is particularly interesting to try to discover what the most important sources of attitudes are.

By concentrating our attention on the attitude of educated groups, we have seen in the previous two sections that the level of education does seem to play a role in determining current public opinion on important political and strategic issues. Age has been at least as important among the highly educated as in the population at large and the two taken together frequently produce important variance in response patterns.

This pattern is confirmed in the following table that shows the attitude of people with university education regarding the installation of Euromissiles in Italy. Support for the installation of Euromissiles in Italy is very low among students (20 vs. the national average of 35 percent). But support constantly increases wth age, climbing to 53 percent, a higher percentage than the national average (41 percent). Opposition reaches its highest point among the youth (71 vs. a 60 percent national average), while hostility toward the Euromissiles progressively decreases in older age groups; it is only 34 percent in the oldest group (vs. a national average of 48 percent). In this case, education accentuates attitudes that are already conditioned heavily by age (Table 5.39).

Opposition to INF deployment also depends very much on political preference. A survey in December 1981 showed an average opposition to INF of 54 percent, a support of 20 percent, and a high degree of uncertainty (26 percent, (Demoskopea)). The strongest opposition was registered by followers of leftist parties (almost 100 percent for Radicals and Proletarian Democrats, and 81 percent for Communists); Socialists and Republicans were slightly above average (58 percent), but with a higher percentage also in favor of INF (25 to 30 percent). The same degree of support was registered by Christian Democrats (26 percent), but opposition to INF was lower (47 percent). The Liberals were the only party in which a clear majority favored INF deployment (59 percent).

Table 5.40   Attitudes toward INF deployment in Sicily by political affiliation (DXUS 7/83)

	PCI Commu- nists	PSI Social- ists	PSDI-PRI-PLI Lay Group	DC Christian Democrats
Unconditional opponents	76	54	35	42
Conditional supporters if there is agreement at Geneva talks	17	32	40	34
Unconditional supporters	5 22	10 42	24 64	17 51
Opponents if stationing proceeds	84	68	47	52
Supporters if stationing proceeds	14	32	51	46
British and French missiles should be included in INF talks	77	69	68	72

Opinion was fairly divided among Social Democrats (33 percent in favor, 34 percent against, and 33 percent uncertain).

The decrease of unconditional opposition to INF during 1982 and its increase again in April 1983 to the levels of early 1981 (just after the so-called Star Wars speech by President Reagan) probably indicate that Italian attitudes toward INF deployment do not depend primarily on the perception of the Soviet threat, but rather on the perception of trends in U.S. nuclear and defense policy. This latter perception is very much influenced by public statements and in general by the declaratory policy of the U.S. government.

More recent data from another survey (Table 5.40) taken just after the Italian general elections of June 1983, seem to show a slight decrease in opposition to INF across the political spectrum. This evolution was probably due to the U.S. interim proposal at the Geneva negotiations. An interesting aspect is that more than two-thirds of Italians supporting all political parties thought that also British and French missiles should be included in the INF talks. This implies a certain success of the Soviets on this particular issue and a failure of the British and French governments to defend their case in a more convincing way.

ALLIES

As we have already seen earlier, the Italians still have a generally good opinion of the United States, but less than in times past. Significantly, the

Table 5.41   Attitudes toward the United States among educated Italians by age (DXUS 5/82)

	University students	−34	People holding degrees 35–44	44–54	55+	Average
Favorable	39	43	55	56	71	54
Unfavorable	54	45	38	29	19	35
Neutral	4	7	5	8	5	6
Uncertain	4	5	3	7	5	5

progressive deterioration of the U.S. image is more evident if we examine the opinions of educated Italians. Table 5.41 shows that positive attitudes toward the United States co-vary directly with the age of respondents. In 1982 a negative opinion was very common among young people, while pro-Americanism was very strong especially among those older than 55. In both cases the extreme percentages were much higher than the national averages (71 percent favorable opinion, compared with a national average of 65 percent; 54 percent unfavorable, compared with a national average of 25 percent).

In the same survey, confidence in American foreign policy among educated Italians also proved to be lower than the national average, which is also generally decreasing (Table 5.42). The same variations according to age were also present.

When asked whether the United States should exercise strong leadership in world affairs, the distribution of attitudes among Italians with university education showed the same pattern of distribution. Interestingly, only the oldest group approached (but was still below) the national average (61 vs. 62 percent). All the other groups showed a clearly negative attitude, which varied inversely with age. In other words, Italians with a university education—unlike the rest of the population—did not wish the United States to hold a strong leadership position in international affairs (42 percent were in favor and 55 percent against, compared with 62 vs. 29 percent in the national average). Acceptance of U.S. leadership thus seems

Table 5.42   Confidence in US foreign policy among educated Italians by age (DXUS 5/82)

	Born in the fifties	Born in the forties	Born before the forties
High/fairly high confidence	54	58	78
Low/no confidence	45	41	20

Table 5.43 Desirability of US leadership among educated Italians by age (DXUS 12/81)

	University students	−34	People holding degrees 35–44	45–54	55+	Average
Yes/to a certain extent	28	31	38	45	61	42
A little/no	68	66	60	52	35	55
Uncertain	4	3	2	3	4	3

to be decreasing in Italy, with the highly educated ahead of the population at large (Table 5.43).

Some other interesting indications of this Italian attitude toward the United States emerge from an analysis of the degree of confidence in the U.S. political system. Images of the U.S. political system do not necessarily coincide with perceptions of U.S. foreign policy but nevertheless are relevant to the general image of the United States. The picture emerging from Tables 5.44, 5.45, and 5.46 shows in general a plurality of Italians (45 percent) having confidence in the U.S. political system, but also a sizeable proportion (31 percent) lacking confidence (with 24 percent uncertain). Once again, U.S. standing is not bad, but not as good as in the past. The degree of confidence varied by 18 percentage points according to sex, education, and social class, but surprisingly this survey showed little variation by age. Variation according to political affiliation emerged as the key factor. Confidence was highest among men, with women mainly being more uncertain. Confidence in the U.S. political system increased with education and social class, but so did the lack of confidence (although to a lesser extent). For highly educated Italians and the upper classes the level of uncertainty was lower, which slightly benefitted confident responses.

Turning to political affiliation, it is no surprise that the highest degree of confidence in the U.S. system is registered among adherents of the lay parties, and especially Republicans and Liberals (75 percent); it is also high among Christian Democrats (58 percent) and among Socialists (50

Table 5.44 Confidence in the US political system by sex and age (DXSO 5/83)

	Total	Sex Men	Women	18–34	Age 35–54	54+
Great confidence	11	14	8	12	9	12
Moderate confidence	34	41	29	36	36	32
Little confidence	22	25	20	25	23	20
Non/Almost none	9	9	9	8	9	9
Don't know	24	12	35	20	24	28

Table 5.45   Confidence in the US political system by education and social class
(DXSO 5/83)

	Education			Social Class		
	High School or University	Junior High School	Elementary Schooling or none	Upper Upper Middle	Middle	Lower Lower Middle
Great confidence	14	15	7	17	11	8
Moderate confidence	41	39	30	37	39	29
Little confidence	25	24	21	27	23	21
None/Almost none	11	6	9	10	8	9
Don't know	9	16	33	9	18	33

percent). It then drops to 29 percent for the Communists, who have one of the highest percentages of little or no confidence (47 percent), but not the highest (60 percent for Radicals and Proletarian Democrats). Thirty-four percent among Socialists lack confidence in the U.S. political system, and 16 percent are uncertain. Finally, just as in the Soviet case, we have the same pattern of a relatively high degree of uncertainty for the two largest parties, the Communists and the Christian Democrats (about 24 percent). Uncertainty is highest (35 percent) among those with no party identification (Table 5.46).

These data, especially the tendency among the young and highly educated, does give some cause for concern that the future may bring some changes in Italo-American relations. Time alone might be sufficient to generate these changes. On the other hand, age can also moderate attitudes, so that in the future we could find patterns of opinion and a

Table 5.46   Confidence in the US political system by political affiliation (DXSO 5/83)

	PCI	PR-PDUP	PSI	PSDI	PRI-PLI	DC	MSI	No party
Great confidence	5	11	9	4	21	17	15	9
Moderate confidence	23	23	42	45	55	41	45	28
Little confidence	30	26	28	30	19	14	24	20
None/Almost none	17	34	6	4	3	4	5	8
Don't know	24	6	16	18	3	25	11	36

Table 5.47   Attitudes toward NATO among educated Italians by age (DXUS 3/81)

	Born in the fifties	Born in the forties	Born before the forties
NATO is essential	62	63	80
NATO is not essential	34	34	20

situation similar to the present one. Unfortunately, we do not have the data necessary to compare today's attitudes with those of a generation ago.

Turning to NATO itself, 62 percent of Italians considered NATO essential to national defense in 1981, and 27 percent opposed NATO (Table 5.47). On this issue attitudes of those with university education were near the national average, with the exception of the percentage of the oldest group (80 percent). When compared with other issue areas analyzed earlier, we do not find the same significant attitude differences according to age. This probably means that, most of those who are against NATO acknowledge that, for the time being, NATO is still essential to Italian defense. In this regard, it is also important to note the attitudes of the Italian Left and especially of followers of the Communist party. This can be clearly seen in Table 5.48.

Confronted with the complex choices offered by the possible evolution of Italian defense either within or outside NATO, it is significant that the highest percentage of uncertainty was to be found among PCI voters: one-fourth of Communist supporters did not know what to answer. Uncertainty was also high among Socialists and Christian Democrats (20 percent). This may be partially ascribed to a lack of information and low personal relevance of strategic affairs. Nevertheless, it is at least a common assumption that Communist supporters follow closely their party press and therefore are better informed on the main issues. Uncertainty is highest (almost 42 percent) among those who indicate no party affiliation, confirming again the relevance of political preferences in determining Italian public opinion.

Perhaps the most interesting fact is that 29 percent of Communists favored an independent Western European defense force, although 17 percent preferred to stay in NATO as it is now, and a remarkably low eight percent wanted to withdraw from NATO. The European options, either inside or outside NATO, were most strongly favored among Socialist supporters (38 percent) and voters of the lay parties (37 percent), whereas they were weaker among Christian Democrats (21 percent). But the majority, except the Communists, preferred a Western European defense linked with NATO. Loyalty to NATO was highest among Christian Democrats (50 percent) and lay parties (Republicans, Liberals and Social Democrats: 46 percent); it decreased considerably among Socialists (28 percent). There was a great consistency of attitudes, the percentage of

Table 5.48 Attitudes on the future of NATO and of Italian defense by political affiliation (DXSO 5/83)

	PCI	PSI	PLI-PRI-PSDI	DC	PR-PDUP	MSI	Total
Concerning national defense, it is better for Italy to							
Stay in NATO as it now operates	17	28	46	50	17	39	31
Establish a Western European defense force within NATO	9	27	30	18	20	27	17
Withdraw from NATO	8	4	3	4	14	7	5
Establish an independent Western European defense force	20	11	7	3	20	11	11
Rely on Italy's own defense force	12	8	2	5	6	8	7
Reduce Italy's defense force	9	3	5	1	11	2	4
Don't know	25	20	8	21	11	7	26

those who wanted to withdraw from NATO being lowest among lay parties, Christian Democrats, and Socialists. Among all political parties, the option to rely on Italy's own defense forces or even to reduce them was considered to be the least attractive. This tendency is generally weak among the Italian public at large (see Table 5.49). Again we detect familiar patterns, such as higher degrees of uncertainty among women, older people, the less educated, and those from the lower social classes. What is remarkable is that, with very few exceptions, fewer than one-third of respondents considered the best option to be in NATO as it now operates.

Withdrawal from NATO receives very little support, but the reformist trend toward the establishment of a Western European defense can be termed as rather sizeable. The two variants average around 28 percent for public opinion in general and have strong support among the younger generation and among the better-educated Italians, as well as those belonging to the upper- or upper-middle class. Clearly some reform of the present Western defense arrangements seems to be a desired development in future Euro-American relations.

One other set of data helps us refine this picture somewhat further. When confronted in 1981 with a direct choice between NATO and neutrality, 58 percent of Italian respondents were in favor of NATO membership, while 34 percent advocated neutrality (Table 5.50). When broken down by age, a pattern emerges in which the national average

Table 5.49 Attitudes on the future of NATO and of Italian defense by sex, age, education and social class (DXSO 5/83)

		Sex		Age			Education			Social class		
	Total	Men	Women	18–34	35–54	+54	High School or University	Junior High School	Elementary Schooling or none	Upper Upper Middle	Middle Middle	Lower Lower Middle
Concerning national defense, it is better for Italy to												
Stay in NATO as it operates now	31	32	30	30	31	32	31	36	29	35	31	30
Establish a Western European defense force, within NATO	17	21	14	20	18	14	25	23	11	26	21	11
Withdraw from NATO	5	5	4	5	5	3	7	5	4	7	5	4
Establish an independent Western European defense force	10	13	8	16	10	6	19	10	7	14	13	7
Rely on Italy's own defense forces	7	7	7	7	6	7	6	6	8	8	6	7
Reduce Italy's defense forces	4	5	3	5	4	3	4	4	3	2	4	4
Don't know	26	17	34	17	25	35	7	15	38	7	20	36

214   SERGIO A. ROSSI

Table 5.50   Support for neutralism (DXUS 3/81)

	Born in the sixties	Born in the fifties	Born in the forties	Born before the forties
In favor of NATO	51	54	64	63
In favor of neutrality	43	37	30	27

actually falls roughly in the middle of the age distribution. Majorities in all age groups favored the Alliance, but there was a clear tendency toward greater support for NATO with increased age and a corresponding decrease in the attractiveness of neutrality. The actual spread, however, is not in fact all that great, and perhaps most interesting is the relatively low average support for the Alliance when compared with other member states.

The spread in responses increased substantially when the sample was limited to those with a university education (Table 5.51). Interestingly, the support for NATO among university students was equal to that among the same age group outside the universities, as was the support of neutrality. It is the sharp increase in support for NATO that occurs with age among the highly educated that is most remarkable. Older, educated Italians are strongly pro-NATO and anti-neutralist.

One final interesting set of data is worth examining. When Italians were asked whether Western Europe should make more efforts to strengthen its defense, an even more pronounced distribution of attitudes emerged. Among those with university education, age proved to be a major discriminating factor of responses. One thing seems clear: European defense is less popular than maintenance of current Alliance arrangements, especially among the young and well educated (Table 5.52).

Conclusions

Any brief summary of data such as analyzed above is bound to oversimplify the complex reality of Italian public perceptions in the area of

Table 5.51   Support for neutralism among Italians with university education by age (DXUS 3/81)

	University students	People holding degrees				Average
		−34	35–44	45–54	55+	
In favor of NATO	50	50	60	71	82	63
In favor of neutrality	43	40	31	24	12	29
Uncertain	7	10	9	6	7	8

Table 5.52   Attitudes toward common European defense among Italians with
university education by age (DXUS 3/81)

	Born before the forties	Born in the forties	Born in the fifties
Positive	50	24	13
Negative	43	62	75

foreign and defense policy. One reason, of course, is the lack of significant time series data over extended periods for all but a very limited number of questions. Security policy simply has not been a major subject of inquiry for public opinion research until very recently in Italy. Moreover, the work that has been done does not allow one to go beyond a very general description of public preferences, with the real factors conditioning attitudes remaining as yet inadequately explored. Nevertheless, there are certain identified tendencies that do permit one to pull together a composite picture that is meaningful, though lacking the sharp resolution that one might desire.

With regard to the Soviet Union, there has been a generally negative image that has prevailed over the post-war period, one that nevertheless improved considerably during the détente years, only to deteriorate again in 1980–1981. A partial recovery in 1982–1983 seems to have been set back in Italian public opinion by the shooting down of the South Korean airliner over Sakhalin Island in September 1983, but the general tendency appears to be toward an improvement.

The Soviet military threat has been perceived as growing in the eighties. According to recent polls, nearly 40 percent of Italian respondents held the Soviet military buildup responsible for current international tensions. This perception is fairly widespread in all sectors of public opinion, even though it is much stronger among upper and middle class Italians and among Christian Democrats. Awareness of Soviet military power, however, does not translate into real fear of a Soviet attack against Western Europe, because the majority of respondents seems to be convinced that military parity between the United States and the USSR is lasting and essentially stable. Moreover, one-quarter of respondents consider U.S. aggressive policies toward the USSR as responsible for international tensions. Only a small minority considers a Soviet attack to be likely. The political dimension of the Soviet image thus appears to be predominant. The Soviet political system holds few attractions for most sectors of public opinion, with the exception of more than one-third of those respondents who express preference for the Italian Communist party. Nevertheless, about 30 percent of respondents who identify themselves as PCI supporters do favor reducing ties with the USSR. At the same time, a majority of respondents continues to favor trade and business relations with the USSR and does not seem to believe in the usefulness of commercial sanctions against Moscow. This orientation is fully reflected among the Italian business community, which, since the 1920s, has developed broad business ties with the USSR.

When one turns to broader security concerns, an increasing percentage of Italians point to a fear of war, making this the third major concern after unemployment and crime. This sentiment is overrepresented among women, older age groups, as well as among Christian Democrats and Communists. Yet only a small minority of Italians consider a world war probable during the next ten years. A majority of respondents, especially the young and those with higher education, do not regard inadequate defense as one of their major concerns and oppose increases in the Italian defense budget. In case of external aggression, slightly more than half of those polled indicate a willingness to resist militarily, and almost 40 percent incline toward nonresistance.

A significant majority of those polled favors negotiating arms control agreements with the USSR as a means to enhance Italian security. This represents considerably more support than for strengthening NATO and especially NATO's nuclear forces. The preference is very strong among young respondents with a university education (85 percent). On the other hand, a certain degree of scepticism regarding the chances of arms agreements is clearly discernible in public opinion in general.

Concern about nuclear weapons has risen, especially in 1982–1983, and is now shared by about one-third of Italians. Concern is higher among young people, those from a middle-class background, and Socialists; it is highest among Communists.

Opinion is almost evenly split on the issue of INF deployment, with opposition to INF deployment in Italy (54 percent in spring of 1983) being strongest. Attitudes do not seem to depend significantly on the degree of information on nuclear issues. The opposition is highest among university students and graduates under 34 (about 70 percent), but decreases significantly in the older age group with academic background. Political party preference is the other crucial determinant of attitudes toward INF: opposition is highest among the leftist parties, close to average among Socialists; it decreases somewhat among Christian Democrats and is lowest for Social Democrats, Liberals, and Republicans. Respondents' attitudes toward INF deployment seem to correlate more strongly with perceptions of U.S. nuclear and defense policies than with all other issues addressed in the data available.

Perceptions of the United States generally are in fact more negative than in earlier years. From a two-thirds majority of favorable opinion in the fifties and the sixties, the U.S. image declined to a low of 41 percent during the mid-seventies. A certain recovery has since taken place, though there is evidence that critical attitudes toward the United States have tended to reappear more strongly in the early eighties. The erosion in the image of the United States is confirmed by the decreasing degree of confidence in the U.S. political system. Confidence is still relatively strong among 45 percent of Italians but is low or lacking among almost one-third of the public. Confidence increases with education and social class, but the opposite seems to be true in the case of the young. Here again, political affiliation is the main determinant. Followers of lay parties, such as the Republicans and Liberals, have the highest confidence in the U.S. system; confidence is stable and substantial among Christian Democrats and Socialists, and is lowest among Communists.

If preference for a close relationship with the United States is still expressed by one-third of respondents, almost half consider it important that national political choices (e.g., trade relations with the USSR) should not be influenced by concern about U.S.-Italian relations. The United States is nevertheless still considered a reliable ally by a large majority of those polled, with nearly 60 percent expressing confidence in U.S. willingness to bear the risk of defending Italy militarily against an external aggression.

Most respondents still consider the NATO alliance essential for national security, but support for leaving NATO has grown to over one-third of the Italians polled. Surprisingly, however, fewer than eight percent of those supporting the PCI want to withdraw from NATO. Confidence in NATO's ability to deter a Soviet attack is also fairly high, and confidence in NATO's ability actually to defend against such an attack has somewhat decreased (to some 50 percent). Support for NATO is weakest among all strata of the young generation. Perhaps more important is that only 31 percent prefer Italy to stay in NATO in its present form, while almost 28 percent prefer the establishment of a Western European defense community, if possible within NATO, but outside if need be. The propensity for a "European option" is strongest among adherents of the Socialists and lay parties, substantial among Communists, and weakest among Christian Democrats. This "reformist" view is shared by one-third of male middle-class respondents; it is strongest among the respondents with academic background, the upper class, and the younger generation.

The general picture is thus mixed and anything but reassuring. The Soviet military buildup seems not to have produced growing support for NATO and national defense but rather stronger support for arms control as well as closer business and industrial cooperation with the USSR. This result is certainly consistent with the perceived unlikelihood of a Soviet military attack and with lack of concern about growing Soviet influence in Europe and in the world at large. Soviet ideological influence is not particularly feared, as indicated by the low confidence in her political system. The unwillingness to support greater defense burdens or to strengthen NATO defense seem to be correlated with a perception of an enduring strategic and military parity between the United States and the USSR.Confidence in NATO's ability to defend Italy seems to be more or less equated with confidence in U.S. willingness and ability to defend Italy.

The different sets of DXUS data indicate that opposition to nuclear weapons and especially to INF deployment is mainly linked to perceptions of American deterrent policies, to the credibility of the U.S. nuclear guarantee for Europe, and to the state of health of U.S.-European relations in general. The high strategic credibility of the United States, combined with a certain scepticism regarding U.S. policies, may in fact be reinforcing each other in increasing opposition to INF deployment in Italy (or in general).

Yet it remains clear that until now key decisions on foreign and defense policy, even the latest ones concerning Italian troops in Lebanon, have been taken more on the basis of political rather than popular consensus. Moreover, it is also clear that a dominant factor in determining most public attitudes is party preference. The high degree of political polarization and identification throughout Italian society is a given and traditional fact, not likely to disappear. Yet as long as the political fault-lines remain as they are today, it is unlikely that foreign and defense policy will become a major source of political dispute that could promote much larger popular interest and involvement, despite the fact that the seeds for a more ambivalent set of Italian policy preferences appear to exist. Considerably more systematic work needs to be done, however, before the real basis of these possible preferences becomes clear along with their eventual impact on political choices.

References

Bechelloni, G., "Opinione pubblica e Politica Internationale," in *La Politica Estera della Repubblica Italiana* (Milano: Edizione di Comunita (IAI), 1967) Pp. 968–995.

Flynn, Gregory, "Seven Myths that are Muddying the Debate on Missiles," *International Herald Tribune*, 25 Feb. 1983.

Rossi, Sergio and V. Ilari, "Pacifisme à l'Italienne," in Pierre Lellouche, ed., *Pacifisme et Dissuasion* (Paris: IFRI, 1983) Pp. 141–152.

Appendix D Sources and Acronyms

Acronyms for sources of data are as follows:

DOXA: Data from different surveys conducted by the Doxa Institute and published in the periodical "Bollettino Doxa," Milan.

DXEB: Data from the regular survey conducted by the Doxa Institute for the "Eurobarometer" of the European Economic Community.

DXLS: Data from the survey conducted by the Doxa Institute for *La Stampa* May 1983.

DXSO: Data from the survey conducted by the Doxa Institute for *Il Sole 24 Ore*, March-April 1983.

DXST: Data from the survey conducted by the Doxa Institute for the "Institut International de Géopolitique", Paris, sponsored and published in Italy by the daily *La Stampa*, April 1983.

DXUS: Data from surveys regularly conducted by the Doxa Institute for the United States Information Agency.

LHAI: Data from the two surveys conducted by Louis Harris, France, for the Atlantic Institute for International Affairs in Paris, in autumn 1982 and spring 1983.

MAKNO: Data from the survey conducted by the Makno Institute for Italian Radio Television.

6 Public Opinion on Nuclear Weapons, Defense, and Security: The Case of the Netherlands

PHILIP P. EVERTS

Introduction

The foreign and security policy of the Netherlands in the post-1945 period rested for a long time on a multipartisan consensus at the level of political decision making and on a strongly permissive mood at the level of public opinion. Public interest in foreign policy by and large remained restricted to rather small groups of individuals, such as representatives of political parties. Foreign policy was made according to a classic elitist model.

All this has greatly changed since the late sixties. The prevailing public consensus began to crumble and has even broken down in some areas, especially that of security policy. Public interest in international politics has increased considerably, according to most observers. Parliament has become involved in foreign policy discussions to a much greater degree. These developments have become most marked in the past few years, an important role having been played by the peace movement (or antinuclear movement, as some prefer to call it), whose impact ranges from the radical left to parts of the political center, including the Christian Democratic party.[1]

This chapter is based upon an abbreviated and updated version of Chapter 7, "The Mood of the Country—Public Opinions on Nuclear Weapons and Other Problems of Peace and Security," in Philip P. Everts, *Public Opinion, the Churches and Foreign Policy—Studies of Domestic Factors in the Making of Dutch Foreign Policy*, Leiden: Institute for International Studies, 1983, 225–302. Data up to July 1983 have been included. Most of the data have been discussed and analyzed earlier and somewhat more extensively in Everts (1981, 1982).

The assistance of the institutions which have provided me with data and other material is gratefully acknowledged. These include the Embassy of the United States of America, the Polls Archives of the Baschwitz Institute, University of Amsterdam, and the Steinmetz Archives, Amsterdam. I also wish to acknowledge the comments and advice of those who have read earlier versions of this paper, including the members of the Interuniversity Working Group for the study of domestic factors in the making of foreign policy. The interpretation of the data is, of course, entirely my own and cannot be identified with the institutions which have provided the data.

1. A survey of Dutch foreign policy is Voorhoeve (1979). The role of domestic factors in foreign policy making, especially the churches and the peace movement, is discussed in Everts (1983). Other recent relevant studies are Domke (1983), Leurdijk (1983), Eichenberg (1983), Siccama (1983).

Recent developments in the Netherlands have gained a certain international notoriety and are seen abroad either as a subject for worry and concern or as a source of inspiration, depending on political preferences. The term *Hollanditis* is used to describe this evolution, suggesting some kind of infectious disease spreading from the Netherlands to other countries (Laqueur 1981).

The purpose of this paper is to describe and analyze to what extent these alleged changes in the mood of the country are reflected in available data on public opinion. To what extent are the views promoted by the peace movement supported by public opinion at large? Is there evidence of a shift in public opinion which could be linked to this movement? And if we discern such a shift, does it portend to be a major and fundamental change or rather a temporary affair? What do the data from public opinion surveys tell us about these and related questions?

Earlier research has led to the conclusion that, at the level of the mass public, public opinion with respect to international problems has a direct impact on policy and decision making only under exceptional circumstances. Even then, this impact seems to be mainly passive. Its major instrument is the threat or application of electoral punishment. But even if considerable pressure exists on all levels, only one condition of influence is fulfilled. Indeed, recent events in the Netherlands have underscored the conclusion that, as long as a parliamentary majority is unwilling to force a government either to abide by its wishes or to abdicate (and with respect to foreign policy, according to experience, this willingness is even smaller than with respect to other problems), active resistance from within society is bound to peter out in the end. In a longer-term perspective, however, governments can probably not ignore or can only partially resist the influences which emanate from more fundamental changes in the climate of opinion.

Developments mentioned briefly above suggest that, with respect to foreign and defence policy, the Netherlands is undergoing just such a change in the climate of opinion, affecting a fundamental reorientation of foreign policy, which began toward the end of the sixties and is still going on. Involved in this reorientation appear to be deep-seated attitudes and values of people and their images of the world. Unfortunately, however, despite the wealth of opinion surveys in recent years time series of data that allow comparisons across time are generally not available, apart from a few topics on which such comparisons are possible—these shall be discussed later. In all other cases, differences in the wording of questions—which, as I shall show, are no minor matter—preclude any firm conclusions on the degree of change or continuity in attitudes. One can, in most cases, do no more than speculate when differences or similarities are observed.

Another reason why it remains difficult to judge whether changes in fundamental attitudes and values have really occurred is that such changes are more difficult to establish than opinions on concrete events and issues.

Indeed, much opinion research suffers from the weakness, often forced by lack of funds and personnel, that it only scratches the surface of people's attitudes. More analytical questions that could uncover these attitudes and emotions are often not asked; at the same time, analyses of existing data (see Appendix E) that would allow such explorations are often not undertaken in the reports of such surveys. This is also the reason why available data offer little help in exploring apparently contradictory elements.

In the second section of this chapter we shall review the available evidence on the way in which the Soviet Union is perceived as a threat to peace and security, including perceptions of the military balance between East and West. The next section discusses the available data on images of security and on perceived threats to security. In particular, it discusses attitudes on the acceptability of the use of conventional and nuclear weapons in response to such threats. In this section an effort is also made to gauge the intensity of public involvement in the nuclear weapons issue.

Next, a description and evaluation of public opinion data on attitudes on nuclear weapons, their presence in the Netherlands, and the desirability of their removal is discussed. The data discussed in this section focuses on the NATO double-track decision of 1979 and its consequences. In the fifth section attitudes on the United States and on NATO are discussed. The question to what extent a movement towards neutralism can be detected in the Netherlands is also addressed. Finally, some conclusions are drawn regarding the contents and trends of public opinion in the Netherlands.

Images of the Soviet Union

PERCEPTIONS OF THE SOVIET THREAT

Until recently hardly any serious research was done with respect to perceptions of the Soviet threat and the salience of this threat compared with other threats. The few available data from public opinion surveys cannot be compared easily because of differences in the wording of questions (see Roschar 1975). The evidence suggests, however, that since the Second World War a negative or even very negative image of the Soviet Union has prevailed in Dutch public opinion. Together with China, the Soviet Union was most often mentioned as the source of potential threats to the security of the country (Table 6.1). The data also suggest that the number of those perceiving such a threat has declined over the years. As opposed to this decline for the Soviet Union and China, one sees an increase for the United States. Other data, however, show that while the perception of an acute threat has perhaps diminished, a feeling that the Soviet Union may become such a threat has remained widespread (Table 6.2).

A more extensive survey of the "image of the enemy" in Dutch public

Table 6.1   Are there any countries that want to dominate the world?

		NIPO 1948	NIPO 1968	NIPO 1972	VARA 1973
Yes		75	79	62	77
If yes, which country?	Soviet Union	75	72	48	51
	China	–	30	29	32
	United States	25	26	35	54

opinion, devoted primarily to perceptions of the Soviet Union, was undertaken in 1979 (Projectgroep Vijandsbeeld 1980). The perceived military threat was concentrated on the Soviet Union (mentioned by 23 percent), with the Arab countries second (nine percent). China had almost disappeared as a threat to Dutch security. An additional question, on the most important threat, revealed a similar picture, with 43 percent mentioning the Soviet Union and an additional 15 percent separately mentioning the countries of the Warsaw Pact.

This does not imply that respondents were very afraid of a Soviet occupation. Only two percent of those who saw the Soviet Union as a threat were afraid of such an event, while 18 percent only imputed to the Soviet Union the intention to dominate other countries militarily. What people seemed to fear was political and ideological expansionism. Of those who saw the Soviet Union as a threat, 79 percent agreed that it wants to extend its power in the world. Of those who saw the Soviet Union as "the enemy," 50 percent thought that this image would not change in the future. Apparently the "enemy image" was firmly rooted. When respondents were asked to characterize the Soviet Union, negative characteristics prevailed over positive ones. This was only slightly less true for those who did not see the Soviet Union as a military threat. That the Soviet Union was perceived as a (potential) threat to security, did not imply identical answers from all respondents to the question how one should react to this threat. No less than 44 percent said they would prefer to search for other ways to react to the threat rather than to risk a nuclear war (nine percent),

Table 6.2   Perceptions of present and future Soviet threat

	Intomart 1967		Intomart 1974		VARA 1978	
	Present	Future	Present	Future	Present	Future
Threat	41	41	31	42	32	44
No threat	53	49	62	44	49	33
Don't know/no answer	6	10	7	14	23	23

Table 6.3   Perceptions of relative strength of the United States and the Soviet Union (USICA)

	Total				Best educated[a]			
	3/81	4/81	10/81[a]		3/81	4/81	10/81[b]	
United States somewhat/ considerably ahead	10	16	16	15	6	23	24	12
United States and USSR about equal	43	48	40	38	61	56	40	56
USSR somewhat/ considerably ahead	29	28	35	37	25	18	32	28
Don't know/ no answer	19	8	9	11	8	2	4	4

Note:
[a]See Appendix E for definition
[b]In October 1981 separate questions were asked for nuclear (first column) and conventional (second column) strength

increase nuclear armaments (24 percent), or increase only conventional armaments (20 percent).

PERCEPTIONS OF THE MILITARY BALANCE

A major point of debate, when the possibilities of particular arms control proposals or the necessity of deploying new generations of nuclear missiles are discussed, is the question how the two blocs (and the superpowers in particular) relate in nuclear or total military strength. Indeed, one of the major claims of advocates of strengthened Western defense efforts is that people would accept the necessity of increased armaments if they would only know what the military facts are, that is, that the balance of forces is shifting rapidly in favour of the East.

Apart from the question whether this assumption is correct, it does not seem as if people believe that the balance is shifting in favour of the East. There is no discernible trend towards increased acceptance of the view that the Soviet Union is ahead in military strength. In October 1979 (NIPO), when asked about the relative strength of NATO and the Warsaw Pact, 13 percent said that NATO was stronger, 33 percent considered both equally strong, and 44 percent said that the Soviet Union was ahead in military strength. But early in 1981, these figures (from USICA) were rather different and more or less similar to results obtained in 1977 and 1978 (Adler and Wertman 1981), and they remained at the same level throughout that year, as is shown in Table 6.3. Remarkably enough, even fewer among the better educated seemed to be impressed by the argument that the balance was shifting toward the East (except for estimates of

Table 6.4   Concern about a Soviet attack on Western Europe in the next five years (USICA)

	3/81 Total	3/81 Best-educated	7/81 Total	7/81 Best-educated	10/81 Total	10/81 Best-educated
Very concerned	8	7	6	2	10	8
Fairly concerned	24	13	22	19	32	21
Not very concerned	36	54	34	34	25	25
Not at all concerned	18	20	35	44	17	30
Don't know/no answer	15	6	4	1	7	5

conventional strength in October 1981). The same picture more clearly emerged when respondents were asked what they expected the military balance to be in five years. Fewer people projected the Soviet Union ahead, and more did so in the case of the United States. The military balance was clearly seen as either remaining in a state of equilibrium or shifting in favor of the West.

With respect to estimates of present military strength, similar results were obtained in another survey held in November 1981 (SP). This survey helps us to answer the question whether there is a relationship between perceptions of the military balance and attitudes toward unilateral disarmament, as proposed by groups such as the Interchurch Peace Council (IKV). People favoring the removal of nuclear weapons, irrespective of what other West European countries do, were indeed less likely to perceive a Soviet military advantage. Regarding the perceived goals of the United States and the Soviet Union in the military field, a large majority believed that the USSR seeks military superiority. A smaller group—but still a majority—believed that this is also the case for the United States. Support for the view that the United States seeks (only) parity increased, however, from 24 percent in October 1981 to 35 percent in December of the same year (USICA).

THE SOVIET THREAT TODAY

Whatever people may think about the alleged shift of the military balance in favor of the Soviet Union, they are, by and large, not very concerned about a Soviet military attack in the next five years, as is illustrated by data collected in 1981 (Table 6.4). There is little variation over time, and among the better educated even lower percentages are concerned. These outcomes are similar to July 1980, when 53 percent thought that the Soviet Union does not constitute a very serious danger to the countries of Western Europe, only ten percent believed the opposite ("very serious danger"), while 29 percent considered it a "fairly serious" danger. Also

Table 6.5   Concern over political pressure on the Netherlands by the Soviet Union
(SP 11/81)

	Total	Best-educated
Very concerned	5	7
Fairly concerned	20	13
Not very concerned	37	51
Not at all concerned	21	25
Don't know/no answer	17	5

according to USICA, few (12 percent) believed that "in the end the Soviet Union will dominate the world"; 79 percent did not believe this would happen. One may argue, however, that even though a direct Soviet attack against Western Europe may be unlikely the Soviet Union could use its military power to exercise political pressure. What do people think about this possibility?

The relative lack of concern shown in Table 6.5 may be misleading. Only 15 percent expressed agreement with the following statement: "There is no danger to be afraid of coming from the Soviet Union, even if we would be in a weaker military position. The Soviet Union would not misuse a possible preponderance or interfere with our domestic affairs and respect our independence." Eighty-three percent disagreed. Among the supporters of unilateral nuclear disarmament 75 percent disagreed, and 23 percent agreed.

Table 6.6 presents results from an effort to investigate perceived sources of threat. The wording of response categories and their overlap make it rather difficult to interpret the data; one can do little more than speculate. The fact that the poll was held early in 1981 explains why a Soviet invasion in Poland was among the threats most frequently mentioned. Nevertheless, while 25 percent saw the long-term buildup of Soviet military forces as the greatest threat, many more pointed to the more general increase of tensions between the United States and the USSR as a threat to the security of the Netherlands. Worth noting is also the number of those who were afraid of the buildup of U.S. military forces: 12 percent at the mass level and 21 percent among the best-educated. There is some evidence, therefore, that it is the general buildup of weapons on both sides, with the resulting tensions, that seems to be worrying people in addition to the threat of a Soviet attack. This conclusion is underscored by the responses to a related question in the same poll (Table 6.7). While more respondents blamed the Soviet Union than the United States for current tensions, more than one-third blamed both sides equally.

While many blame the Soviet Union for its perceived aggressiveness, the danger of war, according to the public, seems to emanate to a considerable extent from the bipolar confrontation between the two

Table 6.6   Threats to the security of the Netherlands (USICA 3/81)

	Total	Best-educated
Economic demands by developing countries	9	5
Cut-off access to Middle East oil	25	28
Long-term buildup of Soviet military forces	25	26
Soviet intervention in Poland	36	38
Increased competition with the United States and Japan over raw materials	8	2
Soviet military presence in Afghanistan	7	6
Increased tension between the United States and the USSR	41	55
Long-term buildup of US military forces	12	21
No answer	10	5

Note: Percentages sum to more than 100 as respondents were asked to choose two items.

superpowers, from the system in other words, rather than from one particular troublemaker. This is also underscored by an international poll undertaken by *Newsweek* (31 January 1983) early in 1983. Only 31 percent (much less than in other European countries) of the Dutch public named the Soviet Union in reply to the question "Who is more likely to initiate a nuclear attack in Europe, the Soviet Union or the United States?" 20 percent named the United States, and 49 percent could or would not answer (we will return to this issue).

Images of Security

THE FEAR OF WAR AND OTHER CONCERNS

It is often said, especially by opponents of the peace movements, that resistance to nuclear weapons is mainly based on an unjustified fear of war or on a more general and vague anxiety, which, as some of them argue, is skilfully manipulated to undermine the will to defend and confidence in

Table 6.7   Responsibility for current East-West tensions (USICA 3/81)

	Total	Best-educated
United States	11	20
USSR	45	36
Both are responsible (volunteered)	37	43
Don't know/no answer	7	2

Table 6.8   Expectations of world war within the next ten years

1945	32
1948	52
1950	41
1953	11
1957	18
1960	10
1962 (Oct.)	10
1962 (Nov.)	19
1967	10
1971	10
1977	7

Source: Oorlogsverwachtingen (1978)

the system of war-prevention through deterrence. The apparent shift in deterrence theory away from pure deterrence and toward the possibility of fighting a nuclear war (together with the perceived increase in the likelihood of a limited nuclear war in Europe) plays a major role in this discussion. But what do we actually know about perceptions of the likelihood of a new world war? One series of data suggests that fear of a new world war has decreased strongly since the late forties and has since then fluctuated around ten percent with only little variation (Table 6.8).

Other sources, however, suggest an increase in the fear of war (Table 6.9). Similar results were reported by KRO-Brandpunt TV in February 1981: 68 percent felt that the danger of war had increased in the past ten years, and only three percent felt that they had decreased. The number of those who saw little or no danger—a small majority—seems, however, not to have changed in the last ten years. The fluctuations in the don't know/no answer category are intriguing, moreover.

Results pointing in the same direction (but from a somewhat different question) were obtained in 1982. Replying to the question "How large do

Table 6.9   Likelihood of a new world war within next ten years (Eurobarometer)

	7/71	10-11/77	4/80	10/81
Likely (chance over 50)	9	16	20	19
50	13	19	9	21
Unlikely (chance under 50)	37	45	47	41
No danger	27	17	10	13
Don't know/no answer	14	3	14	6

you think is the chance that war will break out within the next ten years between the countries of NATO and those of the Warsaw Pact?" ten percent said "very large," 31 percent "fairly large," 37 percent "fairly small," and 22 percent "very small" (Stichting Krijgsmacht 1982 en Maatschappij). In response to a question concerning the likelihood that U.S.-Soviet hostilities would escalate into a third world war, ten percent of the Dutch sample answered "very likely," 21 percent "somewhat likely," and 60 percent "unlikely"; nine percent did not know (*Newsweek* 31 January 1983). Other data concerning the likelihood of a (nuclear) war will also be discussed.

These outcomes do not support the conventional wisdom that countries like the Netherlands are in the grip of a "war scare," utilized by a movement skilfully manipulating people's fears for their own purposes. That fear of an imminent war dominates people's feelings is certainly an overstatement. While people do not, in general, think that the chance of a nuclear war is very great, they see little chance of personal survival if a nuclear war would occur: 32 percent expected certain death, 36 percent expected a very small chance of survival, and only four percent saw a large chance to survive a nuclear war (NIPO). In another survey (KRO-Brandpunt TV 1/81) 71 percent thought they would not survive a nuclear war.

Although far more people consider domestic problems such as unemployment as the greatest concern to them, the problem of nuclear weapons was mentioned by about half of all respondents in the Netherlands as the greatest threat to them in two international polls, undertaken at the initiative of the Atlantic Institute for International Affairs in late 1982 and in March 1983. Together with the Norwegians, the Dutch showed a relatively large number of people concerned about nuclear weapons (49 and 53 percent, respectively) and the threat of war (32 and 33 percent) compared to the other countries in the survey. In all of the other countries, more people were worried in 1982 by crime than by nuclear weapons. This seems to contradict the findings mentioned earlier. When it comes to assessing the factors responsible for international tensions the Dutch do not, however, deviate consistently from the other countries. They are not less worried by the Soviet military buildup than is the case in other countries.

In the attitudes examined here, there are interesting differences between adherents of the various political parties. Respondents on the left are relatively more worried by the danger of war and the problems of nuclear weapons than those on the right, which, in turn, are relatively more concerned by law and order. An impression of the relative salience of issues of peace and security can be gained from the factors mentioned by people as decisive for their voting behavior. Results obtained in 1982 are shown in Table 6.10.

There are remarkable differences between voters of the parties of the left and center left (PvdA and D'66) and those of the center and center

Table 6.10   Factors influencing voting behavior (NIPO 1982)

	Percentage mentioned as decisive for voting
Unemployment	24
Protection of lowest incomes and social security	16
Security in the streets and at home	13
New nuclear weapons in the Netherlands	11
Protection of the environment	10

Rank order of decisive items by party preference (percentage in brackets)

	PvdA	D'66	CDA	VVD
Protect lowest incomes and social security	1 (23)	2 (19)	2 (14)	3 (14)
New nuclear weapons	2 (15)	1 (20)	8 (6)	6 (6)
Security in the streets and at home	3 (13)	3 (15)	1 (16)	2 (15)
Nuclear power reactors	4 (10)	4 (14)	7 (7)	10 (4)
Maintain health care	5 (9)	7 (7)	4 (9)	9 (4)
Protection of the environment	6 (9)	5 (11)	5 (9)	5 (9)
Reduce government expenditures	7 (7)	6 (8)	3 (11)	4 (12)
Strengthen business and industry	8 (6)	8 (6)	6 (8)	1 (17)
Reduce working hours	9 (4)	10 (2)	9 (4)	7 (5)
Freeze incomes	10 (3)	9 (2)	10 (4)	8 (5)

right (CDA and VVD). The first were much more inclined to mention the deployment of new nuclear weapons as a decisive factor for their voting behavior. Of all respondents, 68 percent rejected deployment, while 25 percent were willing to accept it. Of the first group, 14 percent said the issue was decisive for them. For the second group, this was the case only for five percent.

HOW TO RESPOND TO INTERNATIONAL THREATS

Despite a strong reluctance to use military force and a widespread rejection of the use of nuclear weapons, there is a general, though perhaps grudging, acceptance in the Netherlands of the need to maintain a military equilibrium between East and West and to maintain armed forces for this purpose. Let me first review a few questions that have been asked repeatedly and thus permit comparisons across time. One of the major means by which NATO tries to fulfil its function to maintain peace and defend the allies against aggression is to pursue a military equilibrium between East and West. This goal is subscribed to by a two-thirds majority of the population, and there is very little fluctuation over time since 1974

Table 6.11   Need for military counterweight against the East (NIPO)

	7/74	11/74	1/79	1/80	12/80	10/81
Military counterweight is needed	70	66	67	65	68	65
Military counterweight is not needed	14	24	21	22	21	19
Don't know/no answer	16	10	12	13	11	16

(Table 6.11). The same continuous support for the necessity to maintain armed forces is visible in Table 6.12.

Other data (*Elseviers Magazine* 4 December 1982) also support the conclusion that the idea of military defense as such is only rejected by rather small minorities: 71 percent agreed with the statement "a country should defend itself against a military attack." In response to the statement "a people which does not defend itself is not worth its freedom" 47 percent agreed, 31 percent disagreed, and the others did not reply. In response to the statement "(compulsory) military service is necessary," 61 percent agreed, 18 percent disagreed, and 21 percent did not reply. Seventy percent disapproved of the statement that everyone should refuse military service; only 11 percent agreed. The statement "an occupation, like that by the Germans in 1940–1945, would still be better than to wage war" was rejected by 54 and accepted by 28 percent. Similarly, even among those who thought they had no or only a very small chance to survive a new European war, sizeable majorities would prefer to fight rather than capitulate. These figures contrast rather starkly with data on the willingness actually to *use* military force, as will be shown.

ATTITUDES ON THE USE OF CONVENTIONAL AND NUCLEAR WEAPONS

Dutch membership in NATO has never been—as we shall see—a matter of serious controversy in the Netherlands. We have already found that a

Table 6.12   Attitudes on the armed forces

	1963	1964	1965	1966	1967	1968	1974	1982
The armed forces are								
necessary	59	48	46	46	40	47	45	52
a necessary evil	34	35	35	34	40	35	41	30
hardly necessary	3	5	4	6	7	6	8	9
superfluous	3	7	8	6	9	6	6	9
don't know/no answer	1	5	7	8	4	6	0	0

Source: Stichting Krijgsmacht (1982)

sizeable majority has continually subscribed to the idea that military equilibrium between East and West should be maintained. There also is considerable support for the view that the preservation of peace in Europe is at least partly due to the existence of an equilibrium of (nuclear) deterrence (some surveys, however, have offered contradictory evidence on this latter point (ISEO, 1981 and Krijgsmacht en Maatschappij, 1982)).

Belief in the necessity of the Atlantic Alliance and the need of a military equilibrium, including nuclear weapons, does not automatically lead to a willingness to use the available weapons should deterrence fail and war occur. But it is not obvious that people are making a distinction between possession and use of nuclear weapons, a distinction that is often made in ethical debates. In order to find out what people's attitudes on these topics are one has to dig deeper, and even then one probably only gets hypothetical answers. Support for the possession of nuclear weapons can be given today, but the preparedness actually to use them is always conditional and would only be put to the test if and when the decisive moment would arrive. Still, the available evidence is interesting: it does contradict the widespread support for NATO.

If the question is asked in general terms, the use of nuclear weapons is almost completely rejected. In 1977, 72 percent of respondents did not agree that the use of nuclear weapons could be acceptable under certain circumstances (De Nederlandse Kiezer 1977). Another survey, for VARA radio, revealed that only 12 percent agreed that our security should be based on nuclear weapons, while 81 percent rejected this. In 1974, these figures were 13 and 82 percent, respectively (VARA). Support for the proposition that people do distinguish between possession and use of nuclear weapons can be found in the results of a survey held in 1974. Respondents were confronted with four cases of military threats and asked which countermeasures they would support (Table 6.13).

It appears that the hypothetical preparedness to use nuclear weapons and to accept the consequences of the threats inherent in NATO's strategy, which could be deduced from the support of NATO membership, dwindles when confronted with the alternatives available if deterrence were to break down. People do make a distinction between nuclear and conventional force, a larger number accepts only the latter, as is also evident in Table 6.14. One wonders whether the futility of "defense" prevails in people's minds or the fact that retaliation would have to be carried out by nuclear weapons.

Both elements were contained in the following question, asked in 1981 (NIPO): "Some people say that a nuclear war would be so terrible that it would be better to be conquered by the Soviet Union than to fight and defend the Netherlands with all the possible consequences." Thirty-seven percent agreed, 53 percent did not and would be prepared to fight and accept the consequences. That something in the order of 35 percent (in 1981, the number seems to have increased to 45 percent in 1983) is a good estimate of the share of "nuclear pacifists" also appears in Table 6.15. The same number of 36 percent appears for statement I in the 1981 poll. While

Table 6.13   Use of military force in various scenarios

	No counter-measures	Alert forces	Use armed forces	Use nuclear weapons
One or more countries concentrate troops at the borders of our allies Denmark and Western Germany	19	69	13	–
One or more countries cut off all roads of access to West Berlin, including access by air	41	50	9	–
One or more countries undertake an attack with tanks, aircraft and rockets on Western Europe, including the Netherlands	9	26	62	4
One or more countries undertake a nuclear attack on Western Europe	19	20	21	40

Source: Stichting Volk en Verdediging (1977)

logically the 32 percent opposing statement II could include those who also are in favor of the use of nuclear weapons in circumstances other than a first use by the other side, it appears from the responses to statements I and III that this is not generally the case and that they consist largely of the same group of nuclear pacifists. From statement III, one can conclude that the option of first use of nuclear weapons is accepted only by a very small minority. The general trend is unmistakable: There is a group of complete nuclear pacifists and a group who does not reject all use of nuclear weapons. The latter is subdivided into those who would accept nuclear use in retaliation only and a small minority who would be willing also to consider first use by NATO in response to a conventional attack.

At first sight these results seem to reveal a discrepancy between the

Table 6.14   How to react if the Netherlands were attacked by the Soviet Union (USICA 10/81)

	With conventional weapons	With nuclear weapons
We should		
Resist	73	56
Not resist	18	33
Don't know/no answer	9	12

Table 6.15   Attitudes on the use of nuclear weapons

| | (I) | | | (II) | (III) | |
	KO 1972	ISEO 1981	ISEO 1983	ISEO 1981	ISEO 1981	ISEO 1983
Agree (completely)	36	36	45	51	9	11
Disagree (completely)	49	44	41	32	74	77
Don't know/no answer/undecided	16	21	14	18	17	11

Note:
Question wording:

I.The use of nuclear weapons is not acceptable under any circumstances, not even if we are attacked with nuclear weapons ourselves.

II. Nuclear weapons in Western Europe should only be used to defend the West, if the East would attack with nuclear weapons.

III. If the Eastern bloc would attack Western Europe without using nuclear weapons, we would be justified in using nuclear weapons to bring about an end to the war quickly.

support for NATO membership and the almost total rejection of the actual use of nuclear weapons. This calls for explanation. Various possibilities are at hand. Respondents may, for instance, try to "reconcile" their attitudes by making a distinction between NATO as an organization and its strategy and policies, or between possession and actual use of nuclear weapons. It may also be the case that the attitudes which we find are separate aspects and are not mutually related. In that case, the relations between these partial aspects have not entered respondents' attention. This results in acceptance of present security policies for lack of a better alternative, as long as the threat to use nuclear weapons is not put to the test.

DEFENSE EXPENDITURES

One other measure of the salience of security problems is the degree to which people are willing to spend money on defense. It is often argued, especially by those who see the military balance shifting to the advantage of the Warsaw Pact, that the West should strengthen its military forces and increase expenditures for defense. But despite the opinion of a majority that the Netherlands should follow majority decisions on defense and armaments in NATO, there is very little sympathy with proposals to increase defense expenditures, even by those who share the perception that NATO is weaker than its opponents (see Figure 6.1).

That lack of support for increases in the defense budget is not something new but rather the continuation of an existing trend is shown in Figure 6.1. This figure should be seen against the background of a persistent feeling that government expenditure in general ought to be reduced. This position was supported by clear majorities in 1967 and 1972

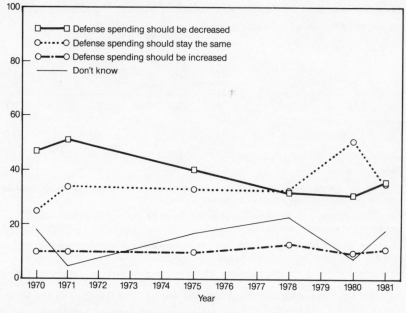

Sources: NIPO (1970, 1971); Dutch Continuous Survey (1975, 1978);
         USICA (1980, 1981)

Figure 6.1
Attitudes on the defense budget 1970-1981

(Nederlandse Kiezer 1967, 1972) and by as much as 80 percent in 1980 (NIPO). In 1967, 58 percent thought that the government should cut back on defense expenditures rather than on expenditures in other areas. One recent study concluded that while support for reducing defense expenditures may have decreased, this had not resulted in a willingness to spend more. The Dutch accept the present level of defense spending, but they do it "contre coeur" (Eichenberg 1983).

Recent data support this conclusion. In 1980, only 21 percent agreed that it is more important to maintain our national defense than our social security, and in 1983 only 27 percent were against reducing military in favor of social expenditures (Eichenberg 1983). In January 1981, however, 55 percent favored the proposition that the Netherlands should stick to the NATO agreement annually to increase defense expenditures by three percent (40 percent disagreed). A somewhat larger degree of sympathy (21 percent) for strengthening Dutch defense efforts rather than pushing for arms control negotiations first (44 percent) also appears to exist when questions are phrased more generally, the need to maintain a balance of power is mentioned specifically, and when no direct reference is made to defense expenditures (USICA 3/81). Attitudes on defense spending were surveyed more recently in yet another way (Table 6.16). The view that too much money is spent on defense was shared by 40 percent. When we look

Table 6.16   Attitudes on defense expenditures

	A	B	
Agree completely	15	17	Disagree completely
Agree	25	34	Disagree
Neither agree nor disagree	22	20	Neither agree nor disagree
Disagree	24	19	Agree
Disagree completely	6	4	Agree completely
Don't know/no answer	7	6	Don't know/no answer

Source: Krijgsmacht en Maatschappij (1983)

Note:

A: "In the Netherlands far too much money is spent on defense"
B: "If need be we should spend more money on defense"

at the opposite statement we find that it was rejected by even more respondents, 51 percent. That there is a strong correlation ($r = -.57$) between the two patterns of responses is not surprising. The answers, however, may be misleading. It could be that respondents feel that all government expenditures should be reduced, but defense expenditures less than others. That turns out to be the case for only 8 percent of the respondents.

INTEREST AND INVOLVEMENT IN THE NUCLEAR WEAPONS ISSUE

It is often said that public opinion data should be treated with care because surveys usually do not distinguish between those who are interested in and/or knowledgeable on the subject and those who are not. It is necessary to make this distinction, as uninterested people may just say what comes to their mind, what they have just heard, or what they perceive to be the socially "correct" answer.[2] It is also necessary if one wants to explore the possible impact on the political behavior of respondents and the political significance of the distribution of opinions one finds. Are people willing to

2. In addition to the wording of the questions and the context in which these are presented, the larger societal situation also may have an important influence on the outcomes of opinion polls: "Often a certain opinion happens to be fashionable, and thus it seems decent to join that opinion (. . .). We too easily assume that everyone has a well-founded opinion about everything. That assumption often implies that one gets a lot of nonsense. Never having thought about the problem in question, people give the fashionable answer." (Interview with P. H. van Westendorp, De Volkskrant 16 May 1981.)

If this is true and people answer according to what they perceive to be the current (and hence desirable) view, it is nevertheless remarkable that the image of the general opinion climate is one in which rejection of nuclear weapons is considered to be the common view. Thus, we indirectly find an argument for the proposition that there really is a rather fundamental reorientation of views on the security policy and the role of the Netherlands, which is no longer perceived as "a loyal ally."

Table 6.17   Concern about the arms race (SP 12/82)

	Concerned	Trust governments	Don't know / no answer
PvdA	70	30	0
D'66	91	9	0
CDA	33	65	2
VVD	38	62	0
Small left parties	100	0	0
Small right parties	35	65	0
Total	52	47	1

Note:
Question wording:

"There is concern about the official policies of governments. It is feared that ever more weapons are deployed which could lead to a catastrophe. Therefore, in many different ways and from different angles, people try to bring about changes and force the governments to other policies. Irrespective of what you think about the peace movement and its tactics, do you share this concern or do you trust that governments will act responsibly?"

act upon their conviction, or is their interest marginal compared with other issues? Are they willing to support initiatives to bring about changes in the desired direction?

In one survey (USICA 1981) 48 percent said that they follow news about national defense and security issues either fairly or very closely (an equal number said the opposite). This was confirmed by another poll (ISEO 1981), in which 40 percent said that they followed all developments in the field of nuclear weapons as closely as possible. That these percentages were even higher among the best-educated is not surprising. Three out of four people said that they were seriously concerned about nuclear weapons.

As can be seen in Table 6.17, there are remarkable differences in concern between voters of the left and the right. On the left there is general concern, while on the right majorities tend to trust their government instead. What does this really mean? How strong is this sentiment? What will happen in politics? In this respect the opinions of those who are involved in the problem and strongly committed to a particular opinion may be more relevant than the views of those who have only a marginal interest or are ill-informed. But even assuming that these figures give a reliable indication of true interest, people may still feel that they lack the necessary information and that these matters are too complicated for the layman and ought to be dealt with by the experts. In an earlier survey (Nederlandse Kiezer 1977), for example, 64 percent agreed with the statement: "Problems such as the relations between East and West, the unification of Europe, and other such problems are too complicated for people like myself."

In 1982, a number of questions were devoted to perceptions of the complexity of questions of security and the consequences to be attached to this in terms of making political decisions on these questions. The results are ambiguous and show a divided public (Stichting Krijgsmacht en Maatschappij 1982). Forty percent agreed that defense problems can well be understood by those who are not experts, 32 percent disagreed. But when it came to a more concrete example of such problems, an opposite picture emerged: 46 percent affirmed the difficulty of weighing the pros and cons of removal of nuclear weapons for the layperson. A similar inconsistency in answers can be discovered with respect to two other questions: 61 percent felt that the opinions of the majority of the popula-tion should be decisive for what happens with nuclear weapons in the Netherlands. This seems to be a clear vote of confidence in the democratic process. But only 32 percent faced up to the consequences by concluding that the final decision should, therefore, not be left to the parliament; 49 percent thought that it should.

This evidence that one-third of all respondents would not be willing to leave the final decision to parliament also appears from answers to another question: "(If it is decided to deploy new nuclear weapons in the Nether-lands) should one abide by that decision or continue to oppose it?" The question was only put to those who earlier had said they were completely opposed to the missiles. Eighty-two percent (or one-third of all respon-dents) said they would continue opposition (NIPO 9/82). The question was asked again in a somewhat different form in December 1982 (SP). Almost a majority (49 percent) now was prepared to continue to oppose the decision. This came primarily from the left, but even among the right there was about one-third that would not acquiesce in the decision. A small minority (seven percent) would consider civil disobedience to stop the missiles.

One also sees that concern about the arms race does not imply that one would continue to oppose government decisions one dislikes, nor that trust in government implies a willingness to follow whatever it decides. One effort to establish a reliable measure of interest, involvement, and action disposition with respect to problems of public concern has been developed by van Westendorp (1981). His method allows one to study the development of involvement over time, to evaluate the meaning of opin-ions expressed by people on social problems, and to study groups of people with different degrees of involvement.[3]

---

3. The measure of involvement is derived by calculating scores for (subjective) levels of interest and knowledge, topical perception (which issues preoccupy many people?), cognitive involvement (issues read or spoken about), and emotional involvement (issues concerned about). Action disposition is also measured.

Every three months, involvement with thirty-six "standard" problems and nine "current"

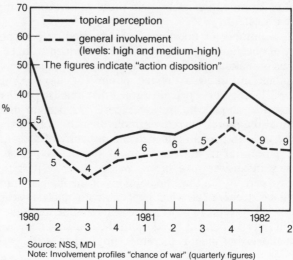

Source: NSS, MDI
Note: Involvement profiles "chance of war" (quarterly figures)

Figure 6.2

An interesting result of the application of this method is the following. One of the items in the list of standard problems is armaments and disarmament, which is described as "the arms race between countries, atomic armaments, Netherlands and NATO, disarmament and peace negotiations, etc." By way of experiment the reference to atomic weapons was left out in one of the regular surveys. Results show that involvement in problems of armament and disarmament drops considerably if this reference is not made. This drop cannot be explained by general variations in involvement over time, which remained constant over the period that was investigated (Nederlandse Stichting voor Statistiek 1981).

The profile of involvement with regard to armaments questions (including atomic weapons) was very similar to the profile for nuclear energy, while the profile for armaments questions (without mentioning atomic weapons) was different and more similar to the profile for the danger of war. Modernization of nuclear weapons showed a similar profile to the first, and the profile for Netherlands and NATO was similar to the second. The authors concluded that it is a general concern with "the atom" which leads to a high degree of involvement with both the problems of nuclear

---

problems is measured, which enables to judge to what degree topics remain on or disappear from the "public agenda." By extracting from raw data those with the lowest degree of interest, involvement, and action disposition one can get at the hard core of people who are committed and/or have strong opinions on a particular topic and separate them from those that are not involved. By comparing involvement with one topic with the general level of involvement with a whole range of topics, one can arrive at a measure of relative involvement.

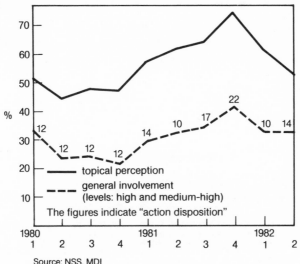

Source: NSS, MDI
Note: Involvement profiles "armament/disarmament" (quarterly figures)

Figure 6.3

weapons and nuclear energy. Concern with the more general problem of armaments and chances of war is weaker and it leads to much less involvement. Modernization of nuclear weapons is characterized by a high level of emotional involvement and a high action disposition among relatively few people, which supports the view that this matter mainly appeals to a restricted group of people (represented by special interest groups).

This study also led to a confirmation of the frequently heard argument that involvement in foreign affairs is relatively low compared to domestic problems. How "topical knowledge" (the perception of general interest in and concern with a specific problem), "general involvement" and "action disposition" vary over time is portrayed in Figures 6.2, 6.3, and 6.4, which show these variations for war and peace in general, nuclear weapons, and nuclear energy. These profiles show how involvement, especially concerning the last two problems, gradually increased until it reached a maximum toward the end of 1981 (coinciding with the demonstration in Amsterdam on 21 November 1981), and then decreased again, while remaining at a higher level than in 1980, however. These profiles, moreover, underscore previous remarks on the linkage between nuclear weapons and nuclear energy issues.

SUPPORT FOR THE PEACE MOVEMENT

Bearing in mind that surveys that combine the problem of nuclear weapons with problems of war and peace in general or which focus on

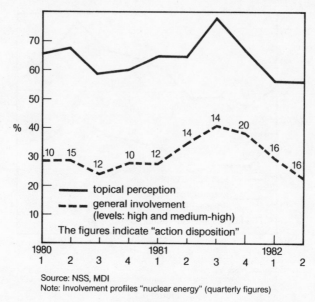

Source: NSS, MDI
Note: Involvement profiles "nuclear energy" (quarterly figures)

Figure 6.4

nuclear weapons probably lead to an overestimation of concern with war in general, one must turn to other data which gives additional information on the degree and character of concern with nuclear weapons. They deal in particular with the degree of support for demonstrations as a means to show one's opposition to established policies and support for the peace movement (Table 6.18).

One the one hand, the problem is apparently so frightening and so overwhelming that many people turn to apathy rather than to action: 38 percent said that they do not think about nuclear weapons at all. But there was also a group of some 50 percent that not only rejected nuclear weapons but also expressed a remarkable show of sympathy with people demonstrating against them; only a somewhat smaller group thought that everyone should follow the example of the demonstrators. But a group of the same size held opposite views. Sympathy with the demonstrators increased considerably between 1981 and 1983: from 48 to 60 percent. The same is true for the view that everybody should take to the streets to demonstrate against nuclear weapons. Agreement increased from 37 to 47 percent.

Results of another poll also show that there is an amazing degree of support for those who actually do take part in demonstrations. It was held shortly after the demonstration in Amsterdam of 21 November 1981. Ninety-four percent of all respondents stated it had made a favorable impression on them (NIPO 12/81). This result is confirmed by a some-

Table 6.18 Attitudes on nuclear weapons and the peace movement (ISEO)

	Agree com-pletely	Agree	Neither agree nor disagree	Dis-agree	Disagree com-pletely	Don't know/no answer	
I rather do not think about nuclear weapons at all	15	23	10	37	12	2	(1981)
All this fuss about nuclear weapons is greatly exaggerated	5	16	16	46	15	2	(1981)
The antinuclear movement is paid by the Russians	1	5	31	38	20	5	(1981)
I have admiration for people who take part in a demonstration against nuclear weapons	14	34	16	25	10	2	(1981)
	28	32	15	16	9	0	(1983)
Everybody should take to the streets to demonstrate against nuclear weapons	15	22	16	33	11	2	(1981)
	24	23	16	26	12	0	(1983)
If the government and parliament decide to deploy new nuclear missiles in our country demonstrations against this should stop	14	21	17	28	20	0	(1983)
If the government and parliament should decide to deploy new nuclear missiles in our country I would not really mind if acts of sabotage were carried out against this	10	16	15	36	23	0	(1983)

what earlier poll comparing views in four Western European countries (Table 6.19).

Demonstrations are only one particular form of action, and the fact that one rejects demonstrations does not necessarily imply that one is not prepared to undertake any action at all. Attitudes toward demonstrations are correlated with attitudes toward nuclear weapons in general (tau = .36), fear of nuclear war (tau = .31), and—to a lesser extent—with

Table 6.19 Sympathy for peace demonstrations in Western Europe

	Netherlands	France	Great Britain	West Germany
Totally sympathetic	46	22	23	23
Mostly sympathetic	33	28	29	36
Mostly unsympathetic	9	13	15	22
No sympathy at all	8	21	24	16
Don't know/no answer	4	16	9	3

Source: *Nouvel Observateur* 11/81

attitudes toward the Eastern bloc (tau = −.17). It is evident that the problem is taken seriously by many people and that few people believe in the accusation that the peace movement is but a tool of Soviet foreign policy.

Although the group which actually takes part in demonstrations or other forms of pressure may constitute only a minority, it is surely not without reason that it is seen as the tip of the iceberg rather than as an isolated minority. Majorities show sympathy with demonstrators in all four countries, but this sympathy is strongest in the Netherlands. Support in words or in an opinion poll, however, is not the same as acting upon these words. Thus, for instance, there is little evidence that the nuclear weapons issue played an important role in determining behavior of voters in the 1981 and 1982 parliamentary elections in the Netherlands, in spite of the fact that this issue was among the most discussed items in the campaign preceding the elections (Everts 1983).

The degree of sympathy for the peace movement and its activities may actually also be somewhat less if we consider the fact that, in reply to the question "what is your attitude to the Dutch peace movement; think of IKV, Stop the Neutron Bomb, Women's Peace Camps, Pax Christi, that sort?" nine percent answered "very sympathetic," 35 percent "sympathetic," 34 percent "somewhat suspicious," and 20 percent "very suspicious" (ISEO 2/83). Contrary to the figures quoted earlier, there seems to be less than a majority which is sympathetic to the peace movement, but still 44 percent, at least as defined in this question. More people (48 percent), however, rejected the idea that demonstrations should stop once a decision to deploy the missiles would be taken. About one-quarter can be considered to be the hard core of the opposition. They say they would not mind if acts of sabotage were to occur against deployment (Table 6.18). Although expressions of sympathy are not the same as concrete action, the latter figure still gives some indication of the degree of opposition to be expected if the government of the Netherlands were to proceed with deploying cruise missiles.

Images of Deterrence

NUCLEAR WEAPONS AND THE DANGER OF WAR

Official policies on nuclear weapons are based on a number of assumptions. One such assumption is that peace is maintained only through an equilibrium of strength and deterrence. It is also contended that without nuclear weapons military defense is not possible and that one will have to learn to live with them. The question now is to what extent the movement against nuclear weapons can capitalize on a general rejection of these nuclear assumptions, or whether it is fear and moral outrage which primarily form its basis.

A number of questions on this topic were included in the 1981 ISEO survey "Meningen over kernwapens" (see Table 6.20). There was rather firm agreement that the present equilibrium between East and West is conducive to the maintenance of peace. On the question whether nuclear weapons help to prevent or rather add to the danger of war, however, opinions were divided into almost equal parts. When it came to the question what additional nuclear weapons would do to the chances of war, scepticism about their war-preventing role reached a majority (which has become even more pronounced since 1981).

Although it is often argued that the plans to introduce new nuclear weapons into Europe should be seen as evidence of an effort to create the option of confining nuclear war to Europe, it was not generally believed that this would actually be possible. A firm majority believed that a nuclear war in Europe would escalate into a world war. This belief was less firm with respect to a war between India and Pakistan, should nuclear weapons be used there: only 30 percent held that this would lead to a world war, compared with 55 percent in the case of war in Europe.

On the basis of four items included in this survey, ISEO was able to construct a scale (items two through five in Table 6.20) to obtain a measure of the fear of nuclear war. It appears that 40 percent tended to agree with most of these statements, 37 percent scored predominantly neutral, and 23 percent tended to disagree with most of these statements. Fear of war, as measured by these four variables, was correlated with the political left-right dimension: The more leftist the stronger the fear of war. It was also possible to construct a general scale for attitudes on nuclear weapons. By cumulating item scores a general score was calculated. It appeared that 36 percent could be considered to be opposed to nuclear weapons, 27 percent obtained a neutral score, and another 36 percent were favorable toward nuclear weapons. High scores against nuclear weapons were obtained for people of age 25 to 34, persons with a higher education, humanists, those without a religion, and those with leftist orientation. Supporters of CDA and VVD were predominantly in favor of nuclear weapons (52 and 77 percent, respectively). Not surprisingly, opposition to nuclear weapons was closely related to the fear of war (Table 6.21).

Table 6.20   The role of nuclear weapons and the likelihood of war (ISEO 7/81)

	Agree totally	Agree	Neither agree nor disagree	Dis- agree	Disagree totally	Don't know/no answer
The present equilibrium between East and West is the best guarantee for peace	15	36	21	20	5	3
The use of nuclear weapons on a small scale in Europe will lead to a world war	15	40	23	16	3	3
A war between India and Pakistan in which nuclear weapons would be used will lead to a world war	6	24	31	32	3	3
The presence of nuclear weapons in Europe only increases the chances of war	14	29	16	31	7	3
The increase of nuclear weapons in Europe only increases the chances of war[a]	16	33	17	27	5	3
	24	28	17	25	6	3
If there would be no nuclear weapons in the Netherlands, our country would not be attacked with nuclear weapons	1	7	14	49	25	3
If the Netherlands should decide no longer to admit any nuclear weapons on our territory, this would decrease the chances of a nuclear war	3	17	22	43	12	3

Note:
[a] Second row: ISEO 1983

NUCLEAR WEAPONS IN THE NETHERLANDS

Although it has been overshadowed in recent years by the more pressing issues of the introduction of neutron warheads and the modernization of NATO's intermediate range nuclear weapons, whether nuclear weapons should be deployed in the country at all remains a central topic of the public debate on security policy. There are really two questions at issue here. One concerns the presence of nuclear weapons on Dutch territory, the second concerns the way they should be removed, if one is in favor of removal. The IKV has proposed immediate and unilateral removal, others

Table 6.21   Attitudes on nuclear weapons and fear of war (ISEO 7/81)

| | Attitude on nuclear weapons | | | | |
Fear of war	Strongly against	Against	Neutral	Favorable	Very favorable
Much afraid	39	31	19	9	2
Afraid	18	31	30	17	4
Neutral	5	19	38	28	10
Not (so) afraid	3	10	6	41	29

Note:

tau = .42, p. = .001

stress a more gradual process and do not wish to take steps outside the NATO framework. Related is also the question of the nuclear tasks of the Dutch armed forces. In this section, the results of a number of recent polls on these questions will be presented.

One should begin with the presence of nuclear weapons in the Netherlands as well as Western Europe in general. In the discussion on the removal of nuclear weapons from the Netherlands some people are accused of being hypocrites or "free riders," in the sense that they wish to enjoy the protection of nuclear weapons but are unwilling to pay the costs and accept the risks. Is this criticism justified? Answers to three related questions throw some light on this question (Table 6.22).

It can be argued that there are sound strategic and political arguments to restrict the deployment of nuclear weapons to the United States, and therefore the "free rider" argument does not carry as much weight in the case of the first statement as it does in the case of the second, that is, to be in favor of the deployment of nuclear weapons elsewhere in Western Europe but not in the Netherlands. A plurality of 46 percent disagreed with the first statement. This group could include the hypocrites and "free riders," as well as those who really are against nuclear weapons in the United States as well as in the whole of Western Europe. The second question should provide the answer. The number of those who rejected that statement is very large indeed: 74 percent refused an exclusive position for the Netherlands and only ten percent pleaded for such a position. If one cross-tabulates responses to the first and the second statement, it appears that most respondents have answered consistently. Only five percent of the whole sample can truly be called hypocrites: They disagreed with the first statement and accepted the second one. Strangely enough there also was another still smaller group (some three percent of the total sample) that agreed with both statements (Table 6.23).

The same pattern emerges if one cross-tabulates answers to the first and the third question. A few disagreed with the first and agreed with the third

Table 6.22   Attitudes on deployment of nuclear weapons (ISEO 7/81)

	Agree totally	Agree	Neither agree nor disagree	Dis- agree	Disagree totally	Don't know/no answer
Nuclear weapons should be deployed in the Netherlands, as well as in the rest of Western Europe and in the United States	9	27	15	27	19	3
Nuclear weapons should be deployed in Western Europe as well as in the United States, but not in the Netherlands	2	8	13	49	25	3
Nuclear weapons should be deployed in the United States only and not in Western Europe	4	9	15	49	20	3

statement, also there were some who agreed with both statements. In addition to the 46 percent who disagreed with the first statement, there were another seven percent who accepted one of the other two statements or both and thus partially rejected the deployment of nuclear weapons, which brings the share of rejecters to a total of 53 percent. It seems safe to conclude that a majority rejects the presence of nuclear weapons in the Netherlands, while some 40 percent also reject their presence in Western Europe. The question then is how to remove these weapons.

An unpublished survey by NIPO for the Ministry of Defense revealed that already in October 1978, 58 percent of respondents agreed with the

Table 6.23   Attitudes on deployment of nuclear weapons in Western Europe and the United States by deployment of nuclear weapons in the United States and Western Europe, except the Netherlands (ISEO 7/81)

Nuclear weapons in United States and Western Europe, except the Netherlands	Nuclear weapons everywhere				
	Agree totally	Agree	Neither agree nor disagree	Disagree	Disagree totally
Agree totally	5	1	1	2	2
Agree	3	8	8	12	4
Agree nor disagree	2	10	47	10	8
Disagree	36	69	36	66	53
Disagree totally	55	13	8	11	54

Table 6.24   Attitudes on removal of nuclear weapons from the Netherlands: The IKV
slogan (NIPO 10/79)

Only after consultation and in agreement	74
Unilaterally by the Netherlands	13
Don't know/no answer	13

Note:
Question wording:

"The IKV has presented the following slogan: 'Free the world of nuclear weapons, and begin in the Netherlands.' IKV thinks that in the coming cabinet period nuclear weapons should be removed from the Netherlands. Do you think that such a decision can be taken unilaterally by the Netherlands, or only after consultation and in agreement with the other NATO countries?"

IKV slogan "help rid the world of nuclear weapons, let it begin in the Netherlands" which was launched in 1977. In a NIPO survey of October 1979 a more detailed question was asked about the IKV proposal (Table 6.24). The outcome seems disastrous for IKV. But the stimulus did not differentiate between the wish to see nuclear weapons removed from the Netherlands and the way in which this should be done. The question asked whether this could be done unilaterally by the Netherlands, which can be read as "is this allowed according to the rules of NATO?" but also as "is this morally allowed?" In the first case, it is a knowledge question and lack of information about the formal procedures may have played a role in the answers. NIPO too, has felt some uneasiness: The title of the relevant section in its report reads "Unilateral decision concerning nuclear weapons can, should not (be taken), thinks a majority."

More recent polls indicate a much larger degree of support for the IKV proposals. Since 1979 discussions have become more intense, and consequently the public mood may have changed. Differences in the wording of questions may be equally as important, however. In a survey held in November 1979 (NOS Kijk-en luisteronderzoek) one can see how adding an in-between category affects outcomes. When asked whether NATO should unconditionally keep nuclear weapons, keep nuclear weapons under certain conditions, or should abolish nuclear weapons, 29 percent chose the first, 36 chose the second, and only 24 percent chose the third option. More people, but not a majority, spoke against allowing nuclear weapons to be stationed on Dutch soil in another poll held in March 1981 (USICA): 35 percent felt that this should be allowed; 43 percent said no. The highest percentage of opponents to nuclear weapons in the Netherlands was obtained in October 1980 (Table 6.25).

On the whole, two-thirds of respondents supported the idea that nuclear weapons should disappear from the Netherlands. Among women there was even more support for this idea. The breakdown according to

Table 6.25   Attitudes on nuclear weapons on Dutch territory by sex and political
preference (ISEO 10/80)

	Nuclear weapons may be in the Netherlands	Nuclear weapons should disappear	Don't know/ no answer
Men	35	59	7
Women	21	70	9
CPN	24	77	–
PSP	–	91	9
PPR	10	84	7
PvdA	14	82	5
D'66	25	70	5
CDA	39	53	8
VVD	59	34	7
SGP/GPV	56	39	5
Total	28	65	8

Note:
Question wording:

"Do you agree that there may be nuclear weapons on Dutch territory or do you think that nuclear weapons should disappear from the Netherlands?"

political preference shows a neat left-right pattern again. It seems as if the IKV demand was supported by a solid majority. But this conclusion is not entirely justified, and the results should be treated cautiously.[4] The stimulus can well be interpreted as a long-term goal which, in addition, has to be tied to a number of conditions, such as approval by NATO. It seems better, therefore, to base conclusions on another survey of January 1981 in which respondents were asked whether or not they supported the IKV slogan. The results produce evidence of strong support for the IKV proposal (Table 6.26) and confirm the doubts raised in connection with Table 6.22. This support is found primarily among the left, the parties now in opposition, but it is less strong (about 15 percent less) than Table 6.22 would have led us to conclude. This is so for each of the four major parties. Again, a gap appears between the government parties and the opposition. In another poll (ISEO 7/81), however, support for the IKV

4. Another poll, held in 1981 (KRO-Brandpunt TV, September 19), produced similar results: On the question "What do you think of the idea 'all nuclear weapons out of the Netherlands'?" 61 percent were in favor, 32 percent disapproved, and 7 percent gave no answer. This poll was held among Catholics only, but we know that these do not deviate in their answer patterns from the population in general. See for evidence Projectgroep Vijandsbeeld (1980) and Goddijn (1979).

Table 6.26   Support for IKV slogan by party preference (KRO-Brandpunt TV 2/81)

		Agree	Disagree	Don't know/ no answer
Total	54	41	5	
PvdA		68	27	5
D'66		58	37	5
CDA		39	56	5
VVD		25	70	5

proposal was slightly lower (30 percent agreed and 18 percent completely agreed).

Regarding nuclear weapons the question is not only whether they should be deployed in the Netherlands or not, but also whether the Netherlands' armed forces should carry out nuclear tasks. Even before the debate on this question took full force it had already appeared that a majority of the population rejected such tasks (Table 6.27). It is remarkable that this was already the case in 1975, before the peace movements began their campaign for removal of nuclear weapons. This confirms the notion that not so much the content but the intensity of attitudes has changed, which probably has increased disposition for action. The fact that in 1975, 11 percent considered nuclear tasks to be the most important aspect of the defense problem (compared with 23 percent in 1979) also shows that one has to do with increased intensity of feeling rather than with changes in the content of opinions.

What do we know about the motives of those opting for removal of nuclear weapons from the Netherlands or for a halt to further deployment? It has already been noted that the supporters of such a move would only to a limited extent like to see the Netherlands loosen its ties to NATO and adopt a neutral position (34 percent compared to 18 percent of the whole population). They did not believe more than others that this would help either to prevent a war in Europe or a nuclear war (NSS telephone survey for *Haagsche Courant*). This argument is rejected by large

Table 6.27   Attitudes on nuclear tasks of the Dutch armed forces (KO)

	1975	1979	1980
Should fulfill nuclear tasks (1980: remain equipped with nuclear weapons)	23	20	26
No nuclear tasks (no nuclear weapons)	60	53	56
Don't know/no answer	17	27	17

Table 6.28   Would other West European countries follow Dutch example to ban nuclear weapons (by opinions on deployment of nuclear weapons in the Netherlands)

	Total	In favor of deployment	Condition- ally in favor of deployment	Uncondi- tionally against deployment	Don't know/ no answer
Yes I expect so	24	12	13	38	10
No I do not expect so	64	84	82	48	43
Don't know/no answer	12	4	5	14	47

Source: *Haagsche Courant*, 24 April 1981

majorities among all groups. Nor did they believe more than others that the removal of nuclear weapons would increase chances of survival in a nuclear war. One can safely discard the thesis that these arguments play a major role in determining people's attitudes in favour of removal. This is underscored by the 1982 survey for Stichting Krijgsmacht en Maatschappij that included the following statement: "Whether there are nuclear weapons on Dutch territory or not has hardly any influence on international security." Forty-two percent agreed, 34 percent disagreed, and 24 percent took a position in between.

The proponents of removal of nuclear weapons often argue that such a step would lead other countries in the West, but in the East as well, to follow the Dutch example. Tables 6.28 and 6.29 show that this expectation plays only a limited role in considerations about deployment of (new) nuclear missiles. Fewer proponents of modernization expected such a reaction, opponents expected somewhat more imitation, but only to a limited extent. Very few had any illusions about reciprocation on the part

Table 6.29   Would East European countries follow Dutch example to ban nuclear weapons (by opinions on deployment of nuclear weapons in the Netherlands)

	Total	In favor of deployment	Condition- ally in favor of deployment	Uncondi- tionally against deployment	Don't know/ no answer
Yes	17	5	8	29	5
No	66	84	81	54	38
Don't know/no answer	17	11	11	17	57

Source: *Haagsche Courant*, 24 April 1981

Table 6.30   Attitudes on unilateral removal of nuclear weapons from the Netherlands
by party preference

	Total	PvdA	D'66	CDA	VVD
			Party preference		
Remove	38	48	45	26	17
Do not remove	58	49	51	70	81
Don't know/no answer	4	3	4	4	2

Source: NCRV Hier en Nu TV, 4/81

of Eastern Europe. This is also confirmed by ISEO data of June 1981 and the survey for Stichting Krijgsmacht en Maatschappij of January 1982.

At the same time, there was no widespread agreement with the argument often heard from opponents of removal, that is, that by removing nuclear weapons the Dutch would betray their allies. Thirty-two percent agreed wholly or in part to such a statement, 43 percent disagreed, and 24 percent either did not want to take sides on this issue or abstained from expressing an opinion (ISEO 6/81). If such arguments are not generally shared, what then are the decisive arguments for the opponents? Or in other words, is their number as large as the figures quoted above suggest?

When further questions are asked adding specific conditions the number of opponents diminishes indeed. A majority of respondents agreed that the presence of nuclear weapons in this world is no guarantee for peace and security (64 percent no and 32 percent yes). However, while 85 percent agreed that the Netherlands should remove all nuclear weapons from its territory provided that the other countries of East and West were prepared to do the same, the percentage of agreement was reduced considerably if other countries in East and West would not do the same (Table 6.30).

This is more or less confirmed by another poll, which asked respondents whether they would want to keep nuclear weapons anyway, abolish them if the other side were to do the same, or abolish them irrespective of what the other side would do (SP 12/82). A small minority would prefer to stick to nuclear weapons (nine percent). A majority (57 percent) would prefer the second option, and about one-third would like to see nuclear weapons abolished unilaterally. The latter option was most popular among the 18 to 34 age group and leftist voters. By adding the conditions mentioned in the questions, the share of supporters of removal of nuclear weapons from the Netherlands is reduced by about one-third among all parties (compare Tables 6.26 and 6.30). That data from public opinion surveys should be judged carefully and with a considerable deal of scepticism is underscored by these findings.

THE 1979 DOUBLE-TRACK DECISION

Because of the concrete nature of the choices to be made the political debate since 1979 has concentrated on the question whether the Netherlands should cooperate with the decision taken by NATO and deploy 48 new nuclear missiles, unless the results of arms control negotiations with the Soviet Union make this deployment unnecessary. A considerable number of polls on this issue was undertaken in recent years. One of the first was held before the NATO decision of December 1979 (SP). It asked whether NATO should or should not modernize its nuclear weapons. Thirty-seven percent said it should and 25 percent said it should not. Apparently the public was not yet fully informed about the issue or had not made up its mind then, because 27 percent gave no opinion and 12 percent said it would depend. Opposition was stronger among those with a leftist preference and among the younger part of the population.

Further questions asked during 1981 showed that opposition had become stronger after the decision had been made and seems to have increased during that year. Polls held in February and April showed rejection of modernization by margins of 62 to 30 percent and 68 to 28 percent, respectively (see Table 6.33). Again considerable variation between the supporters of different parties could be observed, with opposition ranging from 83 percent among PvdA voters to 30 percent for VVD voters. The public had also become more outspoken; only a few abstained from giving an opinion.

Comparing these data with those of another survey held at about the same time demonstrates, however, how forcing a dichotomy can distort the picture (Table 6.31). Opposition to deployment seemed to be much smaller here, but a closer inspection reveals that this was caused primarily by supporters of the political center. Some material is also available on the breakdown of these attitudes. Resistance against modernization was relatively strong among women and the young, the religious factor does not seem to have had an impact. It could not be demonstrated that those who opposed modernization had an overly positive image of the military efforts of the Soviet Union. For example, in November 1979 (NIPO), 73 percent agreed that it was probably or certainly true that the Soviet Union was engaged in improvement of nuclear weapons which could be used against Western Europe.

Before looking at the fluctuations in attitudes throughout 1981-1982 in more detail, one should first examine two other questions. The first deals with actual knowledge, the second with expected results of deployment of the new missiles. The public did not seem to be fully informed whether there actually already were missiles on Dutch territory which could reach the Soviet Union. In July 1981 46 percent said yes while 48 percent said no; in October 1981 these figures were 42 and 48 percent, respectively (USICA). Among the best-educated these percentages were 32 vs. 52 and 33 vs. 46. Would the deployment of nuclear weapons in Western Europe

Table 6.31   Attitudes on deployment of nuclear missiles in the Netherlands by sex and political preference

	Total	Men	Women	Right[a]	Middle[b]	Left[c]	Will not vote
Unconditionally in favor	12	16	9	27	14	8	7
Conditionally in favor	36	34	37	50	50	21	38
Unconditionally against	46	46	47	18	30	71	41
Don't know/ no answer	6	4	7	5	6	—	14

Source: *Haagsche Courant* 24 April 1981

Note:

[a] VVD, SGP, GPV, BP
[b] CDA, DS'70
[c] PvdA, PPR, PSP, D'66

help to prevent Soviet attack? In July 1981 56 percent said that indeed new nuclear weapons would make a Soviet attack less likely. But in October 1981 this figure had fallen to 42 percent, and the number of those who thought it made a Soviet attack more likely had increased from 32 to 40 percent. Are people therefore more worried by the missiles on their own side than by those of the Soviet side? This sentiment is in fact comparatively stronger in the Netherlands than elsewhere in Western Europe (Table 6.32).

Returning to public attitudes on the deployment of new missiles, it is unfortunate that differences in question wording make comparisons with earlier data from the same year difficult. In the USICA poll of October 1981 questions on attitudes toward deployment of cruise missiles were preceded by the following statement: "The Russians have 450 nuclear warheads on new medium-range nuclear missiles—the SS-20s—aimed at Western Europe, while NATO has no such missiles aimed at the Soviet Union." The suggestion implied by this statement is clear and it is interesting to see whether and how it did affect responses. Based on these various surveys is Table 6.33.

One may argue that the political decision is not phrased in terms of a yes-or-no choice, the question rather is whether one wants to reject or accept the missiles unconditionally, only if negotiations are going on at the same time, or when these have demonstrably failed. This also is what has been asked in several polls (Table 6.34).

Unconditional opposition to new missiles increased in 1981 and reached a majority in December; it was clearly strongest among the best-educated.

Table 6.32   Nuclear threats to the security of Western Europe

	France	West Germany	Great Britain	Netherlands
The presence of nuclear missiles in Eastern Europe	41	58	43	29
The future deployment of new US missiles in Western Europe	19	33	29	24
Both	7	2	0	31
Don't know/no answer	33	7	28	16

Source: *Nouvel Observateur*, 11/81

In addition (USICA 7/81) one notes that opposition was very pronounced among those opposing any use of military force (86 percent), those who would stay out of U.S.-Soviet disputes (71 percent), those preferring neutrality over NATO (83 percent), those not at all worried about a Soviet attack (61 percent), those who prefer arms control negotiations over strengthening NATO first or doing both simultaneously (70 percent), those who oppose any use of nuclear weapons (87 percent), those who think that having nuclear weapons in Western Europe makes a Soviet attack more likely (78 percent), those who want to give up all nuclear weapons on Dutch soil (90 percent), those who believe that the United States could stay out of a nuclear conflict in Europe (68 percent), those who believe it is better to be conquered by the Soviet Union than to risk nuclear war (77 percent), and, finally, among the 18 to 24 year-olds (61 percent).

The above data definitely indicate a hard core of opposition of some 40 to 50 percent of the population. An additional 30 percent or so was

Table 6.33   Attitudes on the deployment of new nuclear missiles in the Netherlands

	KRO Brand- punt TV 2/81	NCRV Hier en Nu 4/81	USICA 7/81	USICA[a] with additional information 10/81	without information 10/81	NIPO 8/82
In favor	30	28	44	36 (29)	26 (23)	25
Opposed	62	68	51	56 (67)	67 (77)	68
Don't know/no answer	8	4	5	8 (4)	7 (0)	7

Note:

[a] Figures in brackets refer to the best-educated group

Table 6.34   Attitudes on deployment of new nuclear missiles in relation to arms control negotiations (USICA)

	3/81[a]	7/81[a]	10/81[a]	12/81	7/82
Under no condition should we agree to station these new nuclear missiles in the Netherlands	39 (39)	38 (57)	47 (55)	52	44
We should accept stationing of the new nuclear missiles only if arms control negotiations with the Soviet Union have failed	15 (20)	20 (11)	21 (23)	42	20
We should accept stationing of the new nuclear missiles in the Netherlands only if there are arms control negotiations with the Soviet Union at the same time	16 (21)	22 (20)	18 (21)		15
We should accept stationing of nuclear weapons without pushing for arms control negotiations	8 (10)	9 (8)	7 (1)	7	8
Don't know/no answer	21 (11)	11 (3)	8 (−)	−	13

Note:

[a] Figures in brackets refer to the best-educated group

wavering and likely to be influenced by information and the chances of arms control negotiations. Half of these tended to join the opposition if faced with a direct question. Yet another series of questions (NIPO), asked repeatedly (eight times in all) during 1981 and 1982, suggest a somewhat different conclusion. The text of the question was as follows: "If the (new) government would ... decide to replace, within the framework of NATO, the old nuclear weapons on our territory by new ones, would you consider that a wise decision, regrettable but acceptable, or a wrong decision to which you would remain opposed?" The share of those who said they would consider this a good decision decreased slowly, from 18 to 11 percent, paralleled by an increase of those who would consider the decision regrettable but acceptable. The percentage of unconditional opponents hardly changed and fluctuated around 40 percent. One may object, however, that this question was misleading. Plans were not and are not to replace old missiles by new ones, but rather to add a number of nuclear weapons to existing ones, at least as far as the Netherlands are concerned. For respondents this does not seem to have mattered since the same proportions expressed support or disapproval when faced with the

Table 6.35   Deployment of new nuclear missiles in Europe if arms control negotiations fail

	Yes	No	Don't know/ no answer
Netherlands	33	51	16
France	34	29	37
Great Britain	43	34	23
West Germany	37	35	28
United States	45	31	24

Source: *Newsweek*, 31 January 1983

last question in the series (September 1982) which was phrased somewhat differently and more accurately. Putting all these data together one can conclude that in 1981 and 1982, if faced with a simple question, two out of three respondents rejected deployment. If the question allowed more than a simple yes-or-no answer the number of opponents dropped considerably. Faced with the eventuality that INF negotiations between the USSR and the United States would fail a majority of the Dutch would still oppose deployment, unlike those polled in the United States, France, Germany, and Great Britain (Table 6.35).

The most recent data suggests comparable attitudes. Early in 1983 half of all respondents thought that the Netherlands should not make its decision dependent on the outcome of the Geneva negotiations. But even among those who did support this linkage, there was little sympathy with

Table 6.36   Attitudes on (new) nuclear weapons in the Netherlands by attitude on the Geneva negotiations (ISEO 2/83)

	Those who think that the Netherlands should decide independently (50 percent)	Those who think that the outcome of the negotiations should be awaited (49 percent)
Increase the number of nuclear weapons/deploy new cruise missiles in the Netherlands	4	14
Keep the same number of nuclear weapons on our territory	17	45
Reduce the number of nuclear weapons on our territory	22	20
Remove all nuclear weapons from our territory	59	20

Table 6.37   Expectations of deployment of cruise missiles by party preference (NIPO)

	Deployment expected		Deployment not expected		Don't know/ no answer	
	8/81	9/82	8/81	9/82	8/81	9/82
PvdA	43	70	41	23	16	7
D'66	59	82	34	14	7	4
CDA	45	70	40	17	15	13
VVD	58	74	30	17	12	9
Total	48	70	36	19	16	11

the idea that the Dutch should accept more nuclear weapons on their territory (Table 6.36). One related item that is hotly debated at present is whether the Netherlands should proceed with preparatory measures to deploy the missiles. Contrary to the government's policy there is currently no majority (54 percent opposed) for such measures because not only adherents of the opposition but also about one-third of supporters of the present government coalition reject them (SP 11/82).

Scepticism over the likelihood that government and parliament would follow public opinion is evident in a survey (SP 11/81) that showed that only 28 percent expected that the government would probably (seven percent certainly) prevent the deployment of new missiles in the Netherlands; 50 percent expected that this would probably not (13 percent certainly not) happen. If anything, this scepticism seems to have increased in the course of 1982 (Table 6.37).

THE NEUTRON BOMB

A specific target of the growing resistance against nuclear weapons in the Netherlands was the plan to introduce the so-called neutron bomb into the NATO arsenals. Opposition to this plan was particularly strong in the Netherlands. Indeed it seems that the Dutch have been witnessing since 1977 the manifestation of opinions and attitudes which had been latent but growing for some time and which only surfaced and contributed to political action after a suitable catalyst presented itself. The neutron bomb was such a catalyst.

The massive support for the campaign against the introduction of the neutron bomb in 1977 and 1978 (Maessen 1979) cannot be explained away by reference to skilful exploitation of the revulsion against the inhuman aspects of a weapon which "kills people and leaves buildings intact," and even less as a result of manipulation by the Soviet Union. More probably, the campaign succeeded in bringing to the surface a latent revulsion against nuclear weapons—which had existed for a long time and had

Table 6.38   Attitudes on deployment of neutron bomb (USICA)

| | 3/81 | | 10/81 | |
	Total	Best-educated	Total	Best-educated
In favor of deployment	17	25	11	14
Against deployment	58	59	69	80
Don't know/no answer	14	12	5	3
Not heard of neutron bomb	12	4	15	3

grown gradually—by focusing on one concrete decision, which, in addition, was perceived as possibly affecting the Netherlands.

In April 1978, NIPO asked the following question: "Do you think that America should in any case not produce neutron bombs *or* produce them in any case *or* not produce neutron bombs provided Russia does not reinforce its nuclear armaments?" Of all respondents, 48 percent thought that America should not make the neutron bomb in any case, nine percent thought that it should do so in any case, and 34 percent thought that it should make its decision dependent on Soviet restraint. As expected, sympathizers of the left showed more resistance to the neutron bomb than those of the parties of the right.

In recent surveys, a number of questions were again included on this issue. In contrast to the question of new nuclear missiles the public is relatively well-informed about the neutron bomb. In November 1981, 85 percent said that they had heard about this weapon (USICA). Those who had heard of the neutron bomb were then asked whether they thought that its introduction would increase the likelihood of a nuclear war with the Soviet Union. Fifty-nine percent said that they felt this to be the case. Forty-one percent thought that the neutron bomb would make a Soviet attack more likely, while only 40 percent thought that it would help to prevent such an attack. Nineteen percent were undecided on this score. These figures help to explain why large majorities rejected both the U.S. decision to produce the neutron bomb and its deployment in Europe. Opposition increased still further after President Reagan's decision to proceed with production of this weapon as planned (Table 6.38).

ATTITUDES ON ARMS CONTROL AND
DISARMAMENT NEGOTIATIONS

The data suggest that there is a fairly general belief in the necessity to seek security not so much in additional (nuclear) weapons, but rather in measures of arms control. While there is considerable distrust of Soviet motives and gestures, it is not generally felt that the conduct of negotiations should be made conditional on Soviet good behavior in other areas. Faced with a choice between pushing harder for arms control negotiations to try to reduce military forces on both sides and strengthening its military forces to help NATO maintain a balance of power vis-à-vis the East, the Dutch clearly prefer the first course (by a margin of 44 to 21 percent (USICA 3/81)). Similarly, in July 1981 (USICA) 56 percent expressed support for the statement that the West should begin arms control talks as soon as possible, while only ten percent thought that it should strengthen its nuclear forces first (26 percent preferred to do both simultaneously). There was an even division over the question whether the West should accept the Soviet proposal of a moratorium on medium-range nuclear missiles in Europe (USICA 4/81): 43 percent (and 34 percent of the best-educated) said that the West should reject this proposal "because the Soviet Union already has many missiles which can hit West European cities, while NATO has no missiles on the European continent which can hit Soviet cities" (sic). However, 46 percent (62 percent of the best-educated) preferred that the West should accept this proposal "because stationing new nuclear missiles in Western Europe which could hit the Soviet Union would increase the danger of war."

While a clear majority (61 percent) thought it unlikely in July 1981 (USICA) that results of the East-West talks would be forthcoming in the next two years, there was also a considerable belief (contrary to most other countries where this question was also asked) that both the Soviet Union and the United States were making serious efforts to reach agreement: 62 percent said this about the United States, and 56 percent about the Soviet Union. Somewhat earlier, 46 percent had said that they considered the various Soviet proposals to be an attempt to divide and weaken the Western Alliance rather than an effort to show a genuine concern for peace (38 percent (USICA 4/81)).

Other data also supports the conclusion that while the Dutch public supports efforts to reach arms control agreements it is also profoundly sceptical of the likelihood of success. In December 1981 (NIPO), only eight percent expected an early successful conclusion of the Geneva negotiations, and one year later this scepticism seemed only slightly lower (*Elseviers Magazine* 4 December 1982). To the question "Do you expect that these (the Geneva) negotiations will be successful through goodwill on both sides, or are you somewhat more careful but you would not exclude small results, or are you sceptical about the course of the negotiations and do you not expect any results?" four percent replied optimistically, 34 percent expected no success at all, and a majority (60 percent) expected only some small successes (SP 12/82). Those who said they were not so concerned but trusted their governments (Table 6.17) were slightly more optimistic than those who showed themselves very concerned.

A controversial element in discussions about the best way to disarmament is the degree to which one is willing to rely on the conventional method of bilateral or multilateral negotiations or is convinced that only unilateral initiatives can bring about a multilateral disarmament process. Much of the data presented above suggests considerable support for the unilateral removal of nuclear weapons from the Netherlands and the Dutch armed forces. At the same time, however, it was noted that fewer people expect such a move to result in similar steps by other Western countries or in reciprocation by the Warsaw Pact. This becomes even more clear if the question of unilateralism vs. bilateralism is addressed in the context of international negotiations. Conventional ideas, such as not giving something away without getting anything in return, not to trust your opponents, and the need to maintain a military equilibrium between East and West, are still firmly entrenched (*Elseviers Magazine* 4 December 1982).

Images of Allies

ATTITUDES ON THE UNITED STATES AND U.S. LEADERSHIP

At the basis of Dutch foreign and defense policy lies the conviction that its security and other interests are very much in agreement with those of the United States, that U.S. security guarantees to Europe can be relied upon (or, at least, should not be questioned openly), and that American leadership of the "free world" is desirable. At the same time, some of these beliefs have come under scrutiny and criticism, and it has been argued that the Netherlands are more and more in the grip of virulent anti-Americanism. What do people think about these and related questions?

According to one survey held in July 1981 (USICA), a majority was still sympathetic to the United States, though this sympathy seemed to be diminishing, if not crumbling. In 1971, 83 percent said that their feelings toward the United States were friendly or very friendly, while 12 percent had negative feelings (NIPO). In 1978, 80 percent had a favorable and 18 percent an unfavorable impression of the United States. In 1981, this had changed to 55 percent favorable, 28 somewhat favorable, and eight percent very unfavorable. Comparable data for the Soviet Union were 16, 52, and 24 percent, respectively (USICA 10/81). A similar difference could be observed if the question were phrased in terms of "respect." Again more people showed respect for the United States than for the Soviet Union; the differences were small, however (USICA 3/81).

Another series of data—that unfortunately covers only a brief period—also suggests a deteriorating image of the United States. In various polls held between 1971 and 1973, the percentage of those who mentioned the United States as the country that was the major threat to world peace increased from six to 13 percent (NES 1971, KO 1972–1973). This evolution is confirmed by a survey held in 1982. Fifty-five percent then said that they had become more critical of the United States than a few years ago (*De Volkskrant* 6 March 1982). This was the case especially among supporters of the left (PvdA and D'66: 70 percent), and among those under 30 years (65 percent). Respondents also seemed to agree (68 percent) that it matters who is president of the United States. They clearly had President Reagan in mind, as is shown by responses to another question asked in April 1981: "As best as you can judge, do you think that the foreign policy direction taken by the United States under President Reagan is more likely to improve or more likely to harm East-West relations?" Forty-eight percent of the population and 68 percent of the best-educated chose the second option, while only 14 percent of the population and 16 percent of the best-educated chose the first (USICA 4/81). While majorities among the best-educated as well as among the total population thought it desirable for the Netherlands' interest that the United States should exert strong leadership in world affairs (USICA 3/81), it appears that confidence in U.S. ability to deal responsibly with world affairs has suffered (USICA 3/81, 10/81, 12/81). The percentage of those who had no such confidence increased in 1981 from 37 to 50 percent.

In the course of 1981, the public became more outspoken. The don't know/no answer category shrank considerably and, consequently, those who had little or no confidence in U.S. ability to deal responsibly with world problems gained the upper hand. Criticism of U.S. policies also appears from other data, which allows us to compare the degree to which the United States and the Soviet Union were seen as dangers to world peace. More than one-third thought that the United States constitutes a great danger to world peace, in the case of the Soviet Union this was almost a majority. Equal shares considered both to be a small danger, only seven percent considered the Soviet Union to be no danger, while this was 20 percent for the United States.[5] In another survey 49 percent agreed that the United States presents an equally large threat to world peace as the Soviet Union (NSS-opinie-analyse 1983).

Early in 1983 a fairly extensive survey was carried out which confirmed earlier findings and showed the extent to which negative feelings toward the United States, especially with respect to the policies of the current administration, had come to be shared by a plurality of the Dutch public (NSS-opinie-analyse 1983). The existence of a strong degree of anti-Americanism could no longer be denied or neglected. Scores on a specially constructed attitude scale revealed that while 25 percent expressed a positive attitude toward the United States, 29 percent expressed a rather negative, and 18 percent a very negative attitude; 28 percent were ambivalent or had no particular view. Negative feelings prevailed among those under thirty (59 percent) and in the 30 to 44 age group (51 percent). A majority (52 percent) felt that Dutch attitudes toward the United States had changed in 1982, of which 85 percent (or 44 percent of all respondents) felt that attitudes had become more negative. When asked which reasons could account for this change, 51 percent mentioned the problems

---

5. *De Volkskrant* 6 March 1982. Differences in the context (the question concerning the United States was preceded by a reference to criticism of President Reagan, the question concerning the Soviet Union was not preceded by a similar reference) may have had an effect on the answers to these questions.

Table 6.39 Support for NATO membership

	NATO 1967	NIPO 1969	a 1970	NES 1970	NES 1971	NES[b] 1972		c 1974	NIPO 1974	d 1976	NIPO 1979	NES 1979	NIPO 1980	NIPO 1981	KRO TV 1981	NIPO 1981	NIPO 1982
Remain member	85	65	66	60	71	66	63	71	76	81	76	57	76	73	78	69	76
Remain member under certain conditions	e	e	e	e	e	e	e	17	e	14	e	22	e	e	e	e	e
Leave NATO	7	13	14	18	12	16	21	8	9	4	12	3	14	17	14	12	13
Don't know/ no answer	7	22	21	23	16	19	16	5	15	1	12	17	10	10	8	19	11

Note:

[a] Survey Progressiviteit en conservatisme
[b] First column older, second younger respondents
[c] Survey Volk en Verdediging
[d] Baehr et al. (1978, elite survey)
[e] response not offered

of armaments, nuclear weapons, the cruise missiles, and so on; 21 percent referred to the policies of President Reagan in general.

The division of opinions concerning the roles of the United States and the Soviet Union with respect to world peace is reflected in answers to a question put in March 1981, concerning the extent to which the security interests of the United States and the Netherlands are in agreement. Thirty-five percent thought that these interests are in agreement, 40 percent thought they were different, and 26 percent were undecided (USICA 3/81). But still 22 percent expressed a great deal and 39 percent a fair amount of confidence that the United States would come to the aid of the Netherlands in case of a threatening Soviet attack. These percentages were even higher among the best-educated (USICA 7/81). This may be related to the fact that few believed that U.S. territory could stay out of a nuclear war in Europe.

NATO AND NATO MEMBERSHIP

Membership in NATO has always been the "cornerstone" of Dutch foreign policy, or, as it was once put by a government official, "the Dutch have no foreign policy: we have only NATO" (Russell 1969). Despite differences in the wording of questions it seems unmistakable that at least this aspect of Dutch foreign and security policy has continued to enjoy massive support. Support for leaving the Alliance has never exceeded 20 percent. As shown in Table 6.39, fluctuations over time have been very small (Roschar 1975). The 69 percent of October 1981 obviously was the result of a sampling error or a temporary deviation. In January 1982 the situation was back to "normal."

The same impression of continuity emerges from a comparison of data from the 1977 National Election Survey with earlier data from 1967. In 1967 (VARA 12/67) 73 percent of people were convinced that because of the existence of NATO no war had broken out between East and West in Europe since 1949, 84 percent were convinced that, through NATO, the United States contributed to the security of Europe, and 72 percent subscribed to the notion that the NATO countries had succeeded in maintaining a balance of power in Europe. In 1977 (Nederlandse Kiezer 1977) this image had hardly changed: no fewer than 75 percent thought NATO necessary for our security, and 57 percent agreed with the statement that security in Europe can only be guaranteed by an alliance with the United States. Four years later (USICA 3/81) at least six out of ten considered NATO membership still essential; this number has not changed since October 1980 when the question was first asked. Thus, it seems that there is a continuous and stable majority in favor of NATO and the policies which it pursues.

Other data indicate, however, that these conclusions are misleading—or at least premature. It may be that the questions discussed so far are not valid in the sense that they do not measure the changes that are taking

Table 6.40 Security options for the Netherlands (USICA 3/81)

	Total	Best-educated
NATO as it now operates among the countries of Western Europe, the United States and Canada	31	41
NATO reformed, so that Western Europe has more to say in NATO, in return for paying more of the costs	15	11
Withdraw our military forces from NATO, but otherwise remain in NATO for such things as policy consultations	11	15
Establish an independent West European defense force not allied to the United States	11	17
Rely on greater accommodation to the interests of the Soviet Union	6	5
Don't know/no answer	27	13

place and only touch the surface of people's attitudes but not the relevant level. To give an example of a contradictory trend, the number of those who agreed that NATO is promoting détente in Europe decreased from 65 percent in 1967 to 39 percent in 1978. Attitudes on NATO membership could also be compared to those on alternative forms of providing for Dutch security (Table 6.40). Both among the mass public and the better educated in 1981 a majority preferred NATO as it is or was at least undecided about the alternatives, each of which enjoyed the support of only small minorities. This is remarkable to some extent because at the same time there was only a plurality which had either a great deal or a fair amount of confidence in NATO's ability to prevent an attack on Western Europe (Table 6.41). There was much less confidence that alternative security options would improve the present situation. This may be due to the fact that options and attitudes on the nuclear question and related aspects are by now well-developed, but alternative security arrangements and defense systems are seldom discussed. Consequently, opinions about possible alternatives are almost randomly distributed.

Table 6.41 Confidence in NATO's ability to prevent an attack on Western Europe (USICA 3/81)

	Total	Best-educated
A great deal	8	14
A fair amount	38	39
Not very much	28	32
None at all	8	7
Don't know/no answer	19	9

Table 6.42   Attitudes on NATO membership

	USICA 1977	USICA 3/81	USICA 7/81	SP 11/81
Stay in NATO	78	62	56	72
Become neutral	11	17	25	26
Don't know/no answer	11	21	18	2

A TREND TOWARD NEUTRALISM?

Given the hesitations about the contradictions in NATO's policy of deterrence—prevention of war as long as deterrence "works," but possibly total destruction should it fail—and the unwillingness actually to carry out the (nuclear) threats inherent in the present strategy of the Alliance, it would not be surprising if a tendency toward staying aloof from the big power confrontation, toward some degree of neutralism could be observed. While sizeable majorities still prefer NATO membership over neutrality, such a tendency is indeed suggested by data collected in 1981 (Table 6.42). This is also confirmed by a more recent poll, which showed that neutralist tendencies are by no means restricted to the smaller European countries. While 53 percent opted for neutralism in the Netherlands, figures for countries such as France and Great Britain were not very much lower (Table 6.43).

Summary and Conclusions

At the outset of this chapter questions were raised about the impact of the activities of peace organizations in the Netherlands on the development of

Table 6.43   Should country move toward neutralism in the East-West conflict?

	Favor	Oppose	Don't know/ no answer	Total
Netherlands	53	32	15	100
France	43	41	16	100
Great Britain	45	48	13	100
West Germany	57	43	a	100
United States	41	45	14	100

Source: *Newsweek* 31 January 1983

Note:

a German respondents were pressed to give an answer

public opinion vis-à-vis security in general and nuclear weapons specifically. While only the plausibility of such a link could be shown, it seemed possible to demonstrate shifts in public opinion pertaining to these problems. The intensification of public debates within political parties and other social groups and the opinions presented in these debates seem to suggest that the political mood about issues of international politics and the role of the Netherlands has been undergoing a rather fundamental reorientation. At first sight, however, the available data that allow comparison across time reveals a picture of continuity rather than of change. It also suggests that established ideas on security policy continue to enjoy widespread support. There is, for example, almost unanimous and unchanging support for NATO membership, the need to maintain a military counterweight to the East is still subscribed to by a majority, and these figures have not fluctuated over time. Attitudes on defense expenditures have not changed much either.

At the same time, some of the policies that NATO stands for, in particular the threat to use nuclear weapons in case of attack, are strongly rejected. Majorities oppose the deployment of new nuclear missiles and favor the removal of nuclear weaponry from the Netherlands. Unfortunately, little data allows one to ascertain whether changes have occurred in this respect in recent years. One poll (Table 6.27) suggests, however, that opposition against the nuclear roles of the Dutch armed forces was just as strong already in 1975 as since 1977 when the intensive campaign for their abolition got started.

There are therefore two discrepancies for which one must account. One concerns the difference between perceived changes in the general climate of opinion and the actual data on mass opinions, the second refers to the discrepancy mentioned above between support for NATO and rejection of its policies. With respect to the first, it could be that mass opinion as measured in the traditional way does not show the changes which one infers from the increased public debate and current actions to express disagreement with conventional policies. Although it is difficult to find empirical evidence for this, it may well be that what one sees in the Netherlands is not so much a change in the distribution of opinions as a change in the intensity with which they are held. On several occasions it could be noted that the number of those who could or did not want to express an opinion had decreased and that polarization had set in. The political battle seems to revolve around the doubters in the middle of the political spectrum. Also, opinions may have changed but these changes may have remained latent until a suitable catalyst presented itself to make them manifest. Concrete issues such as the introduction of the neutron bomb and NATO's double-track decision of 1979 may have served as such catalysts.

Various explanations are available for the second discrepancy. First, it is possible that people are really not terribly interested in this sort of problem and just answer randomly or express what they consider to be the "correct" answer (social desirability effect). Corrections for the level of knowledge and involvement could possibly control this problem, as could further detailed questioning after introductory general questions. A second possibility is that different questions measure different aspects of a complex of attitudes which may be inconsistent but each of which is equally important and serious for the individual. What would be lacking in this case is a logical structure into which these attitudes fit and in which they are reconciled to one another. Because of the unstructured character of these attitudes, that might be due to low personal salience, they could also be very susceptible to outside manipulation. More detailed research could possibly throw some light on the real degree of inconsistency in response patterns. Finally, inconsistencies recorded by the researcher may not be perceived as such at all by respondents. In order to explore to what extent these discrepancies only appear to outside observers, one would need in-depth interviews and better formulated questions which would allow the structure in which the respondent places his attitudes to be brought to light.

On the contents of public opinion in the Netherlands a number of conclusions can be drawn. First, while the perception of an acute Soviet threat has diminished fear in a more latent form has remained. This fear is focused on the Soviet Union as an ideological-political threat rather than as a military threat. Likewise, the argument that the military balance of power is gradually shifting in favor of the East is not generally believed. Consequently, few are seriously concerned about a Soviet military attack in the near future. The Dutch are not in the grip of a war scare. While many still blame the Soviet Union for current tensions in the world, many others point to the confrontation between the big powers as a source of tensions. This is confirmed by the large number of those who see the Soviet Union and the United States as equally large threats to world peace. In general, though, fear of an imminent war has diminished. Nevertheless, about half of all Dutch respondents still see the existence of nuclear weapons as the major threat to their security. This seems to be undoubtedly connected to the belief that they would not survive a nuclear war. This fear of nuclear weapons is more pronounced in the Netherlands than in many other European countries.

There is generally a strong reluctance to respond to (increased) international tensions by a show or use of force. While the need to be able to defend oneself is generally acknowledged the willingness actually to carry out military threats seems severely limited. Few adhere to the view that the actual use of nuclear weapons could ever be justified; first nuclear use is generally rejected. About one third of the public can be considered to be nuclear pacifists.

Rather than a show of military strength, people opt for a policy of reconciliation and arms control negotiations to deal with military imbalances. In addition to disbelief in a shifting military balance and an obvious preference for butter over guns, a sense of futility with respect to defense expenditures may be at play in the general unwillingness to increase these expenditures. Even among those who perceive an unfavorable imbalance only 29 percent want to increase defense expenditures. A majority wants to keep them at the present level.

Proponents of unilateral nuclear disarmament also tend to hold these views. Thus, the argument that reduction of conventional armaments is likely to be the next item on the "shopping list" of the peace movements finds little support in the available data, at least at this moment any such proposal would find little support in public opinion. This applies also to the issue of NATO membership.

Public interest and involvement in security issues is very much concentrated on the nuclear weapons issue. This concern, however, is much more evident among leftist than among the more conservative voters. Those on the right tend to have more trust that their government will solve the problem, mainly through international negotiations. Survey data show considerable support for the peace movement and its activities. More people than before seem to be willing to act upon their convictions that strong measures are called for in order to express disapproval of the current course of events. Besides those who are seriously concerned about nuclear weapons there is also a sizeable group of people (more than one-third) who would rather not think about nuclear weapons at all, but the first group is certainly larger. While only a minority is actually involved in actions against nuclear weapons, these actions seem to enjoy very considerable and increasing support. Thus, 46 percent said they were totally in sympathy with the recent demonstrations across Europe, and a further 33 percent said they were mostly sympathetic; 48 percent in 1981 and 60 percent in 1983 responded that they admired people who took part in a demonstration against nuclear weapons, and 37 percent in 1981 (47 in 1983) agreed that everybody should take to the streets to demonstrate against nuclear weapons. About one quarter of the public seems to be unwilling to abide by a future decision to deploy new nuclear missiles in the Netherlands.

While a majority still believes that the United States will come to the aid of Europe in case of war, confidence in the reliability of the United States as an ally, in its leadership, and its capability to deal responsibly with world affairs is decreasing. The number of those who have a generally favorable opinion of the United States has also diminished considerably. It does not seem too far-fetched to conclude that the policies of the present administration in Washington have much to do with this shift. Of all respondents 37 percent considered "the present America" to be a great danger to world peace. Yet, at the same time, a majority supports the view that the Netherlands and other countries cannot do without American support to ensure their security. While 48 percent think that Western Europe should be able to do without American aid for its defense, there is little indication where the preferences with respect to possible alternative security arrangements may lie. Opinions are either very much divided or the alternatives have simply not been seriously considered yet. The unwavering endorsement of NATO as an institution and Dutch membership therein is therefore perhaps less an indication of positive support than of a rejection of possible alternatives, including a turn toward neutralism.

Indeed, while membership in NATO continues to enjoy strong support, the policies that the Alliance stands for, especially with respect to the threat to use nuclear weapons in case of attack, are by and large rejected: 28 percent turned out to reject all use of force, and the nuclear pacifist position seems on the increase. One poll showed an increase from 36 percent in mid-1981 to 50 percent at the end of that year. Two out of three respondents reject the deployment of new nuclear weapons in the Netherlands. This proportion decreases somewhat (but it is still a majority) if deployment is tied to arms control negotiations or if the question is preceded by information stressing the imbalance in land-based Eurostrategic missiles. The number of people rejecting the introduction of the neutron bomb is even greater. Depending on the way the question is phrased, between 40 and 55 percent opt for unilateral removal of nuclear weapons from the Netherlands. But the hope that such a step would be followed by other countries is not shared by more than 30 percent. Even fewer believe that such a move would decrease the danger of a nuclear war. There were certain differences in response patterns related to background variables. The least important proved to be gender. Fewer women tend to be favorably disposed toward the deployment of (new) nuclear weapons in the Netherlands than men. They are also more critical of the United States and U.S. policies. Fewer women show an interest in international problems than men. But on the whole, these gender differences are not very strong.

The same seems to be the case with respect to age differences. Where we do find (small) distinctions, they are all in line with the general hypothesis that those who have not lived through the experiences of World War II and the cold war are less likely to support NATO and the policies for which it stands (Adler and Wertman 1981). They are more inclined to reject nuclear weapons in general, support their (unilateral) removal from the Netherlands, and to be critical of the United States. It is not warranted, however, to explain the opposition against established security policies in terms of a "generation gap." It should be recalled here that the same explanation was already given twenty years ago for the rise of the ban-the-bomb movement in the early 1960s. Also, at least as far as the Netherlands is concerned, the peace movement is not predominantly a movement of young people (with the possible exception of participation in demonstrations and the like). All age groups are represented.

Education makes somewhat more of a difference. The best-educated tend to differ on a number of issues from the population as a whole. They tend, for example, to be more optimistic about the balance of forces and less concerned about a possible Soviet attack or threat. More of them regard increased tensions between the Soviet Union and the United States as such as a threat. They are less favorably disposed towards nuclear weapons in general and (consequently) tend to be less willing to deploy new nuclear weapons in the Netherlands. They are more against any use of nuclear weapons and more of them support a neutralist course. Like the young, the best-educated tend, in general, to be more critical of NATO and of "tough" policies toward the East (USICA 9/81).

A question that arises in this connection is whether party preference and foreign policy attitudes are to some extent independent variables or whether these attitudes merely reflect and reproduce party positions. The latter does not seem to be the case. The available evidence suggests (1) that voters are not very well-informed about the positions of the various parties on the nuclear weapons issue; (2) that confronted with the position of the party of their preference on this issue not less than 40 percent tend to disagree with it; and (3) that even though the issue is much more salient for leftist than for rightist voters and for opponents of nuclear weapons than for supporters of established policies, even among the first categories very few indicated that the issue was for them decisive in their voting behavior in the 1981 and 1982 parliamentary elections. The general left-right cleavage in "images of the world" seems just as relevant in explaining differences of opinion on international as on domestic issues.

Many studies have shown that a plurality of the population is (potentially or actually) sympathetic towards a foreign policy which would no longer be based on what until recently were considered the requirements of loyal membership of NATO. At the level of the mass public—especially on the left side of the political spectrum—there is unmistakably considerable support for a policy which would reject the introduction of new nuclear weapons into Western Europe and their deployment in the Netherlands, which would opt for the repeal of some or all of Dutch nuclear tasks, and which would aim at the removal of nuclear weapons from the Netherlands. On the other hand, there is also a smaller group of committed and convinced NATO supporters which function as a veto group. However, the data showing support for alternative policies should be treated carefully. Sometimes considerable discrepancies were found to exist between various polls which cannot be explained by differences in timing or inadequate sampling. When questions are more detailed and conditions are added, for example, the much cited majority support (55 to 65 percent) for the IKV proposal is reduced considerably. Discrepancies, therefore, seem to be caused primarily by differences in the wording of questions. More research controlling that effect is necessary before more definitive conclusions can be drawn.

References

Adler, K. P. and D. A. Wertman, "West European Security Concerns for the Eighties: Is NATO in Trouble?" *Public Opinion* (August/September 1981): 8–12, 50.
Domke, K., "Kompromiss, Konsens und Populismus: Die Niederlande," in W. D. Eber-

wein and C. M. Kelleher, eds., *Sicherheit, zu welchen Preis?* (Muenchen/Wien: Olzog Verlag, 1983) Pp. 253–274.

Eichenberg, R. C., "The Myth of Hollanditis," *International Security* (1983): 143–159.

Everts, Philip P., "The Mood of the Country—New Data on Public Opinion and Other Problems of Peace and Security," *Acta Politica* 17 (1982): 497–553.

Everts, Philip P., *Public Opinion, the Churches and Foreign Policy, Studies of Domestic Factors in the Making of Dutch Foreign Policy* (Leiden: Institute for International Studies, 1983).

Everts, Philip P., "Wat vinden 'de mensen in het land'? Openbare mening en kernwapens," *Acta Politica* 16 (1981): 305–354.

Goddijn, W. et al., *Opnieuw God in Nederland* (Amsterdam: De Tijd, 1979).

Laqueur, W., "Hollanditis: A New Stage in European Neutralism," *Commentary* vol. 72, no. 2 (1981): 19–27.

Leurdijk, J. H., "Die Niederlaende, ein treuer Verbuendeter," in W. D. Eberwein and C. M. Kelleher, eds., *Sicherheit, zu welchen Preis?* (Muenchen/Wien: Olzog Verlag, 1983) Pp. 227–252.

Maessen, P. J., *Wie stopt de neutronenbom?* (Leiden: Vakgroep Politieke Wetenschappen/ Instituut voor Internationale Studën, 1979).

De Nederlandse Kiezer 1967 (Alphen a/d Rijn: Samsom, 1967).

De Nederlandse Kiezer 1972 (Alphen a/d Rijn: Samsom, 1973).

De Nederlandse Kiezer 1977 (Voorschoten: VAM. 1977).

Nederlandse Stichting voor Statistiek, "Betrokkenheid bij atoombewapening: het atoom centraal, of de bewapening?" (Den Haag: 1981).

NIVV-notice, *Oorlogsverwachtingen en overlevingskans* (Den Haag: January 1978).

NSS-opinie-analyse, *Nederland en Amerika* (January 1983).

Projectgroep Vijandsbeeld, *Vijandsbeeld in Nederland—Eindverslag van een onderzoek naar het vijandsbeeld in de publieke opinie* (Nijmegen: Studiecentrum Vredesvraagstukken, 1980).

Roschar, F. M., ed., *Buitenlandse politiek in de Nederlandse publieke opinie, 1960–1975* (Den Haag: Nederlands Instituut voor Vredesvraagstukken, 1975).

Russell, R., "The Atlantic Alliance in Dutch Foreign Policy," *Internationale Spectator* 23 (1969): 1189–1209.

Siccama, J. G., chapter on the Netherlands for the project "Overlooked Allies: The Northern Periphery of NATO" (Paris: Atlantic Institute for International Affairs, forthcoming).

Stichting Krijgsmacht en Maatschappij, *De publieke opinie over krijgsmacht en maatschappij* (The Hague: 1982).

Stichting Volk en Verdediging, *Defensie in de publieke opinie. Samenvattend verslag van een onderzoek naar houdingen en opvattingen van de Nederlandse bevolking inzake veiligheid, verdediging en krijgsmacht, gehouden in mei/juni 1974* (Den Haag: 1977).

Voorhoeve, J. J. C., *Peace, Profits and Principles: A Study of Dutch Foreign Policy* (The Hague: Nijhoff, 1979).

Westerndorp, P. H., "A New Dimension in Public Opinion Research—Standard Multidimensional Measurement of Involvement with Social Problems: Technique and Application" *Journal of the Market Research Society* vol. 23, no. 3 (1981): 161–180.

Appendix E Sources

All surveys have been held in Dutch. In most cases the translation of the questions is my own—the reader should be aware of this source of possible errors. All polls were held with representative nationwide samples of the adult population (eighteen years and above) of the Netherlands. Figures in all tables are percentages.

For several research and survey institutions or studies that are frequently referred to the following acronyms have been used:

ISEO: Instituut voor Sociaal-wetenschappelijk en Economisch Onderzoek
KO: Kontinu-onderzoek, FSW Amsterdam
NES: National Election Survey
NIPO: Nederlands Instituut voor de Publieke Opinie
SP: Het Schaduwparlement, regular polls by Lagendijk Opinieonderzoek for AVRO broadcasting organization
USICA: United States International Communications Agency

Much of the material discussed in this chapter comes from the United States International Communications Agency. In the available form it unfortunately contains only sparse breakdowns by demographic variables and political preferences. The breakdowns by education (a separate group of some ten percent of the "best-educated" was distinguished) have been used whenever they allowed interesting comparisons.

Data for a number of surveys discussed in this chapter are available for further analysis at the Steinmetz Archives, Amsterdam. They include National Election Surveys, NIPO weekly opinion polls, 1962–1981, Eurobarometer data, 1974–1982, ISEO, *Meningen over kernwapens*, 1981.

7 Norwegian Attitudes Toward Defense and Foreign Policy Issues

RAGNAR WALDAHL*

Introduction

Norwegian postwar politics was for a long time characterized by a strong consensus on foreign policy. The Communist Party (NKP), which was the only party to oppose Norwegian membership in NATO, soon lost the large following it had enjoyed during the first postwar years, and the internal opposition against the NATO membership in the Labour Party (DNA) never succeeded in changing the party line.[1] It was not until the anti-NATO group on the DNA's left wing seceded in 1961 to form the Socialist People's Party (later the Socialist Left Party (SV)) that Norway got a foreign policy opposition group of any political significance.

Initially, however, the institutionalization of the opposition against NATO had little impact on the general foreign policy debate in Norway, and it did not lead to any noticeable increase in the general public's interest in foreign policy issues. It was not until the conflict over the proposed Norwegian membership in the European Communities (EC) that these questions really became part of the Norwegian political debate.

---

*Shortly before I started working on this paper, Mr. Bernt Olav Aardal of the Institute for Social Research in Oslo concluded a systematic review of opinion polls in this field for the Norwegian Ministry of Defense (Aardal 1983). His study proved invaluably useful to me, and if I had not also had access to his basis material, it would not have been possible to write this paper within the given deadline. I have also drawn extensively on a recently published review of public opinion polls on defense issues in the time period 1945–1981 (Ringdal and Nergaard 1982). The chapter is translated into English from the Norwegian manuscript by Mr. Jon Gunnar Arntzen.

1. The Norwegian political parties will be referred to by their common Norwegian abbreviations:

NKP:	Communist Party of Norway
SV:	Socialist Left Party
DNA:	Norwegian Labour Party
V:	Liberal Party
KrF:	Christian People's Party
Sp:	Center Party
H:	Conservative Party

As a foreign policy issue, however, the EC conflict was very special. It not only concerned Norway's relationship with the rest of Europe but also had direct relevance for a number of specific domestic political issues. It is worth noting that the EC debate had a far greater and more direct impact on domestic policies than on foreign policy in Norway (Valen 1973).

It is not really surprising to find that matters of foreign policy receive relatively little attention from the general public, in spite of the relatively great attention which is accorded to it by the mass media. Most foreign policy issues have little direct bearing on people's everyday life, and they often touch on questions which seem rather remote from the general public's point of view. It is a well-known fact that people's interest in different matters will increase as an issue comes closer: geographically, culturally, and timewise. Thus, foreign policy issues will only receive general attention if they also touch on questions which are of a more immediate interest to substantial sections of the population.

Such an interest could either be related to structural antagonisms, that is, conflicts stemming from relatively stable social group interests such as those that are present in the labour market, or it could relate to ideological differences over general issues that are important to the nation as a whole (Valen 1980). The EC conflict in Norway undoubtedly comprised both structural and ideological elements, but for most people the structural elements must have seemed the most important and most imminent ones. Other foreign policy issues, such as for instance the question of Norway's membership in NATO and the debate about nuclear free zones, are largely of an ideological nature.

There is no recent data available which enables us to measure *how great* an interest Norwegians in general have in foreign policy issues, but since 1965 the Norwegian Election Research Programme has been measuring people's *relative* interest in local politics, national domestic politics and foreign policy.[2] The interest in foreign policy has the lowest relative score throughout the whole period, and all up to 1977—with an exception for the time around the 1972 referendum on EC membership, which of course generated a somewhat increased level of interest—fewer than 20 percent of the respondents stated that they are most interested in foreign policy. The results from 1981 do, however, show a certain increase, in that about one quarter of the respondents ranked foreign policy highest among the three issues.

The increasing awareness of—and perhaps also concern over—foreign policy issues is demonstrated in several ways in the surveys of the election

---

2. The election research programme, which was initiated in 1956 by Stein Rokkan and Henry Valen, carried out nationwide representative interview surveys on the occasion of the 1957 parliamentary election, and later surveys in connection with all parliamentary elections from 1965. Further details of the research programme and a discussion of the main topics which have been included in the surveys, can be found *inter alia* in Henry Valen's "Electoral Research in Norway," in *Research in Norway 1981*, Oslo (Universitetsforlaget).

research programme. Both in 1977 and 1981, the respondents were asked to state which controversial political issue they thought was most important for their voting preferences. In 1977, only nine percent mentioned foreign or defense policy issues, but in 1981, the proportion had increased to 20 percent. In the 1981 survey, the respondents were also asked to indicate which of the following issue areas they felt was most important in society today: "public taxes and duties," "Christian faith and morality," "conservation of nature and environment protection," "defense and foreign policy," "equal opportunities for men and women," and "public control and steering of private enterprise." The respondents were then asked to name and rank the three most important issues, and "defense and foreign policy" received the second highest score, both in the ranking for "most important," and in the general ranking, being mentioned by one-sixth of the respondents in the former context, and by just over one-half of the respondents in the latter.

Taken as a whole, this can be regarded as an empirical confirmation of the general observation that foreign policy issues have gained a more prominent place in Norwegian public opinion over the last three to four years. More detailed surveys have revealed, however, that this increasing prominence does not affect all segments of the population, but that it is primarily apparent on the left wing of Norwegian politics. In Figure 7.1, the respondents who were most interested in foreign policy issues in the 1977 and 1981 surveys, have been grouped according to their own placing

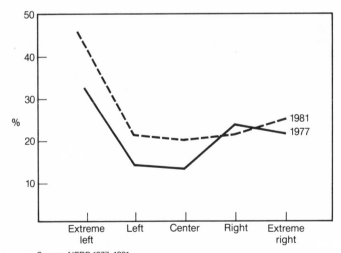

Source: NERP 1977, 1981
*Respondents expressing no opinion have been excluded from the data

Figure 7.1
Political interest and left-right position, 1977 and 1981: the curves
describe proportion indicating most interest in foreign politics*

of themselves along a nine-point scale that indicates their position on a left-right (radical-conservative) axis.[3] For practical reasons, in this presentation, the original nine-point scale has been condensed to one of five positions.[4]

The electorate's interest in foreign policy is distributed along the left-right axis in the shape of a U curve with the highest interest scores at both ends of the scale. There is no doubt, however, that in both surveys the actual interest displayed by voters on the left wing was considerably higher than that of right-wing voters, and that the difference in scores increased from 1977 to 1981. In fact, the general increase in foreign policy interest which took place between 1977 and 1981 was almost exclusively due to increasing interest among centre and left-wing voters; voters on the right display a remarkable stability in this respect.

The Norwegian public opinion's ranking of defense policy issues is high also when seen in an international perspective. In two comparative studies, which were conducted in the United States and seven European countries in October 1982 and in May 1983 (Norwegian fieldwork by NOI), the respondents were asked to indicate which issues out of a list of ten were most important for them and their countries in the present situation. Three of the issues were pertaining to defense policy: "threat of war," "inadequate defense," and "nuclear weapons." Together, these issues were mentioned by about 80 percent of the respondents in the Norwegian sample in both surveys (the percentages add up to more than 100, since the respondents were permitted to mention more than one issue), and "nuclear weapons" and "threat of war" were ranked in second and third place, respectively, only surpassed by "unemployment" both times. It was only in the Netherlands that the three defense policy issues were mentioned by more respondents than in Norway in both surveys, and in only one other instance were two of the three most frequently mentioned issues defense policy issues (Spain in the 1983 survey).

Even if domestic political problems such as unemployment, inflation and tax policies still dominate both the political debate and the public's attention, there can be little doubt that foreign and defense policy issues occupy a more prominent place in the Norwegian public's awareness than they used to do. This means, first of all, that the political parties will have

---

3. The question has the following wording: "There is so much talk about radicalism and conservatism these days. Here is a nine-point scale. Suppose that people ranking most to the left on the radical side should be given the value 9, while those most to the right on the conservative side should have the value 1. Where would you locate yourself on this scale?"

4. The new index has been composed in the following way:

		Scale Values
1	Extreme right	1 + 2 + 3
2	Right	4
3	Center	5
4	Left	6
5	Extreme left	7 + 8 + 9

to take foreign policy attitudes and reactions of the electorate more into consideration than they have done in the past. They cannot give the same exclusive prominence to purely foreign policy-related considerations as they have been used to doing, but must also consider in what way such issues may be linked up with certain domestic political interests. In this way there is today a stronger linkage between domestic and foreign policy issues, and a greater need for accommodation between them. Second, it means that the electorate's attitudes on foreign and defense policy issues are more important than before. The objective of this chapter is to present an overall picture of Norwegian public opinion on central matters of foreign and defense policy, with an emphasis on issues which have been topical during the last three to four years.

The presentation of Norwegian public opinion that follows is organized around the four main axes used in each chapter of this book in order to increase cross-national comparability. Since the analysis will show that there are only relatively small variations in attitudes toward defense and foreign policy issues between groups with different socio-demographic characteristics such as sex, age, education, income, residence, and so on, I shall not endeavor to make any systematic subdivision along these lines. In those instances where the variations are significant, they will be presented and commented upon. Furthermore, on issues where it is generally thought that different attitudes are present in the population, I shall emphasise if and where this, in fact, is seen not to be the case. Otherwise, the omission of a reference to demographic variations should be taken to indicate that such variations are not significant. In order to facilitate the readers' overall insight into the subject matter, I shall, however, give a short general summary of the impact of the most significant social characteristics and examine closely the importance of party affiliation for the attitudes in question.

Before moving on to this analysis, a brief word about data is in order. This paper is based on two sources of data. The first are the surveys that have been carried out under the auspices of the Norwegian Election Research Program in connection with every parliamentary election in Norway since 1965. Second are the opinion polls that have been conducted by the commercial opinion polling agencies in Norway. The material from these agencies is presented as it appears in their own reports.

These two data sources differ in quality both as regards the sampling and the phrasing of the questions. The election research program conducts interviews with random samples with certain persons being drawn for inclusion among the respondents. The commercial polling agencies use quota sampling with start addresses, which means that the interviewers have a significant influence on who will actually be interviewed.

The election research program's questions on foreign and defense policy issues have been phrased and thoroughly tested by experienced social scientists, in order to give as correct and objective a picture as possible of people's attitudes. The commercial agencies, on the other hand, include questions commissioned by various clients, and it is usually the client who phrases the questions, on the basis of his particular interests in the matter. This fact has a number of unfortunate consequences. *Inter alia*, the phrasing of the questions will frequently be too strongly influenced by the intended use of the results in the political debate. Openly leading questions, ambiguous phrasing that may produce unintended associations, long and complex questions, and inadequate response categories are not uncommon. In the media's presentation of opinion polls, these weaknesses are usually overlooked, and the results are uncritically accepted. We have not carried out an explicit evaluation of the reliability of all the questions that are included in this study, but the discussion of the results does, of course, take into consideration both the phrasing of the questions and of the response categories.

The material that will be presented unfortunately consists mainly of isolated surveys. Time series, in which the same questions have been asked repeatedly over longer periods of time, are the exception. It is thus very difficult to map longitudinal development trends. Normally, every survey only contains a few questions with reference to defense and foreign policy, and in the few cases where the number of questions in this field has been larger, the agency reports very seldom contain any cross-tabulation between these questions. This again means that the material does not lend itself very well to an analysis of interrelationships and patterns in people's attitudes to these matters.

Taken as a whole, this means that a thorough, unified analysis of public opinion is impossible, and that one should be very careful not to draw too wide-ranging or general conclusions on the basis of single (or even a few) opinion polls. Nevertheless, a great number of surveys have been conducted in this field over the last three to four years, and they do give a good overview of current Norwegian public opinion on defense and foreign policy issues.

Images of the Soviet Union

NORWEGIAN ATTITUDES TOWARD THE SOVIET UNION IN A COMPARATIVE PERSPECTIVE

Traditionally, Norway has always had its strongest international inclinations, both commercially and culturally, directed toward the Western world. The political developments in the first years after the Second World War, with increasing tension between East and West, the creation of NATO and the Warsaw Pact, and the cold war of the 1950s and 1960s helped to maintain and reinforce these inclinations. Two opinion polls conducted by NMD in 1978 and 1980 and presented in Table 7.1 serve to confirm that this remains the case.

One can observe that the Soviet Union receives the poorest score by far among those five countries included in this survey. Whereas about 40

Table 7.1   Perceptions of Norway's relationship with foreign countries
(NMD, 8/78 and 3/80)

	Sweden		West Germany		Poland		USSR		US	
	1978	1980	1978	1980	1978	1980	1978	1980	1978	1980
The relationship is:										
Very good	33	38	14	20	4	6	1	1	22	25
Quite good	55	53	58	60	34	38	14	16	59	58
Neither good nor bad	10	6	24	16	50	46	43	40	16	13
Quite bad	1	1	2	2	8	6	30	31	1	2
Very bad	0	0	1	0	1	1	9	9	0	0
Don't know	1	2	1	2	3	3	3	3	2	2

percent of the respondents think that Norway's relationship with the Soviet Union is poor, and only about 15 percent think that it is good, there is practically nobody who thinks that Norway has a poor relationship with any of the other countries. One may also note that Norway's relationship with Poland is perceived as being considerably better than its relationship with the Soviet Union, something that most probably reflects the notion—held by many—of the Soviet Union as a kind of occupation power in Poland. The differences that can be discerned between the results in the two polls are generally insignificant. In other words, there has not been any significant development in public opinion during this time, which would suggest that public opinion in this area is quite stable.

General attitudes of this kind will, of course, also be reflected in opinions on issues of defense and foreign policy, for example, in terms of which countries are believed to constitute a possible threat to Norway's national security. In two surveys in 1980 and 1981, NOI asked respondents from whom they expected an eventual attack on Norway. In both surveys the answers point unambiguously in the same direction: approximately 80 percent mention the Soviet Union or the Eastern bloc, only about five percent mention the United States or other Western countries. Two questions that were asked in a NOI poll in February 1983 did, however, yield somewhat different results, and they indicate that Norwegian public opinion evidently distinguishes to a certain extent between the country which represents the greatest military threat to Norway and that which constitutes the most serious threat to peace in general. When asked "Which country do you consider would be most likely to launch a nuclear attack in Europe, the United States or the Soviet Union?" roughly 50 percent mentioned the Soviet Union, about ten percent the United States, about ten percent mentioned both countries, and the rest did not voice an opinion on the matter. But when the question was posed in terms of who could launch a large-scale nuclear war, there was much less distinction between the superpowers: 46 percent feared that the Soviet Union might do this, while 36 percent thought the United States capable.

On this latter point, there is a greater tendency among women than among men to believe that both superpowers might start a nuclear war, but there is no difference between men and women in their perception of relative threat of nuclear war from the two superpowers. This reflects a higher general level of fear of war among women than among men, which is something which I shall touch upon later. There is also a difference in the relative perception between different age groups: the youngest respondents tend to believe that nuclear war could be started by either superpower, whereas the oldest respondents to a greater extent have focused their fears on the Soviet Union.

These results clearly show that the Norwegians' fear of an attack against their territory is oriented toward the east, and that the Soviet Union is regarded as the only real direct threat against the country's security. The data do not, however, give any direct indication as to *how strongly* this threat from the Soviet Union is perceived. But when, in the same surveys, people are asked to state whether they think the risk of an attack from a foreign power is rather great or rather small, about 60 percent state—in both surveys—that they think the risk is rather small. Therefore, this threat does not appear to be perceived as very serious by a majority of the population.

The Soviet Union is also seen as the most likely initiator of an eventual nuclear war in Europe, but Norwegian public opinion does not think that the Soviet Union represents a significantly greater threat than the United States, in the question of a worldwide nuclear war.

PERCEPTIONS OF THE BALANCE OF POWER

Ever since the two opposing military alliances were formed in the years after the Second World War, the relationship between the Soviet Union and the Warsaw Pact on one side and the United States and NATO on the other has been based on the notion of an approximate balance of power. Two NOI surveys from 1981 and 1982 show that the opinions are divided on the question of whether the superpowers have succeeded in their endeavours to maintain such a balance of power. When asked about which of the two alliances is the stronger in military terms, slightly less than half of the respondents stated that they believe the two blocs enjoy equal military strength; 30 percent believed that the Warsaw Pact is stronger, and 15 percent believed that NATO is stronger. However, when they were asked whether the United States or the Soviet Union is the stronger in terms of nuclear weapons in Europe, only 40 percent of the respondents believed that a parity existed; just over 40 percent believed that the Soviet Union is stronger in terms of nuclear weapons in Europe; and only ten percent believed that the United States is the stronger party in this respect. In general, this would indicate that a significant portion of Norwegian public opinion thinks that the military balance is currently skewed in favour of the Soviet Union, and that this imbalance is particularly noticeable as regards nuclear weapons in Europe.

Again, there are certain variations in the responses from men and women, and between different age groups. It is primarily the men who consider the Warsaw Pact to be superior in military strength. Women are partly more uncertain about the actual state of affairs in this field, and partly they tend more to see the two blocs as being equal in strength than do men. The youngest respondents have a stronger tendency than the older respondents to perceive military parity between the two superpowers, and this again *may* be one reason why (as was shown earlier) the young people tend to believe in the capability of either power starting a nuclear war.

In summary, what little data are available on how Norwegians perceive the Soviet Union are primarily concerned with how the country is regarded in comparison with other countries. In this respect, there is no doubt that the country ranks low. But there are virtually no concrete data as to exactly *what* the Norwegians think of the Soviet Union and its political system. One survey, however, probably provides a good indication of general attitudes. When a sample of Norwegian children was asked which country they would move to if they were compelled to leave Norway, not one child mentioned the Soviet Union (Werner 1980).

Images of Security

FEAR OF WAR

In all the surveys that have been conducted by the Norwegian Election Research Program since 1969, the following question has been asked: "How great do you think the risk is that Norway may be involved in a new war in the next few years: do you think it is great, considerable, or quite small?" Table 7.2 shows that the war issue has become a cause for more concern during this period. Between 1969 and 1977 an average of 60 percent believed that the risk of war was small, and fewer than ten percent believed it to be great. But from 1977 to 1981 there was a marked increase in the fear of war. During the whole period from 1969 there was a slightly, but consistently higher, fear of war among respondents over 50 years of age. Up to 1977 there were no significant differences in attitudes between men and women on this issue, even if the women did tend to have a somewhat greater fear of war than the men. In 1981, however, the difference between men and women was considerable, and the increasing fear of war which is shown in the table, is mostly accounted for by a rising fear of war among women.

The years 1969–1977 were characterized by a relatively good atmosphere between East and West, but the 1981 parliamentary elections in

Table 7.2   Fear of war 1969-1981 (NERP)

	1969	1973	1977	1981
The risk that a war may break out is				
— Great	7	4	8	13
— Considerable	18	16	16	30
— Rather small	54	65	60	51
— Don't know	21	15	16	6

Norway coincided with increasing disquiet over the relationship between the United States and the Soviet Union, an uneasiness that in part was related to the outcome of the American presidential election of 1980. The increasing fear of war among the Norwegian general public is probably more closely linked to such a general deterioration in the international political climate than to any specific international events, although one should not totally disregard the possible significance of, for instance, the Soviet intervention in Afghanistan. Another contributing factor undoubtedly is the increased focus on nuclear weapons and on the devastation that would result from a nuclear war. Later in this chapter we shall see that the issue of nuclear free zones was very prominent in the Norwegian political debate in 1981.

There are no more recent studies available that could substantiate the results from 1981 or reveal if the trends have changed since then. But the international situation today, as well as the Norwegian domestic debate about NATO's nuclear strategy in Europe, would suggest that the fear of war probably has not diminished since 1981; a small increase would seem more likely.

ATTITUDES TOWARD MILITARY DEFENSE

The buildup of the Norwegian military defense after the Second World War was not an issue that created much dissent, and as we will see later, the overall consensus also included NATO membership. For the period up to the end of the 1960s there are only a few studies concerning the Norwegian public's attitudes toward military defense, but the available data suggests that public opinion was not much concerned with these matters.

Since 1969, the NMD agency has been carrying out annual surveys, commissioned by the Norwegian "People and Defense" association, in which the following question has been asked: "Do you feel that Norway ought to have a military defense in the present situation?" The results are presented in Table 7.3.

In a time series of this kind, there will always be a number of minor

Table 7.3 Desirability of a Norwegian defense (NMD)

	1969	1971	1973	1974	1975	1976	1977	1978	1979	1980	1981	1982	1983
Yes	75	77	75	79	75	79	79	79	84	86	80	86	87
No	10	9	10	7	6	5	7	6	6	4	6	6	6
Uncertain	8	8	8	9	11	9	8	10	7	5	6	3	0
Don't know	7	6	7	5	8	8	6	5	4	6	8	5	7

Table 7.4   Attitudes toward a proposed reduction of defense expenditures (NERP)

	1977	1981
A good proposal, very important that it is implemented	12	14
A good proposal, quite important that it is implemented	16	16
I am not very concerned about the issue	22	16
A bad proposal, quite important that it is not implemented	26	28
A bad proposal, very important that it is not implemented	24	26

variations, partly due to statistical errors, and partly due to short-term oscillations caused by specific international events. Considering these factors, the time series presented here displays a remarkable stability, with a slight increase during the 1970s in support for a Norwegian military defense. There can be no doubt that a large majority in the Norwegian population wants the country to have a military defense, and (when taken in the context of results that will be presented) that this should be done within the NATO framework. The outright opposition against a Norwegian military defense is very tiny, and there are no signs of its increasing.

The support for a military defense has been stronger among men than among women throughout the whole period, but during the last three to four years there are some indications that this difference is diminishing slightly. The youngest respondents (i.e., those under 30 years of age) are always most sceptical about military defense, whereas the 30 to 60 age group is the most positively inclined. The general trend suggested in the table is the same in all age groups. The minor variations that can be observed, therefore, seem to be life-cycle-related: particularly the youngest but also the oldest respondents will normally tend to be more sceptical about a military defense than the middle-aged.

While most respondents believe that Norway ought to have a military defense, such a defense force may vary greatly in size and strength, and it would be interesting to know how much the Norwegian public thinks one should spend on defense. Recent data tell us something about how people regard the size of the defense budget and something about how they rate these expenditures in relation to spendings in other public sectors.

In the 1977 and 1981 election surveys, the respondents were asked to state their opinions about a number of proposals for specific policies. One of these proposals was to "reduce defense expenditures." The response alternatives, together with the actual scores for 1977 and 1981, are presented in Table 7.4.

When they were presented with the question in this phrasing, about 50 percent stated that the defense expenditures must not be reduced; about 30 percent said that they ought to be reduced; the rest did not have a strong opinion on the issue. However, these results do not tell us anything about how many of those who believed that a reduction in expenditures was a bad proposal actually think that the present level of expenditure is adequate and how many of them would, in fact, prefer an increased level of expenditure on defense. Two surveys carried out by NOI in 1979 and 1981 phrased the question differently and indicate that about 60 percent of the respondents considered current defense expenditures to be adequate, about 20 percent preferred a reduction in expenditure, and about 15 percent wanted to increase expenditures.

The results from the NERP and NOI surveys are not more at variance than is to be expected on the basis of the different phrasing of the questions, and taken together they do show that a majority of the population believed that defense expenditures at least should be maintained at the current level. The proportion of respondents who preferred a cut in expenditures, however, was larger than one might expect, judging by the results presented in Table 7.3, and it is obvious that a number of those who supported the general idea of a Norwegian military defense believed that Norway could do with a less costly defense force than the one it has today. In another respect, both surveys displayed a remarkable stability in attitudes over time, and there is no indication that the increased discussion about central defense policy issues (such as nuclear free zones and the NATO double-track decision) in recent years has produced increased opposition to current defense expenditures.

Both surveys revealed the following variations according to the age and sex of the respondents: the proportion of respondents who wanted to reduce defense expenditures was the same among men and women, but among the men there was a higher proportion in favor of maintaining (or increasing) the current expenditures. This was because a higher proportion of women did not state specific preference. The youngest respondents were somewhat more inclined to prefer a reduction in expenditure, but the difference was not significant enough to suggest any strong generation conflict in this respect.

Although we also find a considerable minority (about 20 percent) among the NATO supporters who believed that a reduction in defense expenditure was a good proposal, most of the subscribers to this attitude were, of course, found in the anti-NATO camp. In 1977, the survey results showed no correlation between fear of war and a preference for reduced defense expenditures. Such a correlation was, however, present in the 1981 results, but the relationship was inverse to what might be expected, that is, the wish for a reduction in expenditure was positively correlated to the fear of war. This "illogical" tendency was probably related to the fact that, in the wake of the debate about nuclear weapons and the concern over the consequences of a nuclear war, there has emerged a pattern of attitudes which combine strong fears of war with a resignation to the fact that it is not possible to defend oneself against a nuclear attack, and that one therefore can draw the consequences of this and reduce defense expenditures.

The question of what is a preferable level of expenditure in different public sectors is, however, only one aspect of the matter. Another aspect is people's reactions if they are asked to accord economic priority to different public tasks. In the 1981 election survey, the following question was also asked: "From time to time, demands for reductions in public expenditure are expressed. I have here a list of a number of public sectors that might be considered for such reductions. Can you select three of these sectors where you feel reductions should be effected?"

When the question was phrased in this way, one received a somewhat different impression of people's attitudes toward defense expenditures. Defense was the sector mentioned by the highest proportion (27 percent) as the first sector in which savings should be effected. Altogether 42 percent of the respondents mentioned defense as a suitable sector for reductions, and only "public subsidies to agriculture" was mentioned by a higher proportion of respondents. This does not necessarily imply that such a large number of people in fact want an actual cut in defense expenditures. Their priorities may also reflect a belief in the possibility of rationalization, that the same level of defense may be maintained at lower cost. Whichever interpretation one chooses, the fact remains, however, that a considerable portion of the population sees the defense sector as the most suitable area for expenditure reductions. Such a low priority on defense expenditures has also been demonstrated in an NMD survey in 1969 and an MMI survey in 1977. It is thus not a "new" attitude.

Taken as a whole, the results presented in this subsection indicate that there is a strong will to defend the nation in the Norwegian population and that a very large majority wants the country to have a military defense. However, the proportion of people who want to maintain defense expenditures at the current level is not quite as high, and when it comes to the priorities among different public sectors, people seem to consider the defense sector as a strong candidate for retrenchment measures.

This apparent inconsistency between, on the one hand, people's desire to defend the country, and their priorities when it comes to allocating funds to this purpose on the other, must be considered in relation to people's interest in different political questions as well as to the question of which political issues have the highest relevance for their everyday situation. There is little doubt that, in this respect, defense rates rather differently from, for example, health service, the educational system, care for the aged, or social security. Most people tend to have a clear understanding of what the effects of cutbacks would be in these areas, simply because they themselves or their families would be directly affected by the reductions. Only very few people, however, would be directly affected by reductions in defense expenditures, and consequently, the general public will have less understanding of the possible consequences. Seen in conjunction with the fact that most people only have a vague notion of the requirements of a modern defense system, this seems to make defense expenditure cutbacks a natural choice if one contemplates reductions in public spending. Therefore, one should perhaps not accord too much weight to the fact that defense usually ranks high on the priorities list of possible targets for public expenditure reductions. By the same token, it is evident that such attitudes can easily gain a certain popularity in public opinion, and may become politically significant—especially in times of strained economic conditions—if they are unchallenged in the political debate.

PRE-POSITIONING OF ALLIED MILITARY EQUIPMENT

The Norwegian accession to the NATO treaty in 1949 was to a great extent based on the desire to protect the country against expansionist policies of the Soviet Union. At the same time, Norway wanted to maintain a friendly and positive relationship with the Soviet Union. This dual objective has guided Norwegian defense policies during the whole postwar era, and it is the cornerstone of, among other things, the Norwegian policy regarding the deployment of allied military personnel and equipment on Norwegian soil. This policy rests on two main principles: no foreign country shall be permitted to have military bases in Norway as long as it is not under attack or threat of attack, but military installations may be constructed for use by allied military forces in the event of a crisis, and allied military forces are permitted to participate in military training maneuvers in Norway.

When the question of pre-positioning of heavy military equipment for eventual use by 8,000 to 10,000 American infantry troops was brought up in 1980, the Norwegian policy on allied bases was again brought under scrutiny, and in the autumn of 1980 and the spring of 1981 there was considerable public debate on this issue. As has been customary in recent years, this debate on defense policy was followed up by the opinion polling agencies in a series of surveys. Table 7.5 presents the most important of these surveys (a few minor surveys based on telephone interviews have been left out).

These surveys, just like those on nuclear free zones and the NATO double-track decision (which will be discussed later), are characterized by considerable variation in the phrasing of questions and in the sequence of questions. In analyzing and evaluating the survey results one must take this into consideration.

Table 7.5   Attitudes toward pre-positioning of NATO military equipment in Norway

	NMD 9/80	MMI 10/80	NMD 12/80	NOI 1/81
In favor/We should approve it	42	32	40	56
Against/We should reject it	34	35	41	40
Don't know	24	33	19	4

The substantially lower proportion of "don't know" answers in the NOI survey is attributable to the fact that the "don't know" alternative was not specified in the NOI interview form, and this probably has made the pollsters press the respondents for a response that could be fitted into the prescribed format. The other surveys undoubtedly give a much more correct representation of people's interest in the issue, and it is obvious that a considerable number of people do not have any specific opinion on the matter. Altogether, experiences from opinion polls on defense policy issues in recent years do suggest, however, that those respondents who are in doubt or uncertain about their attitudes, primarily tend to come down on a pro-NATO and pro-Western attitude if they are pressed for a specific answer. This may be a contributing factor in explaining the solid majority in favor of pre-positioning that was shown in the NOI survey. Another explanation could be that the NOI survey employed the wording "allied military equipment," whereas the NMD and MMI survey used the words "American military equipment"; for some people, the word *American* may have a more negative connotation in this context than the word *allied*. The fact that the question about pre-positioning was preceded in the NOI survey by questions about the risk of war and whether pre-positioning may reduce this risk, may also have influenced the responses, but it is difficult to draw any firm conclusions in this respect.

In a total assessment, which takes into account all the differences between the surveys, one may conclude that there was a small majority in favor of pre-positioning early in the autumn of 1980; that the difference in scores between the pro and anti camps probably was reduced somewhat later in the autumn; but in early 1981 the supporters of pre-positioning increased their lead again. This last change may be explainable by the fact that the Norwegian Storting voted in January 1981, with a large majority, to approve the plans for pre-positioning. Experiences from other political issues, both in Norway and in other countries, show that a political decision in itself may frequently have a certain impact on further developments in public opinion. An example of this is the interplay that undoubtedly occurred in the 1970s between the Norwegian laws on abortion (where, over a period of five to six years, three different laws succeeded each other) and the concurrent developments in people's attitudes toward the proposed introduction of self-determined abortions.

Men have a greater tendency to support pre-positioning than women, who tend in part to be more outright opponents to the scheme, partly not to have any specific opinion on the matter. On a geographical division, the supporters of pre-positioning are overrepresented in the Oslo area and underrepresented in Trondelag (central Norway) and northern Norway. The geographical variations are relatively moderate, however, especially considering the fact that Trondelag and northern Norway were most likely locations for storing the equipment.

The question of where the equipment should be stored was in fact the other main issue in this debate. At first, northern Norway was the most likely location, but the government finally decided that Trondelag would be a more suitable area. The reasoning behind this is not quite clear, but it seems reasonable to assume that political considerations—particularly the risk of doing something that might be interpreted as a provocation by the Soviet Union—have outweighed specifically military considerations.

Three of the surveys mentioned above also included questions about preferences with regard to the location of storage. Table 7.6 shows that a great many respondents had not made up their minds on this issue. This is not very surprising, considering that, for many people, this must have seemed a rather technical question, about which they felt insufficiently informed to voice an opinion. Of those that had, about twice as many preferred northern Norway as preferred Trondelag. That so few respondents chose southern Norway, reflects the fact, of course, that this was never a realistic alternative. The results seem to show that people attached great importance to the fact that northern Norway would be the most exposed area in case of war. A majority of those who had a specific preference with regard to location, preferred the area where they believed the equipment would be most useful. This means that these people presumably did not subscribe to the government's view on the political aspects of the issue. There were no great variations in people's preferences for the different alternative locations, only a slight tendency among respondents in Trondelag and northern Norway to favor southern Norway as a location for the storage.

DISARMAMENT

The question of war and peace will, of course, always be a central issue to most people, and I have already touched upon this in my discussion of their fear of war and their opinion with regards to who constitutes the most serious threat against Norway's security and independence. As mentioned, Norway has, as a member of NATO, to a great extent based its security on the existence of a balance of power between NATO (United States) and the Warsaw Pact (Soviet Union). Table 7.7, which presents

Table 7.6   In case of pre-positioning of NATO military equipment in Norway, where should the equipment be stored?

	NMD 9/80	MMI 11/80	NMD 12/80
Northern Norway	34	39	32
Trondelag	16	21	16
Southern Norway	4	3	4
Different locations	15	—	16
Don't know	30	37	33

Table 7.7 Importance of NATO-Warsaw Pact balance for world peace (NMD)

	2/81	6/82
Very important	49	43
Quite important	22	25
Slightly important	7	7
Quite unimportant	3	4
Totally unimportant	3	4
Don't know	15	17

two NMD opinion polls from 1981 and 1982, reveals that a substantial majority of the Norwegian population share the politicians' and the military strategists' view that a balance of power is essential in order to preserve world peace.

The unambiguous attitude of the Norwegian public in this respect is also clearly demonstrated in a comparative survey which was carried out in the United States and seven Western European countries in October 1982. In this survey, respondents were asked to state which of seven specific factors they believed to be most important for the future security of the Western countries; "military balance with the Soviet Union" was one of the factors listed. In the Norwegian sample, military balance shared the second highest number of responses (28 percent). Its ranking was the same in West Germany, Great Britain, and the Netherlands, and it was only in the West German sample that this factor was mentioned by a larger proportion of the respondents than in Norway.

Nevertheless, although the maintenance of a balance of power must be regarded as having been a success up to now, most people will still maintain that a reduction in the large weapons arsenals which are held both by East and West is a necessary precondition for permanent peaceful coexistence. In the same poll just mentioned, the factor chosen more often than military balance as being important for Norway's future security was "productive arms control talks" (34 percent). Only in this way will the threat of war (especially nuclear war) really be reduced. While the postwar era has seen a long series of disarmament negotiations, primarily between the United States and the Soviet Union, they have not been able to prevent a continuous growth in military strength on both sides.

A small country like Norway has limited means of making independent contributions on these issues, and the relationship of Norway to the continuous dialogue on disarmament has not been a very outstanding feature in the Norwegian foreign policy debate, or in opinion polls in this field. Two NOI surveys, in 1979 and 1981, did, however, ask people whether they thought Norway did enough to promote disarmament or whether it should do more. The results are presented in Table 7.8.

Table 7.8   Norway's contribution to arms control (NOI)

	10/79	6/81
Norway does enough	45	28
Should do more	43	55
Don't know	12	17

In this field one can discern a noticeable change from one poll to the next: in 1981, fewer respondents stated that they thought Norway did enough, and more respondents said it ought to do more. The trend in this direction is marked among both men and women, but it is stronger among the women. The trend is noticeable in all age groups, but in both surveys there is a higher proportion in the youngest age bracket who thought Norway should do more. There was also a tendency that, with increasing distance from Oslo, more people thought that more should be done to promote disarmament. In contrast to what is the case in most political questions, the periphery was more concerned with the peace issue than the center.

Taken as a whole, the variations on this point—and in some other parts of the data—point to an interesting trait of public opinion on defense and foreign policy. Whereas general interest in political matters shows a significant increase with higher social status and position in society, the involvement in peace and disarmament-related issues is strongest in those groups which traditionally occupy a more peripheral position with regard to the political aspects of society: women, the very young, and people who live on the geographical periphery. In other words, it seems as if much of the initiative in this field comes from people who normally play a more unobtrusive role in the political arena, and one might be tempted to regard this as an apolitical reaction against the prevailing policies.

The growing discontent which many people feel about Norwegian contributions to the efforts at disarmament is, naturally, closely linked to the increasing awareness of the peace issue which has manifested itself over the last three to four years. This awareness has also found an expression through the peace movements that have flourished in most Western countries and that have gained a large following in Norway. One of the concrete results of the peace movement's work has been the "peace march" phenomenon. The most extensively publicized—and controversial—of these marches, in terms of the Norwegian opinion, was the peace march to Moscow in 1982, which had participants from the Nordic countries and the Soviet Union. An NOI survey that was carried out the same year throws some light on the attitudes held among the Norwegian general public toward this peace march.

In June 1982—before the peace march started—the following question was asked: "There is going to be a peace march in the Soviet Union, with some Nordic and Soviet participants. Do you believe that this peace march will (a) have an impact on the Soviet authorities? (b) have an impact on the people in the Soviet Union? (c) be exploited for propaganda purposes?" About one-third of the respondents said they believed the march would have an impact on the Soviet authorities; about 60 percent thought it would have an impact on the people of the Soviet Union; and about two-thirds believed that the march would be exploited for propaganda purposes. In other words, there was a stronger belief in the effect the march might have on ordinary Soviet citizens than on the political authorities of their country, and only a minority thought that the march would not be exploited by Soviet government propaganda.

The women in the survey had a generally more positive outlook on the effects of the march than did male respondents, in that the women tended more to think that it would have an impact both on the Soviet authorities and on the Soviet people and were less inclined than the men to believe that it would be exploited for propaganda purposes. By the same token, younger people had a stronger belief in the effects of the march than older people. Both these trends are obviously explained by the fact that the march was arranged by "Nordic women for peace," and that most of the participants were younger people.

NUCLEAR FREE ZONES

The question of nuclear free zones is closely related to the general issue of disarmament and has become increasingly more topical in recent years. In Norway, the question of declaring the Nordic area (the three Scandinavian countries plus Finland and Iceland) a nuclear free zone was raised in September 1980 by the former Norwegian Minister for the Law of the Sea, Mr. Jens Evensen of the Labor party. The idea was pursued both by the Labor party and by the Norwegian trade union congress. At the 1980 national convention of the Labor party, the issue was incorporated into the party program, and in the spring of 1981 it looked as if this would be one of the hottest issues in the election campaign before the national elections in September. This would not have benefited the Labor party, however, where the proposal had obviously stirred a lot of diverging opinions among party members. Hence, when the matter was discussed in the Storting in July, the Labor party and the nonsocialist opposition parties reached an agreement that negotiations about nuclear free zones should be conducted within the NATO framework. A contributing factor in making such a compromise acceptable to the Conservative party (which undoubtedly did not favor the proposal) may have been that its leadership also did not want a public debate on this issue immediately before the elections. A couple of minor opinion surveys based on telephone interviews had already revealed that the idea of a nuclear free zone in the Nordic area tallied well with the general public rejection of nuclear weapons.

This parliamentary decision helped dispose of the issue as an election campaign topic, but it did not, of course, mean that the issue was taken off the general political agenda. In many quarters, voices were raised in favor of a direct Norwegian initiative in the matter, and in June 1982 the "NO to nuclear weapons" association presented the Storting and the government with an appeal, signed by 540,000 Norwegians, asking the Storting to take a decision that nuclear weapons never be used from Norwegian territory and asking the government to work actively to promote the establishment of a Nordic nuclear free zone. Similar appeals have come from half of Norway's provincial assemblies, and from about 50 municipal councils. During 1982, however, this issue was more and more overshadowed by the debate on NATO deployment of new missiles in Europe.

The Norwegian debate on nuclear free zones comprised three main aspects: Should nuclear free zones be established? If so, which geographical areas should they cover? And how should negotiations about the establishment of such zones be conducted? All these questions (and some other related issues) have, in one form or another, been subject to public opinion surveys.

The 1981 election survey opened the investigation of this issue by asking the respondents how interested they have been in the discussion about nuclear free zones. One-quarter said they were very interested, one-half were somewhat interested, and the remaining one-fourth were not very interested. These results correspond well with the answers given to two comparable questions which were asked by NMD in September 1981 and September 1982, and they show that there was considerable interest in this issue among the population. Men were somewhat more interested than women, and interest increased with age and level of education. However, the differences here are less pronounced than is usually the case with public interest in political issues, and this may imply that the question of nuclear free zones also engaged groups that normally are less interested in political matters. Seen in the context of party preferences, only two parties stand out from the general picture: the Socialist Left (SV), about two-thirds of whose supporters said they were very interested, and the Liberals (V), almost one-half of whom were very interested in the issue. For the other political parties, scores correspond to the general picture.

In the election survey, the respondents were asked whether they believed Norway's present policy on nuclear weapons (i.e., no nuclear weapons in time of peace) should be maintained or whether they supported the idea of a nuclear free zone in the Nordic area and in Europe. One-half of the respondents said they were in favor of nuclear weapons free zones, while just over one-third wanted to maintain the present nuclear weapons policy. In a NOI survey in which people were asked only if they were for or against nuclear free zones, a much larger majority came out in favor of the zones (69 percent for, 14 percent against). The variations in the population are small on this issue, but the stronger general opposition to nuclear weapons among women makes them less inclined than the men to support present policy.

Even if these two surveys reveal slightly different results, there can be no doubt that a large majority of the Norwegian population ideally would like to see the country as part of a nuclear free zone. But within this majority there are certainly wide differences in opinion as regards which areas should be included in such a zone and about how the negotiations on the establishment of the zone should be conducted. And it would primarily be questions of this nature, which touch on the conditions for establishing a nuclear free zone, that would be the focus of the political debate if the issue were to be put onto the agenda again.

With regard to which area should be included in a nuclear free zone, the Norwegian debate has been focusing on the Nordic area and the northern part of the Soviet Union (especially the Kola Peninsula), and less on the rest of Europe. Two NMD surveys (September 1981 and September 1982) showed that just over half of the respondents feel that a zone, which should be operative also in the event of war, must include the northern parts of the Soviet Union; one-fourth of the respondents advocated a unilateral Nordic zone; and almost one-fourth did not have any specific opinion. These results stand in some contrast to the results from two minor NOI telephone surveys, which showed a clear majority in favor of nuclear free zones, in spite of the fact that the question specified that the zone would not comprise any part of Soviet territory. Although one should not accord too much importance to such telephone surveys, the results taken together may indicate that even if a majority among the population basically rejects the idea of a unilateral Nordic zone, parts of the population would still be willing to consider such a zone if it were to prove impossible to establish a zone including parts of the Soviet Union.

In the population as a whole, there is a clear majority in favor of conducting eventual negotiations about a zone within a unified NATO framework. Both the two NMD surveys from 1981 and 1982 and a NOI survey from 1981 show that about two-thirds want negotiations within such a framework, and only about one-quarter preferred direct bilateral negotiations. In the 1981 election survey, where the question about negotiations was put only to those respondents who had indicated that they were in favor of nuclear free zones in the Nordic area and Europe, there was, however, a small majority who would prefer direct negotiations between Norway and non-NATO countries. This difference in opinion shows that the question of negotiations is closely linked to the attitude toward nuclear free zones in general: Those respondents who strongly favored such zones had a much more positive attitude toward direct negotiations than the zone opponents, who maintained that if there were to be negotiations, then they must take place under the auspices of NATO.

So much for the main issues of the debate, but some connected issues throw further light on the matter and on its prospective importance for Norway. First, would a zone which includes the Nordic countries, but not the Kola Peninsula, increase or reduce the risk of an attack against Norway? On this issue, opinion was highly divided. About 40 percent think it would increase the risk, and about 40 percent think it would reduce the risk, according to a NOI survey from 1981. And while the youngest respondents strongly believed in the usefulness of such a zone, scepticism increased with age. According to the same survey, however, there was much scepticism about whether the Soviet Union would agree to a zone that would include the Kola Peninsula. This was expressed by as much as 75 percent of the respondents, while only 20 percent believed that the Soviet Union might agree to such a zone. And on this issue there were no variations in opinion between different population groups, nor with respect to party preference.

Second, if a nuclear free zone were established in the Nordic area, backed by guarantees from both the United States and the Soviet Union, would the two superpowers stand by their guarantees? As one might expect, on the basis of the public's general attitudes toward the two countries, they are not regarded with equal confidence in this respect. In another NOI survey from 1981, one-quarter of the respondents believed that the Soviet Union would honor such a guarantee, and two-thirds believed it would not honor it. The corresponding figures for the United States were 50 percent and 40 percent, respectively. These results reveal in other words, a considerable amount of scepticism with respect to Norway's ally as well. Furthermore, considering the rather strong general scepticism about the usefulness of a nuclear free zone, one may wonder why the support for such a zone is as strong as it is.

In general terms, Norwegian public opinion in 1981–1982 was undoubtedly in favor of a nuclear free zone in the Nordic area. Viewed against the background of official Norwegian policy with regard to nuclear weapons during the whole of the postwar era and the firmly established opposition of the Norwegian people against having nuclear weapons as part of national defense, this result is actually as one would have expected. Furthermore, many people would maintain that such an attitude is, in fact, not much more than a confirmation of the already existing situation. However, the conditions for the establishment of such a nuclear free zone—both as regards the negotiations and the role of the Soviet Union and Soviet territory in an eventual treaty—will have a decisive influence on people's attitudes on this issue, and in this respect opinions are highly divided in the Norwegian population.

Images of Deterrence

DETERRENCE

The concept of nuclear deterrence is an integral part of the military strategies which form the foundation of the East-West balance of power.

Each side wants to appear strong enough that the other will not risk launching an attack for fear of the consequences. The adversary should always be aware that any attack will be met by an unavoidable counteraction.

The building up of the nuclear forces of the superpowers through an increased number and sophistication of missiles, missiles that could only be countered with great difficulty by an opponent's defensive systems, have brought to a head for many people the question of whether there does not exist a threshold, beyond which any further buildup and modernization would serve no purpose. Such a notion enjoys considerable support in Norwegian public opinion. This is shown in a NOI survey from February 1983, in which people were asked whether they agreed or disagreed with the following statement: "Those people who strive to freeze the nuclear arsenals at their present level claim that both the United States and the Soviet Union already have enough nuclear weapons to be able to destroy each other, and they therefore wish to ban any further testing, production or deployment of nuclear weapons on both sides. What is your opinion on this? Do you strongly agree, agree, disagree, or strongly disagree?" 43 percent said they strongly agreed, 28 percent agreed, 15 percent disagreed, and only four percent strongly disagreed with this statement (ten percent did not have an opinion).

In the same survey, the deterrent effect of nuclear weapons was linked to the conditions for peace through the following question: "Do you think it is realistic or unrealistic to believe that peace can be secured if (a) the West reduces the number of its nuclear weapons? (b) the West modernizes its nuclear weapons without increasing the number? (c) the West increases its number of nuclear weapons?" A majority of almost two-thirds of the respondents thought that an increase in the number of nuclear weapons in the West would be a poor means to secure continued peace. The two other alternatives were also received with scepticism; there was a small majority (about 50 percent vs. about 40 percent) of respondents who thought it unrealistic that peace could be secured through modernization of the West's nuclear arsenal, and an equal majority doubted that a reduction in the number of nuclear weapons in the West could bring about the desired result.

These results undeniably seem to some extent contradictory, and one could possibly interpret this as an expression of an uncertain and disillusioned public opinion which does not know how to react to the future turns of the nuclear weapons issue. This is, however, probably not a correct interpretation. The problem lies primarily in the fact that the question is poorly phrased, in that it focuses unilaterally on possible Western initiatives, and does not give the respondents any opportunity to take into consideration what the other side might do. A more balanced question would undoubtedly have yielded different results, and the best conclusion that can be drawn from the answers is that a majority of the public sees deterrence (and disarmament) as a *two-sided* issue, where the strategies and reactions of one party must be considered in the context of what the other party does. Nevertheless, there can be little doubt that Norwegian public opinion is sceptical to the deterrent effect of a further nuclear buildup and considers such an option to be a dubious means of preserving peace.

THE USE OF NUCLEAR WEAPONS

Ever since the 1950s, when the question of possible deployment of American nuclear weapons on Norwegian soil was first raised, official Norwegian policy on this issue has been stated in no uncertain terms: nuclear weapons shall not be stored or deployed in Norway; Norwegian military personnel shall not be trained in the use of nuclear weapons; and no preparations shall be made for an eventual use of nuclear weapons from Norwegian territory in the event of a crisis or a war. Norwegian military defense is, without exception, based on conventional forces, and there has been no political debate about this principle.

Norwegian policy on nuclear weapons has strong support in Norwegian public opinion. In an NMD survey from November 1979, 80 percent of the respondents said they believed Norway should maintain its present policy on nuclear weapons; only ten percent said that one should allow the deployment of nuclear weapons in Norway. In an MMI survey from November 1980, just over 60 percent were against preparing for eventual allied use of nuclear weapons from Norwegian territory in the event of a war; only ten percent favored this option. A question regarding whether American aircraft carrying nuclear weapons should be permitted training opportunities in Norway yielded the same result. And in December 1980, 90 percent of the respondents in a NOI survey answered that under no circumstances should Norway resort to the use of nuclear weapons; only about ten percent said that it would be advantageous for Norway to have nuclear weapons as part of their defense. As much as the Norwegian public wants the country to have a military defense, its determination is just as strong that nuclear weapons should not be part of this defense.

The strong antipathy against nuclear weapons manifest in the Norwegian population also finds more concrete expressions than simply replies to questions in opinion surveys. As mentioned earlier, the "NO to Nuclear Weapons" organization gathered approximately 540,000 signatures for their appeal against nuclear weapons in the spring of 1982. And, according to an NMD survey that was conducted in June/July 1982, many more people would have signed the appeal if they had been approached. The results show that, in addition to the 21 percent who stated that they had signed the appeal (a proportion that tallies well with the actual number of signatures), almost 50 percent said that they would have signed, whereas only about 20 percent stated that they would not have signed the appeal.

The support for the appeal in the different segments of the population corresponds well with previous observations about the strength of support for the peace and disarmament issues. There was a smaller proportion of supporters among men than among women, and there was also a greater proportion of men who said they would not have signed the appeal. There were more supporters for the appeal among young people than among the elderly, and more people in the central region of eastern Norway stated their disapproval of the appeal than was the case in other parts of the country.

The actual participation in rallies against nuclear weapons is, naturally, significantly lower. This is partly because there are fewer opportunities for using such a form of expression and partly because it is a more cumbersome form of participation. In a NOI survey from April 1982, seven percent of the respondents said that they had participated in such demonstrations. Participation was most frequent among city dwellers (where a greater number of demonstrations are held), and it is particularly among young people with relatively high levels of education that one finds the participants in these demonstrations. In a follow-up question, respondents were asked to state if they approved or disapproved of such demonstrations. About 60 percent said they approved, and it is worth noting that there was a majority for this attitude among followers of all political parties except the Conservatives and Fremskrittspartiet. Even for these two parties, about 40 percent approved of demonstrations against nuclear weapons.

These results serve as a further confirmation of the very strong opposition to nuclear weapons among the Norwegian people, and they show that a significant number of people are prepared to let their attitudes be manifested through various forms of action. This means that the attitudes in question are firmly established and regarded as important by those who hold them, and that they are not easily changed.

THE NATO DOUBLE-TRACK DECISION

Recently, the Norwegian debate on defense and security policy has been dominated by the so-called double-track decision of NATO of December 1979. This question has focused the Norwegian political debate on defense policy to an extraordinary degree. Opinion polls have gradually come to play an important role in the discussions, and this is the first time since the 1971–1972 debate on Norwegian membership in the EC that a political issue has generated such fierce competition for support in the public.

The NATO double-track decision determined that NATO in the future should pursue a double strategy that combined the modernization of NATO's nuclear arsenal in Europe with arms control negotiations with the Soviet Union. If these negotiations produced acceptable results, NATO would not deploy the new American missiles; if not, then the missiles would be deployed.

The double-track decision is a complex political issue, and one needs a lot of information and insight to get an adequate overview of the facts and of the different political linkages and implications. A considerable part of the population is unlikely to possess this insight, and this poses a serious problem to the pollster and analyst. Simple questions about attitudes toward the double-track decision, without any reference to the substance of the issue, will yield both a high percentage of "don't know" answers and a great many answers which are not based on any specific attitudes. Questions that attempt to include specific references to the substance of the issue tend to become too long and complex, and they usually also run the risk of emphasizing some aspects of the matter more than others and may therefore lead the answers in certain directions. One may, in fact, justifiably ask whether this issue lends itself to analysis through interview surveys based on representative samples. This objection would be particularly relevant in the early stages of the process of opinion formation, when there would be great variations in the level of information, and when substantial portions of the population probably would not yet have formed any personal opinions about the issue.

In autumn 1982 and spring 1983, a large number of different questions about the double-track decision were included in different surveys. Most of the questions have been commissioned by clients who have had a more or less direct interest in the matter (newspapers, various institutions). The phrasing of the questions varies greatly, which clearly reflects that the issue is a complex one and that there is no one natural and simple form of questioning available, as well as the fact that the clients wish to focus on different aspects of the matter. This has led to two undesirable consequences: First, the picture that emerges is a rather blurred one. The results undeniably present considerable variations, and disagreement about which poll gives the most accurate picture has been a prominent feature in the public debate on this issue. Second, it becomes almost impossible to study the evolution of public opinion. Since the questions that were asked at different points in time, with one exception, have been phrased differently, one has no way of knowing whether changes from one poll to the next were caused by an actual shift in opinion or whether they should be attributed to variations in phrasing.

Any complex political issue is bound to have linkages to a number of different aspects of society, and people's attitudes toward the various issues will, to a great extent, depend on which aspects they associate with the issue at hand, and what emphasis they put on these aspects. A review of the most common frames of reference that seem to apply when people form opinions about an issue would form an important basis for the interpretation of the public opinion on that issue. It is not easy to give a complete directory of all the possible frames of reference that may apply to the NATO double-track decision, but there are three aspects that seem to stand out, and they will be discussed here.

First, one may focus on the fact that the issue concerns nuclear weapons. In Norwegian public opinion, this would almost automatically bring forth objections. As has been pointed out before, there is a long tradition in Norway of opposition to nuclear weapons, and this opposition draws legitimacy from official Norwegian policy in this field, which is supported by all political parties. To many people, this in itself is sufficient reason to regard the NATO double-track decision with scepticism and resistance. To others, the crux of the matter may be whether the decision should be considered as an increase in NATO nuclear forces or just as a modernization of these forces.

Second, one may focus on the implications of the double-track decision for the relative military strength of East and West. In this context, one would expect the opinions to come out more strongly in favor of the double-track decision, at least if one believes that the Soviet Union enjoys military superiority in Europe, and that the measures that are prescribed in the double-track decision are necessary in order to recreate (or possibly maintain) a desirable military balance.

Third, one may focus on the negotiations aspect. In this case, people's attitudes toward the double-track decision will probably depend on how they judge the conditions for real negotiations between the United States and the USSR. Is the threat of deployment necessary in order to evoke a genuine willingness to negotiate from the Soviet Union? Would the Soviet Union enter into negotiations even without such a threat? Or would the threat of deployment in fact be a provocation which might cause the Soviet Union to build up their own nuclear forces even further?

Various interpretations are possible, and for people who are conscious of one or more of these aspects, and have formed their opinions on the basis of these aspects, variations in the phrasing of the questions will be of little significance. They would probably give the same answers irrespective of question wording. On the other hand, for people who are not distinctly aware of the different aspects of the issue, the phrasing of the question will, in many cases, shape their approach to the problem, and consequently it will also to a great extent determine the content of their answers. The distribution of responses which can be observed in the many surveys of attitudes toward the double-track decision must, therefore, be closely examined in light of the phrasing of the questions, and of those aspects of the issue that are emphasized in the questions.

The first survey question that touched on the subject matter of the double-track decision was asked by NMD in November 1979, that is, before the decision itself was actually taken. The question read as follows: "It is maintained that new Soviet weapons systems have altered the military balance in Europe in favor of the Soviet Union. The NATO countries are, therefore, planning to modernize the alliance's nuclear weapons, also with a view to achieving a stronger bargaining position in the event of disarmament negotiations. Do you think that Norway ought to support the plans for a modernization of NATO nuclear weapons, on the understanding that these weapons will not be deployed in Norway, or do you think that Norway ought to oppose these plans?"

We see that the question refers to a Soviet military superiority in

Europe, without mentioning that opinions may differ on this issue. Further, it is specified that eventual deployment of the new NATO missiles will not affect Norwegian territory. Both these aspects may be expected to bias the question in a way that would produce responses in favor of the double-track decision. Nevertheless, the responses show a small majority of opposition to NATO's modernization plans (44 percent against, 37 percent for, and 19 percent who did not have an opinion). A follow-up question, which asked "whether it is necessary for NATO to have concrete rearmament plans in order to make any headway in the disarmament negotiations with the Soviet Union, or whether one might achieve just as much in the disarmament negotiations without first having decided on a plan for nuclear weapons modernization," gave as a result a clear majority who said one might get just as far without such plans (43 percent against, 29 percent for, and 28 percent who did not have an opinion). Taken together, these two questions would indicate that a small majority of Norwegian public opinion was opposed to the nuclear weapons modernization plans of NATO at the time when the double-track decision was taken.

At first, the double-track decision attracted little attention in Norwegian public opinion. It was not until 1982 that the issue really found a prominent place on the political agenda. This fact is reflected in public opinion surveys, and with the exception of two minor telephone surveys in 1981—which in this context are of little importance—direct questions about the double-track decision were not included in the surveys until late in the autumn of 1982. At that point in time, the public's interest in the issue had been roused, and, in a NOI survey of November 1982, 29 percent of the respondents said they were very interested in this issue, 40 percent said they were quite interested, and 35 percent said they were not particularly interested. The public interest in the double-track decision at this time was, in other words, almost as great as the public interest in nuclear free zones was in 1981. There is reason to believe that interest in the double-track decision increased as the public debate about the issue swelled in the beginning of 1983, and that these two issues (nuclear free zones and the double-track decision) together are indicative of the level of interest that central matters of foreign policy can attain in Norwegian public opinion.

From November 1982 to April 1983, five surveys were conducted on the issue of the double-track decision, in which the questions (in somewhat varying form) explicitly mentioned both the deployment and the negotiating aspects of the decision. Table 7.9 summarizes the results from these surveys, giving the exact phrasing of the questions.

The NMD survey distinguishes itself with a considerably higher percentage of "don't know" answers than the other surveys, something that undoubtedly reflects the fact that the "don't know" alternative was specifically mentioned in the question. It is a well-known phenomenon in interview research that the proportion of respondents who have no specific

Table 7.9   Attitudes toward the NATO double-track decision

	NOI 11/82	NMD 12/82	NOI 1/83	NOI 2/83	NMD 4/83
For	51	34	48	53	38
Against	44	33	39	34	35
Don't know	5	33	13	13	28

Note:
Question wording:

NOI, 11/82:
"In the Norwegian debate, some people maintain that nuclear weapons are such a special and terrible type of weapon that we in the Western world ought to reject the idea of deploying new missiles, regardless of the position of the Soviet Union in their negotiations. Others say that if we reject beforehand a nuclear modernization in the West, we will lose an important bargaining advantage. Then the Soviet Union would not believe it necessary to diminish their nuclear forces. Which of these two positions are you most in agreement with?"

NMD, 12/82 and 4/83:
"NATO is planning to modernize its defense capabilities in Western Europe by deploying a number of new nuclear missiles, because it is felt that the Warsaw Pact has a greater striking power in this field. Briefly stated, the double-track decision implies that these NATO missiles will only be deployed if the Soviet Union does *not* agree to reduce its number of new nuclear missiles. Would you say that you support this double-track decision, or do you believe that the NATO missiles should not be deployed, regardless of what the Soviet Union does, or do you not want to take a stand on this issue?"

NOI, 1/83 and 2/83:
"In accordance with the unanimous double-track decision of NATO in December 1979, NATO is going to modernize its nuclear forces, but without increasing the total number of NATO nuclear weapons in Europe. The deployment of the modernized NATO nuclear weapons will, however, only be carried out if the Soviet Union in negotiations refuses to reduce the number of its nuclear weapons aimed at targets in Western Europe. Are you in favor of or against this double-track decision?"

opinion on an issue is considerably higher in surveys where the respondents are given a legitimate opportunity to say just that. The differences between the surveys in this respect suggest, therefore, that in the other surveys there must be a larger number of respondents who give answers that must be characterized as rather random.

It is especially the response alternative expressing support for the double-track decision that benefits from a low "don't know" ratio. This suggests that, with this form of questioning, a number of persons will choose the supportive response alternative, probably on the basis of a general pro-Western or pro-NATO attitude, even if their actual knowledge of this issue is rather scanty. Another factor that may influence some doubters in the same direction is the form of questioning that employs phrases like "lose an important bargaining advantage," "Eastern Europe has a greater military striking force," and "modernize their nuclear

Table 7.10   Attitudes toward deployment of new NATO missiles (NOI)

	11/82	12/82
For	27	34
Against	69	62
Don't know	4	3

Note:
Question wording:

"Since 1979, a number of NATO member countries have discussed a modernization of the alliance's nuclear missiles. A possible course of action would be the deployment of 572 new missiles in five countries: West Germany, Italy, Great Britain, The Netherlands and Belgium. Are you in favor of or against such deployment?"

weapons, but without increasing their total number," phrases that may to some extent be seen to favor supportive responses.

In contrast to the 1979 survey, these surveys (with the exception of the NMD survey) all show a majority in favor of the double-track decision. This may indicate that there has been an actual shift in opinion between 1979 and 1982/1983, but the different phrasing of the questions makes it difficult to draw any positive conclusions about this. The two surveys that used identically phrased questions (NOI, January and February 1983, and NMD, December 1982 and April 1983) also indicate that there has been a shift in this direction in public opinion. Admittedly, the differences in scores between the two polls are very small in both cases, but the fact that they both show the same trend increases the probability that the figures reflect an actual change in public opinion. However, a third survey on the same question from at least one of the polling institutes would be needed before one could draw a certain conclusion.

A NOI survey from February 1983, which does not explicitly mention the negotiations aspect but which asks whether or not NATO should deploy their new missiles if the United States and the Soviet Union do not reach an agreement on disarmament, shows a small majority against deployment (46, 40, and 14 percent). This deviation from the trend of the other surveys is probably related to the fact that this question focuses more on the actual deployment and less on the content of the double-track decision, and it is, therefore, an appropriate illustration of the importance of the question wording.

The importance of this is expressed even more clearly in the two NOI surveys that were carried out in November and December 1982 and are presented in Table 7.10. This table shows that there is a clear majority in Norwegian public opinion against deployment of new nuclear weapons when the question focuses on this aspect alone, although the specific mention of "572 new missiles" may also have had some effect on the

Table 7.11   Attitudes toward NATO's double-track decision by respondents' knowledge of the issue (NMD 12/82)

| | Knowledge about the double-track decision | | | |
	Very good	Know what it is about	Have heard about it	Have not heard about it
In favor of the decision	60	48	24	13
No deployment under any circumstances	32	36	32	25
Unsure	8	16	44	62

outcome. In this case too, however, we can discern a shift toward less outright opposition against the NATO plans, and this supports the assumption that there has been a real shift of opinion. This particular question can be regarded as representing one extreme in the opinion surveys on the double-track decision; the other extreme is represented by a question, which NOI asked in January 1983, about what people would choose if they were faced with a choice between continued Norwegian membership in NATO and a Norwegian rejection of the double-track decision. In this case, 70 percent prefer NATO membership; only 20 percent support an unconditional Norwegian "no" to the double-track decision.

The opinion surveys that have been conducted on the issue of NATO's double-track decision do undeniably present a rather confusing picture of Norwegian public opinion on this question, and it is not surprising that the surveys have been the subject of considerable debate and controversy. The primary reason for this is not necessarily the complexity of the issue or the technical problems this complexity causes for the phrasing of the questions, but may rather be the fact that the double-track decision is related to two questions that most people consider important, and about which they have formed opinions: the question of nuclear weapons and nuclear disarmament, and the question of Norwegian membership in NATO and the foundations of Norwegian security policy. Normally these two questions do not clash in any serious way, but in the case of the double-track decision they are brought together in a way that is bound to create problems for a public opinion where there is strong sentiment against nuclear weapons and a desire to reduce the risks of a devastating nuclear war and—at the same time—a strong sentiment in favor of Norwegian membership in NATO.

For that majority of the population that is neither so strongly supportive of NATO or so strongly opposed to nuclear weapons that the choice is self-evident, their attitudes to the double-track decision will reflect a dilemma, the resolution of which is sought in a way that does not entail an "either-

or" stance. This gives room for a number of individual considerations, some of them concerning premises—What is the actual distribution of military force in Europe today? Are the missiles necessary to ensure real negotiations?—others concerning consequences—Will nuclear weapons' modernization increase the security of NATO and Norway? Will modernization of the nuclear arsenal increase the risk of a nuclear war? Some people will consider these factors of their own accord; others will take decisive direction from the phrasing of the questions. Where issues as complex as the double-track decision are concerned, there are no "correct" questions, in the sense that they measure real public opinion on the issue more exactly than other questions could. In the final analysis, it is always a question of subjective interpretation, both on the part of the interviewer and on the part of the respondent.

Nevertheless, we may conclude first, that a clear majority of the Norwegian public is opposed to the deployment of new nuclear weapons, if this issue is regarded separately. Second, an equally large majority prefer NATO membership to a rejection of the double-track decision if these are the only options. Between these extremes, the picture of public opinion is more diffuse, and the opinion is probably divided almost down the middle. All things considered, it does seem as if the proponents of the strategy implied in the double-track decision constitute a small majority.

In the December 1982 survey of NMD, respondents were also asked to indicate how well informed they were about the double-track decision. Such a self-evaluation of knowledge should not be given too much weight, but the trend in Table 7.11, which correlates people's attitudes to the double-track decision with their level of information, is still clear enough. The opposition to the decision shows almost no correlation with the level of information, but there is a strong positive correlation between support for the double-track decision and the level of information.

This result has led some commentators to maintain that increasing support for the NATO decision is a question of improving the level of information. Similar arguments were also introduced in the debate about Norwegian membership in the EC, and the experiences from that debate show that this is a too simplistic conclusion. It is always going to be difficult to judge beforehand what impact increased knowledge and insight into an issue will have on attitudes toward that issue, for this will depend both on the person's attitudes toward other aspects of the issue and related issues, and on which groups the persons in question belong to and identify with.

The diffuse picture of public opinion notwithstanding, the results reveal two clear and consistent patterns, which are not significantly influenced by variations in phrasing of the questions. First, as was to be expected on the basis of previous results, the men in the sample are generally more positive to the double-track decision, while the women are both more sceptical and less inclined to have any specific opinion. Second, we find the strongest opposition against the double-track decision among persons under 30 years of age.

Images of Allies

ATTITUDES TOWARD THE UNITED STATES

A general impression of Norwegian attitudes toward the United States has already been presented in Table 7.1, which shows that more than four-fifths of the Norwegian population regard their relationship with the United States as being good. The United States, in other words, does not fare much worse in this respect than our closest neighbor country, Sweden. There is little other data describing how Norwegians evaluate different aspects of American society, but the general popularity of the United States is clearly attested to by the survey (mentioned earlier) of the relocation preferences of Norwegian children. After Sweden, the United States was mentioned by most children (altogether almost one-quarter) as the country they would prefer if they had to leave Norway (Werner 1980).

The good relationship with the United States is also confirmed by the fact that practically nobody perceives that country as a potential threat against Norway's freedom and independence (according to the two NOI surveys). A similar result was found in a 1980 NOI survey, in which three-fourths of the respondents stated that they had confidence in American support if Norway were to get involved in a war. According to another NOI survey from February 1983, an equally large proportion of the respondents think that an American security guarantee vis-à-vis Western Europe is still necessary.

In sum, a significant majority of Norwegian public opinion perceives its relationship with the United States as good, is confident that Norway will receive help from the United States in the event of a crisis, and regards an American security guarantee as an important factor in the Norwegian defense system.

ATTITUDES TOWARD NATO

After Norway regained its independence in 1905, the country pursued a policy of armed neutrality aimed at staying out of international conflicts. During the First World War this policy worked well. This was not the case in the Second World War, however, and this experience caused Norway to abandon its neutral stance. In 1949, when Norway joined the NATO alliance, it happened without much internal political controversy, although the Communist party, of course, was strongly against it, and there was also some oppostion from Labour party voters.

The issue of Norwegian membership in NATO is one of the few foreign policy issues about which good time series data about public opinion are available. First, ever since 1965, the NMD polling agency has been conducting surveys—commissioned by the Norwegian "People and Defense" association—in which the respondents have been asked whether they think that Norwegian NATO membership serves to reduce or

Table 7.12   Attitudes toward Norwegian membership in NATO 1965-1981 (NERP)

	1965	1969	1973	1977	1981
Norway should continue as a NATO member	44	54	67	66	72
Norway should cancel its NATO membership	15	13	9	8	8
Don't know	41	33	24	26	20

increase the risk of an attack from another country, or whether it does not make any difference. These surveys reveal a high degree of stability of public opinion: over the last 10 years, the proportion who believe that NATO membership serves to reduce the risk of an attack against Norway has been more or less constant in the range between 60 percent and 65 percent. The number who believe that our membership increases the risk of an attack has increased slightly, from six to seven percent ten years ago to about ten percent in the last three or four years.

The other time series data focuses more directly on Norwegian NATO membership. Within the scope of the Norwegian Election Research Program, in surveys held at the time of every parliamentary election from 1965 to 1981, a specific two-part question has been included. The question presented two alternatives: that Norway should withdraw from the alliance or that Norway should maintain its membership. Respondents were first asked whether they had formed any opinion on this issue. If the answer was affirmative, the interviewer would repeat the alternatives and ask the respondent to state a preference. In this way, respondents were given a legitimate opportunity to state that they did not in fact have an opinion on the matter. Table 7.12 shows that the attitudes toward Norwegian membership in NATO have undergone an interesting development.

In 1965, the "don't know" score was very high. Later, it has dropped steadily. The reduction in the number of "don't know" answers from 1965 to 1969 can—at least in part be explained by the fact that the membership treaty was up for review in 1969, at the end of 20 years. In June 1968, a large majority in the Norwegian Storting (national assembly) voted to continue Norway's NATO membership. This means that since 1969, respondents in these surveys have stated opinions on an issue that had recently been reconsidered by parliament. The increasing propensity to state a specific preference may thus reflect, at least to some extent, an acceptance of a parliamentary determined policy. But it may also reflect a general increase in the public's interest in foreign policy issues.

Public support for Norwegian membership in NATO has shown a steady, uninterrupted growth, even during the years from 1969 to 1973 when the EC debate was going on. The opposition against Norwegian NATO membership, however, has been reduced to half of its original strength from 1965 to 1981, and today fewer than ten percent of the respondents are against membership in the alliance.

During the whole period, women have had a considerably higher "don't know" score than men. In the first surveys, this meant that women had a low propensity to state a preference for either of the two alternatives. But in later years, the opposition against NATO membership was equally low among both women and men. At no time during this period have there been any significant differences between the various age groups in support for NATO membership. Thus, the relatively widely held notion of a stronger opposition against NATO among younger people is not corroborated by this data (time series data from MND yield similar results).

The percentage of "don't know" answers is significantly inversely correlated with respondents' level of education, but the differences seem to have diminished over time. As a consequence of this, we also find that the higher the respondents' level of education, the higher is the occurrence of outright support for NATO membership. There is a less strong correlation between level of education and opposition to NATO. It is well worth noting that whereas in the beginning of the period, the highest proportion of NATO opponents could be found among those respondents who had the least education, the tendency is exactly the opposite in the latter part of the period. This is due to the fact that while opposition to NATO has diminished among the groups with low and medium levels of education, it has remained almost unchanged among the highly educated. In other words, the opposition against NATO in intellectual, radical circles is not decreasing.

Taken as a whole, the socio-demographic variations in attitudes toward NATO have been moderate during the whole period, and there is no population segment that stands out as particularly diverging from the main trends on the NATO issue. The next section demonstrates, however, that variations according to party preferences are considerably greater.

Correlates of Attitudes Toward Defense

SEX

The previous discussions have shown clearly that the greatest socio-demographic variations in people's attitudes toward defense are between men and women. This difference is most manifestly expressed by a greater uncertainty among women with regard to these issues. To a much greater extent than men, women tend to state that they either have not formed an opinion or that they are in doubt. This is a response pattern that may in part be the result of a lesser degree of interest in issues of this kind, and in part be the result of less factual knowledge about the issues. Such a difference between men and women is also found where general political issues are concerned (although the difference has decreased over time), and it is only to be expected that it would be significant in this particular field, which traditionally has been strongly dominated by men.

The substantial differences between men and women can best be summarized by stating that women in general express stronger opposition against all forms of war and growth of armaments. They are less inclined than men to favor military defense, although the differences in this respect have decreased somewhat, and the support for NATO is about the same among men and women. On the concrete defense issues that have been on the political agenda in Norway in recent years, we find that women are more inclined than men (1) to express opposition against the proposed pre-positioning of allied military equipment in Norway; (2) to support the idea of a nuclear weapons free zone in the Nordic area; (3) to take a negative attitude toward the NATO double-track decision; and (4) to have a positive opinion of peace marches and their effects.

In spite of this, it is primarily among women that the fear of war has increased in recent years, and women are more dissatisfied than men with the Norwegian endeavors for disarmament. From a military point of view, it may seem illogical that a strong fear of war coexists with a significant opposition against proposals that are aiming at increasing the defense capabilities of the West. For those women (and men) who display such attitude patterns, this is probably not the case. On the contrary, there is every reason to believe that it is just the fear of war that is the motivation behind what these people regard as endeavors to promote the possibility of continued peace.

AGE

Second only to sex, age is the demographic variable that is associated with the greatest variations in attitudes, and the 20 to 30 year age bracket stands out as the most atypical group. This tendency is manifested in several ways:. First, the youngest respondents are more inclined to believe in a military parity between East and West, and they are also more inclined than their seniors to think that either side could initiate another war. These attitudes probably stem to a great extent from the fact that the younger generation does not have the same direct experience of the cold war of the 1950s and 1960s as do the older respondents. This difference, combined with personal experiences of World War II, probably explain the higher occurrence of fear of war among the older age brackets.

Furthermore, young people tend to be more sceptical of military defense, and they are somewhat more inclined to favor reductions in defense expenditures. They also come out more strongly in favor of disarmament, they have a more optimistic outlook on the possible impact of peace marches, and they are more supportive of nuclear free zones. There are, however, no variations according to age in the support for Norwegian NATO membership.

Having said this, I should add that all of these differences are generally rather small, and the present material does not reveal any significant generation gaps as regards attitudes toward defense and foreign policy issues. On the contrary, the differences are clearly much smaller than one might expect when observing the public debate.

Table 7.13 Attitudes toward NATO according to party preferences 1965–1981:
Percentages in favor of Norwegian membership in NATO (NERP)

	SV	DNA	V	KRF	SP	H
1965	9	40	52	50	45	67
1969	17	43	69	56	64	86
1973	33	62	82	73	77	89
1977	9	62	70	63	73	89
1981	25	70	66	69	78	89

PARTY PREFERENCE

In foreign policy issues, which often are perceived as being rather "distant" from people's everyday life, the general public needs a substitute for the practical references that would be available in most issues concerning domestic policies. This usually comes in the form of an ideological reference. One should also bear in mind that significant international events during the postwar years may have been instrumental in shaping attitudes toward foreign policy. The 1956 Hungarian crisis, the Vietnam War, the Soviet invasion in Afghanistan, and the present United States involvement in Latin America are just a few such events.

The main features of the evolution of Norwegian opinion are probably not essentially different from what one would find in other Western countries. Among the Norwegian political parties and their supporters, attitudes toward foreign and defense policy issues are, to a great extent, determined by the position on the ideological right-left axis, which constitutes the dominant political cleavage in Norwegian politics (Rokkan 1970; Rokkan and Valen 1971; Valen and Rokkan 1974). This trend has grown stronger in recent years. Multidimensional analysis of the 1977 election data shows that, at that time, defense and foreign policy attitudes represented a distinct dimension that existed alongside the right-left dimension. Similar analyses of the 1981 election reveal that the two dimensions by then had merged into one. Defense and foreign policy issues now constitute an addition to the traditional right-left factors that make up the dimension (Valen 1981; Valen and Aardal 1983).

The opposition against official Norwegian foreign and defense policy in the postwar era has primarily come from the left wing of the political spectrum. In the first few years after the war it was particularly expressed through the Communist opposition to Norwegian membership in NATO. In later years, the most articulate and broadly based opposition in foreign and defense policy matters has come from the Socialist Left. The political background for this situation should probably be sought in the long-standing pacifist tradition that prevails in the Socialist parties and in the general Socialist scepticism against the capitalist system of the Western countries.

Regarding people's attitudes toward the superpowers and their international positions, there is a pronounced difference between Socialist Left (SV) voters on the one hand, and all other voters on the other. This is reflected in a number of ways: SV voters are the only respondents who believe that the United States constitutes a more serious threat to Europe, when it comes to the risk of a nuclear attack, than the Soviet Union. The SV voters also perceive the United States and the Soviet Union as being about equal in military strength, while a majority of respondents supporting other parties consider the Soviet Union to be stronger. Whereas a very large majority of the respondents loyal to other parties state that they believe the American security guarantee to be indispensable for Western Europe, only 33 percent of the SV voters subscribe to this opinion. The differences between the other political parties are minor on this issue, but as a rule, Conservative (H) and Center party (SP) voters tend to be somewhat more pro-American than Labor (DNA) and Liberal (V) voters.

The support for NATO within the different political camps is shown in Table 7.13. This support has always been strongest among Conservative voters (a consistent score of nearly 90 percent since 1969), while voters of the Socialist Left have represented the other extreme. Among the latter, however, the actual strength of support has fluctuated considerably, and the surprisingly high number of NATO supporters among them in 1973 reflects that, in this election, which was held in the wake of the EC debate in Norway, the party received a considerable influx of Labor voters who for the most had returned to their old party by 1977. The increase in NATO support among the Socialist Left in 1981 is not as easily explained, and in relation to the other results it seems rather odd. The actual number of SV voters in these surveys is rather small, however, and random statistical variations may be partly responsible for the results.

The differences between the other political parties are not as dramatic, and it is especially worth noting the pronounced increase in support for NATO among Labor voters. The increased support for NATO in the population as a whole is due to a considerable degree to the shift in opinion among Labor voters, and the difference in scores between Labor and Conservative voters on this issue is much smaller now than it used to be. Among Liberal voters, however, support for NATO has diminished during the last decade. Despite the fact that their number in the samples is also small, there is reason to believe that the scores reflect an actual trend. A number of results that will be presented later in this section seem to corroborate this interpretation.

There is little dissension between the different political camps with regard to the importance of having military defense. Voters of the Socialist Left (SV) do diverge slightly from the others in this respect, but today even the SV can muster a clear majority in favor of a military defense. However, on the issue of the size of defense expenditures, opinions differ much more, and the proportion of respondents who believe that expenditures ought to be reduced, varies from about 80 percent among SV voters to some 15 to 20 percent among the supporters of the Conservatives, the

Christian People's party, and the Center party. In between these extremes, the Labor and Liberal voters are almost evenly distributed between support for and opposition against a reduction of the defense expenditures.

Among the SV, DNA, SP, and H voters, there were almost no differences between their respective attitudes in 1977 and 1981 on this issue, but we can observe an interesting development among voters for the Liberal and Christian People's parties. First of all we find that in the 1977 survey there was a high proportion of respondents from these parties who said they were not particularly interested in this issue. At a time when defense issues were not yet really on the political agenda, those voters who belong "somewhere in the middle" along the right-left axis thus tended to be less interested in these issues than the voters toward the two poles. This, of course, is a tendency that can be observed in most public opinion surveys. However, when the proportion of "not particularly interested" responses drops among supporters of both parties in 1981, the changes go in different directions. Among the Liberal voters, the result is an increase in the proportion of respondents who favor a reduction in defense expenditures, while among those voting for the Christian People's party there is a corresponding increase in the proportion of respondents who think this would be a bad proposal. What this seems to indicate is that the previously uncommitted respondents tend to take that attitude that most clearly reflects the official party line. This again corroborates well-documented processes and trends in the forming of political opinions and shows that the electorate, especially where less salient issues—and also new issues—are concerned, often will adopt the attitudes expressed by political parties and leaders whom they already trust and identify with.

The three defense policy issues that have dominated the Norwegian debate during the last three to four years (pre-positioning of allied military equipment, nuclear free zones, and the NATO double-track decision) also offer a consistent pattern of alignment along party cleavages that, with a few minor distinctions, can be summarized as follows. The Socialist Left party has adopted a strong and unambiguous "anti-NATO" attitude. Its supporters are almost unanimous in their rejection of pre-positioning of allied military equipment in Norway; they are equally united in their support for nuclear free zones in the Nordic area and in Europe. If such zones are to be established through negotiations, Norway should negotiate directly and not through NATO. They are also opposed to NATO's double-track decision and the deployment of new missiles in Europe.

The Liberal party is closest to the Socialist Left on issues of defense policy. A clear majority of Liberal voters are opposed to pre-positioning (about two to one). An even larger majority favors the idea of nuclear free zones, but most of them prefer the negotiations to be conducted within the NATO framework. Liberal voters' attitudes toward the double-track decision seem to vary according to which premises are specified in the question, but there is, undoubtedly, a substantial majority among the party's followers against the NATO decision.

The Labor party seems to be divided almost down the middle over the pre-positioning issue, but a majority of its supporters would like to see Norway become part of a nuclear free zone. On both these issues, Labor voters' attitudes are clearly more pro-NATO than those of the Liberal voters. The differences between the two parties are less pronounced over the double-track decision issue, but if one makes a composite analysis of all the surveys, the Liberal voters come out as being somewhat more sceptical than the Labor voters, who are divided into two almost equal factions (albeit with a slight majority against the double-track decision).

Voters for the Christian People's and Center parties both seem to share the same interests in issues of defense policy. This is especially the case for the pre-positioning issue, which is supported by the voters of both parties, and the nuclear free zones, where both groups are strongly in favor of negotiations within the NATO framework. As regards the double-track decision, however, the Center voters are more positively inclined than those of the Christian People's party, although there is undoubtedly general support for the official NATO policy among voters of both parties on this issue.

If the Socialist Left represents the one extreme where attitudes toward defense policy issues are concerned, the Conservative voters clearly represent the opposite extreme. However, it is also clear that there are more Conservative voters who are negatively inclined on the three issues that are discussed here than there are positively inclined voters in the opposite camp. And it is worth noting that when the nuclear free zones issue is presented as a simple question of for or against, the Conservative voters also come out with a majority in favor of such zones. In general terms, however, a considerable majority of the Conservative voters stand firmly behind official NATO policy on all the three issues.

In the cases of Socialist Left, the Christian People's party, the Center party, and the Conservatives, there is a clear correlation between their voters' attitudes toward NATO in general and their attitudes toward the three issues that recently have been dominating the Norwegian relationship with NATO. In the case of Labor voters and Liberal voters, the correlation is less clear, and these voters are undoubtedly expressing a higher degree of scepticism than might have been expected, considering their general support for Norway's NATO membership. Among Liberal voters, this discrepancy has already resulted in an increasing opposition against Norway's membership in NATO. Only the future will show whether this trend will continue, and whether it will also spread to Labor voters. Judging from the debate about NATO's double-track decision and the considerable opposition against nuclear weapons, such a development would not come as a surprise.

The purpose of the discussion in this section has been to demonstrate the strong linkages between the prevailing attitudes toward defense and foreign policy in Norwegian public opinion and the dominant left-right dimension in Norwegian politics in general. In fact, there is complete correlation between the variables. For those who have previous knowledge of Norwegian politics, this may seem to be an incorrect observation, insofar as the Liberal voters undoubtedly display the strongest opposition to official Norwegian defense policies, with the exception of the voters of the Socialist Left. Traditionally, one finds the Liberal voters to the right of Labor voters, not to their left, as is the case here. However, unpublished data from the 1981 election survey shows that between 1977 and 1981 Liberal voters have moved clearly toward the left, with the result that in 1981, for the first time, the self-evaluation index mentioned earlier places Liberal voters to the left of Labor voters, and next to those of the Socialist Left. The main reason for this realignment along the left-right dimension would seem to be a substantial influx of young and radical voters into the Liberal ranks. But clearly specific defense and foreign policy issues have also played an important part in this development.

Conclusion: The Dilemma of Norwegian Defense Policy

Most of the themes that are discussed in this chapter are very complex, touching on issue areas that most people are not normally exposed to to any great extent and that traditionally have been regarded as the domain of political leaders. One must not overrate people's knowledge of and information about these issues. Only very few opinion surveys have attempted to make objective measurements of people's levels of information, but the studies that do exist (for example, one concerning the double-track decision) have in some cases revealed very low levels of factual information in substantial segments of the population. Such low levels of information, combined with generally low proportions of "don't know" answers, must necessarily mean that many of the responses given are of an ad hoc nature: responses that do not reflect firmly held or deliberated opinions.

This fact has a number of implications. First of all, the responses probably include a relatively high proportion of what is often known as "non-attitudes" or "pseudo-opinions" (Converse 1968; Robertson and Meadow 1982). Second, in this particular context, people's feelings will play a greater part than actual knowledge, than is usually the case. The importance of the emotional aspect would increase with increasing complexity in the issues concerned. In such issues, therefore, it is important to know which linkages exist between the concrete issue and other issues and issue areas that may have a great emotional significance for large segments of the population.

Third, it means that political leadership is important, and it gives the established political leaders a central role in the opinion-making processes. The above has demonstrated how people's attitudes are influenced by the official standpoints of their respective political parties. The fact that public opinion is in need of political guides on these issues does not mean, however, that the political leaders have a completely free hand. It is, in fact, just in questions which appeal strongly to central sentiments in the population that other elite groups also have considerable opportunities to meet with the public's approval, if they can play their cards right. The EC debate in Norway is a typical example of the formation of nonestablishment leadership groups, which in turn came to represent a serious challenge to the established political parties in their endeavors to influence public opinion. In such cases, it becomes important to take an "aggressive" approach in the political debate, and the political parties must make sure that their respective standpoints gain a foothold in public opinion, if they want to succeed. Public opinion will undoubtedly be strongly influenced by political leaders; the question is just who the leaders will be.

It is, of course, impossible to state exactly the interplay and relative importance of these different factors in relation to the foreign and defense policy debate in Norway in recent years. However, it is important to remember that, where these issues are concerned, public opinion is, at least partially, impressionable (especially in questions of some detail and complexity), and it can be led by whoever is capable of marketing his views in such a way that they are linked up with issue areas that are familiar and salient to the individual. Both the detailed review of Norwegian foreign and defense policy, which I have presented in the earlier parts of this chapter, and the concluding analysis that follows must be considered against this background.

Norwegian public opinion on defense and foreign policy issues in 1983 is characterized by two main traits: first, a strong will to defend the nation and a substantial support for NATO membership; second, a strong fear of and opposition to nuclear weapons. Both these attitudes have long traditions in Norwegian politics, and up to the late 1970s they did not present serious problems to most people. In the 1980s, however, several defense policy issues that reveal the inherent conflict between these attitudes have been put onto the political agenda. Public opinion has focused increasingly on the means and methods being used to maintain our security and to preserve peace, and, at the same time, public awareness with respect to defense policy is greater than it used to be. This situation creates a dilemma for many people in the form of the conflict between, on one hand, the desire to secure Norwegian independence through links with the West and its membership of NATO, and, on the other hand, a scepticism regarding the methods that the Alliance uses in its endeavors to realize this objective.

The essential problem in all three current defense issues—pre-positioning, nuclear free zones, and the NATO double-track decision—is, in fact, a reflection of this dilemma and of the notions it evokes. Has Norway reached a point where a change of direction may be the best option? Should it still rely on the balance of power and on the arms race that seems to be its inevitable result? Or should new paths be sought, for instance, in the form of nuclear free zones or unilateral nuclear disarmament, in the hope that such an alternative may work?

Up to now, such attitudes have primarily been expressed on individual, specific issues. There is no suggestion in the survey results that these specific attitudes have affected the public's general attitudes on foreign policy in any significant way. On the contrary, we can show that, in recent years, there has been an increase in the general will to defend the nation, as well as in support for Norwegian membership of NATO. Yet, public opinion on matters of foreign and defense policy is less perspicuous today than it was only a few years ago, and the most important question today concerns the actual significance of the perception of a poor relationship between ends and means.

On the one hand, it is difficult to imagine that there would not be a spill-over from specific attitudes to general attitudes in the longer run—at least to a certain extent. A continuous focus on such aspects of Norwegian defense policy where, as in the case of the double-track decision, there is considerable opposition in the population against official Norwegian policy, cannot but lead to major effects in the long run, unless other domestic or international factors were to counteract this influence.

On the other hand, Norway's links to the Western world, to the United States, and to NATO have long traditions in Norwegian politics. They are regarded favorably by most political parties, and they are reflected in a set of firmly established attitudes in large sections of public opinion. Such attitudes are not easily influenced by singular, specific events that may be topical for just a short period of time. It would take a lot to bring about a major shift in public opinion.

One must not overrate the importance of this contradiction. It is not yet known what impact the concrete issues that have dominated Norwegian defense policy debate in recent years will have over time. For the moment they appear to be very important, but how relevant will they be in the long run? First of all, it is a well-known fact that inconsistencies in attitude patterns create relatively few problems if parts of the patterns are of little direct importance to the people concerned. Second, there have also been other substantial controversies over important international issues (e.g., the Vietnam War) without their having had any longterm effects on Norwegian public attitudes toward foreign policy. Third, the great number of opinion surveys concerned with defense policy issues is a relatively recent phenomenon. This could possibly be significant in itself. Could it be that the inconsistencies that have been demonstrated in this field are not new, but simply that they have not been visible before, because of the lack of attitude surveys and measurements in this field? This doubt notwithstanding, the central question in the study of Norwegian public opinion on defense and foreign policy issues in the years to come will be to try to disclose the interplay between attitudes toward the specific defense issues of the day and more fundamental attitude patterns pertaining to defense policy in general.

References

Aardal, *Bernt Olav, Meningsmalinger om forsvars-og sikkerhetspolitikk med hovedvekt pa* NATO's *dobbelvedtak. En oversikt og evaluering* (Oslo: Institutt for samfunnsforskning, 1983).

Converse, Philip, "Attitudes and Non-Attitudes: Continuation of a Dialogue," in E. Tufte, ed., *The Quantitative Analysis of Social Problems* (Reading, Mass.: Addison-Wesley Publishing Company, 1970).

Robinson, John and Robert Meadow, *Polls Apart* (Cabin John, Md.: Seven Locks Press, 1982).

Ringdal, Kristin and Trude Nergaard, *Opinionen om forsvarssporsmal i perioden 1945–81* (Trondheim, Norway: Institutt for sosiologi og samfunnsfag, Universitetet i Trondheim, 1983).

Rokkan, Stein, *Citizen, Elections, Parties* (Oslo: Universitetsforlaget, 1970).

Rokkan, Stein and Henry Valen, "Regional Contrasts in Norwegian Politics," in Allandt and Littuen, eds., *Cleavages, Indologies and Party System* (Helsinki: Westermarch Society, 1964).

Valen, Henry, "No to EEC," *Scandinavian Political Studies*, vol. 8 (1973).

Valen, Henry, "Internal Conflicts and Reactions Toward Foreign Politics: A Case Study of the Norwegian Electorate," in Otto Buesch, ed., *Waehlerbewegungen in der Europaeischen Geschichte* (Berlin: Colloquium Verlag, 1980).

Valen, Henry, *Valg og politikk* (Oslo: NKS-forlaget, 1981).

Valen, Henry and Stein Rokkan, "Norwegian Conflict Structure and Mass Politics in a European Periphery," in R. Rose, ed., *Comparative Electoral Behaviour* (New York: Free Press, 1974).

Valen, Henry and Bernt Olav Aardal, *Et valg i perspektiv: En studie av stortingsvalget i 1981* (Oslo: Statistisk Sentralbyra, in press).

Werner, Anita, *holdninger til andre land og fjermsynsseing blant barn i Finnmark* (Oslo: Institut for Mass Communication Research, 1980).

Appendix F Sources

NERP: The Norwegian Research Program
NMD: Norges Markedsdata
NOI: Norsk Opinionsinstitutt
MMI: Markeds-og Mediainstituttet

8 Peace and Strength: American Public Opinion on National Security

WILLIAM SCHNEIDER

Introduction

The United States is both a democracy and a military superpower. This means that the American public's attitudes on foreign policy and national security have significance far beyond the arena of American national politics. The American public has undergone substantial, and sometimes quite rapid, shifts of foreign policy temperament over the past twenty-five years, and these shifting moods have reshaped the agenda of international politics.

It has often been argued that the period between, roughly, 1948 and 1968 was one of bipartisan consensus in U.S. foreign policy. Following World War II, despite the temptation to reject an activist role in world affairs and "return to normalcy" as the United States did after World War I, American leaders from both political parties drew together around a new internationalist consensus. "The dominant view from the late 1940s through the early 1960s," one historian of American public opinion writes (Levering 1978,104), "had such powerful influence even on its critics that it may be called the cold war consensus." The foreign policy values that prevailed during this period were those that will be described below as conservative internationalism: a continuity of goals—essentially containment of Soviet power accompanied by a two-track foreign policy strategy, confrontation, and cooperation.

The argument of this chapter is that this foreign policy consensus broke down after 1968. The principal reason was ideological polarization over foreign policy within the activist segment of American political life. Counterelites emerged on both the right and the left to challenge the supremacy of the old foreign policy establishment, which included the traditionally moderate leaders of both political parties who supported the foreign policy consensus of the cold war years. The result, it will be shown, has been a split at the elite level between conservative and liberal internationalists. Both groups have acquired substantial influence within the two major political parties.

The mass public in the United States continues to support a two-track policy, which it sees as meaning peace and strength. However, ordinary Americans have become increasingly impatient with and distrustful of foreign policy leadership. The dominant trend in mass public opinion has not been ideological but antiestablishment, a growing hostility toward political parties and leaders as corrupt, incompetent, and ineffective. A public that was once passive about foreign policy and generally willing to grant political leaders a great deal of leeway in managing foreign affairs has become suspicious and distrustful. Instead of elite consensus and mass followership, the United States now has an unstable system of competing coalitions in which the mass public swings left or right unpredictably in response to its current fears and concerns. A stable, two-track foreign policy has given way to a system of erratic alternation from one track to the other.

That is why the Reagan administration has so often been surprised by the failure of the American public to support a tougher and more aggressive foreign policy. A sense of military weakness and insecurity was the prevailing public mood during the 1980 presidential campaign. Both major parties proposed some version of a return to the cold war doctrine of containment in response to a decade of perceived U.S. defeat and decline in world affairs. The "tougher" candidate, Ronald Reagan, won the election with surprising ease, carrying a Republican majority with him into the Senate for the first time in 28 years. It appeared that the American public was giving its enthusiastic endorsement to a new foreign policy of self-assertion.

That is how the Reagan administration chose to read the foreign policy mandate of 1980. In fact, however, the data reveal considerable ambiguity in the public's foreign policy mood. A Gallup poll taken in September 1980 showed Jimmy Carter ahead of Ronald Reagan by no fewer than 25 points as the best candidate for keeping the United States out of war. Reagan had an equally strong lead, however, as the best candidate for strengthening the national defense. Reagan was also felt to be the more capable of increasing respect for the United States overseas. But Carter was preferred for dealing with the Arab-Israeli conflict. Generally, peace issues worked to Carter's advantage, and Reagan held a clear lead on defense issues.

In an ABC News/Harris survey, Reagan led Carter by 35 points as the candidate who would "keep U.S. military strength at least as strong as or stronger than the Russians." Americans also felt, by a margin of 23 points, that Reagan would "stand up most firmly if the United States were threatened by the Soviet Union." By a margin of 28 points, however, the public felt that Reagan "might be most likely to get the United States into another war." The result was that Carter led Reagan as the candidate who "would best handle foreign policy"—but by only two points. Thus, the evidence suggests that Ronald Reagan won the 1980 presidential election despite widespread public reservations about his foreign policy.

This ambiguity showed up at the end of Reagan's first year in office, when the public's foreign policy mood appeared to shift abruptly. At the end of 1981, a sequence of foreign policy crises, beginning with the declaration of martial law in Poland, brought foreign policy to the center of public attention. The American public became deeply concerned about the dangerous situations in Poland, Central America, the Falkland Islands, and Lebanon. In every case, polls revealed a strong public preference for keeping the United States out of these conflicts and a persistent fearfulness about President Reagan's desire to get the United States involved.

The most striking evidence of the rapid shift in the American public's foreign policy mood was the sudden emergence, at the end of 1981, of a mass popular movement in support of a bilateral U.S.-Soviet nuclear freeze. The nuclear freeze campaign, which began at New England town meetings and spread quickly throughout the country, gained impetus with the proposal of Congressional resolutions calling for a freeze. Congressman Timothy Wirth of Colorado called the nuclear freeze movement "the most powerful, spontaneous grass-roots movement I have ever seen since I was elected to Congress" in 1974. An aide to Senator Edward M. Kennedy, who co-sponsored the nuclear freeze resolution in the Senate, observed that the Senator was engaged, not in leading public opinion on the issue, but in "catching up with the country."

Poll after poll taken during 1982 and 1983, as will be seen below, showed enormous majorities in favor of a joint U.S.-Soviet agreement to ban the testing, production, and deployment of all nuclear weapons. Nuclear freeze resolutions appeared on one-fourth of the state and local ballots cast by American voters in the 1982 midterm elections. These resolutions were passed by voters in eight out of nine states and 28 out of 30 localities. The popularity of the nuclear freeze, along with the public resistance to President Reagan's interventionist tendencies in Central America and other parts of the world, seem to indicate a rapid shift in the public's foreign policy mood. Are we, therefore, observing a cyclical phenomenon whereby American public opinion swings back and forth between hawkish and dovish extremes?

The next sections of this chapter offer an interpretation of American public opinion and foreign policy that attempts to explain this vacillation. It will be argued that there is a continuity of basic values—peace and strength—on the part of the public, but a polarization of elite attitudes between liberal and conservative world views. Subsequent sections describe the "rightward" shift in American foreign policy attitudes from 1974 to 1980, which culminated in Reagan's election. It is shown that this shift was in a conservative but not an internationalist direction; Americans were concerned about their own national defense and military security but did not endorse a more interventionist stance in world affairs (except, very briefly, in early 1980). According to the general outline of this book, this chapter will examine American public opinion in more detail on four specific image clusters: of the Soviet Union, of national security, of nuclear deterrence, and of the Western Alliance. Particular attention will be paid to the development of public attitudes since 1980. A modest effort will also be made to explain the many ambiguities and inconsistencies of public opinion that inevitably emerge.

Images of the Soviet Union

A major component of the increasing conservatism of American public opinion has been growing antipathy toward the Soviet Union since the early 1970s. This trend can be seen in Table 8.1. Feelings about the Soviet Union were almost unanimously unfavorable during the cold war period of the 1950s. About 90 percent of the public regularly reported strongly negative attitudes, while fewer than two percent were favorable. Attitudes began to improve in the period between the nuclear test ban treaty of 1963 and the full flowering of détente in the early and mid-1970s. Even at the height of détente, however, public attitudes toward Russia were never very positive. Between 1972 and 1975, about 19 percent of Americans said they felt favorable toward the Soviet Union, while about 36 percent were unfavorable. A plurality of about 45 to 50 percent reported "mixed" feelings.

The late 1970s, however, saw a rapid decline of favorability. The majority position once again became unfavorable. Negative feelings reached a peak of 73 percent in January 1980, just after the Soviet invasion of Afghanistan; they then diminished gradually to 61 percent in 1982 and 53 percent in 1983 (before the shooting down of the Korean Airlines passenger plane in September). Thus, by the early 1980s, the preponderance of sentiment was once again negative, but not quite as negative as had been the case in the 1950s. About a third of the American public in 1980–1983 reported "mixed" feelings toward the Russians, compared to only about ten percent in 1953–1956.

One question in the 1978 and 1982 Chicago Council on Foreign Relations surveys asked respondents to rate various countries on a "feeling thermometer" running from zero degrees (very cold or unfavorable) to 100 degrees (very warm or favorable). The average rating for the Soviet Union dropped from 34 degrees in 1978 to 25 degrees in 1982. The public's favorability toward Cuba, a close Soviet ally, also declined, from 32 to 25 degrees. However, the public's feelings toward Poland became more positive (from 50 to 53 degrees). The trend seems to have been specifically anti-Soviet rather than generally anti-Communist. This is confirmed by the shift in attitudes toward the People's Republic of China; China's image improved between 1978 and 1982, from 44 to 48 degrees.

Moreover, the 1982 Chicago Council results revealed an eight point increase since 1978 in the percentage of Americans willing to use U.S. troops "if Japan were invaded by the Soviet Union" and a ten point increase in willingness to use U.S. forces "if Soviet troops invaded Western Europe." As will be noted below, public support for restricting

Table 8.1 Attitudes toward Russia, 1953–1983 [a]

	GAL 10/53	GAL 8/54	GAL 9/54	GAL 12/56	GAL 12/66	GAL 5/72	GAL 4/73	GAL 7/73	NORC 3/74	NORC 3/75	GAL 6/76	NORC 3/77	GAL 2/79	GAL 1/80	NORC 3/82	NORC 3/83
Favorable	1	2	0	2	17	19	16	19	19	19	8	12	14	4	7	5
Mixed	11	11	9	12	30	38	44	51	45	45	34	40	38	23	32	39
Unfavorable	89	88	91	86	63	43	40	30	36	36	58	48	49	73	61	56

Note:

[a] People were asked to rate on a scale from –5 to +5 how strongly they disliked (liked) the Soviet Union: favorable +3 to +5, mixed +2 to –2, unfavorable –3 to –5.

U.S.-Soviet trade and for limiting the sale of advanced computers to the Soviet Union also rose significantly between 1978 and 1982.

The public's ability to differentiate among communist countries can also be seen in polls taken by the Roper Organization in which people were asked to classify various countries as either "a close ally of the United States," "a friend but not a close ally," "more or less neutral," "mainly unfriendly toward the United States but not an enemy," or "an enemy of the U.S." Here is how Americans saw the Soviet Union in June 1983: close ally one percent, friendly two percent, neutral seven, unfriendly 43, and enemy 42 percent. Clearly the division of public sentiment was between those who saw the Soviets as unfriendly, but not an enemy, and those who saw them as an enemy. Both categories were slightly larger than had been the case in June of 1982, when 39 percent called the Soviets unfriendly and 40 percent called them an enemy.

Cuba was seen in almost exactly the same way. In the 1983 Roper poll, 39 percent called Cuba unfriendly and 47 percent called it an enemy of the United States. On the other hand, only 22 percent called mainland China unfriendly to the United States, while seven percent said China was an enemy, 21 percent described China as friendly, and 37 percent shared the prevailing sentiment that China is more or less neutral. Similarly, in the 1982 poll, 33 percent described Poland as friendly to the United States, 34 percent as neutral, and only 18 percent as either unfriendly or an enemy (two percent). In other words, there are communists and there are communists. It is the Soviets, along with the Cubans, who are seen in the most negative terms.

Negative attitudes toward "communism" in general, as distinct from the Soviet Union, did grow during the 1970s but at a relatively gradual pace. Between 1973 and 1982, the almost-annual General Social Surveys taken by the National Opinion Research Center of the University of Chicago asked people how they felt about "communism as a form of government": "it's the worst kind of all," "it's bad, but no worse than some others," "it's all right for some countries," or "it's a good form of government." The dominant view has always been that it is the worse kind of all. That view increased steadily from 44 percent in 1973 to 51 percent in 1974, 54 percent in 1977, and 61 percent in 1982. The attitude that tended to lose support was that it is all right for some countries. Twenty-five percent of Americans felt that way about communism in 1973, only 12 percent felt that way in 1982.

Nevertheless, it is clear that anti-Soviet feeling was setting the pace. In 1972, 1974, and 1976, Gallup polls (commissioned by Potomac Associates) asked people how they would characterize two problems facing the United States: "the problem of the Soviet Union" and "the threat of communism." Over these four years, the percentage of people who said they felt a great deal of concern about communism increased from 41 to 50 percent, while concern about the Soviet Union more than doubled, from 24 to 50 percent. In 1972, Americans were far more worried about communism in general than about the Soviet Union in particular. In 1976, they were equally concerned with both.

Most Americans feel that Russia is seeking global domination, but there are doubts about whether Russia is willing to risk a major war for that objective. Six times between 1978 and 1983 the Roper poll asked the respondents to choose among four descriptions of Russian objectives in the world. These attitudes have been fairly stable over the past five years, except for February 1980, when anti-Soviet feeling temporarily intensified. On the average, about seven percent of Americans felt that Russia seeks only to protect itself against the possibility of attack by other countries. Twenty-three percent held the view that Russia seeks to compete with the United States for more influence in different parts of the world. Over 60 percent were of the opinion that Russia seeks global domination, but they were split over how far the Soviets will go: An average of 35 percent said "Russia seeks global domination, but not at the expense of starting a major war," while an average of 28 percent felt that "Russia seeks global domination and will risk a major war to achieve that domination if it can't be achieved by other means."

As noted earlier, one source of increasing anti-Soviet sentiment in the United States was the perception of a massive Soviet military buildup. Table 8.2 traces the public's perceptions of the relative military strength of the United States and the Soviet Union from 1976 to 1983. Of course, the mass public has very little factual knowledge by which to judge the two superpowers' actual military capabilities. Indeed, military experts cannot agree on this issue, which has stimulated a good deal of political controversy. What the data in Table 8.2 measure is not factual understanding but public impressions: basically whether Americans feel secure with respect to Soviet military power.

Since the end of 1976, when polls began asking this question, Americans have never felt stronger than the Soviet Union. After 1976, belief in United States military superiority diminished even further, from over 20 percent of the public to about ten percent. The prevailing sentiment has shifted back and forth between the feeling that the United States is weaker than the Russians and the feeling that the two superpowers are about equal in military strength. The view that the United States is weaker—that is, the feeling of military inferiority and insecurity—rose from 30 percent in 1976 to over 40 percent in 1978–1983. The Reagan military buildup, however, appears to have had an effect on public attitudes. In late 1982 and early 1983, the data show an increase in the perception that the United States and the Soviets are about equal. The most recent polls, both dated April 1983, do not settle this issue, however. The CBS News/*New York Times* poll taken that month shows a plurality once again holding the view that the United States is weaker, while the Harris survey indicates an increase in perceived American military strength.

The instability of these assessments reflects the fact that they are not based on factual information. A news story, a major foreign policy event,

Table 8.2   US-Soviet military strength compared

		United States stronger	About equal	United States weaker
LH	12/76	23	47	30
LH	7/78	20	47	34
LH	11/78	15	42	43
CBS/NYT	6/79	11	30	43
CBS/NYT	1/80	14	34	42
LH	1/80	16	37	41
CBS/NYT	6/81	11	39	42
CBS/NYT	1/82	9	37	44
LH	10/82	17	40	35
CBS/NYT	1/83	11	47	32
LH	3/83	13	47	33
CBS/NYT	4/83	12	36	42
LH	4/83	20	40	29

or a speech by the president can shift opinion one way or the other. President Reagan himself generates mixed signals on this issue. His increases in defense spending tend to make Americans feel that the United States is catching up with the Russians. At the same time, the president calls for still higher defense budgets by arguing that the United States remains in a position of military inferiority. What the polls over the past seven years consistently demonstrate is that the feeling that the United States is weaker than the Russians always outweighed the feeling that the United States is stronger. However, the share of those who felt that the United States is equal or stronger was always greater than the proportion who said the United States is weaker. It seems clear to the public that the United States has lost military superiority over the Russians; it is not clear, however, that the United States is in a position of military inferiority.

These same generalizations hold for the public's characterization of U.S. *nuclear* strength vis-à-vis the Soviet Union (Table 8.3): although more people felt that the United States is weaker than that it is stronger, the overall majority did not feel the United States to be weaker. The trends also show a basic similarity. Between 1977 and 1982, the sentiment that the United States was weaker than the Soviet Union in nuclear strength tended to increase. In late 1982 and 1983, there was a shift back toward the view that the two superpowers are about equal. If we average the responses in Tables 8.2 and 8.3, the basic comparability of these estimates is obvious. On the whole, 15 percent regarded the United States as stronger on both counts, 40 percent perceived both sides as equal; 38 percent judged the United States inferior in general military capability, 34 percent in nuclear capability.

Table 8.3   US-Soviet nuclear strength compared

		United States stronger	About equal	United States weaker
ROP	11/77	18	38	28
ROP	6/78	17	36	31
ROP	1/79	18	38	31
LH	3/80	12	47	34
ROP	10/80	15	29	43
ROP	10/81	16	35	41
ROP	4/82	12	32	41
LH	10/82	17	47	27
ROP	12/82	14	39	39
LH	3/83	12	52	29
LH	5/83	19	43	27

Do Americans think it is necessary for the United States to be stronger than the Soviet Union, or would they be satisfied with rough military parity? It turns out that a substantial number of Americans do not think the United States has to be stronger. Between 1978 and 1981, the CBS News/*New York Times* poll asked whether the military strength of the United States should be superior to that of the Soviet Union, about equal, or whether the United States does not need to be exactly as strong as the Soviet Union. In 1978 and 1979, about 50 percent of the public said that the United States does not have to be stronger than the Russians, 46 percent said they should be about equal, and four percent said that the United States need not be as strong as the Russians. This attitude outweighed the opinion that the United States should be stronger than the Russians, which was held by about 44 percent. The 1979–1980 "shocks," however, shifted the balance in the other direction. In the polls taken in 1980 and 1981, a majority (slightly above 50 percent) said the United States should be stronger. However, the proportion who felt that military superiority was not necessary still remained high, at about 44 percent.

The same has been true in Roper polls, which asked whether the United States should be stronger than the Russians in nuclear arms capability. Between 1979 and 1981, a majority (averaging 53 percent) said that the United States should be superior, but a substantial minority (averaging 43 percent) said that nuclear parity was adequate. The latest poll on this issue, taken at the end of 1982, shows a significant shift, possibly reflecting the impact of the nuclear freeze movement: Only 41 percent said that the United States has to be stronger than the Russians in nuclear arms capability, and 56 percent felt that superiority was not necessary. Indeed, 15 percent of the latter group took the most extreme position, that the United States does not need to be as strong as Russia as long as it has enough nuclear arms to knock Russia out. This sentiment was also reflected in a CBS News/*New York Times* poll from May 1982, in which Americans felt, by 67 to 24 percent, that the United States and the Soviet Union both have so much nuclear strength it does not matter which one has more.

Does the American public still support détente? The answer, perhaps surprisingly in light of the trends noted above, is that they do. The most recent evidence comes from the November 1982 Chicago Council survey: In the area of cultural and scientific cooperation, the American public favored a resumption of cultural and educational exchanges with the Soviets (70 to 19 percent) and joint efforts to solve energy problems (64 to 23 percent). The public opposed prohibiting the exchange of scientists between the United States and the Soviet Union (52 to 35 percent). In the area of trade, the public opposed a ban on grain sales to the Soviets (57 to 28 percent). However, limiting the sale of advanced U.S. computers to the Soviet Union, which has obvious security implications, was supported 59 to 28 percent. The position to restrict U.S.-Soviet trade produced a divided public response: 47 percent in favor, 40 percent opposed. In the area of security, finally, the American public strongly favored the negotiation of arms control agreements between the United States and the Soviet Union (77 to 13 percent). If détente is understood to mean measures that would reduce tensions between the two superpowers, then the American public remains basically favorable.

On the other hand, it has definitely become more wary of détente in recent years. Exchange of scholars and cultural groups, which was favored by about 80 percent of the public in 1970–1972, in 1982 was supported only by 70 percent. Support for exchanging scientists fell from 73 percent in 1973 to 65 percent in 1974 and 51 percent in 1975. Between 1974 and 1975, support for joint U.S.-Soviet space missions dropped from 82 to 46 percent. Joint efforts to solve the world energy crisis were favored by 90 percent in 1973, 82 percent in 1974, 68 percent in 1978, and 64 percent in 1982.

Support for expanding trade between the two countries dropped from 75 percent in 1970–1972 to 72 percent in 1973 and 68 percent in 1974 (Harris). Between 1974 and 1975, the idea of giving the Soviet Union the same trade treatment we give other countries declined in popularity from 63 to 56 percent. Public support for two restrictive trade measures tested in the Chicago Council surveys (limiting the sale of advanced computers and restricting U.S.-Soviet trade) in both cases increased by eight percent between 1978 and 1982.

The deterioration of détente can be seen in a Harris question asked between 1970 and 1975: "Do you think it is possible for the United States and Russia to reach long-term agreements to help keep the peace, or do you think this is not possible?" Optimism reached a peak at the end of 1973, when a 69 to 20 percent majority said that such agreements were possible. By the end of 1974, that margin was 59 to 26 percent. By the end of 1975, it had narrowed considerably: 45 percent now felt it was possible to reach such agreements, while 39 percent said it was not possible.

As will be shown in the following section, public support for the SALT II treaty also diminished at the end of the 1970s. The message seems to be that, while Americans are ever hopeful about détente and prefer to relax tensions whenever and wherever possible, the growth of anti-Soviet feeling during the late 1970s has made the American public notably more cautious about U.S. dealings with the Soviets.

Table 8.4, based on data from the 1982 Chicago Council survey, breaks down attitudes toward the Soviet Union by two types of factors: first, mass-elite differences, as indicated by differences between the mass public and opinion leaders[1], by education, by attentiveness to news about foreign affairs, and second, political differences, as indicated by partisanship and self-ascribed ideology.

Basic feelings about the Soviet Union show very little variation by either status or ideology. Virtually all Americans have deeply negative feelings toward Russia. However, on questions of U.S. policy toward the Soviets, there are noticeable mass-elite differences. Opinion leaders, the college-educated, and Americans who are attentive to foreign affairs tend to see the United States as stronger militarily and are less supportive of anti-détente measures (trade restrictions). There are also predictable differences by ideology, but these are relatively weak. To a considerable extent Table 8.4 indicates that the sense of military weakness and anti-Soviet feeling are shared by non-internationalists and conservatives. The better educated and those most involved with foreign policy are less doubtful about America's military strength and more supportive of détente.

The next section, which deals with security policy, introduces issues that are more ideologically controversial. Left-right differences are stronger on questions relating to defense spending and troop intervention than on questions relating to the Soviet Union. In the area of security policy, as we shall see, elite opinion in the United States is often divided and inconsistent.

Images of Security

Beginning with the Arab oil embargo at the end of 1973, the United States, along with other Western democracies, entered a ten-year economic downturn. Gallup polls taken in the United States reveal an abrupt shift in public priorities. For most of the postwar period, foreign policy issues (Korea, the cold war, nuclear arms control, Vietnam) had dominated the agenda of national concerns. After 1973, however, economic problems became paramount (inflation, the energy crisis, unemployment).

---

1. Opinion leaders comprised a sample of 341 prominent individuals from government, international business, labor, academia, the mass media, religious institutions, private foreign policy organizations, and special interest groups.

Table 8.4 Attitudes toward the Soviet Union for opinion leaders and for the public by interest, education, political orientation (CCFR 1982)

	Opinion Leaders	Public	Attentiveness to foreign news			Education			Partisanship			Ideology		
			Low	Average	High	Grade School	High School	College	Democrat	Independent	Republican	Liberal	Moderate	Conservative
Very negative feelings toward the Soviet Union	a	64	62	65	65	62	67	55	65	60	67	61	64	67
US-Soviet military strength														
—United States equal/stronger	82	63	59	62	69	62	61	70	70	58	60	66	64	62
—United States weaker	15	29	27	32	26	26	31	26	23	34	33	30	28	33
Favor restricting US/Soviet trade	28	47	47	48	45	44	50	41	48	46	48	46	45	54
Favor ban on US grain sales to Soviet Union	16	28	28	28	27	32	28	22	29	25	29	26	27	33

Note:
aNot surveyed

Table 8.5 Goals of US foreign policy (CCFR)

	1974	1978	1982
Protecting the jobs of American workers	74	78	77
Keeping up the value of the dollar	a	86	71
Securing adequate supplies of energy	75	78	70
Worldwide arms control	64	64	64
Containing communism	54	60	59
Combatting world hunger	61	59	58
Defending our allies' security	33	50	50
Matching Soviet military power	a	a	49
Strengthening the United Nations	46	47	48
Protecting the interests of American business abroad	39	45	44
Promoting and defending human rights in other countries	a	39	43
Helping to improve the standard of living of less developed countries	39	35	35
Protecting weaker nations against foreign aggression	28	34	34
Helping to bring a democratic form of government to other nations	28	26	29

Note:

a Not surveyed

The 1970s represent the longest sustained period of economic stagnation in the United States since the 1930s. The American public's obsession with the economy did affect foreign policy attitudes; Americans became more self-absorbed, more security-conscious, and less internationalist-minded.

In its 1974, 1978, and 1982 surveys, the Chicago Council on Foreign Relations asked respondents to rate the importance of various foreign policy goals for the United States. The results, displayed in Table 8.5, provide a picture of the foreign policy priorities of the American public.

Self-interest is the factor that most clearly separates the top-ranked from the bottom-ranked goals. The three objectives at the top of the list, those considered very important by 70 percent or more of the American public, are all self-regarding: protecting American jobs, keeping up the value of the dollar, and securing adequate energy supplies. The goals considered least important all relate to "other countries": promoting human rights in other countries, improving the standard of living in less developed countries, protecting weaker nations against aggression, and bringing democracy to other nations.

Two security objectives, worldwide arms control and containing communism, are rated fairly high in importance despite their apparent ideological inconsistency. Americans value peace (arms control) and strength (to contain communism) in about equal measure. Two other security-related goals, defending the security of America's allies and matching Soviet military power, are not quite as highly valued; about half of the public rates the latter objectives as "very important." Americans appear to support defending their allies' security and matching Soviet military power to the extent that they contribute directly to the security of the United States.

Security consciousness rose noticeably between 1974 and 1978. As noted earlier, this period saw an increase in public support for containing communism and protecting weaker nations against foreign aggression, as well as a marked increase in support for defending the security of U.S. allies. During the same period, non-security-related goals such as combatting world hunger, improving the living standard of less developed countries, and bringing democracy to other countries did not increase in importance. The 1982 data show little change from the 1978 figures (except for a decline in public concern over energy supplies and the value of the dollar). The mood of security consciousness that emerged in the mid-1970s appears to have been sustained through the early 1980s.

One convenient index of the American public's security consciousness is its attitudes toward defense spending. As was the case with estimates of U.S.-Soviet military strength, attitudes toward defense spending do not reflect real information. Very few people—and not many politicians—have the knowledge on which to base an informed judgment of whether the government is spending too much, too little, or just about the right amount on national defense. What such questions measure is not knowledge but security consciousness. When the public feels uneasy about the country's military security—usually not because of news about the defense budget but because of news about Soviet adventurism or a Soviet military buildup—people demand more defense spending.

That is exactly what happened in the mid and late 1970s. Beginning in 1974, support for higher defense spending began to increase (see Table 8.6). By the spring of 1980, a majority of Americans for the first time felt that the United States should spend more money on the military, armaments, and defense. As noted earlier, the beginning of 1980, just after the seizure of American hostages in Iran and the Soviet invasion of Afghanistan, was the time when concern over military security reached near-panic proportions in the United States. By the time President Reagan took office in January 1981, the proportion of Americans favoring higher defense spending had reached an all-time high of 65 percent, according to the CBS News/*New York Times* poll. Table 8.6 shows that this trend had been building gradually for some time before it exploded in 1980. The late 1970s was also a period when support for domestic spending was declining in the United States.

That mood was sustained through President Reagan's first year in office. In May 1981, Gallup asked people whether they approved of the president's proposal for substantially increased defense spending in the 1982

Table 8.6 Support for domestic and defense spending (NORC)

	Too little	About the right amount	Too much
Domestic spending			
1973	48	29	17
1974	49	30	15
1975	48	30	16
1976	44	30	21
1977	41	31	21
1978	42	31	21
1980	42	30	21
1982	45	29	19
1983	47	31	16
Defense spending			
1973	11	45	38
1974	17	45	31
1975	17	46	31
1976	24	42	27
1977	24	45	23
1978	27	44	22
1980	56	26	11
1982	29	36	30
1983	24	38	32

Note:
Question wording:

"We are faced with many problems in this country, none of which can be solved easily or inexpensively. I'm going to name some of these problems, and for each on I'd like you to tell me whether you think we're spending too much money, too little money, or about the right amount."

The percentages for "domestic spending" are the average of the responses for five items: "improving and protecting the environment," "improving and protecting the nation's health," "solving the problems of the big cities," "improving the nation's education system," and "welfare." The defense item was "the military, armaments, and defense."

budget. They did, very strongly: 64 to 29 percent. Four times between April 1981 and January 1982, the ABC News/*Washington Post* poll asked people whether they thought Reagan's plans to increase military spending were going too far, not far enough, or were just about right. In every case, majorities of between 52 and 57 percent called the increases just about right. Minorities of below 20 percent felt they did not go far enough, and 18 to 28 percent thought they went too far. The picture one gets is of general public satisfaction with Reagan's initial increases in defense spending; he did exactly what the people elected him to do.

After the 1983 budget was announced, however, the public began to draw the line. In February 1982, the Harris survey told its respondents that "President Reagan has proposed an 18 percent increase in defense spending for 1983. This is $33 billion more than was spent for defense this year." Only 19 percent said they favored giving the president the full increase he was asking for, 20 percent felt that defense spending should be increased, but by less than the amount the president was requesting. The largest group, 36 percent, wanted to keep the 1983 defense budget at about the same level as 1982. On the other side of the issue, only 23 percent wanted to reduce defense spending below the 1982 level, that is, to undo the increase obtained during President Reagan's first year in office.

The basic picture was approval of Reagan's initial defense buildup, no desire to revert to the perceived weakness of the Carter period, but no desire to push the defense buildup any further. At the end of 1981, NBC News and the Associated Press reported that the proportion of Americans favoring an increase in defense spending had fallen by almost half, from 65 percent in January to 34 percent in November. For the first time in almost two years, a plurality of the public wanted to keep military spending at about the same level. This pattern is confirmed by the evidence in Table 8.6. In the spring 1982 NORC survey, the proportion favoring higher defense spending dropped sharply, from 56 to 29 percent. For the first time since 1976, more people said the United States was spending too much than said it was spending too little on the military, armaments, and defense, with a plurality of 36 percent expressing the opinion that military spending was just about right.

Through most of 1982, the public seemed to be basically satisfied with the level of defense spending that resulted from President Reagan's initial increases. By the end of that year, however, the view that the United States was spending too much for defense had become the prevailing one. The public's ambiguity on this issue can be seen in the discrepancy that results from two different formulations of the question. The opinion that the United States is spending *too much* on defense (45 percent in January 1983, according to Gallup) was considerably stronger than the desire to *decrease* the present defense budget (28 percent in March 1983, according to Harris).

It is not clear that the public actually wants to cut defense spending. What is clear is that few people agreed with the president that the United States should continue to spend more. Only 24 percent of the public in 1983, according to Table 8.6, felt the United States was spending too little on defense. Moreover, in three surveys taken by ABC News and the *Washington Post* during 1983, a majority (50 to 54 percent) repeatedly endorsed the view that President Reagan was going too far in his plans to increase military spending.

The data suggest, therefore, that after the first year of the Reagan administration public opinion began to shift from a paramount concern with military strength and security to increasing apprehension over peace.

It has been noted that, whereas Ronald Reagan was strongly preferred over Jimmy Carter as the candidate who would do the most to strengthen America's military security, Reagan was always vulnerable on the issue of keeping peace. That concern intensified during Reagan's presidency. In February 1981, just after Reagan took office, 32 percent of the American public said they were concerned that President Reagan might get the United States into a war (NBC News/Associated Press). One year later, in January 1982, that fear had increased to 48 percent (CBS News/*New York Times*). The beginning of 1982 was also the time when the nuclear freeze movement began to gather strength.

The most recent figures, from April and June 1983, showed 40 percent of the American public continuing to express fears about President Reagan getting the United States involved in a war. In ABC News/*Washington Post* data from August 1983, 34 percent held the opinion that the way Reagan is handling relations with the Soviet Union is increasing the chances for war, while 47 percent said his policies were decreasing the likelihood of war. Thus, a substantial minority of Americans, between one-third and two-fifths, express fearfulness about a war resulting from Reagan's policies. Of course, not all the blame for this concern lies with Reagan. In May 1983, the American public was evenly divided, 45 to 46 percent, over whether it is likely that a foreign country such as Russia will attack the United States in the next twenty years. One quarter of the American public said it was very likely that a third world war using nuclear weapons would break out in the next twenty years, an additional third said such an event was somewhat likely.

Americans have become increasingly security conscious, but that security consciousness has more of a defensive than an aggressive character. Americans show little interest in engaging in foreign policy crusades. It was noted earlier that the period 1974–1978 was one of increasing conservatism but declining internationalism in American public opinion. A poll question that has been asked regularly by Gallup, NORC, and others since 1947 is "Do you think it will be best for the future of the country if we take an active part in world affairs or if we stay out of world affairs?" The proportion who said the United States should take an active part in world affairs went from 68 percent in 1947 to a peak of 72 percent in 1955, at the height of the cold war. It then diminished to 66 percent in 1974, 59 percent in 1978, and 54 percent in 1982. In the latter year, fully 35 percent of Americans, the largest proportion since World War II, expressed the opinion that it would be best for the future of the country if the United States stayed out of world affairs.

That trend, which was certainly influenced by America's catastrophic experience in Vietnam, helps to explain why Americans are extremely reluctant to support military involvement in other countries. Approval of military aid to other nations, for example, is extremely low. In the 1982 Chicago Council survey, only 28 percent of Americans favored giving military aid, while 65 percent wanted to cut back military aid, which was the least popular of seven different government spending programs evaluated by respondents. To be sure, these figures were slightly more favorable than those obtained in 1974, when only 22 percent supported military aid and 70 percent wanted it cut back. That shift probably reflects the increase in the security consciousness of the American public, since foreign economic aid became less popular over the same period. Nevertheless, the preponderance of public sentiment on military aid remains strongly negative.

Americans also remain quite negative toward the idea of sending U.S. troops to other countries. Table 8.7 shows only two foreign crises in which most Americans are willing to countenance the use of U.S. troops: a Soviet invasion of Western Europe and a Soviet invasion of Japan. Both involve Soviet aggression against a major U.S. ally. Most Americans continue to oppose the use of U.S. troops in other situations, including an Arab invasion of Israel and an Arab oil boycott of the United States. To be sure, Table 8.7 does demonstrate an increase in interventionist sentiment between 1978 and 1982, particularly in cases involving the Soviet Union. However, the data cited earlier suggest that interventionist sentiment moved in two directions during this period.

Americans' support for interventionism crested at the time of the Iranian and Afghanistan crises in 1980 and began to subside shortly thereafter. Gallup reported a 20 percentage point decline from February 1980 to July 1981 in the public's willingness to employ American forces if Western Europe were invaded by the Soviet Union. Willingness to use American forces if our oil supply in the Middle East were disrupted fell by 15 points between October 1980 and July 1981. Support for sending American troops to help defend Israel against an Arab invasion declined seven points from February 1980 to July 1981. The Iran and Afghanistan crises appear to have occasioned only a temporary surge of interventionist sentiments. By 1982, the public had become more conscious of the risks involved—and suspicious of the administration's interventionist rhetoric.

Thus, the public's reactions to the crises in Poland, El Salvador, the Falklands, and Lebanon were decidedly noninterventionist. Survey after survey in each of these situations revealed a strong public desire to avoid direct American involvement, even though the public indicated definite favoritism for one side over the other in each case. In the Polish situation, according to Harris surveys, the public supported sanctions against the Soviet Union but not against Poland. When the *Los Angeles Times* asked a national sample what, if anything, the United States should do if Russia invaded Poland, the answer most often volunteered by respondents was "nothing" (28 percent), only five percent suggesting the dispatch of U.S. troops. In the Falklands crisis, NBC News and the Associated Press reported 53 to 35 percent approval of the United States' taking sides with Great Britain and against Argentina. But even among those who favored taking the British side, sentiment was 85 to 12 percent against sending American troops to help the British. In June 1982, CBS News asked those

Table 8.7   Support for the use of US troops (CCFR)

	1978	1982
If Soviet troops invaded Western Europe	54	64
If Japan were invaded by the Soviet Union	42	51
If the Arabs cut off all oil shipments to the United States	36	38
If Arab forces invaded Israel	22	30
If the Soviet Union invaded Poland	a	29
If Iran invaded Saudi Arabia	a	25
If North Korea invaded South Korea	21	22
If the Soviet Union invaded the People's Republic of China	a	21
If the People's Republic of China invaded Taiwan	20	19
If the government of El Salvador were about to be defeated by leftist rebels	a	19
If South Africa invaded Angola	a	8

Note:

a Not surveyed

who had heard or read about the crisis in Lebanon what the United States should do in that conflict. Thirty-two percent said "say or do nothing," while 20 percent wanted the United States to support Israel publicly seven percent wanted the United States to criticize Israel publicly, and 24 percent wanted the United States to reduce military aid to Israel.

The El Salvador issue brought these sentiments into sharpest relief. In a March 1982 ABC News/*Washington Post* survey, respondents agreed by 64 to 27 percent that a procommunist government in El Salvador would endanger the security interests of the United States. But by 79 to 18 percent, they disapproved of sending U.S. troops to fight in that country. The public disapproved of the way the administration was handling the situation in El Salvador, 45 to 40 percent. They were evenly split (42 to 42 percent) over whether the Reagan administration was in fact telling the truth when it claimed it had no intention of sending American soldiers to fight in El Salvador. And by 51 to 42 percent Americans said they would support young men who refused to go to El Salvador if the United States were drafting soldiers and sending them to fight there.

None of these attitudes had changed significantly a year later, after President Reagan delivered a nationally televised address before a joint session of Congress on the subject of Central America on 27 April 1983. The view that a procommunist government in El Salvador would endanger U.S. security went up slightly, according to a poll taken in May 1983 by ABC News and the *Washington Post* (69 percent agreed, 22 disagreed). Opposition to sending U.S. troops to fight in El Salvador remained strong, however (80 over 14 percent). The public was almost as strongly opposed to President Reagan's request for increased military aid to the government of El Salvador (70 over 19 percent). When asked which side the United States should support in El Salvador, only 15 percent said the government, three percent said the rebels, and fully 69 percent replied that the United States should stay out of the situation. The ABC News/*Washington Post* survey also asked people which they saw as the greater danger to the United States: "the spread of communism in Central America because the United States doesn't do enough to stop it" or "the United States becoming too entangled in internal Central American problems as a result of trying to stop the spread of communism." A majority, 55 percent, saw U.S. entanglement as the greater danger, compared to 34 percent who were more concerned about the spread of communism.

Thus, increased security consciousness of the American public during the 1970s and 1980s has not produced an aggressive or interventionist attitude. The American public's security concerns are clearly defensive in character. The public is highly selective about the conditions under which it is willing to endorse the use of military force. Basically, these amount to a direct military action by the Soviet Union against the United States itself or one of their principal allies. This anti-Soviet security consciousness of the 1980s is quite different in character from the anticommunist and interventionist cold war mentality of the 1950s.

How does the American public prefer to deal with the Soviet Union? The data cited earlier make it abundantly clear that Americans do not trust the Soviet Union. Also, in 1978 and 1979 the NBC News/Associated Press poll pointed out that for the past few years the United States and Russia have had a policy of trying to reach agreements that will relax tensions between them, and asked, "Do you think the Russians can be trusted to live up to such agreements or don't you think so?" The answer was definitely no, by margins of over three to one.

Even if it cannot be trusted, this does not mean that Americans oppose negotiations with the Soviet Union. In 1981 and 1983, Roper asked respondents to choose one of three ways of dealing with the Soviet Union. About one in four chose the hardest line: "It's clear that Russia can't be trusted and that we have to rely on increased military strength to counter them in the future." One in four endorsed the softest line: "We should do nothing that is likely to provoke a U.S.-Russian military conflict but instead try to negotiate and reason out our differences." About half of those interviewed in 1981, and again in 1983, took the middle position: "We should take a strong position with the Russians now so they won't go any further but at the same time we should try to re-establish good relations with them." In other words, the American public does not favor strength over peace or peace over strength. They favor a "two-track" policy that engages both values. Therefore, Americans approve of Ronald Reagan's policy of "toughness" toward the Soviet Union, but they also want the United States to negotiate with the Russians. A policy of strength is not sufficient; Americans also want to see action on the "peace" front.

By a two-thirds majority Americans told a recent CBS News/*New York Times* poll that a U.S. military buildup will have the effect of making the Soviet Union want to produce more weapons rather than of convincing them to negotiate seriously about arms control.

The SALT II treaty, signed in 1979 but never ratified by the United States Senate, is a particularly instructive case for examining American public opinion on a major issue of national security (see Robinson and Meadow 1982,42 ff.). SALT II was a highly technical treaty about which experts were in basic disagreement. Yet public opinion criticized that the treaty required a two-thirds vote of approval by the U.S. Senate in order to be ratified. How could an ordinary American citizen make a judgment about such a complex and technical issue?

Table 8.8 shows three measurements of American public opinion taken repeatedly between 1975 and 1980 by three different polling organizations. The NBC News/Associated Press question was the most general: "Do you favor or oppose a new agreement between the United States and Russia which would limit nuclear weapons?" Throughout 1978 and 1979, the American public remained strongly favorable to the idea of such an agreement. The Harris/ABC News question was a little more specific: "Would you favor or oppose the United States and Russia coming to a new SALT arms agreement?" Again, public opinion was quite positive, with about three-quarters approving such a treaty throughout 1978 and 1979. The Roper question was much more detailed and indicated that "there's a good deal of controversy about this proposed treaty." It asked specifically whether the U.S. Senate should vote for or against SALT II. In this case, public opinion was much more hesitant. No more than 42 percent ever came out directly in favor of the treaty, and a substantial proportion always said they didn't know how they felt or had mixed feelings about the issue, a voluntary response that was allowed by the polling agency.

Polls that explicitly allowed respondents to opt out of answering the question found that a substantial proportion did just that. As late as October 1979, 44 percent told the NBC News/Associated Press poll, when asked, that they had not heard or read enough about the issue to have an opinion on it, while an additional five percent were not sure how they felt. The remaining respondents were evenly split over the treaty, 25 percent for it and 26 percent against it. A September 1979 Gallup survey asked: "Have you heard or read about SALT II, the proposed nuclear arms agreement between the United States and Russia?" 39 percent of the sample said no, an additional 11 percent had heard about it but still had no opinion. Again, the result was closely divided among those respondents who had heard of SALT *and* had opinions: 24 percent were in favor of the treaty and 26 percent were against it.

What can be said about public opinion in such a case? Two important generalizations can be made. One is that the general *idea* of an arms control agreement remained very popular, while the SALT II treaty itself had much more limited public support. The more abstract the principle

Table 8.8 Support for SALT II Treaty

	1/78	6/78	8/78	10/78	11/78	1/79	3/79	4/79	7/79	9/79
Favor	74	67	71	70	75	81	71	68	65	62
Oppose	19	22	22	21	17	14	18	22	25	30
Don't know	7	11	7	9	8	5	11	10	10	8

Source: NBC/AP

Note:
Question wording:

"Do you favor or oppose a new agreement between the United States and Russia which would limit nuclear weapons?"

	12/75	3/77	5/77	5/78	6/78	1/79	4/79	5/79
Favor	59	66	77	74	72	74	75	72
Oppose	14	8	8	12	17	16	14	18
Don't know	27	26	14	13	11	10	11	10

Source: ABC/LH

Note:
Question wording:

"Would you favor or oppose the United States and Russia coming to a new SALT arms agreement?"

	10/78	1/79	4/79	7/79	9/79	10/79	1/80	11/80
For	42	40	33	31	30	30	22	26
Against	20	21	24	29	39	35	42	36
Mixed feelings	17	19	20	21	15	19	17	20
Don't know	20	20	23	19	17	17	18	19

Source: ROP

Note:
Question wording:

"In June of 1979, President Carter for the United States and President Brezhnev for Russia signed a new SALT treaty. The treaty, which would last until 1985, limits each country to a maximum of 2,250 long-range nuclear missiles and bombers. As you know, there's a good deal of controversy about this proposed treaty. Do you think the US Senate should vote for this new SALT treaty or against it?" (Question slightly different before treaty was signed.)

and the more general the question, the stronger the support. Items that called attention to the specific provisions of SALT II and questions that filtered out uninformed respondents showed a more divided public. Arms control in general is a popular concept, but as soon as the SALT II treaty had become the object of controversy among political elites doubt and scepticism also emerged at the level of mass attitudes, reflecting political strife not over the abstract goal of arms control but over its concrete implementation.

A second and related generalization can be made from Table 8.8: opposition to SALT II tended to increase over time. All three polls showed growing opposition as the political debate, and therefore public opinion, focused more and more closely on the ratification process. In the NBC News/Associated Press question, support diminished from a four to one majority at the beginning of 1978 to a two to one majority in September 1979. The Harris/ABC survey showed support going from almost ten to one in May 1977 to about six to one in May 1978 and four to one in May 1979. In the Roper poll, opinion went from two to one favorable in early 1979 to a roughly even split in mid-1979, and then to a plurality opposed by the end of 1979, when President Carter withdrew the treaty from consideration by the Senate. The margins in the various polls differ widely, as does the exact timing of the downturn. But they all agree that the prevailing trend of public opinion toward SALT II was negative.

It is by no means pointless to examine public opinion on such a topic, but one must be careful about what conclusions can be reached. Arms control (for many respondents probably almost synonymous to "peace") does have widespread support in the American public, but if efforts to achieve this cherished goal get entangled in political debates, as they almost invariably do, the public divides along the lines prevailing in these debates. Continuing consensus on arms control and peace coexists with divided opinion on specific policy proposals.

A similar process may have occurred on the issue of whether or not the United States should build the controversial MX missile system. In June 1983, two polls gave somewhat different pictures of public opinion. The ABC News/*Washington Post* poll showed public opinion narrowly in favor of the MX, 46 to 44 percent, while the Harris survey showed the public 53 to 41 percent opposed. However, both surveys indicated a trend in favor of the MX. In the ABC News/*Washington Post* poll, support had increased from a 51 against 38 percent margin opposed in January 1983. In the Harris survey, attitudes in November 1982 had even been somewhat more negative (58 over 35 percent against it). It appears that the high importance of peace predisposes the public generally to favor arms control agreements and to oppose new weapons systems. An extensive political debate at the elite level, however, can turn public opinion around to a certain extent over time, if segments of the public recognize that political leaders they trust have taken different positions and supply arguments and rationales to support them.

Table 8.9 reveals that national security issues, defense spending and troop intervention, tend to divide Americans along ideological lines. In the 1982 Chicago Council survey, more Republicans and conservatives wanted to increase than to cut back military spending, while the reverse was true for Democrats and liberals. All party and ideological groups favored sending U.S. troops if the Soviet Union invaded Western Europe, but support was noticeably higher among Republicans and conservatives.

Mass-elite differences were not consistent, however. The goal of defending the security of U.S. allies was much more popular among opinion leaders and those attentive to foreign affairs than among the mass public at large. Very little difference could be detected between mass and elite opinion on matching Soviet military power. On the issue of defense spending, however, opinion leaders and those attentive to foreign news were more favorable to cutting back. The same inconsistency showed up on questions relating to interventionism: Elites were much more favorable than the mass public to the idea of sending U.S. troops if the Soviet Union invaded Western Europe, but they were less favorable to sending troops if the Soviet Union invaded Poland. On security issues elite opinion seems to be highly differentiated. On certain issues (notably, the American security commitment to its allies) elites are more supportive than the mass public. On other issues (defense spending and actions outside alliance commitments) the mass public shows stronger security consciousness. The critical factor is internationalism: Elites are more aware and supportive of America's security commitments to others, whereas the mass public is more concerned about both America's vulnerability and the Soviet Union's aggressiveness.

Images of Deterrence

The American public is deeply frightened by the prospect of nuclear war. In polls taken in the spring of 1982, 41 percent according to ABC News/ *Washington Post* and 43 percent according to CBS News/*New York Times* believed that a nuclear war was somewhat likely or very likely in the next few years.

Do Americans believe a nuclear war could be won? They do not. At the end of 1981, 73 percent told a Roper poll that both sides would be annihilated in a nuclear war; only 15 percent thought it would be possible for one side to "win" such a war, that is, "come out of it as a functioning country with a reasonable size population." Sixty percent felt that very few Americans, or none at all, would survive, 55 percent felt that few or no Russians would survive. Would most Americans even want to survive a nuclear war? A majority, 53 to 37 percent, told the *Los Angeles Times* poll in March 1982 that they would rather not survive an all-out nuclear war.

Do Americans believe a limited nuclear war is possible? They do not. Only 15 percent in 1981 (Roper), ten percent in 1982 (NBC News/ Associated Press), and 17 percent in 1983 (Harris) were of the opinion

Table 8.9 Security-related attitudes for opinion leaders and for the public by interest, education, political orientation (CCFR 1982)

	Opinion Leaders	Public	Attentiveness to foreign news			Education			Partisanship			Ideology		
			Low	Average	High	Grade School	High School	College	Democrat	Independent	Republican	Liberal	Moderate	Conservative
Percent "very important"														
Matching Soviet military power	52	49	44	52	51	a	a	a	a	a	a	a	a	a
Defending our allies' security	82	50	39	51	67	a	a	a	a	a	a	a	a	a
Attitude toward defense spending														
Increase	20	21	19	23	23	22	24	12	17	20	32	17	21	26
Cut back	41	24	21	23	29	17	21	43	26	26	14	37	21	18
Percent who favor sending US troops if														
Soviet troops invade Western Europe	92	65	40	64	72	46	67	78	59	66	75	66	63	70
Soviet troops invade Poland	6	31	19	31	29	24	31	28	29	27	32	26	27	30

Note:

a Not available

that, once nuclear weapons were used, a conflict could be limited to something less than a full-scale war. The 1982 *Los Angeles Times* poll asked people what would happen if the United States became involved in a war with the Soviet Union. Twelve percent said such a war would be fought with conventional weapons, 19 percent thought it would be a limited nuclear war with each side only attacking the other's military targets with nuclear weapons, and 60 percent felt it would become an all-out nuclear war. The American public does not believe that superpower conflict is the most likely way a nuclear war would start, however. Twenty percent told the *Los Angeles Times* poll that a nuclear war would most likely happen because one of the great powers believed it could wipe out its enemy before it could retaliate, and 11 percent thought it would start because one of the great powers feared attack and struck first in defense. A nuclear war was considered most likely to occur (36 percent) because some smaller nation started nuclear war against another smaller nation and the situation got out of hand.

The American public is concerned, moreover, that the Reagan administration does not share these views. In April 1982, Americans felt by 46 to 32 percent that the United States could not win a nuclear war with the Soviet Union. By 50 to 29 percent the same people said that President Reagan believes the United States could win a nuclear war. In June 1983, the public felt by 51 to 40 percent that President Reagan has not done as much as he should to limit the buildup of nuclear weapons (ABC News/ *Washington Post*). In the same month, a 54 to 34 percent majority told a CBS News/*New York Times* poll that Reagan had not done enough to try to reach an agreement to reduce nuclear weapons. The public was divided over whether Reagan is sincere when he makes proposals for arms control (44 percent) or whether he makes these proposals simply to quiet his critics (40 percent). Indeed, most Americans blamed both the United States and the Soviet Union for the failure to reach an arms control agreement: 60 percent said they blamed both countries, while 30 percent blamed the Soviet Union and four percent blamed the United States, according to a CBS News/*New York Times* poll taken in April 1983.

The American public's basic preference is for total nuclear disarmament. The Harris survey asked: "Would you favor or oppose all countries that have nuclear weapons agreeing to destroy them?" Support for this proposition was 61 to 37 percent in March 1982, 72 to 22 percent in May 1982, 80 to 17 percent in March 1983, and 80 to 16 percent in May 1983. As the next best option Americans held that every country that has nuclear weapons should ban the production, storage, and use of those weapons. This was favored 73 to 23 percent in March 1982, 70 to 25 percent in May 1982, and 69 to 25 percent in March 1983.

At the other extreme, Americans definitely oppose unilateral nuclear disarmament. The proportion in favor of the United States reducing its nuclear weapons without waiting for the Russians to do the same has been in the range of 13 to 19 percent, with 78 to 82 percent opposed. Americans favor disarmament, but only if it is *mutual* disarmament. The NBC News/ Associated Press poll asked Americans to choose between three types of disarmament policies in 1981–1982. Only 12 to 14 percent thought the United States should disarm on its own. The percentages who opposed *any* nuclear disarmament were in the range of 26 to 28. A majority, about 50 percent, felt that the United States should move toward nuclear disarmament only if the Soviet Union agrees to disarm as well. Public attitudes toward disarmament can probably be explained by a *Los Angeles Times* question from March 1982 that posed the classic "red versus dead" choice: "Would you be willing to risk the destruction of the United States rather than be dominated by the Russians, or not?" The answer was better dead than red, by 60 to 28 percent.

While Americans favor—indeed, deeply desire—nuclear disarmament, they will not endorse a policy that puts the United States at a military disadvantage. For example, a May 1982 CBS News/*New York Times* poll asked: "Do you think the United States would *ever* be justified in using a nuclear weapon first during a war against another country?" (emphasis in original). The public said no by a strong margin, 62 to 26 percent. Does that mean the American public favors a no-first-use pledge? Not exactly. In several polls taken during 1982, the American public opposed such a pledge (55 against 34 percent in the ABC News/*Washington Post* poll, 56 against 33 percent in the *Los Angeles Times* poll, and 43 against 29 percent in the Roper poll). All three surveys, however, had reminded respondents of the potential risks of such a pledge. When a policy of no-first-use was presented as a military disadvantage, Americans were reluctant to endorse a policy they believed in in principle. This sensitivity to question wording might be interpreted, of course, as an indication of rather low salience, of not very strongly held beliefs.

However, the American public is reluctant to endorse the use of nuclear weapons even in extreme situations. What if Western Europe were attacked by the Soviet Union and threatened with a Soviet takeover, would Americans then favor the use of nuclear weapons? The answer is no: 57 to 28 percent in a May 1982 CBS News/*New York Times* poll and 64 to 26 percent in a June 1982 *Los Angeles Times* poll. However, by 49 to 36 percent respondents told the *Los Angeles Times* poll they thought President Reagan would favor the use of nuclear weapons if the Russians attacked Western Europe.

As noted earlier, the public's concern over the likelihood of war and its feeling that the Reagan administration was not being serious enough in pursuing arms control gave rise to the nuclear freeze movement at the end of 1981, more or less in direct imitation of the peace demonstrations that occurred throughout Europe that autumn. Every poll taken since the end of 1981 that has posed the question of a nuclear weapons freeze (usually described as a mutual and verifiable ban on the testing, production, and further deployment of all nuclear weapons) has found a majority, and usually a strong majority, in favor. Five polls taken during 1983 reveal an average of 72 percent in favor of a nuclear freeze and only 20 percent opposed. These results are almost unchanged from six 1982 polls. As indicated earlier, these results were confirmed in the 1982 midterm elections, when nuclear freeze proposals were passed on almost every ballot where they appeared.

This does not mean that Americans favor a freeze unconditionally. It is not difficult to define circumstances that lead Americans to change their minds on the issue. In May 1982, the CBS News/*New York Times* poll found a 72 to 21 percent margin in favor of a nuclear freeze in response to an initial question. Respondents were then asked how they would feel about a freeze under various conditions. Support for a freeze quickly reversed under any of the following conditions: if either the United States or the Soviet Union could cheat on the number of its nuclear weapons without being detected by the other side (71 to 18 percent opposed); if, in order to get the Soviet Union to agree to a freeze, the United States would have to freeze its own weapons first (67 to 26 percent opposed); or if a nuclear freeze would result in the Soviet Union's having somewhat greater nuclear strength than the United States (60 to 30 percent opposed). On the other hand, if cheating could be detected by both sides, support went up to 83 against 12 percent, and if a nuclear freeze would result in the United States and the Soviet Union having about an equal amount of nuclear strength, support rose to 87 percent (nine percent being opposed).

The American public does not seem to agree with President Reagan's precondition for a nuclear freeze: that the United States first build up its own nuclear arsenal to match that of the Russians. In November 1982, the Chicago Council survey asked people whether they favored a mutual, verifiable nuclear freeze right now, if the Soviets would agree, or only after the United States had built up its nuclear weapons more. The answer, by 58 to 21 percent, was "right now." In April 1983, the CBS News/*New York Times* poll asked a similar question, namely, whether people thought building up United States military strength to get the Russians to agree to nuclear arms reductions or seeking agreement on a mutual freeze first and negotiating reductions afterwards would be more likely to prevent nuclear war. Again, the public preferred an immediate freeze, 64 to 25 percent.

Table 8.10 shows the results of two 1982 Roper polls in which respondents were offered five alternative nuclear freeze policies for choice of one. The preferred policy for about one third of the public was to freeze production of all nuclear arms if Russia would agree to cut back to equal nuclear capacity. About one-third of the public favored a "tougher" position: freezing production only when the United States could build up to Russia's nuclear capability (eight percent), freezing production only when the United States is stronger than Russia or no freeze at all (eight and 12 percent, respectively). Finally, about one-quarter of the American public wanted an immediate freeze even if that meant that Russia would have somewhat more nuclear arms than the United States. Table 8.10 substantiates the point made earlier, that the public favors a freeze if it

Table 8.10   Positions on nuclear arms control (ROP)

	4/82	7/82
Freeze production now of all nuclear arms at their present levels, even if that means that Russia will have somewhat more nuclear arms than we do	26	22
Freeze production of all nuclear arms if Russia will agree to cut back to equal nuclear capability	32	34
Freeze production of all nuclear arms when the United States builds up to Russia's nuclear capability	13	16
Freeze production of all nuclear arms when the United States achieves a greater nuclear capability than Russia	8	8
Impose no freeze on the production of nuclear arms by either the United States or Russia	11	8
None	2	3
Don't know	8	9

Note:
Question wording:

"Nearly everyone would like to see a reduction in nuclear warfare tensions between the United States and the Soviet Union. The only disagreement is over how to reach it. Which one of these agreements on nuclear arms production would you most like to see the United States come to with Russia?"

results in U.S.-Soviet equality. Moreover, most Americans oppose an unbalanced freeze with either the Soviets or the United States ahead. Nuclear deterrence from the public's point of view means nuclear parity, and many people see a freeze as a good way to obtain this.

The public is not convinced that building up America's nuclear arsenal actually reinforces its national security. In a March 1982 *Time* Magazine/ Yankelovich, Skelly, and White poll, respondents were closely divided over whether "the nuclear arms race is so dangerous that spending more money on nuclear arms weakens our national security rather than strengthening it"; 45 percent agreed with this statement, and 48 percent disagreed. A March 1982 *Los Angeles Times* poll asked, "If the United States manufactured more nuclear bombs, would that make you feel more secure or would that make you feel more vulnerable?" Put in those personal terms, 43 percent said "more vulnerable" and 34 percent said "more secure." The same poll asked whether the United States needed more nuclear weapons for its defense or whether the United States now possessed enough nuclear weapons to destroy its enemies. By a decisive margin of 50 to 31 percent the public felt the United States did *not* need more nuclear weapons for its defense.

It turns out that the question just cited was strongly related to support for the nuclear freeze. Of those people who said the United States had enough nuclear weapons 69 percent supported the freeze, of those who said America needed more nuclear weapons for its defense only 43 percent supported the freeze. The same survey asked whether the United States should get tougher with Russia, even if that means risking war, or whether we should be more conciliatory, even if that would invite Russia to become more aggressive. Profreeze sentiment notwithstanding, respondents endorsed the tougher stance by a decisive margin, 53 to 27 percent. Opinion on the nuclear freeze, however, was virtually unrelated to the question of how the United States should deal with the Russians. Those who wanted to get tougher and those who wanted to be more conciliatory both almost equally supported the freeze. Thus, the nuclear freeze movement appeared to have little to do with toughness or anti-Soviet feeling, both of which remained very strong. Rather, it had to do with the growing sentiment that a nuclear arms race was dangerous and pointless. Building up the stock of nuclear weapons, to most Americans, today does not signify greater strength, but greater risk.

Table 8.11 reveals another interesting fact about public opinion on the nuclear freeze. It is more a function of education than of ideology. Liberals, moderates, and conservatives all agree that the United States should get tougher with the Russians and that the United States has enough nuclear weapons for its national security; all three groups support a nuclear freeze. The college-educated, however, who are most likely to favor a tough policy toward the Soviets, are also most likely—by a good margin—to feel that the United States has enough nuclear weapons. Since, as was shown, opinion on the nuclear freeze tends to be associated more strongly with the latter view than with the former, the college-educated show the strongest support for a freeze. Indeed, at 69 percent favorable, the college-educated support the nuclear freeze more than people under 30 (54 percent) and even more than liberals (65 percent). Similarly, in the 1982 Chicago Council survey, an immediate freeze was favored by 58 percent of the mass public, 79 percent of opinion leaders, and 77 percent of the college-educated; support was somewhat lower among Democrats and liberals (60 and 65 percent, respectively). What appears to generate support for the nuclear freeze is not ideology but the level of information. Support is strongest among the more knowledgeable and sophisticated segments of the public who are most actively concerned with foreign affairs.

Two surveys, the ABC News/*Washington Post* poll in 1982 and the Roper poll in 1983, have probed the reasons for Americans to support or oppose a nuclear freeze. The pro-freeze arguments that were accepted by most Americans include the following: that it does not matter who is ahead in nuclear weapons because both sides have more than enough to destroy each other no matter who attacks first (79 over 16 percent); that the nuclear arms race increases the risk of nuclear war (70 over 25 percent); that public support for a nuclear freeze will make the Reagan administra-

Table 8.11   Attitudes toward nuclear weapons by ideology and education (LAT 3/82)

	Ideology			Education		
	Lib-erals	Moder-ates	Con-serva-tives	Didn't finish high school	High school grad-uate	Col-lege
United States needs more nuclear weapons	33	29	35	39	32	23
United States has enough nuclear weapons	56	53	45	36	48	65
United States should get tougher with Russia	52	53	58	43	57	58
United States should be more conciliatory	32	26	25	33	23	25
Opinion on nuclear freeze						
Favor	65	60	51	44	57	69
Oppose	33	35	45	46	38	29

tion give higher priority to arms control (64 over 22 percent); and that a freeze would reduce international tensions and the threat of nuclear war (48 over 36 percent). The public even agreed, albeit by a close margin (50 to 41 percent), that stopping the arms race is so important that we should have a nuclear freeze no matter how risky it seems. On the other hand, most Americans did *not* believe that a freeze would cause either United States or Soviet policies to become more reasonable and moderate, that a freeze would establish a stable nuclear arms balance between the United States and the Soviet Union, or that a freeze would encourage the Soviets to agree to a nuclear arms reduction later. Americans support a freeze because they view the alternative, a continuing arms race, as extremely dangerous. They consider a freeze to be the first step, not the last step, in reducing the risk of war.

What is interesting is that Americans also accept many arguments *against* the nuclear freeze: that the Soviets cannot be trusted to live up to a freeze agreement (66 over 26 percent), that a freeze would be a gamble because it would be difficult to verify (65 over 26 percent), that a freeze now would leave the Soviet Union ahead of the United States in nuclear capability (60 over 28 percent), that a freeze would prevent the United States from modernizing and improving its weapons arsenal (55 over 34 percent), and that a freeze might make it easier for the Soviet Union to pursue aggressive policies ("invade other countries, including those in Europe") without worrying about U.S. retaliation (52 over 41 percent). All these arguments are considered quite believable, but Americans favor a freeze *despite* such reservations, which indicates how serious the concern over nuclear war has become. On the other hand, as was the case with the SALT II treaty discussed earlier, it could prove difficult to negotiate a concrete freeze agreement that the American public still would approve of. Once a specific agreement would be proposed, political controversies might produce arguments and polarization at the elite level that, in turn, could also divide public opinion along the familiar trenches, thereby considerably reducing support for a particular freeze arrangement, as opposed to the general idea.

As a final aspect of the American public's images of deterrence, we also encounter its preference for negotiated arms control over nuclear weapons buildup in attitudes on INF. The 1982 Chicago Council survey asked opinion leaders whether they thought the United States and its NATO allies should go ahead and deploy medium-range nuclear missiles in Europe in 1983, cancel the scheduled deployment, or start deploying the missiles but stop if the Soviets would agree to limit their own missiles in Europe. The last position was by far the most popular, winning the endorsement of two-thirds of the opinion leaders. Only one in five wanted to go ahead and deploy the missiles in any case, while one in ten opposed deployment altogether. This question was not asked of the general public on the theory that most Americans knew and cared little about this issue.

Images of Allies

Table 8.12 provides a picture of how the American public viewed the world at the end of 1982. Respondents in the Chicago Council survey were asked to indicate their degree of favorability toward each in a list of 24 countries using a thermometer scale ranging between zero degrees (very cold or unfavorable) and 100 degrees (very warm or favorable). A thermometer rating of 50 degrees was designated as neutral. Respondents were also asked whether they felt the United States does or does not have a vital interest in each country, where "vital interest" meant that the country is "important to the United States for political, economic, or security reasons." Table 8.12 shows the percentage who said the United States had a vital interest in each country as well as the average favorability rating for each country on the thermometer scale.

Western allies came out high in favorability, with Canada, Britain, and France at the top of the list. The public also saw a vital American interest in Canada and Britain. While Americans indicated quite favorable feelings toward France and Italy (60 and 55 degrees, respectively), both countries rated relatively low in terms of vital interest to the United States. Just 58 percent of the public said that the United States has a vital interest in France, and a surprisingly low figure of 35 percent said the United States has a vital interest in Italy. On the other hand, 82 percent saw a vital United States interest in Japan, even though Japan's favorability rating, at 53 degrees, was not especially high. The American public has favorable opinions of its Western allies, presumably because they are culturally

Table 8.12   Foreign countries by favorability and US interest (CCFR 1982)

	Favorability [a]	Vital US Interest (Percentage)
Canada	74	82
Great Britain	68	80
France	60	58
Mexico	60	74
West Germany	59	76
Israel	55	75
Italy	55	35
Brazil	54	45
Japan	53	82
Poland	52	43
Egypt	52	66
Saudi Arabia	52	77
Taiwan	49	51
India	48	30
People's Republic of China	47	64
Jordan	47	41
Lebanon	46	55
South Africa	45	38
South Korea	44	43
Nigeria	44	32
Syria	42	36
Iran	28	51
Cuba	27	b
Soviet Union	26	b

Note:

[a] Mean value of zero-100 feeling thermometer
[b] Not surveyed

similar to Americans (especially the Canadians and the British). On the other hand, being an ally, even a NATO ally, does not guarantee that the public believes the United States has a vital interest in a country. More Americans saw a vital U.S. interest in Mexico, Israel, Egypt, Saudi Arabia, and China than in France or Italy.

Table 8.13 presents a slightly different measurement of the way Americans see the world. Here, in a 1983 Roper survey, respondents were asked to classify each country as either a close ally, a friend but not a close ally, a country that has been more or less neutral toward the United States, an unfriendly country but not an enemy, or an enemy of the United States.

Britain was the only country on the list defined by a majority of Americans as a close ally of the United States, even though a 1983 Harris survey asking the same question found that a majority also defined Canada as a close ally. Most other allied countries—West Germany, France, and Japan, as well as Israel, Mexico, and Egypt—were seen as "friends" of the United States but not close allies. Italy and the Netherlands, however, were characterized by pluralities as "neutral" or slightly friendly. They were the only two Western countries on the list that were not described in positive terms (ally or friend) by a majority of Americans. This may reflect the fact that Italy and the Netherlands are minor powers where American vital interests, as noted above in the case of Italy, are seen to be limited. While Americans may feel favorable toward such countries, their power status does not seem to justify calling them allies or even friends.

Note that both Saudi Arabia and Mainland China were seen as basically neutral countries. As Table 8.12 shows, Saudi Arabia and China were both rated as important to America's vital interests. If they are important to the United States for economic or political reasons, then it is difficult for most Americans to see them as unfriendly. On the other hand, the Reagan administration's claim that the United States has vital interests in Central America does not seem to carry much weight in American public opinion. Both El Salvador, which the U.S. government supports, and Nicaragua, which it opposes, were seen as unfriendly to the United States. At the bottom of the list, as mentioned earlier, Cuba and the Soviet Union were both perceived in highly negative terms, although Americans were about evenly divided between those who considered them enemies and those who described them as simply unfriendly.

Has the commitment of the American public to the NATO alliance diminished? There is no evidence to this effect. Actually, public support for NATO has tended to increase since 1974. As Table 8.14 reveals, a majority of Americans has consistently favored maintaining or increasing the U.S. commitment to NATO. The size of that majority rose from 54 percent in 1974 to 67 percent in 1978 and 1982. The proportion of Americans who want to decrease that commitment dropped slightly, from 20 percent in 1974 to 13 percent in 1978 and 15 percent in 1982. The percentage who said they were not sure how they felt about America's NATO commitment also declined after 1974. Apparently, the increasing security consciousness of the American public after 1974 manifested itself in a stronger commitment to the Atlantic Alliance, despite the trend of declining internationalism.

What about policies that have caused friction among the Atlantic allies? The 1982 Chicago Council survey asked people whether they thought the United States should put diplomatic pressure on its allies or apply economic sanctions if they refused to go along with the U.S. boycott of the Soviet natural gas pipeline to Western Europe. Only 15 percent of Americans favored economic sanctions, and 27 percent endorsed diplomatic pressure. A plurality, 37 percent, said that the United States should

Table 8.13   Foreign countries rated as allies versus enemies (ROP 6/83)

	Close ally	Friend	Neutral	Mainly Unfriendly	Enemy	Don't know
Great Britain	54	31	7	1	1	7
Japan	16	45	24	5	2	8
West Germany	19	40	20	6	2	13
Israel	14	41	20	11	3	11
Mexico	7	47	27	8	2	9
France	12	41	27	9	1	10
Egypt	7	38	27	11	2	15
The Netherlands	8	32	37	2	0	21
Italy	4	33	40	6	1	15
Saudi Arabia	4	25	26	21	5	18
Mainland China	1	20	37	22	7	13
Venezuela	1	16	35	13	2	33
Argentina	2	11	27	28	6	24
Honduras	1	9	25	22	4	39
El Salvador	1	10	18	34	15	21
Nicaragua	1	5	19	34	16	25
Soviet Union	1	2	7	43	42	5
Cuba	1	2	5	39	47	7

let the allies pursue the policies they think best. An additional 21 percent said they didn't know what the United States should do. These data suggest that Americans are not zealous supporters of policies that would pressure U.S. allies.

Perhaps even more revealing, however, is the scarcity of survey data concerning U.S. relations with its allies. American pollsters are tireless in their efforts to probe every aspect of public opinion on timely and controversial subjects, whether or not people really have clearly articulated views on the issues. Hence the abundance of data on SALT II in 1978–1979 and on the nuclear freeze in 1982–1983. The fact that the Atlantic Alliance is seldom the subject of polling inquiries is evidence that it is not an issue of major interest or controversy in the United States. Beyond the ranks of foreign policy specialists, alliance relationships probably are not matters of serious concern to Americans. This does not mean that they do not support the alliance. They do quite strongly, as the evidence in Table 8.14 indicates. It is not, however, an issue of major public attention or debate.

Americans do not evince very strong opinions on the subject of the alliance. In a Gallup survey taken in January 1983, for example, the American public opposed the prospect of West European neutralism by the considerably less-than-overwhelming margin of 45 to 41 percent. By

Table 8.14   Attitudes toward NATO (CCFR)

	1974	1978	1982
Increase US commitment	4	9	9
Keep commitment what it is	50	58	58
Decrease commitment	13	9	11
Withdraw entirely	7	4	4
Not sure	26	20	18

another modest margin of 45 to 31 percent, the American public favored deploying medium-range nuclear missiles in Western Europe if talks between the United States and the Soviet Union failed. In a Gallup survey for the French-American Foundation, respondents in both countries were asked whether they thought the French and American governments generally agreed or generally did not agree on several issues: the Arab-Israeli conflict, détente with the Soviet Union, and limiting the spread of nuclear weapons. In each case the French were more likely than the Americans to perceive the two governments as in agreement. Here again, the American public seems less alliance-conscious than the European public.

Several Chicago Council surveys have included interviews with leadership samples of Americans in senior positions (government, business, labor, education, religion, journalism, and civic service) with knowledge of and influence on international affairs and foreign policy. According to the 1978 and 1982 studies, the principal difference between American public opinion at large and leadership opinion can be stated simply: Leaders are more internationalist. They were much less likely than the public to name protecting American jobs and keeping up the value of the dollar as important foreign policy goals. In the case of protecting weaker nations from foreign aggression, matching Soviet military power, promoting human rights, and promoting democracy abroad, leadership opinion was almost no different from public opinion. Leaders were even less enthusiastic than the public about containing communism and protecting American business interests abroad, two conservative goals, and strengthening the United Nations, a liberal goal.

On questions relating to troop involvement, leaders were more supportive in cases that involve threats to countries allied to the United States: Western Europe, South Korea, Japan, Israel, and Saudi Arabia. In situations in which no alliance commitments are at stake, leaders were less amenable than the public to the use of U.S. troops. These differences emerged quite sharply in the case of Soviet invasions of China and Poland, where over 20 percent of the public, but very few of the leaders, would be willing to involve American forces.

Leadership opinion, being internationalist, is more or less in line with the traditional bipartisan foreign policy consensus of the 1950s and early 1960s. That consensus embraced a continuity of goals (essentially, containment of Soviet aggression) and an acceptance of both cooperative and confrontational strategies. Among political activists, however, that consensus eroded rapidly in the wake of the Vietnam War. As will be described below, activist sentiment tends to be polarized between conservative internationalism, which is interventionist, pro-military, and staunchly anticommunist, and liberal internationalism, which is more concerned with economic and humanitarian issues, suspicious of military power, and preoccupied more with global interdependence than with East-West confrontation.

Conclusion: The Dynamics of Public Opinion on Foreign Policy

Survey researchers regularly discover that 60 to 70 percent of the American public has no sustained interest or involvement in foreign affairs. This large, inattentive public is neither consistently liberal nor consistently conservative in its foreign policy beliefs. Nor is it ideologically isolationist in the sense that many Americans were in the period between World War I and World War II. The inattentive public is best characterized as "noninternationalist." It is predisposed against U.S. involvement in other countries' affairs unless a clear and compelling issue of national interest or national security is at stake. If the United States is directly threatened or if its interests *are* involved in any important way, this constituency will support U.S. engagement but prefers swift, decisive action without long-term involvement.

The other portion of the public is what social scientists have always depicted as the attentive audience for foreign affairs. This audience is better-educated and follows foreign affairs regularly. Historically, it has also tended to be more supportive of government initiatives than the noninternationalist public. When the attentive elite was asked about the Korean War, about American involvement in the rest of the world, or about trade, treaties, or foreign aid, it was consistently more favorable than the rest of the public. Noninternationalists, on the other hand, have revealed a persistent strain of distrust and anti-involvement. At the same time, they only tend to get involved in the foreign affairs debate in election years. Between elections, the noninternationalist constituency usually has little influence over foreign policy.

In the late 1960s, the attentive public split. As described by Mandelbaum and Schneider (1979), one segment became liberal internationalists who dissented from the cold war interventionism that had characterized American foreign policy for most of the twenty years following World War II. They were not isolationists. They simply envisioned a different form of U.S. involvement in world affairs. Another segment of the attentive public, also well educated and heavily involved in foreign policy, took a conservative internationalist line. The issues that split the attentive public were the war in Vietnam and the nature of détente after the Nixon-Kissinger initiatives.

Both segments of the attentive public are basically internationalist in their predispositions. Neither disputes the notion that the United States has a major role to play in world affairs. They part company on exactly what kind of role that should be. Conservative internationalists see the world primarily in East-West terms, with the United States the assertive, sometimes interventionist leader of the anticommunist alliance. Liberal internationalists have a stronger north-south orientation and are more likely to think in terms of global interdependence and mutual cooperation, with the United States again taking the lead.

The large, inattentive public does not consistently support either a liberal or a conservative U.S. world role. Instead, this group swings left or right unpredictably in response to its current fears and concerns. After 1968, for instance, the noninternationalist public turned against the Vietnam War as a wasteful, pointless, and ultimately tragic U.S. involvement. The antiwar coalition of the early 1970s was a potent alliance between liberal internationalists and noninternationalists. The noninternationalists, however, never accepted the more extreme contentions of the antiwar activists that U.S. purposes in Vietnam were evil or corrupt.

The noninternationalist public allies with the left on questions of intervention because it sees no point to American involvement unless U.S. interests are directly threatened. Noninternationalists are profoundly antiforeign aid, anti-troop involvement, anti-anything that suggests foreign entanglement. Traditionally, isolationism in the United States meant ideological opposition to U.S. participation in world affairs. Noninternationalists are not so much ideologically opposed as simply non supportive. Being less well-educated—that is the strongest demographic correlate of noninternationalism—this group has a limited understanding of the relevance of events that are complex and remote from their daily lives. They feel that most of what the United States does for the rest of the world is senseless, wasteful, and unappreciated.

In cases such as Vietnam and El Salvador, noninternationalists find a natural alliance with the left. But that alliance is not automatic or permanent. The noninternationalist public is also oriented toward a strong military posture and will support conservatives on issues of military strength and toughness. As noted earlier, after 1974 the mass public in the United States began to feel increasingly insecure about Soviet adventurism and the Soviet military buildup, and public opinion began to drift toward the right on foreign policy issues. Virtually every month from 1974 to the beginning of 1981 saw greater public support for increasing defense spending. Noninternationalists voted heavily for Reagan, in part because of his promises of a defense buildup and a tougher stand toward the Soviet Union. This constituency approves of strength and toughness in foreign affairs in part because that prevents the United States from becoming involved with the rest of the world. The basic impulse is defensive; the public wants to see the United States increase its military power in order to protect itself from a growing Soviet threat, not in order to assume an interventionist role in world affairs.

As noted in the Introduction, Americans are committed to two foreign policy values, peace and strength. They believe in both of them and do not regard them as inconsistent. In 1981 and again in 1983, the Roper poll asked people to choose one of three ways of dealing with the Soviet Union:

1. "It's clear that Russia can't be trusted and we will have to rely on increased military strength to counter them in the future."
2. "We should take a strong position with the Russians now so they won't go any further but at the same time we should try to reestablish good relations with them."
3. "We should do nothing that is likely to provoke a U.S.-Russian military conflict but instead try to negotiate and reason out our differences."

In both years, about one person in four preferred the "tough" line (option 1). Another one in four endorsed the conciliatory line (option 3). About half of those interviewed (50 percent in 1981, 52 percent in 1983) took the "mixed" position, in favor of a strong stance while trying to reestablish good relations with the Soviets. In other words, the American public does not favor peace over strength or strength over peace. It favors a policy that engages both values.

Asking Americans to choose between peace and strength is like asking an individual to choose between health and financial security. Both are important. But sometimes people are more concerned about health, and at other times they are obsessed with financial security. It depends upon the immediate problems that people are facing. So it is with public opinion. Sometimes Americans are more worried about military security, and at other times, peace is the major cause of anxiety. These concerns have ebbed and flowed in three basic stages since World War II.

The first was the cold war, a period in which the public became increasingly obsessed with the nation's military security vis-à-vis the Soviet Union. That concern developed rather slowly during the late 1940s. In 1945, according to a Gallup poll, most Americans thought the Russians could be trusted to cooperate after the war. The Truman administration, privately alarmed over Soviet aggressiveness, felt it had to be cautious in its public pronouncements. President Truman and his advisers were not convinced that the public (or Congress) would support a policy of global confrontation with the Soviet Union. After all, the American public (and Congress) had defiantly rejected an activist role in world affairs for the United States after World War I.

The turning point came with the Korean War, which tended to alarm Americans less about peace than about the nation's military security. The protest against that war came not from the left but from the right, from those who felt that the United States lacked the strength and determination to win a decisive victory over communism. In fact, there is evidence that American leaders deliberately overstated the nature of the Soviet threat in order to sustain public support for an activist foreign policy. According to diplomatic historian Ernest R. May (1984), "Men of the Truman, Eisenhower, and Kennedy Administrations doubted that the mass of voters could or would reconcile themselves to a long-term, hostile rivalry with the Soviet Union involving continual expense and danger and promising no happy conclusion at any point in the anticipatable future." Given historic American resistance to a world leadership role, leaders of the time felt that the cold war had to be "sold" to the American public.

It was not difficult. As noted, anti-Soviet hostility was extremely intense during the 1950s, with over 90 percent of Americans expressing negative attitudes. In his 1960 presidential campaign, John F. Kennedy stressed the "missile gap" with the Soviet Union, arguing that the United States had fallen behind the Russians in military strength and global influence. That was what most people understood by his promise to "get the country moving again."

The cold war came to a climax with the Cuban missile crisis in October 1962. During the subsequent period, which for our purposes lasted from the Limited Nuclear Test-Ban Treaty of 1963 until the end of 1973, the Soviet Union virtually disappeared from the political agenda in the United States. The nuclear threat seemed much less imminent, and relations with the Soviets gradually took on the character of stable, competitive rivalry. Peace, not strength, was the public's paramount concern between 1963 and 1973. The Vietnam War activated the American public's traditional fears that if U.S. leaders got their way, they would involve the country in wasteful foreign adventures.

The final, "post-détente" period actually began prior to the downturn in superpower relations with the energy crisis of early 1974 and the ensuing inflation and recession. The Soviet military buildup along with Soviet activities in African and the Middle East then heightened the American public's concern over military strength and security. While support for higher defense spending had been increasing gradually after 1973, the dam literally burst in 1980 after the seizure of U.S. hostages in Iran and the Soviet invasion of Afghanistan. The result was a surge of nationalist sentiment in American public opinion. Surveys taken in 1980 showed a marked increase in support for U.S. troop involvement in other parts of the world. According to Free and Watts (1980), the view that the United States should come to the defense of its major European allies if any of them were attacked by the Soviet Union reached an all-time high of 70 percent in February 1980 (it had fallen as low as 48 percent in 1974 and 1975). So did the feeling that the United States should use military force to defend Japan against Russia or China, which rose from 37 percent in 1974 to 57 percent in 1980.

The 1980 data also reveal a decline in unilateralist sentiment. Between

1964 and 1976, according to polls taken by Potomac Associates, unilateralism had been rising in the United States: sentiments to the effect that the United States should "go its own way in international matters, not worrying too much about whether other countries agree," "mind its own business internationally and let other countries get along as best they can on their own," and not cooperate with the United Nations or take into account the views of its major allies in making foreign policy decisions. The figures for early 1980 reveal a sharp reversal in this trend, with more Americans suddenly favoring cooperation with allies and with the United Nations and rejecting go-it-alone attitudes.

Do these results bespeak a new internationalism in American public opinion? What they probably measure is a heightened sense of self-interest following the late 1979 shocks of Iran and Afghanistan. The 1980 survey was taken by Free and Watts at the height of concern over the hostages in Iran, when the American public was exceptionally mindful of the need for support and cooperation among allies. Moreover, the strongest shifts were registered on those questions that measured military opposition to Soviet power (coming to the aid of European and Japanese allies in case of Soviet invasion). There is no evidence of any marked increase in nonmilitary internationalism, on issues such as foreign aid, arms control, human rights, or support for Third World development. It apears that what motivated the surge of international assertiveness in 1980 was a sense of military vulnerability and anti-Soviet hostility. Americans suddenly realised that it was in their own national interest to fortify anti-Soviet military alliances.

Thus, by the early 1980s, strength once again had become a paramount concern to the American public. It was not quite the same as during the cold war, however. Vietnam made a difference. The American public in the 1980s is measurably less interventionist and more sensitive to the risks of foreign entanglement than it was during the 1950s and early 1960s. The "strength" constituency is certainly larger than it was during the Vietnam period. But the "peace" constituency is larger than it was during the 1950s. The nuclear freeze movement of the 1980s is considerably larger than the "ban the bomb" movement ever was in the 1950s, even though their purposes are basically the same. The "ban the bomb" movement included very few mainstream American politicians, whereas the nuclear freeze movement today has been endorsed by the most influential leaders of the Democratic Party.

Events during the fall of 1983 moved foreign policy back to the top of the national agenda: the Soviet destruction of the Korean Airlines jet, the tragic bombing of the U.S. marine barracks in Lebanon followed by the failure of the international peace-keeping effort in that country, and U.S. military intervention in Grenada. As one might imagine, one effect of these events was to further intensify anti-Soviet feeling in the United States. The view of the Soviet Union as an enemy jumped from 52 percent in June 1983 to 63 percent in September. The trend on defense spending also reversed, with more Americans for the first time since 1981 supporting increases rather than decreases in the defense budget.

Nevertheless, the polls continue to reveal concern over peace. Polls taken during the fall of 1983 show a sharp increase in the American public's anxiety over the possibility of war. The threat of war moved up in the polls as a serious national concern, while international problems generally moved to the top of the national agenda. Polls taken by ABC News and the *Washington Post* indicated that, for the first time since the Vietnam war, international issues were perceived as the nation's number one problem. Support for arms control negotiations also rose during the fall of 1983, while endorsement of a nuclear freeze remained extremely high (about 80 percent favorable in the ABC/*Post* and Harris surveys).

The basic commitment of the American public to the values of peace and strength thus continues unabated, as does the public's suspicion of international involvement. Why, then, did the U.S. intervention in Grenada receive widespread public support if Americans are strongly noninternationalist? According to polls taken at the time of the invasion, most Americans were not convinced that American lives were in "a great deal of danger." A CBS News/*New York Times* survey showed that Americans were divided over whether "it was really necessary to go in at that time." The principal reason for the popularity of the Grenada action may very well be that it was a success. Grenada is a good example of the kind of foreign policy action likely to win public approval in the United States: swift, decisive, and relatively costless. The polls reveal that the basic impulses of U.S. public opinion did not change as a result of Grenada. Americans certainly do not want to apply the "lessons" of Grenada to other trouble spots. In a CBS/*Times* survey taken after the Grenada episode, the public overwhelmingly (60 to 21 percent) rejected the notion that the United States "should help people in Nicaragua who are trying to overthrow the pro-Soviet government there."

This abiding commitment to both peace and strength, combined as it is with distaste for involvement abroad, is the principal reason why, despite the surge of nationalist sentiment that helped Ronald Reagan get elected in 1980, he has found precious little public support for his policies of militant anticommunism and interventionism (with the conspicuous exception of Grenada, Reagan's one foreign policy success). The bipartisan, two-track foreign policy consensus of the 1950s was an establishment consensus, and that establishment has lost its hold over the two major political parties in the United States. Jimmy Carter tended to follow a liberal internationalist line until the end of 1979, and he found public opinion moving to the right of him, particularly on security issues. Ronald Reagan is a conservative internationalist, and he finds opinion moving to his left, especially on arms control. Basically, Americans want a president who is as committed to peace as Jimmy Carter and who is as committed to military strength as Ronald Reagan.

The Western alliance stands out in American public opinion because it is one of the few issues that is *not* the subject of intense controversy between liberal and conservative internationalists. And it is an internationalist commitment with which the American public is willing to go along, as long as it seems vital to American security interests. The Atlantic Alliance is precisely the kind of internationalist commitment that originated in and was sustained by the bipartisan foreign policy consensus of the 1950s. Yet, today, liberal internationalists tend to undervalue the Western alliance in favor of globalist policies and north-south dialogue. Conservative internationalist tend to overvalue the Western alliance by viewing it as more than a security arrangement; they see it as an ideological alliance and a challenge to international communism, not just Soviet military power.

These interpretations of the Western alliance tend to divide Americans and antagonize Europeans. Public opinion data from Europe and the United States suggest that the basic concept of the alliance remains sound to most citizens on both sides of the Atlantic. What endangers the alliance are efforts by American political activists to give it an ideological thrust, to make NATO the spearhead of either a globalist or an anticommunist crusade. There is no popular consensus, in Europe or in the United States, behind that kind of policy. In short, the way to weaken the Western alliance is to make it the subject of ideological controversy, which is exactly what has happened to most other issues in American foreign policy.

References

Free, Lloyd and William Watts, "Internationalism Comes of Age . . . Again" *Public Opinion* 3 (1980): 46–50.

Levering, Ralph B., *The Public and American Foreign Policy, 1918–1978* (New York: William Morrow & Company, 1978).

Mandelbaum Michael and William Schneider, "The New Internationalists: Public Opinion and Foreign Policy," in Kenneth Oye, Donald Rothchild, and Robert Lieber, eds., *Eagle Entangled: U.S. Foreign Policy in a Complex World* (New York: Longman, 1979).

May, Ernest R., "American Approaches to Managing Relations with the Soviet Union, 1945–64," in Joseph S. Nye, ed., *Managing the U.S.-Soviet Relationship* (New Haven, Conn.: Yale University Press, 1984).

Mueller, John E., *War, Presidents, and Public Opinion* (New York: John Wiley, 1973).

Rielly John E., ed., *American Public Opinion and U.S. Foreign Policy 1975*, (Chicago: Chicago Council on Foreign Relations, 1975); John E. Rielly, ed., *American Public Opinion and U.S. Foreign Policy 1979* (Chicago: Chicago Council on Foreign Relations, 1979).

Robinson, John P. and Robert Meadow, *Polls Apart* (Cabin John, Md.: Seven Locks Press, 1982).

Stokes, Donald E., "Spatial Models of Party Competition," in Angus Campbell, Philip E. Converse, Warren E. Miller, and Donald E. Stokes, *Elections and the Political Order* (New York: John Wiley, 1966).

Appendix G Sources

ABC:	ABC News
CCFR:	Chicago Council on Foreign Relations
CBS:	CBS News
GAL:	Gallup
LAT:	Los Angeles Times
LH:	Louis Harris Associates
NBC/AP:	NBC News-Associated Press Polls
NORC:	National Opinion Research Center, General Social Surveys
NYT:	New York Times
ROP:	Roper

this key dimension of salience. Without wanting to preempt the discussion below, the importance of "defense" and of the "armed forces" have, for instance, not increased at all, although concepts like security, defense, military balance, etc. are widely endorsed. Moreover, if one looks at the levels of support for specific measures designed to increase defensive capabilities, one almost always finds, with the possible exception of the United States, that opposition clearly exceeds support. This all would indicate that the putative increase in salience does not stem from an increase in the perceived need to maintain or to improve military capabilities.

But the picture is not really clear. If people are asked to rate not the importance of defense and of the armed forces in general, but of "protection" against external threat or attack, this tends to be judged far more important. Yet one should suspect that defense in general and the armed forces have a lot to do with protection against threat and attack. There thus is a considerable degree of uncertainty even in the extent to which we can ascertain what is important to people and why.

This may, of course, be related to the widespread perception that national security can be taken for granted, that there is no clearly visible and imminent threat to the values that are comprised by this notion. It is not at all unusual that demand for public goods is lowest and they are evaluated as least important when their supply appears satisfactorily guaranteed for a foreseeable span of time.

Increases in the importance ascribed to aspects of national security are most clearly visible when it comes to matters of the preservation of peace, the prevention of war, or to nuclear weapons. Even here, however, it is not clear what these increases in salience readings actually mean. First, they are compatible with any substantive orientation toward these problems. If people believe the preservation of peace to have become more important for themselves, they can opt for stronger defense as well as for alternative security arrangements or neutralism. If people rate nuclear weapons as more important than they did earlier, this can reflect either a desire for Western unilateralism in the field of nuclear arms control or, on the contrary, increased concern over Soviet missiles. Second, according to the studies contained in this book, there is little to demonstrate that the levels of information and interest or the feelings of competence to judge these matters have grown. This may suggest that the heightened salience readings are not due to genuine personal concern—which normally should lead to more information seeking and higher interest—but to a kind of "bandwagon" effect. Some people may judge these matters as more important because they are being presented all around them as more important than earlier.

Third, we cannot be sure what this means in terms of disposition toward action. In the field of security-related attitudes we face the particular problem that the important actors are frequently not the individuals themselves, but their governments or the Alliance. When this is the case, for example in the area of Western negotiating strategies on arms control, how are we to look at the interrelationship between salience and predispositions toward action? Moreover, even when the dimension of salience is tapped by investigating directly individuals' own inclination to become active, there are many unresolved problems. This is obvious, for example, if one compares what people say they feel should be done about the introduction of new nuclear missiles into Europe, and what they would be willing to do themselves if they disagree with deployment.

One final aspect of the salience dimension deserves mention. There seems to be an intimate connection between the extent to which these things are rated as important at the mass level, particularly the antinuclear aspect of this problem, and the direction and intensity of elite debates, particularly conflict between competing political parties. In at least three of the countries surveyed here (Britain, Germany, and the Netherlands) the increase in the salience attributed to nuclear issues grew apace with the extent to which the social democratic and labor parties of these countries more or less outspokenly adopted anti-INF positions. This is a variation, of course, on the bandwagon effect and interferes with our assessments of how important people really think issues to be. If you are the person in the street, and you have seldom reflected about an issue, how can you say it is not so important if everybody else, including those political elites you trust, claims it is of utmost importance?

More will be said about the relationship between attitudes and political preferences below. The point to be made here is narrower and related only to our consideration of salience: an increase of partisan activities may not actually bring a behavior-determining rise in the salience of security issues for mass publics. This is best illustrated by a look at the German and British elections of 1983. The impact of the security and missile issues was quite different in the two cases. The chapter on Britain shows that voting behavior was indeed heavily influenced by these issues, which made a major contribution to the Labor party's defeat. The chapter on Germany argues that the impact of the nuclear weapons issue on the outcome of the country's most recent election was only marginal. Thus what one might interpret as a measure of increased salience did not prove in the German case to be behavior-determining and hence may not be a measure of increased salience at all. In the British case, the issue was obviously salient enough to determine voting patterns.

This illustrates clearly how imperfect our knowledge of what determines salience and behavior really is. All we can say about the past few years is that we can observe an apparent rise in the salience of national security issues but that existing data and methods do not allow us to determine exactly what has increased in importance or why. What is certain is that the relative salience of these issues generally remains low and one therefore confronts the double difficulty of, on the one hand, greater uncertainty in how accurately we can measure public attitudes and, on the other, even when we can be relatively certain of our measurements, to determine how significant these are for political decision making because of their presumed minimal effect on behavior. This in no way is meant to deny the relevance of public opinion data in the area of national security policy but to voice a sharp word of caution about its over-interpretation. In spite of these constraints, there are a good number of things one can say about the evolution of public attitudes in this area and some of these do have important implications for policy.

THE SOVIET UNION: A MORE NORMAL ADVERSARY

Analyzing public attitudes toward the Soviet Union is perhaps the most straightforward of the summarizing tasks in this final chapter. While the data are certainly not uniform in quantity or quality across the Allied countries studied here, there is a relatively clear picture that emerges. And the picture is at considerable variance with many current notions about how people see the Soviets.

There are three basic dimensions to popular perceptions of the Soviet Union that must be distinguished in order for one to grasp fully how these may affect attitudes toward Western policy alternatives. In each there have seemingly been important changes from earlier parts of the postwar period, seemingly because in some cases we have the data to trace the changes and in other cases we are reduced to an educated guess as to what the earlier data would have looked like.

The first dimension of perceptions concerns general attitudes toward the Soviet Union as an international actor. There is no ambiguity. The Soviet Union is clearly perceived as an adversary and not as a benign adversary. Since the early 1970s, attitudes in all Western countries have deteriorated markedly. Anti-Soviet feelings are strong and widespread. Levels of trust in Soviet goodwill are minimal. Moreover, to preempt somewhat the discussion below, there is absolutely no comparison between the judgments made of the Soviet Union and the questioning of U.S. policy that has occurred. The larger public does not yet consider the two superpowers as cut from the same cloth. In other words, the evidence, at least at this general level, does not support the contention that if only people understood the nature of Soviet objectives they would in turn support more actively and uniformly efforts to strengthen Western defenses.

The second dimension concerns the surprising absence of a link between perceptions of the Soviet Union and domestic political preference. To be sure, there is some variance in attitudes expressed as one moves from left to right across the political spectrum in each of our countries. But this is simply not of the same order as it must have been in previous periods. While the data are not available to prove this, what one can demonstrate is that there are virtually no remaining pockets of opinion that consider the Soviet Union to be an alternative model of society, and this even includes Communists and leftist intellectuals for many of whom this would have been the case some two decades ago. The final blow undoubtedly occurred at different moments in our various countries, but involved in one form or another what the chapter on France refers to as the Gulag effect. This change is in many ways more important than the first as it indicates that there is no longer the same link between attitudes toward the Soviet Union and attitudes toward domestic political order. Basic attitudes toward the Soviet Union transcend domestic politics and the Soviet Union is viewed as largely irrelevant to the underlying problems of Western industrial society.

Finally, there is the fact that growing scepticism about the Soviet Union does not translate into the perception of a greater direct threat to Western security. The growth of Soviet military power is widely acknowledged, as is the incompatibility of many Soviet and Western security objectives. But this has not resulted in the perception of increased threat. The evidence would indicate that this has less to do with perceptions of the Soviet Union than with perceptions of what it is that can threaten Western security. A threat implies something immediate, and it is precisely this immediacy that is absent in popular perceptions of a Soviet menace. The Soviet military buildup or Soviet behavior is seen to be the primary source of international tensions in most countries but this simply does not get equated with an immediate, tangible threat. And this too is an apparent change from earlier periods. A far-less-powerful Soviet Union was once more widely perceived, or so one can surmise, as a more direct threat to the West than the global superpower that has now achieved equivalent status with the United States.

What seems to have transpired, if one puts these three dimensions together, is that for Western publics, the Soviet Union has become a more normal power; an international actor more like others. This was caused or made possible by the break in the link to domestic political strife. In turn, it seems to have changed entirely the context in which Western security policy must be legitimized.

Perceptions of the Soviet Union no longer appear to be the primary determinant of support for Western policy toward the Soviet Union. Rather it appears to be attitudes toward military power, Soviet or Western, that are the key factor. This will be discussed further but the point to be borne in mind is that popular attitudes toward the meaning of Soviet military power do not seem to stem from attitudes toward the Soviet Union itself and this would appear to be new. As a result, policies to deal with the growth of Soviet military power will have to be justified in terms that go beyond simply evoking a negative image of the Soviet system or Soviet objectives. These already exist.

One of the most critical foci of current policy disputes within the Alliance concerns the most appropriate Western political strategy for dealing with the Soviet Union now that it has become a truly global superpower. As should be eminently clear from the above, this is not simply a continuation of old disputes from earlier times, even though it may frequently appear so. It is revealing that the intensity of debate among policy elites stands in contrast to a considerable multipartisan consensus that our data would indicate exists in the population at large. People are widely convinced that the West will have to live with the Soviet adversary, rather than isolate it or "defeat it," for the foreseeable future, and this is not an issue that distinguishes Europeans from Americans. While one enters much more slippery terrain in trying to measure popular attitudes on specific policy alternatives, it is nevertheless clear that Allied policy toward the East must embody active attempts to regulate East-West competition in order to command the popular support indispensable to its viability.

SECURITY: MORE MAY MEAN LESS

While we have only sparse data for earlier periods, one can say with confidence that the concept of security that we assume dominated the early postwar years—primarily military, primarily East-West—no longer exists. The problem is, it has not been replaced by something concrete but rather by something as yet in constant flux. One is thus reduced to describing specific elements of continuity and elements of change.

A frequently asserted proposition today is that Western societies have grown incapable of defending themselves. The growth of the welfare state has supposedly undermined populations' willingness to spend what is necessary to counter a relentless Soviet military buildup. It is perplexing that anyone should believe there is anything new in popular preferences for spending money on things other than defense. Moreover, the data collected in our country profiles yield a far more nuanced picture of popular attitudes than that implied by the oversimplified premises so frequently heard today.

To begin with, popular majorities do not reject the concept of defense. On the contrary, strong majorities favor the principle of armed resistance if attacked. Military institutions obtain widespread support in most of the countries studied here. And there is broad acceptance of the need to maintain a balance of power between East and West as a basic prerequisite of Western security.

These are key general principles upon which Allied security is based and they all receive substantial popular endorsement. The problem is that public attitudes in this area are characterized by ambivalence: support for the general concept is tempered by scepticism about the consequences that flow from this support, in this case the need to have the means to defend oneself against attack or to maintain a balance of power. Interpreting this ambivalence runs into two interrelated difficulties. First, this illustrates perfectly an area where asking respondents for judgments on specific policy alternatives easily overtaxes their detailed knowledge; their responses will thus most likely be determined by affective considerations. And second, precisely because the affective content of most hypothetical futures in this area are unpleasant (spending more money, fighting wars, and so on), one is likely to heighten the automatic opposition. Where is the reality, in the general support or in the rejection of the specific?

We will never be able to determine through survey research what the responses of populations would be in a real crisis situation. One could hypothesize that the levels of support as reflected in opinion polls for such things as defense spending are actually quite irrelevant to the requirements of a nation if a war were truly to occur. Unless these attitudes were to become so salient that they determined voting patterns of large numbers of people, something which appears unlikely given previous experience, then it is unlikely that declared popular opposition to defense spending will determine the capacity of Western nations to defend themselves should it prove to be necessary. Arguments about guns vs. butter not only seem to misrepresent the considerations that are operative in determining popular attitudes toward defense issues but may simply be missing the point entirely, at least for Western populations at large.

The data gathered in this book would indicate that the point probably does lie elsewhere, and not in a willingness or unwillingness to spend for defense or to defend oneself. The scepticism about spending on defense appears to be linked to two other major considerations, each of which may not actually be all that new but certainly is present today. Both concern the relevance of military power in dealing with today's security problems.

The two considerations are actually the obverse of each other. The first is a general belief, a belief that has become pervasive, that more military power does not mean more security. In Europe particularly the contribution of increased military power to increasing security is widely questioned. The feasibility of defense is not generally considered to be evident. Moreover, the growth of military power is often considered to be the "primary threat to security." More arms make conflict more likely. This is something perceived as more immediate and more concrete than "the Soviet threat." Soviet military power seems to be perceived in terms similar to that of the West: dangerous but no more usable. Military power and the logic that drives its acquisition are being questioned, especially in the nuclear age where it is considered more destructive and less usable than ever. The requirements of security are thus frequently perceived as getting in the way of peace, a concept that has reached the pinnacle in the hierarchy of values. People tend to focus more on how Western policy may threaten peace and less on the military requirements for maintaining security.

The other side of the coin is the belief that increased security can best be achieved by reducing the role of military confrontation in providing that security. Open-ended military competition with the East finds no support whatsoever despite support for general principles such as the balance of power. There seems to be a conviction, and this is obviously an extrapolation from the data, that the system that has provided security remains simultaneously both necessary and, in and of itself, a possible source of insecurity. Hence the system must be improved. The result is a strong preference for arms control measures over defense improvements in all countries surveyed, including the United States. One can surmise that this must stem from something like a desire to control both the enemy and oneself more efficiently.

One thus has support for the general principles of Western defense combined with conviction that matters must be better managed. What is interesting is the multipartisan nature of the belief in both of these points. To be sure, there exist differences in the attitudes of those who support Socialist and Social Democratic parties from the supporters of Conservatives or Christian Democrats. But these differences are greatest in response to specific questions on policy alternatives, in other words, in areas where we are least sure of what exactly we are measuring. The range of support for the more general considerations just discussed is in fact surprisingly broad.

DETERRENCE: THE FALLOUT IS NUCLEAR UNCERTAINTY

Issues of nuclear weapons and deterrence are the primary reason for the increased interest over the past few years in public perceptions of Western security policies. Ironically, this area may in some ways be the least revealing of the four thematic clusters treated in this book. As in the previous section, one finds the dichotomy of support for the general and rejection of the specific. But as in the case of Soviet military power, one is frequently measuring attitudes that are almost certainly determined by factors other than nuclear. And it is unlikely that one has recently been witnessing a profound change in attitudes about nuclear weapons; more likely one has seen attitudes coming to the surface that long existed but have ceased to be latent because of changes in context.

A primary thesis of the protest movements has been that populations are no longer willing to accept the basic premises that have underpinned Western deterrent strategy during the postwar period. Despite the passions that nuclear issues evoke today, the available evidence indicates that this generally is not the case, not yet at least; only in rather well-defined strata in one or two countries (Norway and the Netherlands but not, for instance, in the Federal Republic) does one find deep-seated nuclear rejectionism. To be sure, there are few people who like nuclear weapons, and few people feel comfortable with the idea of more nuclear weapons. But this is probably not new and such general predispositions translate more into a generalized fear and confusion than into well-articulated opposition to Western strategy.

The data indicate that peoples' attitudes toward nuclear deterrence are probably composed of four distinct components. The first emerges as strong support for the general concept. This is not surprising, as deterrence implies avoiding war. Our data are uneven, but this appears to be the state of opinion across the political spectrum for all countries surveyed.

The second component is that the logic of deterrence is seemingly rejected, that is, that a weapon must be usable in order to deter. People tend to believe that nuclear weapons themselves have made war impossible, at least as a "rational" extension of political conflict. The new or renewed confrontation with the nuclear paradox—if a weapon can never be used, the adversary has nothing to fear—has heightened the fear that something may go wrong—if a weapon is usable, it may be used. There is widespread rejection of nuclear weapons as instruments of war fighting.

Which is linked to the third component: that people appear to make no distinction among nuclear weapons. For populations at large, there is only one nuclear threshold to be crossed. Thus, the relentless progress of technology that has unleashed major debates among experts about the meaning of the increased precision of ballistic missiles has as yet not had a similar impact on the attitudes of populations at large. If anything, the expert debate may have reinforced peoples' tendency to treat all nuclear weapons as equal.

The final component is that, in those places where data are available, people continue to believe that they have insufficient expertise to make judgments about issues of military strategy. They regularly look to their governments to make responsible policy in this area. This declared preference is clearly substantiated by the extent to which peoples' attitudes can be influenced on nuclear issues by the way in which survey questions are worded. For instance, depending on whether the need for new INF in Europe is linked to Soviet behavior or the need for balance on the one hand, or to the alternative of an arms control solution on the other, one gets a totally different set of responses. This is normally the mark of relatively low salience and probably indicates that the affective content of the question (Soviet Union, balance, arms control) overrides the specific nuclear considerations.

Nuclear weapons thus are not liked but appear to be accepted as a necessary evil for majorities of populations in most of the countries profiled in this book. Even in Norway the distaste for nuclear weapons seems to be overriden by attachment to the Alliance. Nevertheless, there is growing concern about Western strategy as people have become sensitized by the political debates over the past two years. But most people, even if they have opinions, do not feel particularly strongly about the nuclear issue, at least not strongly enough to influence voting behavior. Most importantly attitudes toward nuclear weapons are for many people clearly a function of other beliefs, the most important of which would seem to be those described in the last section. Nuclear weapons themselves seem to be the effect, not the cause.

ALLIES: WHAT BURDEN? WHICH PROFILE?

It is frequently asserted that the Allies are drifting apart at the grass roots. Conflicts over policies toward the Soviet Union are supposed to reflect the growth of deep-seated neutralist or pacifist tendencies in Western Europe;

the counterpart is seen to be growing American weariness with the frustrations of Alliance engagement, and particularly those pusillanimous Europeans. Moreover, anti-Americanism is also frequently claimed to be on the rise in Western Europe.

Much of this is obviously true for specific segments of elite opinion in the various member states of the Alliance. But the evidence indicates that the grass roots have not yet been affected as dramatically as the above would indicate. Populations at large retain a strong attachment to the Atlantic Alliance, with support for the Alliance actually increasing slightly over the past few years in most countries. Most Western Europeans consider NATO to be essential to their security. Support for alternative arrangements is in fact surprisingly low in all West European countries except Italy, seemingly indicating a rather strong preference for the Alliance rather than simply a resignation to its necessity. Nor has support for NATO diminished in the United States. Moreover, there are even indications that European fears of being abandoned by the United States in a crisis with the Soviets—in other words, the traditional fear that the Alliance won't work—have been on the wane in recent years.

But, as has already been seen in the cases of defense and deterrence, support for the general concept does not always translate into support for specific policies. There remains a belief that NATO is the best way to organize security, but not necessarily that current Alliance efforts are the best way to pursue that security. The best examples of this have already been discussed in the two previous sections: the considerable opposition to spending more on defense, despite the fact that there has been a specific Alliance decision calling for an annual three percent increase in spending; and the equally considerable distaste for the deployment of new nuclear weapons as a part of the December 1979 double-track decision. In both cases, we have argued that these opinions seem to be conditioned by another factor, in fact the same factor: attitudes toward the relevance of military power in dealing with today's security problems. By themselves they do not seem to be salient enough to determine political preferences for more than a handful of people. This may also indicate that at this level, the support for the Alliance is unlikely to be affected by the distaste for these issues.

But there is a different dimension to the conflict between the general and the specific, a dimension that is by no means new but the characteristics of which may be. The stable or increasing attachment to the Alliance on both sides of the Atlantic has been accompanied by a rather dramatic mutual loss of confidence of each side in the other.

Traditionally, Americans have felt that Europeans were bearing far too little of the burden for their own security. The new version of the problem for political leaders in Washington is the "cocoon mentality" they find in European capitals in the face of an expanded Western security problem that touches all corners of the globe. For the moment, it does not appear that these new frustrations of American political elites have significantly penetrated the population at large but the more traditional concern with spending too much to defend the Europeans is real and substantial. Over the last three decades this has been a periodically resurgent concern that has never yet resulted in a sharp drop in support for the Alliance, but then again in earlier periods the United States had an unchallenged military and economic supremacy. It would thus be foolish to predict the future only on the basis of the past record; the concern about equitable sharing of the defense burden may grow rather than dissipate.

The other side of the coin is the seemingly sharper contradiction between European belief in the Alliance and the sharp drop of confidence in the United States. At the level of the mass public, this cannot yet be interpreted as true anti-Americanism, for while there has been a visible decline in respect for the United States, positive opinions regularly outweigh the negative by a factor of two to one. Nor is there evidence to support the contention that the two superpowers are seen in the same terms. Criticism of U.S. policy is not accompanied by the same disavowal of the system as in the Soviet case and America is still considered to be essential to European security.

But there exists a profound concern about the United States and levels of trust seem to have dropped to the lowest point since the Second World War. Unfortunately this is another case in which earlier data are sparse and it is impossible to know whether the figures are really more dramatic or whether it just seems as if they must be. What one can say, however, is that this time it is less U.S. reliability and more U.S. political judgment that is being called into question. This coincides with and perhaps is the source of substantial willingness to see European governments pursue policies different from those of the United States if European and American "interests" are deemed in conflict with one another. While differences in attitude do exist according to political preference on this issue, majorities of all parties are on the same side of the issue. In a sense, one is tempted to argue that for Europeans, the United States has become a more normal ally just as the Soviet Union has become a more normal adversary. If this is in fact the correct interpretation of what has been happening, then policy conflict with the United States is unlikely to spill over into diminishing support for the Alliance but simply into a greater desire to pursue policies, independently if necessary, that are more in tune with perceived European interests. At the same time, common sense would indicate that support for the Alliance will be sorely tested by perpetual policy conflicts that reinforce the perception of different or diverging interests rather than focus on issues where interests remain convergent.

There may in fact be no life-threatening contradiction between strong support for the Alliance and distaste for some of its policies. But this will remain true only under one condition: that the policies disliked are not assumed to reflect a general orientation of the Alliance in an unacceptable direction. And this is where the current risk comes in if we are correct in our analysis that the opposition to increased defense spending or to new nuclear systems is primarily based on deeper concerns about the posture of the Alliance toward the role of military power in dealing with today's security dilemmas.

Popular commitment to the Atlantic Alliance is to a defensive Alliance with no aggressive content. It is hard to believe that overwhelming support for the Alliance will continue to exist if the Alliance is increasingly perceived to stand for the perpetuation of conditions which are the source of widespread popular concern, namely an open-ended arms race and permanent confrontation with the Soviet Union. If the West is incapable of formulating a coherent strategy to shape a less dangerous long-term relationship between East and West, not only Alliance policies, but the Alliance itself may become a source of controversy. If it is successful in conducting such a strategy, the opposition to spending on defense or to necessary modernization efforts is likely to diminish substantially if not disappear. Support for the Alliance will depend on what it stands for.

CORRELATES OF PUBLIC OPINION ON NATIONAL SECURITY

The previous discussion has attempted to draw some general conclusions about what may actually have changed over the past few years in public opinion on national security and what the significance of these changes may be. By its nature, the discussion has concentrated on those factors that are relevant across national boundaries and that are relevant across a broad spectrum of opinion within each of the countries studied. At the same time, we consider it important to give at least a brief review of factors that generally are assumed to explain variations of opinion within countries, even if these variations are less important for the specific points that have been raised in the previous discussion.

Age.   Many people believe that generational change is a major factor determining problems the Western Alliance currently faces regarding popular acceptance of its policies. The new generations born after the Second World War, who have little direct experience of foreign threat, supposedly hold views on national security that are dramatically different from those previous generations that built the Alliance. The analogy often used is that of people living along a river that long ago ceased to be threatening because of the construction of solid dams, and who start to ask whether these oversized dams are really required.

There is some evidence to support the view that it is this "successor generation" that most intensely challenges established Western security policy. But if the community of activists tends to be relatively young, the young do not necessarily tend to be activist. The core groups of current defense-related protest can be defined more precisely in terms of the young with a high level of education. The problem, however, is that this is not at all new or exciting: the younger and better-educated have long been a driving force of protest, at least since student unrest in the sixties, be it directed against nuclear power, imperialism, pollution and destruction of the environment, inequality, or established ways and means for attempting to provide national security.

To the extent that the studies contained in this book report breakdowns of opinions by age, the "selective recruitment" of the young "elite" into political activism is not repeated at the mass level. It is certainly true that attitudinal distinctions between age groups exist. The younger people are, the more likely they are in all of the surveyed nations to view the Eastern bloc as less threatening or superior, the less they believe in military defense and deterrence as prerequisites for peace and security, the less favorable they are toward the United States and the Atlantic Alliance, and finally, the more pessimistic they are about the prospects of maintaining peace and of their own physical survival. However, these differences across age groups are not really dramatic, certainly not as significant as across other background variables, such as sex, and they may even not be new at all. If one compares the data with the apocalyptic visions of the successor generation willing to abandon everything that has been sacrosanct in the field of national security, the differences according to age reported in the previous studies are really rather small. As none of our authors had extended time series data available, we are unable to conclude with any certainty whether observable distinctions are due to cohort effects or to life-cycle effects, whether they will persist into the future or mellow as people get older. But the phenomenon of the successor generation may be no more or less than it always has been, and certainly it is more an issue of emerging elites rather than of the population at large, as with so many of the issues described in this book.

Partisan Affiliation.   In discussing the problems of measuring salience, we have already mentioned that there is a direct relationship between the levels of opposition to established national security policy from a major party and apparent increases in the importance ascribed to these matters in public opinion, but that this does not automatically translate into increases in popular activism. Clearly there is need for a greater understanding of the interrelationship between political affiliation and the development of opinion. Yet, as with so many of the issues raised in this chapter, we do not have the possibility to do more than indicate those factors that deserve to be explored more systematically.

From the studies in this book it has become overwhelmingly clear that of all the background variables by which opinions on national security have been broken down (e.g., sex, age, social class, education), party preference has by far the most discriminating power. This is not at all surprising, and it should be expected for at least two reasons. First, if people feel very strongly about an issue, if this issue dominates their political outlooks, they will tend to prefer the party that is closest to them on this issue. This shift of voter preference clearly increases the association between party preferences and issue positions. Second, it is part of parties' everyday business to clarify their positions and policies on the issues of the day. People who care less intensely about particular issues will thus also receive information about how "their" party—that they prefer for very different reasons—views these problems. If they have not held any opinions on this issue before, or have held conflicting attitudes, they can be "educated" to a certain extent; people who already have believed what they now hear is their party's position have their opinions reinforced. Political parties are institutions that mobilize politically and structure public opinion, and they have the machinery to do so.

This interaction between public opinion and partisan politics can also run the other way: if public opinion is seen as shifting without being led by a major party, one or more parties will be likely to adapt to what they see as a shift in opinion away from previous party positions. In market terminology, this can be regarded as adaption to changes in the structure of demand. In the particular field of protest against established national security policy, such adaptation of partisan positions to perceived changes in public opinion may be an attempt to capitalize electorally on issues of popular emotion, or to avoid the political consequences of failing to satisfy that demand. Preservation of the market, integration of those challenging the system, may in fact be more important than the revenue from satisfying a particular demand. More often than not, all these processes will be at work at once so that in the end it becomes extremely difficult to establish whether the chicken or the egg, changes in public opinion or in parties' positions, started the whole feedback loop. Resolving this problem is not important here, anyway. What matters is that there are clear and indisputable reasons for high covariation between public opinion on national security and party preference.

The differences in defense-related opinions across adherents of different political parties are quite considerable in almost all the countries investigated in this volume. France and the United States, on the whole, exhibit the lowest partisan polarization of defense attitudes, the most important reason probably being that in these countries there have been no parties trying to lead or to capitalize on protest. With all due consideration given to important differences, the situation in France now is somewhat parallel to conditions in Germany before the change in government in fall 1982. With Socialists or Social Democrats in government and carrying the responsibility for official security policy and with bourgeois parties forming the opposition, there are no focal points beyond sectarian groups around which protest and opposition could crystallize.

The differences in defense-related attitudes between followers of different parties in the seven nations investigated here generally are of the same order of magnitude, and they generally follow a neat left-right division. The majority position on a particular issue is frequently reversed for adherents of different parties, with followers of the more right-wing party favoring and with supporters of the more left-wing party opposing specific programs or positions favorable to the Western Alliance or its policies. However, these differences are far from representing complete polarization.

On some issues the majorities of each party are on the same side of an issue. Many of those just discussed fall into this category. Moreover, opinions are seldom expressed in purely black and white terms. Nor do attitudes completely coincide with preferences for the major parties. Even though differences reported in this book for adherents of competing parties sometimes exceed 30 or even 40 percent, substantial proportions of party followers on both sides obviously do not toe the party line. Such "dissidents" can even be majorities among those intending to vote for a particular party. In Germany, the percentages in the summer 1983 of self-professed Green voters who held NATO indispensable as well as of Christian Democratic voters who preferred continuing arms control negotiations to the deployment of new nuclear missiles in Europe were both around 60 percent.

There is only one reasonable interpretation for this. This disagreement with the proclaimed position of the preferred party must be compensated for by other, more salient considerations where one finds oneself in agreement with one's party. Thus, while partisan affiliation is strongly related to opinions on defense matters, more strongly than any of the other background variables investigated in this book, the causation can run either way and considerable shares of the populations manage to live with opinions on defense that they do not share with the party they prefer. In the context of issues raised earlier, this may again be evidence of limited personal importance of these matters.

The Analytical Agenda

We warned readers in the introduction to this book that even the most complete inventory of public opinion data would inevitably provide an imperfect analytic structure or theoretical framework for explaining what has happened in the field of public opinion on national security over the past couple of years, let alone for predicting future developments. We have tried in this book to provide a rather complete overview of existing data, and indeed there are a considerable number of important things one can say about changes in public opinion, although these are not necessarily those things that one has been hearing so often over the past several years. But the task of filling the gaps in our theoretical knowledge must remain for another volume. What one can do on the basis of the work collected here is to demonstrate why one must be extremely careful in interpreting the kind of data presented and to point to those areas where further research is likely to provide key additional insights.

The scope for further research is vast. Perhaps the key area to be explored concerns how people acquire interest in or particular views on foreign policy or national security. We know too little about why people, and what kind of people, become attentive to these issue areas after not having been so for some time. We do not know how attitudes of this kind are structured nor how they depend upon other sets of political or non-political attitudes. We have insufficient understanding of what causes issues of this kind to become the focus of political debate at the elite or mass levels.

It appears that much of what we have observed over the past couple of years, particularly the debates on nuclear issues, may come to be regarded as a classical example of mass-elite interactions in the realm of political opinion formation, but our intellectual grasp of these processes is far from being complete. Political and social elites clearly stimulate the type of debates and activities we have witnessed recently, but we need to be able to disentangle this from other factors that cause shifts in popular concern. The role of the media also deserves close attention in this context.

The list of desiderata is thus long. Unfortunately even very detailed future research will probably not be able to explain definitively one of the key issues considered in this book: whether public response to security questions in recent years signals a genuine departure from previous public images or attitudes. The discrepancy between the abundance of current and the scarcity of earlier comparable data cannot be overcome. We can only submit, on the basis of the contributions to this volume, that many security-related attitudes currently being marketed as novel are really not that different from those observed in earlier years. For many of the more specific attitudes that are being polled today, all we can do is speculate that results would not have been much different had one polled the same items ten, 20 or 30 years ago. This lack of historically comparable data is not exclusively due to negligence or lack of interest in continuous observation on the part of survey researchers but also to the winds of change: as the issues of the day move on, so does the focus of survey research.

Perhaps the most urgent task for future research is the construction of a more adequate conceptual breakdown of the types of attitudes we are dealing with in this issue area. In a study like this, one is dealing with hundreds and thousands of tiny pieces of information that reflect how individuals respond to a wide variety of survey items. The problem for the researcher as well as for the political decision maker is to make sense out of such a multitude of isolated observations. These observations taken by themselves deliver an extremely complex impression, but it should be remembered that at the individual level there are most likely attitudinal structures and a few basic attitudinal dimensions that underlie these confusing myriads of recorded opinions. What needs to be done, then, is to identify these underlying dimensions in order to reduce the complexity of observations by means of an adequate conceptual and theoretical model. Such a conceptual clarification would have to take into account the substantive content of attitudes, not only the basic analytic categories used in social psychology for classifying attitudes. Only in this way would it be possible, in the long run, to arrive at a more useful theoretical representation of this sector of public opinion.

This reduction of many scattered measurements to a small number of basic attitudinal dimensions (e.g., optimism vs. pessimism, aggression, salience) is required not only to get a better notion of the structure of attitudes but also to be better aware of the message the data convey. The studies in this volume make it clear that survey responses on national security items should not carelessly be taken at face value. It is, for instance, mentioned again and again that results, for instance, may have been influenced by question wording. One can assume that this occurs most frequently when people are polled about problems where they have little information or feel personally not very involved. In a more abstract sense, to say that a survey instrument has an impact upon responses implies nothing more than that the particular attitude you want to measure using that particular instrument is wiped out or "overpowered" by another attitudinal dimension that the survey item taps. As we have to expect this to happen quite frequently in our issue area, only a clear conceptual and theoretical framework can make us realize what dimensions of defense-related attitudes can be assessed empirically more or less reliably and validly.

One could speculate, as we have on several occasions, that the one dimension that probably can be measured with some degree of confidence is the *affective* one: How do people feel about actors? What national stereotypes do they have? How do they value overall national goals such as peace, independence, security, etc? The problems seem to begin as soon as we hit the cognitive and behavioral components of attitudes, as happens when one asks the respondent to evaluate policy alternatives. On the basis of the information collected in this volume, we would hypothesize, at a very abstract level, that the more remote cognitions are from individuals and the more remote the behavioral side of the attitude is, (for example, individuals believe that their nation, as opposed to themselves, should do this or that), the more the affective component of the attitude will "overpower" the cognitive and behavioral components.

Without the kind of theoretical and conceptual framework we are calling for, one can do little but report attitudinal inconsistencies and call for further investigation. It must be remembered, to repeat a previous point, that in almost all the nations studied in this book the same type of contradiction could be observed: deterrence, military defense, and the Atlantic Alliance are accepted by majorities of respondents as very general and abstract principles, but specific strategies pursued by nations to further these goals find little enthusiasm (e.g., defense spending, or particular weapons systems). The problem then becomes what is the true measure, consent to the general goals or rejection of instruments to further them? Depending on one's political position, one will seize upon the one or the other. The result is the abuse of public opinion data to which we have already become so accustomed that we almost forget to consider it an abuse.

We have attempted to give some plausible explanations for the apparent inconsistency between acceptance of overall goals and rejection of instruments to implement them. And naturally this is not at all confined to the sector of national security. The same pattern of attitudes can be found, for example, regarding environmental protection, where consensus on the overall goal can coexist with widespread unwillingness to sacrifice personally. However, as the issue of personal sacrifice usually is not at stake in the field of national security, uncertainty over what is really being assessed is much greater here. Perhaps the general answer is straightforward: general political goals that commonly bear positive affective evaluation are endorsed, while everything that would have to be done to promote these goals of deterrence, defense, independence, and so on, carries unpleasant affective connotations (military spending, weapons, war) and therefore is rejected. Most of our arguments above are based on the assumption that it is indeed the affective content that is the determinant. However this may be, only theoretical and conceptual progress is going to help us to sort out the various possible interpretations and to subject them to empirical investigation.

A final point is a word of warning. The difficulties that have been described suggest that the scope for—conscious or unconscious—distortion or manipulation of public opinion data on national security should not be underestimated. The further we move away from the cognitive, everyday experience of individuals and from their own behavioral inventory, the more it is likely that their survey responses will be dominated by a few basic affective attitudinal dimensions. It would be exaggerating to claim that an appropriate choice of question wording can produce almost any survey results at the level of mass public opinion on national security. But the range of findings that already are available for some topics, or that could in all likelihood be produced in the future, is very wide indeed.

The best example is the issue of INF deployment in Western Europe. One could let respondents choose between negotiations and deployment; one could ask them whether the West should refrain from deployment even if SS-20 missiles continued to be targeted on Western Europe; one could tie missile deployment to the notion of a "military balance" (or its re-establishment); one could connect it to the need to evoke compromises from the East during negotiations; one could imply that not deploying means abandoning NATO. Depending on the choice of the stimulus, one receives substantial majorities in favor of deployment or in opposition. It is the business of political decision makers and their administrative, partisan, or consulting foot soldiers to hit each other over the head with these types of data, but it is the job of the serious scholar to find out *why* one observes such different majorities with these different instruments. Much has been said in the chapters of this book concerning these problems in an ad-hoc fashion. What is now needed is a firm theoretical base for the more or less informed speculation we have laid out.

The Political Challenge

The agenda for future research is substantial. But the analyses presented in this volume already advance considerably our ability to identify some important implications for the conduct of policy within the Alliance.

The general question with which we have to deal, of course, is whether popular consensus over national security policies has actually broken down and what this might mean in terms of the leeway political decision makers have for specific policies. Disregarding a number of important national particularities and necessary qualifications, we can say that across the sample of nations studied here, the changes that have occurred at the mass level over the past couple of years in either the salience or the acceptance of established national security policy are far less dramatic than one would have suspected on the basis of the intensity and direction of disagreement among political elites. Restrictions on the range of national security options open to decision makers are far more strongly imposed by the positions taken and articulated by political and social elites and counterelites than by public opinion at large. In terms of popular acceptance, the decision latitude for policy makers still appears to be rather wide.

To project how limitations on national security policy will look during the coming period would thus primarily require predictions about the further development of partisan rivalries over these issues and of the peace movements and their future impact. This is obviously beyond the scope of this study. Moreover, one can only speculate about what is going to happen to these groups of activists and their supporters in important social and political strata once the primary issue around which they have been formed, the deployment of new INF in Europe, has been resolved one way or the other.

That political decision makers enjoy considerable leeway in the field of national security policy in terms of its acceptance by publics at large is certainly bound to displease highly motivated and committed followers of peace movements as this contradicts their notion, employed as a political weapon, that there is a "revolt of the masses" against established national security policy. All we can say is that, judging from the data compiled in this book, such a revolt is not taking place. To be sure, there has been widespread opposition against the deployment of new American nuclear missiles in Europe, but as should have become abundantly clear, this is not surprising, and probably not even new. Very few people are really enthusiastic about nuclear weapons. Moreover, many other aspects of military preparations, for example military spending, are viewed almost equally critically. However, for great majorities of populations at large these sentiments are not personally salient enough to create the urgent desire to express intense disagreement or to oppose actively these components of military preparations for deterrence and defense. There is little indication that most of those who engaged in anti-INF activities over the past few months would not be willing to abide by the rules of the political game.

At the same time, this is not to imply that the public at large places no constraints on Western policy makers. To begin with, relying on a "silent majority" in support of such policies is not a viable long-term strategy.

Politics is not conducted by the body politic, but by political and social elites. A permanent challenge to major components of one's political positions is most likely not endurable. True, public opinion in general tends to be largely permissive on national security issues and, at least initially, passive in the process. But people tend to form their opinions in this area with reference to positions taken by parties with whom they have chosen to identify themselves or whom they at least vote for on the basis of other, usually economic and social considerations. Popular consensus is to a great extent a function of political consensus. Thus, in the longer run, sustained and well-articulated dissent by opinion leaders and publicized groups over key elements of national security policy will almost inevitably show certain effects on public opinion as a whole.

If political views polarize over the conduct of security policy, the public is likely to follow, at least to a point. The public may not be the main wellspring of dissent in foreign and defense policy, but neither is it simply a passive observer. There are thresholds of public tolerance, and if these thresholds are crossed, issues can become salient enough to influence political choice. Even foreign and security policy can thus influence voting patterns for more than small groups of people, as we witnessed in the June 1983 British election.

As yet we do not know precisely what causes this to happen, and the record shows that during the post-war period it is not a frequent occurrence. But in principle it applies equally to those formulating policy and those protesting policy. Those who seek to justify policy decisions and to discount the arguments of protesters risk losing public support as quickly as their opponents if they portray policy requirements in terms which fall outside the framework of public acceptance. Thus, just as it is important not to exaggerate the impact of protest on the public at large, so it is critical to avoid taking Western populations for granted.

A considerable number of good reasons for this are to be found in the earlier description of the four clusters of attitudes. It is impossible to say what it would take for any of these considerations to become salient enough to affect the behavior or choice of large segments of the population. But clearly there are a number of demands populations are placing on Western security policy that if left unsatisfied have the potential for undermining the popular consensus that still does underpin Western Alliance arrangements. Above all, despite its general commitment to deterrence, defense and the Alliance, the public is demanding reassurance—reassurance that Western policies designed to provide security are not also a primary source of insecurity.

There are several guidelines for policy makers that flow from the analyses presented in this book that, if observed, will go a good distance toward providing the necessary reassurance. First of all, Western defense policy choices cannot be justified only or even primarily in terms of a Soviet threat. The reason is that peoples' perceptions of the Soviet Union do not appear to be the key to their perceptions of threat. Rather, the relevance of growing Soviet military power and of the political benefits that are to grow from it must be explained differently if people are to accept that they have a military security problem. In the absence of this, portraying a Soviet threat in terms that are not perceived by the public is not likely to alter their perception of that threat nor increase support for Western policy, and is likely to have the opposite consequences. As long as the Soviets are not the primary security concern of populations at large, it will in fact continue to be possible for Western policies to scare our populations more than the Soviets do.

Moreover, it is going to be virtually impossible to override these considerations by mobilizing rank and file support. In earlier periods, doubts about policy could be compensated for as long as adherence to the party line could be commanded on the basis of internal political consider- ations. But the old link between policy toward the Soviets and domestic political preferences has been broken. As a consequence, invoking images of either nirvana or the evil empire are likely to be counterproductive.

Given the widely perceived excess of military power in the world, support for many elements of Western defense policy will remain prob- lematic unless policy makers are more skilled at demonstrating not only the relevance of growing Soviet military power but that additional West- ern arms will help to preserve peace. Above all, military competition between East and West cannot be presented as an open-ended proposition. Support for the maintenance of a balance of power, which does exist in the abstract, will only be present to the extent that efforts to control military confrontation are plausible.

Regarding nuclear weapons, populations are unlikely to force NATO governments to try to escape from the dilemmas of deterrence. But they will have to be convinced that everything is being done to minimize the likelihood of deterrence failing if this issue is not to grow in importance. They currently are not convinced of this. Moreover, the fastest way to increase nuclear rejection will be to ignore that nuclear strategy poses simultaneously major operational and existential issues. If governments focus only on the former, they will leave the moral high ground to those who would wish away the dilemmas of the nuclear age.

Fourth, evidence shows that the Atlantic Alliance is widely supported but that Alliance policies will be supported by public opinion only if they are regarded as basically defensive. This image has suffered recently, particularly with the harder line American rhetoric that came with the Reagan administration, and is at variance with many Europeans' images of the purposes of the Alliance. There are those who argue that this was only meant for internal U.S. consumption anyway, and that the bark has been harsher than the bite. However, words obviously do make a difference, and Western populations, Americans included, will continue to demand that policies be designed to shape a less dangerous long-term relationship between East and West.

Moreover, there is another lesson in the above: domestic politics cannot be separated from external policies in today's world, not just the reverse. The transmission of information and the conduct of intra-Allied debate over policy is less and less confined to diplomatic channels and communication among top political leaders. The speed with which information is available to all Western publics simultaneously creates new and more direct interactions between the different political cultures existing in Alliance member states. Leaders can no longer afford the luxury of statements for purely "domestic" consumption. Allied decision makers have yet to understand fully how this modifies their flexibility in conducting domestic debates and international negotiations.

Fifth, there is a clear preference within most Western publics for arms control over armaments or new weapons. This does not mean that public opinion at large would be unwilling to tolerate increases of Western arms or new weapon systems in general. However, little such support survives if arms control is allowed to be considered a direct substitute for one's defense policy or if the obstacles to successful arms control agreements are seen as much on one's own side as on the other. Arms control and defense policy must be presented as two sides of the same coin, not as alternative policy tracks. Certain security objectives can only be achieved by controlling East-West military confrontation, others only by defense modernization. Treating the two as trade-offs for one another simply widens the scope for political dispute and fragile consensus.

Finally, Western security requirements must be publicly presented and legitimized in terms of their contribution to the preservation of peace. Only Western governments are to blame if those who protest current policies are successful in creating the image that they have a monopoly on the desire for peace. It may well be true that "the first round of the war for peace will probably be won by those who think the balance of terror is less terrifying than an imbalance of terror" (*The Economist* 8 October 1983). But the task for governments will be to take some of the terror out of the balance.

The catalogue of constraints on policy that stem from existing public attitudes is thus significant. One cannot guarantee that a failure to heed these guidelines will cause the popular consensus underpinning Alliance arrangements to disintegrate but the attitudes described appear firm enough to warrant attention. The constraint is more in the form of a requirement to avoid defining or pursuing Western policy in a way that serves to crystallize political dissent in these areas because the dissent is likely to find a positive resonance in the echo chamber of public opinion.

At the same time, there clearly is leeway for decision makers in the area of public tolerance of new weapons and increases in Western military might. But the implementation of the December 1979 decision demonstrates the limits to that leeway. In the absence of widespread enthusiasm for deployment, the idea that the West could threaten deployment of weapons over four years ignored totally the differences between political and social systems in the East and the West. Without the enthusiasm, one ends up threatening Western populations more than the adversary.

Whether the Alliance continues to be perceived as peaceful, whether it is perceived to give sufficient emphasis to controlling military competition, whether people are convinced that particular weapons systems are required and that it really is the other side that is to blame for Western responses—these all interact with one another. They determine the way essential elements of military strategy are understood by people and interpreted in internal political debates and in exchanges between partners of the Alliance. In order to secure consensus and majority acceptance of Allied policies security issues cannot be allowed to serve as crystallizing points for minority protest. To a considerable degree it has been elite failures that have turned these topics into a focus of such protest. Whether the currently available high level of popular consensus over national security issues at the mass level can be maintained in Western nations into the future will crucially depend upon the extent to which decision makers will be able to heed the constraints imposed upon them by the popular attitudes described at length in this book.

Index

Afghanistan, Soviet invasion of: American attitudes toward, 324, 338, 360, 361; British attitudes toward, 25; French attitudes toward, 73, 74, 75, 77; German attitudes toward, 119; Italian attitudes toward, 184–85; Norwegian attitudes toward, 312

Africa, Soviet activity in, 73

Allies: American attitudes toward, 344, 352–57, 360, 375–76; British attitudes toward, 39–47; conflict among, 374–77; Dutch attitudes toward, 262–67, 270; French attitudes toward, 88–97; German attitudes toward, 138–47, 152, 153–56, 165–67; Italian attitudes toward, 196–201, 207–14; Norwegian attitudes toward, 308–10

American public opinion, 321–64; on allies, 344, 352–57, 360, 375–76; antiestablishment trend of, 322; on antinuclear movement, 323, 337, 347–52, 355, 361; on arms control negotiations, 352; on arms race, 350, 351; on balance of power, 328–30; on China, 324, 326, 353; on communism, 326-27; conservatism of, 323, 324; on Cuba, 324, 326, 354, 355; on cultural/educational exchanges, 330; on détente, 330–31; on deterrence, 344, 346–52; on disarmament, 346–47; dynamics of, 357–63; educational factors of, 331, 332, 345, 350, 351; on El Salvador, 339–40, 358; on foreign policy leadership, 322; ideological factors of, 332, 344, 345, 350, 351; internationalist, 357–58, 361; on interventionism, 323, 338–40, 362; of leaders, 356–57; on military aid, 337–40; on military expenditures, 334–36, 344, 345; on military threat, 327, 337; on MX missile system, 343; on national security, 331–44, 345; on NATO, 352, 353, 354–56; on Nicaragua, 354, 355, 362; on no-first-use policy, 347; noninternationalist, 357, 358–59; on nuclear freeze, 355; on nuclear war threat, 337, 346, 347, 351, 352, 362; on nuclear weapons, 346–52; on peace, 336–37, 359, 362; on Poland, 324, 326, 338; political factors of, 332, 379; on priority concerns, 331, 333–34, 344, 345; on Reagan's foreign policy, 322–23; on SALT II treaty,

331, 341–43, 355; on Union of Soviet Socialist Republics, 324–31, 332, 340-41, 360, 361

Andropov, Yuri, 185, 193

Antinuclear movement: American attitudes toward, 323, 337, 347–52, 355, 361; British attitudes toward, 12, 16, 22, 24, 29–32, 48; Dutch attitudes toward, 221, 222, 241–44, 268, 270; French attitudes toward, 81–83, 87; German attitudes toward, 103, 129–30, 132, 160; Italian attitudes toward, 175; NATO strategy and, 189–90; Norwegian attitudes toward, 293–94, 300, 311

Arab nations: American attitudes toward, 353, 354, 355; Dutch attitudes toward, 224

Armed forces: British attitudes toward, 28–29; Dutch attitudes toward, 232, 251; German attitudes toward, 111, 113, 125, 128–29, 130; Italian attitudes toward, 188; Norwegian attitudes toward, 286; salience of, 367. See also Defense; Military expenditures

Arms control, defense measures vs., 373, 387. See also Disarmament

Arms control negotiations: American attitudes toward, 331, 342–43, 352; Dutch attitudes toward, 257, 258, 260–62; German attitudes toward, 136, 137; Italian attitudes toward, 217; Norwegian attitudes toward, 292. See also North Atlantic Treaty Organization: double-track decision of

Arms race: American attitudes toward, 350, 351; Dutch attitudes toward, 238, 239–40

Atlantic Alliance. See North Atlantic Treaty Organization

Balance of power: American attitudes toward, 328–30; British attitudes toward, 16–17; deterrence and, 297–98; Dutch attitudes toward, 225–26; German attitudes toward, 115–16, 149–50; Italian attitudes toward, 179–81; NATO double-track decision and, 302; Norwegian attitudes toward, 282–83, 291–92, 311, 313; public

The Authors

IVOR CREWE

Dr. Crewe is Professor of Government at the University of Essex. He has written numerous articles on electoral behaviour and public opinion in Britain and is co-author (with Bo Särlvik) of the recently published *Decade of Dealignment* (Cambridge University Press, 1983). From 1974 to 1982 he was Director of the SSRC Data Archive at Essex University. He writes for *The Guardian* and comments on BBC Television on elections and public opinion in Britain.

PHILIP P. EVERTS

Dr. Everts is Director of the Institute for International Studies of the University of Leiden. His present research interest is concentrated on the role of domestic factors in the making of foreign policy and the role of the peace movement in particular. His publications in this field include *Elite & buitenlandse politiek in Nederland* (ed.), (The Hague: Staatsuitgeverij, 1978), *Public Opinion, the Churches and Foreign Policy*, (Leiden: Institute for International Studies, 1983) and *Foreign Policy in the Netherlands* (ed.), (forthcoming, 1984).

GREGORY FLYNN

Dr. Flynn is Deputy Director of the Atlantic Institute for International Affairs and Director of the Institute's research program in International Security Affairs. Among his publications are *The Internal Fabric of Western Security* (Allanheld, Osmun, 1981), "Opinions publiques et mouvements pacifistes", in Pierre Lellouche, ed., *Pacifisme et Dissuasion* (IFRI, 1983), and *Overlooked Allies: The Northern Periphery of NATO* (Rowman and Allanheld, forthcoming 1984).

RENATA FRITSCH-BOURNAZEL

Dr. Fritsch-Bournazel is Senior Research Fellow at the Centre d'Etudes et de Recherches Internationales, Fondation Nationale des Sciences Politiques and Director of Studies at the Institut d'Etudes Politiques, Paris. Among other publications, she is the author of *Rapallo: naissance d'un mythe. La politique de la peur dans la France du Bloc National (1974)*, *L'Union soviétique et les Allemagnes (1979)*, *Les Allemands au coeur de l'Europe (1983)*.

HANS RATTINGER

Dr. Rattinger is Professor of Political Science at the University of Bamberg. He has published widely both on strategy and arms control, and on recent German elections, including a contribution to *Wahlen und Politische Kultur: Studien zur Bundestagswahl 1980*, Max Kaase und Hans Dieter Klingemann, eds. (Opladen: Westdeutscher Verlag, 1983). He is currently directing a major research project on the impact of economic conditions and perceptions on political attitudes and behavior in the Federal Republic since 1949 under a grant from the Volkswagen Foundation.

SERGIO A. ROSSI

Sergio Rossi is Deputy Director of CESDI (Centro Studi e Documentazione Internazionali) in Turin and foreign and defense correspondent for the national daily Il Sole 24 Ore of Milan. His book, *Rischio atomico ed equilibri mondiali: Salt, euromissili, crisi afghana* (SEI, Torino 1980), was the first comprehensive Italian survey of the SALT and INF negotiations. Among his latest publications are the chapters on Italy in *Pacifisme et Dissuasion* (IFRI, Paris 1983) and in *The Structure of the Defense Industry* (Croom Helm, London 1983).

WILLIAM SCHNEIDER

Dr. Schneider is Resident Fellow at the American Enterprise Institute in Washington, D.C. He is also political consultant to *National Journal* and *The Los Angeles Times*, where his articles appear regularly, and coauthor of *The Confidence Gap: Business, Labor, and Government in the Public Mind* (Free Press, 1983).

RAGNAR WALDAHL

Ragnar Waldahl is Associate Professor at the Institute for Mass Communication Research at the University of Oslo. From 1968-1976 he was a Research fellow with the Institute for Social Research, Oslo working within The Norwegian Electoral Research Program.